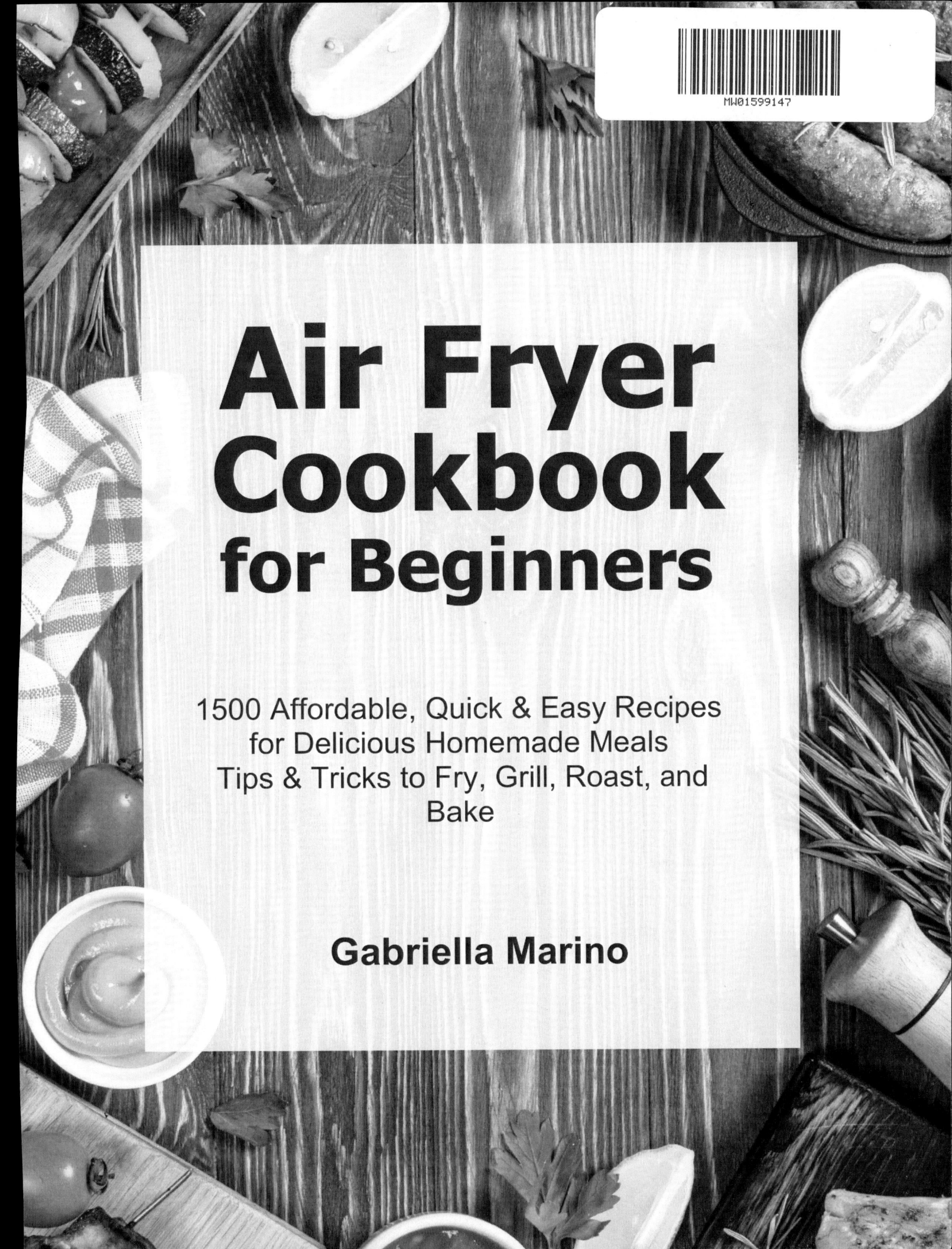

Air Fryer Cookbook
for Beginners

1500 Affordable, Quick & Easy Recipes
for Delicious Homemade Meals
Tips & Tricks to Fry, Grill, Roast, and
Bake

Gabriella Marino

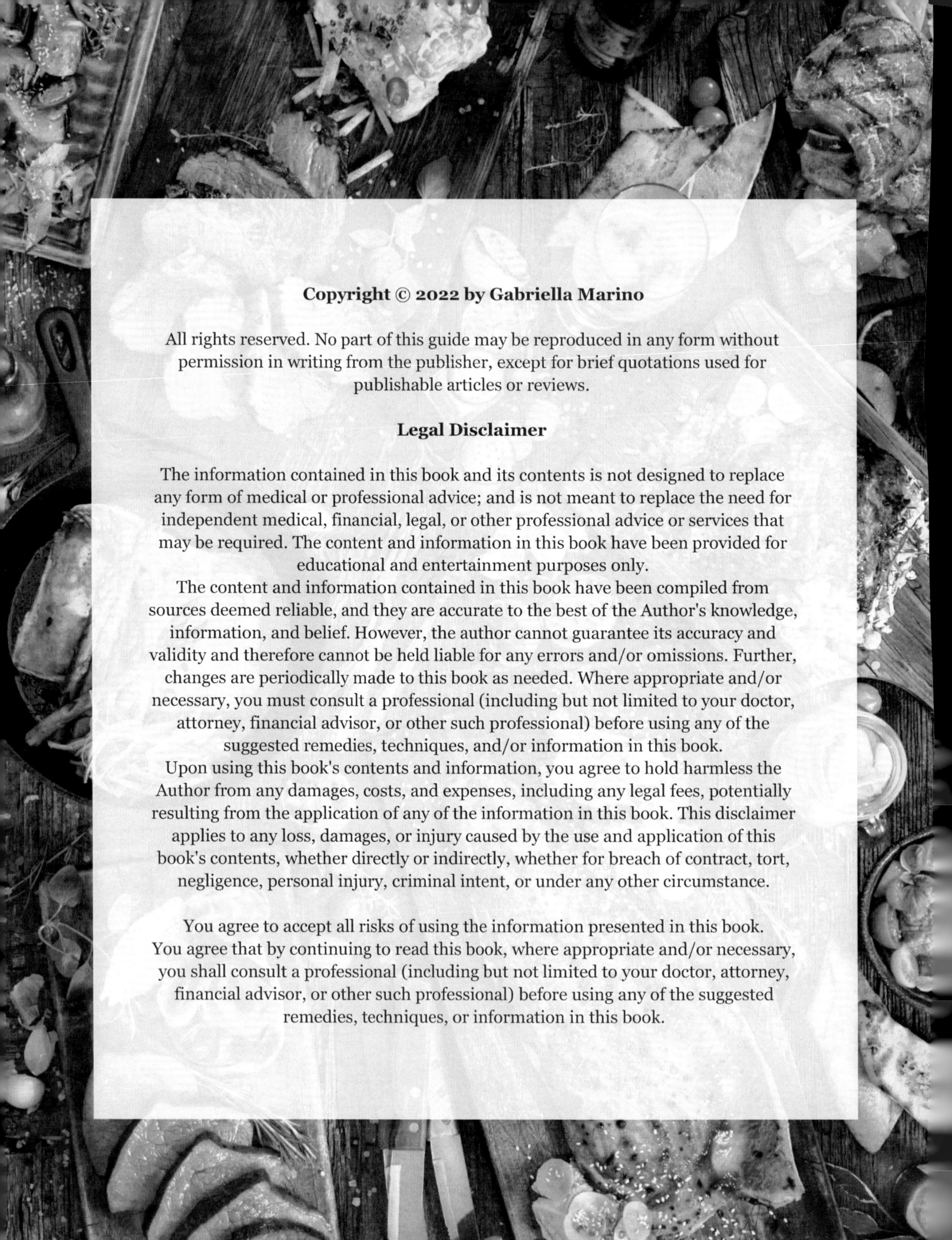

TABLE OF CONTENTS

INTRODUCTION 1

What Is An Air Fryer? 2

How Does An Air Fryer Work? 3

The Benefits Of Using An Air Fryer ... 4

Top Advice For The Best Cooking 5

Common Q&A 5

CHAPTER 1: Breakfast 7

Spinach Mozzarella Baked Eggs 8

Mushroom Kale Frittata.................8

Hard-Boiled Eggs 8

Simple Baked Eggs 8

Bacon & Brie Frittata......................8

Bacon & Eggs 8

Avocado Baked Eggs 8

Bacon & Kale Frittata 9

Yummy Almond Pancake 9

French Omelet 9

Indian Masala Omelet 9

Quick Kimchi Breakfast..................9

Yummy Nutty Granola................. 10

Raspberry Nut Cereal 10

Stuffed Pepper Baked Eggs.......... 10

Bacon Egg Stuffed Peppers.......... 10

Cheesy Egg Stuffed Peppers 10

Easy Egg Stuffed Peppers 10

Quick Brussels Hash 11

Ham, Cheese & Mushroom Melt .. 11

Vegetable Melt 11

Veggie Hash 11

Cheesy Pancake 11

Strawberry Cheese Pancake 11

Breakfast Egg Bowls 12

Air Fried Sandwich Muffins.......... 12

Polenta Bites 12

Tasty Cinnamon Toast 12

Yummy Breakfast Soufflé 12

Yummy Potato Hash..................... 12

Biscuits Casserole 13

Eggs Casserole 13

Cheese Air Fried Bake.................. 13

Oatmeal Casserole 13

Tomato Bacon Breakfast 13

Raspberry French Toast 13

Asparagus Frittata 14

Oatmeal Flax Muffins 14

Turkey Filled Omelets 14

Air Fryer Egg Cups 14

Mediterranean Frittata 14

Air Fryer Breakfast Cottage Pizza ..15

Prosciutto & Kale Egg Cups 15

Greek-Style Frittata...................... 15

Green Casserole 15

Kale, Feta, and Peppers Omelet....15

Air Fryer Vegetable Omelet 15

Air Fryer Egg Bites....................... 16

Sweet Potato Fritters 16

Crispy Quinoa Cakes.................... 16

Mustard, Bacon and Cheese Sandwich 16

Strawberries Jam Filled Toasts 16

Bacon-Wrapped Croquettes 17

Cinnamon-Cake Doughnut Holes ..17

Air Fryer Chocolate Croissants......17

Cheese Stuffed Crescent Rolls 17

Morning Glory Muffins 17

Carrot Raisin Muffins................... 17

Pita Bread Cheese Pizza 18

Loaded Hash Browns.................... 18

Walnut and Cornmeal Muffins 18

Healthy Banana and Chocolate Chip Muffins 18

Savory and Salty Breakfast Muffins 18

Blueberries Oats Muffin 19

English Muffins Pizza 19

Bacon, Spinach, and Eggs Casserole 19

Classic Scrambled Eggs 19

Kale, Eggs and Cheese Frittata 19

Tortillas with Avocado Dipping Sauce 19

Breakfast Hardboiled Eggs 20

Classic Cinnamon and Nutmeg Toast 20

Simple Chicken and Cheese Muffin Quiche....................................... 20

Frozen Sausage Links 20

Breakfast Frozen Hash Browns 20

Cinnamon Rolls 20

CHAPTER 2: Snacks & Appetizers 24

Mexican Apple Snack.................. 25

Quick Banana Snack 25

Coconut Chicken Bites 25

Simple Zucchini Cakes................. 25

Pesto Crackers............................ 25

Beef Jerky Quick Snack............... 25

Tasty Banana Chips 25

Quick Zucchini Chips................... 26

Delicious Spring Rolls................. 26

Crispy Fish Sticks........................ 26

Air Fried Crab Sticks 26

Simple Chickpea Snack............... 26

Fun Sweet Popcorn 26

Cajun Shrimp Appetizer 26

Seafood Appetizer 26

Chicken Breast Rolls...................27
Greek Lamb Meatballs 27
Jalapeno Balls............................27
Beef Patties................................27
Black Olive Balls 27
Spinach Balls 27
Kale & Celery Crackers 28
Tasty Tuna Cakes........................28
Egg White Chips 28
Turkey Pepper Nachos 28
Chicken Pepper Nachos 28
Tasty Chicharrones 28
Cheesy Chicharrones 29
Parmesan Garlic Bread Muffins....29
Herby Cheesy Muffins 29
Brussel Sprout Chips 29
Asian Style Brussel Sprout Chips...29
Honey Brussel Sprout Chips........29
Easy Cauliflower Crunch 30
Easy Broccoli Crunch...................30
Lemon Pepper Broccoli Crunch 30
Cayenne Zucchini Chips 30
Tasty Cucumber Chips.................30
Roasted Paprika Potatoes with Sour
Cream 30
Air Fryer Chicken Alfredo Quinoa
Balls...30
Three Cheese Stuffed Mushrooms 31
Air Fried Cheesy Spinach Crostini .31
Ricotta Fig Crostini 31
Cream Cheese Salmon with
Strawberry Mint Bruschetta 31
Air Fryer Bacon-Wrapped Shrimp
Tapas on Avocado Toast 31
Perfect Crostini 32
Cannoli Stuffed French toast 32
Classic Smashed Potatoes 32
Air Fryer Lemon Potatoes 32

Greek Feta Fries in an Air-Fryer 32
Air Fryer Chicken with Saucy Quinoa
Salad...33
Buffalo Quinoa Bites 33
Tofu Coated with Quinoa Flakes ...33
Air Fryer Zucchini Fries with Tzatziki
Dip 33
Air Fryer Pita Pockets 34
Air Fryer Feta Cheese Appetizer ...34
Air-Fryer Fish Cakes 34
Air Fryer Olives, Garlic & Tomatoes
....34
Mixed Veggies Pancakes 34
Vegan Coconut French Toasts 34
Delicious Lime Tofu.....................35
Crispy Potato Nuggets 35
Vegan Corn Fritters.....................35
Herbed and Spiced Baked Tofu Fries
....35
Mushroom Pizzas with Hummus
Drizzle 35
Delicious Vegan Pasta Chips 36
Buffalo Turkey Pizza 36
Basil Pesto Pizza 36
BBQ Turkey Pizza 36
Christmas Pizza 36
Simple and Classic Marinara Pizza.37
Sweet Cinnamon Plantains 37
Dehydrated Toasted BBQ Almonds
....37
Dehydrated Cashews 37
Maple Glazed Dehydrated Toasted
Almonds 37
Dehydrated Sweet Potatoes 37

CHAPTER 3: Vegetables & Sides..48

Quick Glazed Beets 49
Stuffed Portobello Mushrooms 49
Lunch Special Pancake................49
Asian Style Lentil Fritters............49

Tasty Potato Wedges..................49
Corn, Lemon & Cheese 49
Brussel Sprouts Dish...................49
String Beans Dish 50
Pecorino Button Mushrooms 50
Tasty Garlic Potatoes..................50
Vermouth Mushrooms 50
Quick Eggplant Fries...................50
Tasty Roasted Carrots.................50
Tasty Roasted Parsnips 50
Quick Creamy Endives 50
Roasted Peppers Dish.................51
Creamy Brussels Sprouts 51
Delicious Herbed Tomatoes 51
Delicious Barley Risotto 51
Cheesy Artichokes 51
Beet Salad & Cilantro Dressing 51
Yummy Broccoli Salad 52
Beets Arugula Salad 52
Artichokes With Special Sauce.....52
Brussel Sprouts & Tomatoes Mix ..52
Spicy Cabbage...........................52
Quick Air Fried Leeks 52
Collard Greens & Turkey Wings 52
Okra Corn Salad.........................53
Collard Greens & Bacon 53
Fantastic Radish Hash.................53
Swiss Chard Salad 53
Flavored Air Fried Tomatoes 53
Garlic Tomatoes 53
Stuffed Poblano Peppers.............53
Eggplant With Garlic Sauce 54
Greek Potato Mix.......................54
Air Fried Asparagus 54
Tasty Creamy String Beans 54
Air Fryer Spanish Spicy Potatoes...54

Spinach Croquettes...................54

Roasted Savory Carrots..............55

Smoky Cauliflower....................55

Garlic Parmesan Air Fryer Roasted Radishes...................................55

Air Fryer Spinach.....................55

Orange-Cranberry Butternut Squash with Ginger..............................55

Air Fryer Garlic Aioli Artichokes....55

Herb Air Fryer Butternut Squash..56

Curried Carrots with Dates & Almonds.................................56

Air Fryer Vegetable Kabobs.........56

Air Fryer Pineapple Teriyaki Veggie Kabobs...................................56

Mixed Veggies..........................56

Vegetable Medley.....................57

Roasted Vegetables...................57

Vegetables with Halloumi Cheese.57

Feta Cheese with Roast Vegetables 57

Brined Vegetables.....................57

Simple Jicama Chip....................58

Easy Ratatouille Vegetable Mix....58

Crunchy Vegetable Nuggets.........58

Veggie Tortillas Wraps................58

Garlic Parmesan String Beans......59

Crispy Avocado Fries..................59

Sesame and Vinegar String Beans.59

Spicy Herbed Yellow Squash........59

Coated Carrots Fries..................59

Nuts and Vegetables with Rice.....59

Roasted Asparagus with Tahini Sauce 60

Perfect Stack of Tomatoes..........60

Pumpkin Fries with Sweet Greek Yogurt Sauce...........................60

Lemon Glazed Mushrooms..........60

Poppers Peppers......................60

Pickle Fries............................61

Fried Eggplants Chips................61

Whole Baked Potatoes with Creamy Filling....................................61

Beets in Air Fryer.....................61

BBQ Coated Cauliflower.............61

CHAPTER 4: Poultry.................66

Sticky Chicken Wings.................67

Chicken & Apricot Sauce.............67

Chicken With Coconut Sauce.......67

Chicken With Cilantro Sauce........67

Mexican Chicken......................67

Chicken & Black Olives Sauce.......67

Maple Duck Breasts...................67

Creamy Coconut Chicken............68

Chicken & Asparagus..................68

Delicious Herbed Chicken............68

Chinese Stuffed Chicken.............68

Chicken With Capers..................68

Easy Duck Breasts....................68

Chicken Breasts In Tomatoes Sauce 69

Chicken Thighs With Apple Mix....69

Chicken Creamy Veggie Mix.........69

Air Fried Chicken Mix................69

Chicken Cacciatore...................69

Turkey With Veggies..................69

Lemon Chicken........................70

Cheese Crusted Chicken.............70

Chicken With Garlic Sauce...........70

Pepperoni Chicken....................70

Turkey, Peas & Mushrooms Casserole...............................70

Duck & Veggies........................70

Tasty Greek Chicken..................71

Chicken Chestnuts Mix...............71

Veggie Stuffed Chicken Breasts....71

Duck Breasts & Raspberry Sauce..71

Simple Duck Breasts..................71

Chicken Breasts & Passion Fruit Sauce....................................71

Quick Creamy Chicken Casserole.71

Chicken & Radish Mix................72

Turkey Burgers........................72

Simple Chicken Lunch................72

Chicken Mix Casserole...............72

Duck & Cherries.......................72

Dijon Baked Chicken Breast........73

Air Fried Chicken Quesadilla........73

Cosmic Wings..........................73

Air Fryer Chicken Meatballs with Pasta....................................73

Delicious Turkey Meatballs.........73

Saucy Asian Chicken Wings.........73

Greek Chicken Meatballs............74

Air Fryer Chicken Nuggets...........74

Perfect Alfredo Chicken.............74

Greek Baked Chicken Wings........74

Shake 'N Bake' Style Chicken.......75

Air Fryer Green Chili Chicken Bake 75

Air Fried Loaded Chicken with Potatoes................................75

Creamy Air Fried Chicken Broccoli Rice.....................................75

Chicken Stuffing Casserole..........75

Garlicky Lemon Chicken Drumsticks 75

Air Fried Chicken Shawarma........76

Air Fried Lemon Pepper Drumsticks 76

Chicken Legs...........................76

Air Fried Lemon Feta Chicken......77

Air Fired Greek Chicken.............77

Stuffed Chicken Breasts.............77

Greek Chicken Skewers with Feta Cheese Sauce.........................77

Grilled Chicken Kabobs 77

Greek Chicken and Orzo Pasta Salad 78

Kale and Feta Stuffed Chicken Breasts 78

Mediterranean Chicken Thighs 78

Greek Chicken Bowl 79

Turkey Panini 79

Glazed Chicken Breast with Basil Corn Salad 79

Thanksgiving Turkey 79

Air Fryer Cheesy Chicken Sausage Rolls 80

Air Fryer Crumbed Chicken Schnitzel 80

Air Fryer Japanese Chicken Tenders 80

Air Fryer Whole Turkey with Gravy 80

Classic Hawaiian Pineapple Chicken 80

Air Fryer Whole BBQ Chicken With Baked Potatoes 81

Nashville Hot Chicken 81

Air Fryer Pistachio Crusted Chicken 81

CHAPTER 5: Beef, Pork & Lamb .. 86

Creamy Pork 87

Provencal Pork 87

Easy Air Fried Pork Shoulder 87

Couscous Pork 87

Beef & Green Onions Marinade ... 87

Marinated Lamb With Veggies 87

Air Fried Lamb Shanks 88

Fennel Flavored Pork Roast 88

Mustard Marinated Beef 88

Lamb & Creamy Brussels Sprouts . 88

Crispy Lamb 88

Oregano Pork Roll 88

Beef Strips With Snow Peas 89

Simple Thyme Lamb 89

Chinese Steak & Broccoli 89

Tasty Pork Rolls 89

Garlic Lamb Chops 89

Baked Pork Sausages 89

Lamb Stew 90

Smoked Beef Strips 90

Garlic & Sprouts Pork Stew 90

Beef Vinegar Chops 90

Pork & Okra Stew 90

Ham & Pineapple Sandwich 90

Beef & Tomato Mix 90

Beef Ravioli 91

Cardamom Lamb Mix 91

Mini Pork Burgers 91

Bacon Shrimp Snack 91

Ginger Bacon Partridges 91

Beef Steak & Chimichurri 92

Delicious Beef Kabobs 92

Air Fried Roast Beef 92

Homemade Pork Buns 92

Delicious Lamb Meatballs 92

Hot Paprika Beef 92

Cumin Pork Steak 93

Cheeseburger Pockets 93

Air Fryer Hamburgers 93

Mint Lamb with Toasted Hazelnuts and Peas 93

Empanadas 93

Steak Fajita with Onions and Peppers 94

Air Fryer Nachos 94

Air Fryer Taco Pie 94

Air Fryer Beef and Bean Taquitos .. 94

Keota Kebabs 94

Beef Chimichangas 94

Zucchini Stuffed With Hamburgers 95

Pizza Burgers 95

Roasted Bacon Brussels sprouts ... 95

Roasted Lamb Rack with Lemon Cumin Crust 95

Cabbage and Beef Rolls 95

Steak Kebab 96

Mediterranean Rib eye 96

Skirt Steak with Balsamic Shallots . 96

Quick Kofta 96

Lamb Chops with Dijon Garlic Marinade 96

Pistachio Crusted Lamb Rack 97

Kofta Lettuce Wraps 97

Greek-Style Meat Loves with Arugula Salad 97

Lamb Chops with Lime, Farro and Thyme Vinaigrette 98

Air Fryer Stuffed Pork Chops 98

Easy Pork Chops 98

Mongolian Beef 98

Parmesan and Lime with Schnitzels 98

Pork Schnitzel 99

Beef Crumble Schnitzel 99

Teriyaki Beef and Pineapple Kabobs 99

Steak Bites 99

Vegetables and Sirloin Steak with Sour Cream 99

Spicy Beef Fillet 100

Easy Beef Ribs 100

Sweet Beef Ribs with Baked Potatoes 100

Veal Shank Fricassee 100

Veal Parmigiano 100

CHAPTER 6: Fish & Seafood 110

Savory Lemon Shrimp 111

Asian Style Salmon Cubes 111

Shrimp Celery Salad 111

Cod & Kale Leaves 111

Simple Cajun Shrimps.............. 111

Seafood Mix 111

Basil & Paprika Cod............... 112

Calamari Rings 112

Shrimp Spaghetti.................. 112

Staple Fish & Chips 112

Wrapped Scallops.................. 112

Thyme Catfish...................... 112

Salmon With Creamy Chives Sauce
.... 113

Tilapia With Tomato Salsa 113

Simple Salmon With Sauce 113

Tangy Grilled Salmon 113

Garlic Shrimp Mix 113

Catfish & Spring Onions With
Avocado 113

Smoked Paprika Tilapia............ 114

Delicious Lemon Cod............... 114

Crispy Smoked Fish Fillets 114

Basic Tuna Cobbler 114

Spinach Tilapia 114

Gingered Salmon.................... 114

Coconutty Shrimp................... 115

Pecorino Salmon Fillets 115

Tuna Skewers 115

Cod With Mustard 115

Paprika Cod With Endives 115

Buttered Mussels 115

Parsley Cod Mix 116

Lemon & Oregano Tilapia Mix.... 116

Fried Oregano Crawfish 116

Buttered Lobster 116

Shrimp With String Beans 116

Italian Shrimp 116

Sea Bass With Coconut Sauce 116

Salmon With Olives................. 117

Cajun Salmon...................... 117

Cajun Scallops 117

Mediterranean Style Fish 117

Mediterranean Scallops 117

Salmon Kebob...................... 118

Shrimps and Scallops Pizza 118

Scallops Crab Pizza 118

Korean BBQ Salmon 118

Korean Crab Cakes with Gochujang
Tartar Sauce 118

Korean Spicy Yellow Croaker Fish 119

Bang Shrimp 119

Cheesy Tuna Flautas................ 119

Air Fried Salmon with Hoisin Ginger
Marinade 119

Maple Teriyaki Salmon 119

Korean Grilled Shrimp Skewers ..119

Salmon Patties 120

Blackened Shrimps.................. 120

Bacon-Wrapped Shrimp............ 120

Coconut Shrimp with Honey Sriracha
Sauce 120

Tilapia 120

Blackened Salmon 121

Tuna Patties 121

Oysters............................. 121

Pecan Crusted Halibut 121

Fish Fillet with Onion Rings........ 122

Whitefish with Garlic and Lemon 122

Lime Caper Cod 122

Fried Calamari...................... 122

Mediterranean Fish................. 122

Greek Salmon 122

Crispy Tilapia 123

Spiced Salmon 123

Pistachios Crusted Fish 123

Salmon with Lemon Caper Sauce 123

Eggs Omelet with Tuna and Avocado
.... 124

Steamed Salmon with Lemon and
Herbs 124

CHAPTER 7: Vegetarian 125

Vegan Cheese Green Beans 126

Quick Chickpeas Snack 126

Nutmeg Okra 126

Fried Onion Rings...................126

Spicy Kale 126

Crunchy Tots Snack 126

Paprika Leeks 126

Sweet Potato Chips 126

Broccoli & Cranberries Mix 127

Paprika Jicama 127

Squash Noodles.....................127

Lemon Kale & Bell Peppers Bowls
....127

Paprika Kale & Olives 127

Roasted Cauliflower 127

Cilantro Broccoli Mix 127

Lemon, Olives & Zucchini 128

Wholesome Veggie Snack..........128

String Bean Small Bites 128

Tomato Eggplant Casserole.......128

Tomato Rice Casserole..............128

Lentil & Green Beans Stew.........128

Honeyed Carrots.....................128

Greek Potatoes......................129

Cherries, Farro & Green Onions Mix
....129

Chickpea & Cauliflower Bowl......129

Cheesy Stuffed Vegan Peppers ...129

Vegetable Fritters 129

Easy Lemon Broccoli................129

Easy Eggplant Stew 129

Quick Veggie Paella 130

Easy Apple Chips....................130

Healthy Madagascan Stew 130

Quick Leeks Stew 130

Cabbage Stew.......................... 130

Spinach Salad 130

Turmeric Cauliflower Rice 131

Turmeric Tofu......................... 131

Blacked Eye Peas and Greens 131

Pineapple Crisp....................... 131

Spicy Yellow Squash................. 131

Coated Carrot Fries.................. 131

Olive and Balsamic Vinegar String Beans.. 131

Grilled Vegetable and Couscous . 132

Zucchini Chips 132

Cinnamon Nut Scrolls............... 132

Feta Filo Fingers 132

Crumbed Asparagus................. 133

Roasted Honey Parsnip with Pecans 133

Crispy Chickpeas 133

Garlic and Herb Roasted Chickpeas 133

Garlicky Couscous 133

Black Beans Fitters 133

Vegetable Mirepoix Bites.......... 134

Veggies Tortilla Pizza................ 134

All Olives and Cheese Pizza 134

Frozen Mini Pizza 134

Butter Glazed Pizza.................. 134

Three Cheese Pizza 134

Tortilla Pizza 135

Lentil Tacos 135

Chickpeas Squash Fitters 135

Fried Rice with Sesame Sriracha Sauce 135

Zucchini Corn Fitters 135

Lupine Beans Fitters 135

Egg Fried Rice 136

Buffalo Quinoa Fritters 136

Spiced Chickpeas and Cashew Mix 136

Chickpeas Fitter with Sweet Spicy Sauce 136

Air Fryer Falafel...................... 137

Blacked Eyed Pea Dumpling Stew 137

Vegetarian Pumpkin Schnitzel.... 137

Lentil Fritters with Garlic........... 137

Lentil Ball with Zesty Rice.......... 137

Moroccan Vegetable Couscous .. 138

BBQ Lentil Meatballs................ 138

CHAPTER 8: Desserts 149

Coconut Lime Pie..................... 150

Pecan Cookies......................... 150

Coconut Butter Donuts 150

Simple Banana Rolls................. 150

Perfect Coconut Cookies 150

Vanilla Creamy Cake 150

Lovely Vanilla Cookies 150

Delicious Chocolate Pastry 151

Cream Cheese Bites 151

Easiest Chocolate Mug Cake 151

Healthy Zucchinis Bars.............. 151

Plum Apple Crumble 151

Nutty Pecan Bars..................... 151

Easy Yogurt Treat 152

Chocolate Berry Cake 152

Sweet Cinnamon Toast 152

Almond Aromatic Cup 152

Fantastic Chocolate Ramekins.... 152

Ginger Vanilla Cookies 152

Cinnamon Raspberry Cupcakes .. 153

Lemon Berry Jam..................... 153

Blackberry Cream 153

Coconut Cake 153

Coconut Berries Cream 153

Almond Cookies 153

Simple Air Fryer Brownies 153

Cream Cups 154

Avocado Cream Pudding 154

Almond Bars 154

Healthy Chia Jam 154

Yummy Berry Pudding 154

Plum Almond Cake................... 154

Cinnamon Fried Plums.............. 154

Lemon Berries Stew 155

Toasted Marshmallow Fluff Waffles 155

Air Fryer Cake Box Mix Cupcakes 155

Carrot Coffee cake 155

Raspberry Shortcake 155

Air Fryer Almond Cupcake 155

2 Ingredients Strawberry Cobbler 156

Chocolate Molten Lava Cake 156

Chocolate Cake 156

Angel Food Cake...................... 156

Homemade Coffee Cake 156

Air Fryer Apricot Cake............... 157

Pineapple Cake........................ 157

3 Ingredients Christmas cake 157

Fruit Pudding 157

Peach Cobbler......................... 157

Pecan Strawberry Rhubarb Cobbler 158

Lemon Biscuit 158

Red Velvet Cookies 158

Walnut Chocolate Cookies......... 158

Grill Peaches........................... 158

Air Fryer Cookies 159

Oat Sandwich Biscuits............... 159

Low Sugar Brownie 159

Peanut Butter Cupcake 159

Orange Cornmeal Cake 159

Vanilla Bean Meringues 159

Coconut Meringues 160

Sweet Cookie 160

Oreo Chocolate Pudding 160

Blueberry Pie 160

Honey Goat Cheese balls 160

Easy Donuts 160

Donut Sticks 161

Anzac Biscuits 161

Lime Macaroons 161

Coconut Macaroons 161

Canned Biscuits 161

Cream Puffs 161

CONCLUSION *166*

Are you always seeking out new ways to cook? Can you think of anything that might save you time or add a touch of modernity to your kitchen routine?

You're not the only one!

In today's fast-paced society, people are always looking for time-efficient smart appliances that could help them do their work as quickly as possible while also having minimal to zero drawbacks. Well, your prayers have been answered in the form of an air fryer that enables you to cook, bake, steam, roast, and pretty much do everything from one appliance!

That's right, you heard us!

You can cook healthy fried foods with an air fryer thanks to its rapid air technology, which uses hot air to cook food quickly, retain nutrients, and requires as little as a tablespoon of oil for your favorite fried foods: fries, cakes, crispy chicken wings, etc.!

All of this and more can be accomplished with an air fryer without consuming much oil or risking suffering from several cardiovascular diseases. Even though fried food may be the tastiest thing on earth, we can't deny that it comes with its fair share of health issues. Fortunately, air-fried food eliminates these complications.

Air fryers can be a great addition to any home kitchen, and there are several better reasons to own and use one. Our air fryer cookbook will help you learn everything you need to know about this appliance.

Our cookbook will explain all you need to know about owning and using an air fryer from your morning breakfast to your mighty dinner and a guilty pleasure dessert afterward.

Soups, salads, snacks, stews, puddings, a variety of seafood recipes, side dishes, and more are all covered here so that you can make full use of your air fryer. These recipes will help ease your meal planning and daily cooking decisions, regardless of what model you currently own or plan to purchase.

In a household teeming with humongous tasks, a good air fryer can at least bring you food ease and does it on a brilliant level. Give it a go and see!

You can be sure cooking in an air fryer will be a breeze for you since there is little to no learning curve and the food always turns out to be delicious. However, if there aren't really into your cooking, they will suddenly become fans if you begin preparing food in an air fryer with these recipes!

Air fryers cook using a special method that produces perfect results every time, and there is very little risk of your food burning or spoiling. Experts in the food industry consider this to be the healthiest kitchen appliance, and it will give you a liberating feeling to follow a healthy lifestyle.

Besides, if you love making healthy homemade meals from scratch, this device will surely save you time and bring out your creative side!

An air fryer is a popular kitchen appliance that bears a striking resemblance to an oven. However, their differences lie in their heating elements. An air fryer has its heating element at the top accompanied by a powerful fan that circulates hot air around, known as the rapid air technology to cook your favorite foods.

One of the main reasons air fryers are popular with customers is that they can cook food with very little to no oil.

According to some companies, air frying uses 80 percent less oil than conventional frying. Isn't that incredible?

In addition, it maintains the same crispiness and texture you would expect from fries, chicken wings, cakes, and similar dishes prepared using traditional frying methods

While this is a fairly easy device to use, it has a few learning barriers to be expected with any device. An air fryer, for example, can cook a variety of foods, from fried food to meat to baked goods such as pizzas and cakes.

However, it is important to note that meats generally don't require oil as they are quite juicy on their own. You need to add some herbs and spices and season them with salt and pepper, but make sure you only use dry spices since the less moisture, the crispier the results.

However, if you prefer your meat seasoned with wet ingredients such as sauce, honey, and ketchup, wait to add them only at the very end.

However, if you plan to cook lean meats or foods with little to no fat, you will need to add a little oil to make sure they cook evenly since a little moisture is needed to brown and crisp the food.

Our cookbook suggests brushing oil on the meat or drizzling it on it before cooking, and that applies equally to dry, moisture-free foods. You should use oils with a high smoking point, such as canola or vegetable oil, but olive or sunflower oil will work fine as well since only a small amount is being used.

For vegetables such as broccoli and potatoes, you must always toss them in oil before cooking and precisely follow the recipe. Never forget to season the ingredients with salt and pepper before air frying.

Most air fryers offer toasting and baking functions, which operate more like a small oven, perfect for baking cakes or roasting chicken wings.

However, keep in mind that small ovens can have limitations when it comes to baking since their basket size may not be large enough to cover large quantities of food at a time or even at all with large-cut foods, especially meat.

Make sure you select models you are comfortable using that meet your budget requirements and fulfill your family's needs.

A ir fryers are available in various shapes and sizes, but they all perform the same function: air frying. They vary in terms of their features and looks; some are more advanced, some are simpler, and some are prettier, but their purpose remains the same. You have a wide variety of options to choose from in the market. Keep your needs and budget in mind as you choose, of course.

The basic features of an air fryer that even cheaper models never lack are the timer and temperature dials, which you can use to set the amount of time and the temperature you want to cook food at. In addition, the air fryer has a built-in basket where you can put the food to be cooked and then return the basket into the air fryer to start cooking, baking, or toasting.

A few models come with additional cookware, such as a grill, a rack, a muffin tin, or even thin mesh baskets for cooking small foods.

A drip tray is provided for catching oil and other food spills. In addition, you'll typically find a digital display on air fryers to tell you when to add food and when it's done cooking.

Some even have indicators that alert you when to shake the contents inside for even cooking, and some take care of it. The general idea of an air fryer is very similar to that of an oven. Plug it in, set the timer and the temperature, then add food once it's hot. Yes, you need to preheat the air fryer before using it.

An air fryer is an easy-to-use appliance. Cooking in it becomes second nature once you get used to it.

Like convection ovens, air fryers work even better! It is countertop, compact, and space-saving. It means less work for you.

We know air fryers are mini convection ovens. So we can say they work the same way. Because of their small size, the fans distribute heat quickly, enabling the food to be brown, caramelized, and become crispy in a short amount of time.

As a result of its size, it does not become overpoweringly hot and does not make the entire room hot, making summer cooking almost fun!

To prevent overheating, a vent at the back rapidly releases hot air. As a result, cooking time is reduced by 20% compared to traditional frying, and energy is conserved since it heats up faster.

Oil-free frying is healthier than oil-based frying. Oil is more of a moisture provider than an essential ingredient for frying in an air fryer, and skipping oil is the first step to adopting a healthy lifestyle.

W e all want to enjoy healthy foods without spending all day in the kitchen preparing them. That is exactly what an air fryer is known for quick health! This device is also popular because it introduces a newer, healthier concept of oil frying foods in addition to its convenience and user-friendliness. Below, we have outlined all the advantages of an air fryer for your convenience.

Less Oil, Improved Health
A single tablespoon of oil is all you need to cook with an air fryer to get foods without the oil and unhealthy fats. You don't need much oil if the food is naturally fatty.

While we're on the topic of unhealthy fats, air-fried foods have a lower fat content, which can help you stay healthier and prevent illnesses like cancer, diabetes, high blood pressure, and heart attacks that stem from eating too many fattening, oily foods.

Faster Cooking, Better Time-Saving
Air fryers cook food faster than ovens and stovetops because they heat up quickly and maintain a constant temperature. Because hot air circulates in a small area, the food cooks in a matter of minutes and always turns out perfectly done.

As a result of faster cooking, an air fryer also consumes less energy, lowering electricity bills. Moreover, because it is fast, you can use it for other tasks that you may find more productive.

Easy Operation, Better Learning
In contrast with a stovetop where food needs constant attention, you simply put the ingredients in with an air fryer, set the timer and temperature, and let it do its thing while you do yours.

This device is so simple to use that even kids can easily learn how to make quick snacks and lunches without any need for technical expertise or parental assistance. Furthermore, it is safer to use than a stove which may cause burning or even hot oil spills.

In addition to its simple operation, clean-up is fairly straightforward. Many air fryers come with dishwasher-safe counterparts that can be cleaned using a soapy sponge or placed in the dishwasher.

As a bonus, air fryers cook their food in a closed environment, so there are no chances of outside spills or drips.

It Is Versatile
There's no denying that an air fryer is versatile. It allows you to do everything from one device, including roasting, cooking, frying, baking, grilling, stewing, and even stir-frying, thereby saving you from accumulating multiple appliances and reducing storage space for all your pots and pans.

Whether you're a single person or someone who likes to keep things simple in their kitchen, an air fryer will be right up your alley.

Think of all the foods you can prepare in this appliance without owning special appliances for specific foods. It is also very cost-effective to experiment with this device with different food recipes. Due to all of these benefits, air fryers have become the most coveted and bought kitchen appliances. In addition to the health claims made by air frying, you can conveniently lose weight for you without having to give up your favorite foods because air frying eliminates oil, which raises cholesterol levels and is the main cause of health problems. An air fryer eliminates the need to use high-calorie and high-fat oils.

TOP ADVICE FOR THE BEST COOKING

1. Cook With Little Oil

Oil is indispensable. Fried foods won't be crispy and brown without them. You can prevent food from sticking to the air fryer basket by spraying it with cooking oil beforehand.

When air frying foods with a dry coating, such as breadcrumbs or flour, you should drizzle oil on them first. Foods that are already fatty should not be oiled, nor should they be oiled in advance.

To improve the food's flavor and use the air fryer safely, oil should be drizzled over the basket or the food itself before air frying. Adding a few drops of oil or brushing it on lean meat, vegetables, and potatoes is also a good idea.

Vegetable oils such as canola, avocado, and grapeseed should be substituted for olive oil. Olive oil does not burn well.

2. Avoid Wet Batter

Deep fryers involve dipping the meat in egg and then frying it in a simmering pot of oil, which is not the case with air fryers. Wet batters work well in deep fryers but not in air fryers.

If the fan blows the batter off, a mess will likely occur. As part of our recipes, we mention dipping in egg wash, coating in flour, and finishing with breadcrumbs to start cooking safely with dry ingredients.

The dry batter turns crispy and golden-brown in an air fryer, just like fried food! However, baking requires wet batter. So rather than adding wet batter directly into the air fryer basket, use a cake pan or a different pan instead.

3. Don't Overfill The Basket

Before, we looked at how the hot air is dispersed by exhaust fans used in air fryers. This is what causes browning and caramelization to occur. When there is more room in the basket, the cooking is better. With less space, cooking isn't as even. So, don't overfill the basket to avoid wet and sweaty food due to slow cooking or blockage of hot air. Do it in batches if necessary, but don't overload your appliance.

4. Cook More Than Just Fried Foods

The features of air fryers are there for a reason, and you can prepare all your favorite foods. Use your air fryer to perform all the functions of a convection oven. Make sure the air fryer is not just used for frying food. Try different ways of cooking to get to know your air fryer better!

5. Keep An Eye On Your Food

The convenience of food being snuck in and forgotten until the beeper beeps make air fryers quite popular. Although certain foods like French fries and salmon require constant attention, so they are not undercooked or overcooked, they should be shaken properly.

It is not a good idea to leave everything up to the air fryer, as this may ruin your food. Sometimes, leaving the device on its own can work, especially in an emergency, but depending on it all the time is not the way to cook.

6. Invest In What You Need

It is a fact. To get the most out of your air fryer, choose a model that meets your needs from the very beginning. A small-capacity air fryer can't be able to serve a large family, so research, expectations, usage, and your situation all play a role.

When purchasing an air fryer, keep in mind the features, capacity, and extras you desire. Would you be interested in having an air fryer with a heat-up or dehydration function? Or would you want a much less complex model? If you want the best possible experience with an air fryer, this all counts!

7. Maintain Proper Cleaning Routine

Every time you use your air fryer, you should clean it properly, so that food residues don't stick to the basket and become difficult to remove. The taste of fresh food cooked in the air fryer can also be affected by old food residue, so it is important to clean it beforehand.

To clean your air fryer basket, do not use harsh cleaners, scrubs, or products and if a food is particularly stubborn, soak the basket in water for 30 minutes. The stuck food bits should come loose fairly easily after this. A simple wash with soap and water is sufficient if the parts are handwash and dishwasher-safe. With a soft, dry cloth or kitchen towel, you can wipe away spills or smudges on and inside your appliance. Always keep the drip tray clean, and before using the air fryer basket, make sure it is dry.

COMMON Q&A

Any Safety Precautions To Take With An Air Fryer?

The same safety measures apply to air fryers as to all other appliances. You should always read the instructions before using a product. Nevertheless, we will explain the steps you can follow to ensure your air fryer stays in top-notch condition for a long time.

- Many kitchen appliances, such as trays and pans, have non-stick linings handled with care. Use non-stick accessories with your air fryer's non-stick basket, such as a silicone spatula when flipping food or serving.

- You won't have to worry about the non-stick lining wearing off, chipping off, or getting into your food if you use non-stick accessories & utensils.

- For greasing your air fryer basket, use your sprays filled with oil rather than store-bought cooking sprays. The non-stick lining can be damaged by cooking oil sprays sold in stores that contain propellants. To apply the oil directly, use a pastry brush. Don't be harsh!

- You should keep air fryers away from things and avoid touching them unnecessarily since they get very hot very quickly. For example, to protect your countertop, keep the hot basket under a heat-resistant surface and lay it down on a heat-proof mat every time you remove it.

- You should keep yourself and any items away from air fryers; they have air vents to cool off. The exhaust fans of these appliances can get very hot if they are used. To allow heat to escape, maintain a gap of at least 5 inches between the wall and the appliance. It's the same as setting up a convection oven.

Do Air Fryers Use Special Measurements For Ingredients?
Good question! But measurements never change for any device; they stay the same. To help you out, use the following measurement chart for accurate measuring of the ingredients in the food recipes.

US STANDARD MEASUREMENT CONVERSIONS

Metric to standard Fahrenheit to Celsius Cups to tablespoons Oz to grams	
5 ml = 1 tsp	1/2 cup = 8 tbsp
15 ml = 1 tbsp	3/4 cup = 12 tbsp
30 ml = 1 fluid oz	1 cup = 16 tbsp
240 ml = 1 cup	8 fluid oz = 1 cup
1 liter = 34 fluid oz	1 pint 2 cups = 16 fluid oz
1 liter = 4.2 cups	1 quart 2 pints = 4 cups
1 gram = .035 oz	1 gallon 4 quarts = 16 cups
100 grams = 3.5 oz	1 oz = 29 g
500 grams = 1.10 lb.	2 oz = 57 g
300 F = 150 C	3 oz = 85 g
350 F = 180 C	4 oz = 113 g
375 F = 190 C	5 oz = 142 g
400 F = 200 C	6 oz = 170 g
425 F = 220 C	7 oz = 198 g
450 F = 230 C	8 oz = 227 g
3 tsp = 1 tbsp	10 oz = 283 g
1/8 cup = 2 tbsp	20 oz = 567 g
1/4 cup = 4 tbsp	30 oz = 850 g
1/3 cup = 5 tbsp + 1 tsp	

CHAPTER 1:
Breakfast

Spinach Mozzarella Baked Eggs

Preparation Time: 5 minutes | Cooking Time: 7 minutes | Servings: 1

Ingredients:
- 2 eggs
- ¼ teaspoon salt
- Cooking spray as needed
- 1 tablespoon cooking cream
- ⅛ teaspoon ground black pepper
- Silicone muffin cups or ramekins as needed
- 1 tablespoon grated mozzarella cheese
- 1 tablespoon frozen & thawed chopped spinach

Directions:
1. Set the air fryer to 330 degrees.
2. Grease the muffin cups or ramekins with cooking spray.
3. Mix all the ingredients in a bowl and pour the batter into the cups.
4. Place the cups into the air fryer and bake for 7 minutes.
5. Remove from the air fryer and enjoy it hot!

Mushroom Kale Frittata

Preparation Time: 10 minutes | Cooking Time: 15 minutes | Servings: 2

Ingredients:
- 4 eggs
- ½ teaspoon salt
- 1 cup kale
- 1 cup sliced mushrooms
- Parchment paper as needed
- ¼ cup grated parmesan cheese
- ¼ teaspoon ground black pepper
- 7-inch round baking pan as needed
- 3 tablespoons heavy whipping cream

Directions:
1. Make sure the round baking pan you pick fits into your air fryer — 7 inches is the standard.
2. Set the temperature to 350 degrees Fahrenheit.
3. Line your baking pan with parchment paper
4. Mix the eggs with cream, salt, and pepper in a bowl.
5. Combine the rest of the ingredients and pour the batter into the pan.
6. Transfer the pan to the air fryer and cook for 15 minutes or until done.
7. Cut into wedges and serve immediately.

Hard-Boiled Eggs

Preparation Time: 1 minute | Cooking Time: 16 minutes | Servings: 3

Ingredients:
- 6 eggs
- Ice water as needed

Directions:
1. Set the temperature to 250 degrees Fahrenheit.
2. Put a wire rack into the air fryer and arrange the eggs on top.
3. Cook for 16 minutes and remove once done straight into the ice water bowl to cool.
4. Peel and serve!

Simple Baked Eggs

Preparation Time: 5 minutes | Cooking Time: 6 minutes | Servings: 1

Ingredients:
- 2 eggs
- ¼ teaspoon kosher salt
- Cooking spray as needed
- 1 tablespoon cooking cream
- ⅛ teaspoon ground black pepper
- Silicone muffin cups or ramekins as needed

Directions:
1. Set the air fryer to 330 degrees.
2. Grease the muffin cups or ramekins with cooking spray.
3. Mix all the ingredients in a bowl and pour the batter into the ramekins.
4. Place the cups into the air fryer and bake for 6 minutes.
5. Remove from the air fryer and enjoy it hot!

Bacon & Brie Frittata

Preparation Time: 10 minutes | Cooking Time: 10 minutes | Servings: 2

Ingredients:
- 4 eggs
- ½ teaspoon kosher salt
- ½ cup sliced brie
- ½ cup cooked & chopped bacon
- ¼ teaspoon ground black pepper
- 3 tablespoons cooking cream
- 7-inch round baking pan
- Parchment paper as needed

Directions:
1. Make sure the round baking pan you pick fits into your air fryer — 7 inches is the standard.
2. Preheat the air fryer to 350 degrees Fahrenheit.
3. Line your baking pan with parchment paper
4. Mix the eggs with cream, salt, and pepper in a bowl.
5. Combine the bacon and brie and transfer the mixture into the pan.
6. Put the pan into the air fryer and cook for 10 minutes or until done.
7. Cut into wedges and serve immediately.

Bacon & Eggs

Preparation Time: 5 minutes | Cooking Time: 8 minutes | Servings: 1

Ingredients:
- 2 eggs
- ¼ teaspoon kosher salt
- Cooking spray as needed
- Ramekins or silicone muffin cups
- 1 tablespoon cooking cream
- 1/8 teaspoon ground black pepper
- 2 tablespoons cooked & crumbled bacon

Directions:
1. Set the air fryer to 330 degrees Fahrenheit.
2. Grease the muffin cup or ramekin with cooking spray.
3. Mix all the ingredients in a bowl and pour the batter into a ramekin.
4. Place it into the air fryer and bake for 8 minutes or until set.
5. Remove from the air fryer and enjoy it hot!

Avocado Baked Eggs

Preparation Time: 5 minutes | Cooking Time: 7 minutes | Servings: 1

Ingredients:
- 2 eggs
- ¼ teaspoon salt
- ¼ diced avocado
- Cooking spray as needed
- 1 tablespoon cooking cream
- Silicone muffin cups or ramekins
- ⅛ teaspoon ground black pepper
- 1 tablespoon grated mozzarella cheese

Directions:
1. Preheat the air fryer to 330 degrees Fahrenheit.
2. Grease the muffin cup or ramekin with cooking spray.
3. Mix the ingredients in a bowl.
4. Lastly, add the avocado and pour the mixture into a ramekin.
5. Place it into the air fryer and bake for 7 minutes or until set.
6. Remove from the air fryer and enjoy it hot!

Bacon & Kale Frittata

Preparation Time: 10 minutes | Cooking Time: 15 minutes | Servings: 2

Ingredients:
- 4 eggs
- ½ teaspoon kosher salt
- Round baking pan as needed
- Parchment paper as needed
- ½ cup stemless chopped kale
- ½ cup cooked & chopped bacon
- ¼ teaspoon ground black pepper
- 3 tablespoons cooking cream

Directions:
1. Make sure the round baking pan you pick fits into your air fryer — 7 inches is the standard.
2. Preheat the air fryer to 350 degrees Fahrenheit.
3. Line your baking pan with parchment paper.
4. Mix the eggs with cream, salt, and pepper in a bowl.
5. Combine the bacon and kale and transfer the mixture into the pan.
6. Put the pan into the air fryer and cook for 15 minutes or until done.
7. Cut into wedges and serve immediately.

Yummy Almond Pancake

Preparation Time: 10 minutes | Cooking Time: 8 minutes | Servings: 2

Ingredients:
- 2 eggs
- ⅛ teaspoon salt
- ½ cup almond milk
- 1 ¼ cup almond flour
- 1 teaspoon vanilla extract
- 1 teaspoon baking soda
- Parchment paper as needed
- 2 tablespoons melted butter
- Round baking pan as needed
- 2 tablespoons granulated erythritol

Directions:
1. Make sure the round baking pan you pick fits into your air fryer — 7 inches is the standard.
2. Preheat the air fryer to 400 degrees Fahrenheit.
3. Line your baking pan with parchment paper.
4. Puree eggs, milk, butter, and vanilla extract in a blender for a minute.
5. Follow with the remaining ingredients and blend until smooth.
6. Pour the mixture into the pan and transfer it to the air fryer.
7. Cook for 7 minutes or until golden brown from the top.
8. Slice before serving with a syrup of choice.

French Omelet

Preparation Time: 5 minutes | Cooking Time: 10 minutes | Servings: 4

Ingredients:
- 4 eggs
- ½ teaspoon kosher salt

- Parchment paper as needed
- Round baking pan as needed
- ¼ teaspoon ground black pepper
- 3 tablespoons cooking cream
- 2 teaspoons fresh chopped fines herbs

Directions:
1. Make sure the round baking pan you pick fits into your air fryer — 7 inches is the standard.
2. Preheat the air fryer to 350 degrees Fahrenheit.
3. Line your baking pan with parchment paper.
4. Mix all the ingredients in a bowl.
5. Transfer the mixture to the pan.
6. Put the pan into the air fryer and cook for 10 minutes or until done.
7. Flip the omelet in half and cut before serving.

Indian Masala Omelet

Preparation Time: 5 minutes | Cooking Time: 10 minutes | Servings: 4

Ingredients:
- 4 eggs
- ½ teaspoon salt
- 1 teaspoon curry powder
- ¼ teaspoon garam masala
- Parchment paper as needed
- Round baking pan as needed
- ¼ teaspoon ground black pepper
- 1 tablespoon chopped scallions
- 3 tablespoons cooking cream

Directions:
1. Make sure the round baking pan you pick fits into your air fryer — 7 inches is the standard.
2. Preheat the air fryer to 350 degrees Fahrenheit.
3. Line your baking pan with parchment paper.
4. Mix all the ingredients in a bowl.
5. Transfer the mixture to the pan.
6. Put the pan into the air fryer and cook for 10 minutes or until done.
7. Flip the omelet in half and cut before serving.

Quick Kimchi Breakfast

Preparation Time: 5 minutes | Cooking Time: 10 minutes | Servings: 4

Ingredients:
- 4 eggs
- ¼ cup kimchi
- ½ teaspoon salt
- Parchment paper as needed
- Round baking pan as needed
- ¼ teaspoon ground black pepper
- 3 tablespoons cooking cream

Directions:
1. Make sure the round baking pan you pick fits into your air fryer — 7 inches is the standard.
2. Preheat the air fryer to 350 degrees Fahrenheit.
3. Line your baking pan with parchment paper.
4. Mix eggs, cream, salt, and pepper in a bowl.
5. Transfer the mixture to the pan.
6. Put the pan into the air fryer and cook for 10 minutes or until done.
7. Spread kimchi over your omelet and fold it in half.
8. Cut into wedges before serving.

Yummy Nutty Granola

Preparation Time: 10 minutes | Cooking Time: 18 minutes | Servings: 12

Ingredients:
- ⅓ cup hemp seeds
- 1 whisked egg white
- ¼ cup melted butter
- ⅓ cup sunflower seeds
- ½ cup ground flaxseeds
- 1 teaspoon vanilla extract
- Parchment paper as needed
- 1 cup finely-chopped pecans
- 1 cup finely-chopped almonds
- ½ cup finely-chopped walnuts
- ½ cup peeled & finely-chopped pistachio

Directions:
1. Preheat the air fryer to 325 degrees Fahrenheit.
2. Line the air fryer with parchment paper.
3. Add all the ingredients to a bowl and mix thoroughly.
4. Transfer the mixture to the air fryer basket and cook for 18 minutes.
5. Give a toss after 9 minutes to ensure even baking.
6. Remove the contents of the basket and set them aside to cool.
7. Enjoy with yogurt, milk, or alone.

Raspberry Nut Cereal

Preparation Time: 10 minutes | Cooking Time: 12 minutes | Servings: 12

Ingredients:
- ⅓ cup hemp seeds
- 1 whisked egg white
- ¼ cup melted butter
- ⅓ cup sunflower seeds
- ½ cup ground flaxseeds
- 1 teaspoon vanilla extract
- ½ cup dried raspberry
- Parchment paper as needed
- 1 cup finely-chopped pecans
- 1 cup finely-chopped almonds
- ½ cup finely-chopped walnuts

Directions:
1. Preheat the air fryer to 325 degrees Fahrenheit.
2. Line the air fryer with parchment paper.
3. Add all the ingredients to a bowl and mix thoroughly.
4. Transfer the mixture to the air fryer basket and cook for 18 minutes.
5. Give a toss after 9 minutes to ensure even baking.
6. Remove the contents of the basket and set them aside to cool.
7. Enjoy with yogurt, milk, or alone.

Stuffed Pepper Baked Eggs

Preparation Time: 5 minutes | Cooking Time: 14 minutes | Servings: 2

Ingredients:
- 4 eggs
- ½ teaspoon salt
- 2 tablespoons cooking cream
- ⅛ teaspoon ground black pepper
- 2 tablespoons grated mozzarella cheese
- 1 large seedless & cut half vertically red pepper
- 2 tablespoons frozen, thawed & chopped spinach

Directions:
1. Preheat the air fryer to 330 degrees Fahrenheit.
2. Arrange the halved red peppers in the air fryer basket and cook for 5 minutes.

3. Mix all the ingredients in a bowl.
4. Divide the batter into red peppers and bake for 7 minutes.
5. Serve hot immediately and enjoy.

Bacon Egg Stuffed Peppers

Preparation Time: 5 minutes | Cooking Time: 14 minutes | Servings: 2

Ingredients:
- 4 eggs
- ½ teaspoon salt
- 2 tablespoons cooking cream
- ⅛ teaspoon ground black pepper
- 2 tablespoons chopped cooked bacon
- 2 tablespoons grated mozzarella cheese
- 1 large seedless & cut half vertically red pepper

Directions:
1. Preheat the air fryer to 330 degrees Fahrenheit.
2. Arrange the halved red peppers in the air fryer basket and cook for 5 minutes.
3. Mix all the ingredients in a bowl.
4. Divide the batter into the red peppers and bake for 7 minutes.
5. Serve hot immediately and enjoy.

Cheesy Egg Stuffed Peppers

Preparation Time: 5 minutes | Cooking Time: 14 minutes | Servings: 2

Ingredients:
- 4 eggs
- ½ teaspoon salt
- 2 tablespoons cooking cream
- ⅛ teaspoon ground black pepper
- 2 tablespoons grated cheddar cheese
- 2 tablespoons grated mozzarella cheese
- 1 large seedless & cut half vertically red pepper

Directions:
1. Preheat the air fryer to 330 degrees Fahrenheit.
2. Arrange the halved red peppers in the air fryer basket and cook for 5 minutes.
3. Mix all the ingredients in a bowl.
4. Divide the batter into the red peppers and bake for 7 minutes.
5. Serve hot immediately and enjoy.

Easy Egg Stuffed Peppers

Preparation Time: 5 minutes | Cooking Time: 14 minutes | Servings: 2

Ingredients:
- 4 eggs
- ½ teaspoon salt
- 1 sliced jalapeno
- 2 tablespoons cooking cream
- ⅛ teaspoon ground black pepper
- 2 tablespoons grated mozzarella cheese
- 1 large seedless & cut half vertically red pepper

Directions:
1. Preheat the air fryer to 330 degrees Fahrenheit.
2. Arrange the halved red peppers in the air fryer basket and cook for 5 minutes.
3. Mix all the ingredients in a bowl.
4. Divide the batter into the red peppers and bake for 7 minutes.
5. Serve hot immediately and enjoy.

Quick Brussels Hash

Preparation Time: 10 minutes | Cooking Time: 25 minutes | Servings: 4

Ingredients:
- 4 beaten eggs
- ½ teaspoon kosher salt
- 2 minced garlic cloves
- ½ cup chopped red onion
- 1 oz. quartered Brussels sprouts
- 6 slices of cooked & chopped bacon
- ½ teaspoon ground black pepper

Directions:
1. Preheat the air fryer to 350 degrees Fahrenheit.
2. Mix bacon, onion, garlic, Brussels, salt, and pepper in a bowl.
3. Transfer the mixture to a 7-inch baking pan and place it in the air fryer.
4. Make sure the pan fits inside and cook the ingredients for 15 minutes.
5. Add the whisked eggs to the mixture and return the pan to the air fryer to cook for an additional 10 minutes.
6. Combine thoroughly to break up the hash before serving.

Ham, Cheese & Mushroom Melt

Preparation Time: 12 minutes | Cooking Time: 18 minutes | Servings: 4

Ingredients:
- 2 tablespoons butter
- 1 minced garlic clove
- ½ oz. sliced mushrooms
- ¼ cup diced white onion
- 1-16 oz. cooked ham steak
- 1 cup grated parmesan cheese
- ¼ cup cooked & crumbled bacon
- 1 tablespoon chopped fresh cilantro

Directions:
1. Preheat the air fryer to 350 degrees Fahrenheit.
2. Combine butter and onion in a pan that fits inside the air fryer and cook for 5 minutes.
3. Take out the pan and mix in garlic and mushrooms.
4. Once again, fit the pan in the air fryer and cook for another 5 minutes.
5. Again, remove the pan and place ham and top with cheese.
6. Return the pan to the air fryer and cook for 8 more minutes.
7. Garnish with cilantro before serving!

Vegetable Melt

Preparation Time: 10 minutes | Cooking Time: 14 minutes | Servings: 4

Ingredients:
- 2 tablespoons butter
- 1 minced garlic clove
- 1 cup diced zucchini
- ½ oz. sliced mushrooms
- ¼ cup diced white onion
- 1 cup chopped kale
- 1 cup grated gruyere cheese
- 1 cup diced green bell peppers
- 1 tablespoon chopped fresh cilantro

Directions:
1. Preheat the air fryer to 350 degrees Fahrenheit.
2. Combine butter, onion, and bell peppers in a pan that fits inside the air fryer and cook for 5 minutes.
3. Take out the pan and mix in garlic, zucchini, and mushrooms.

4. Once again, fit the pan in the air fryer and cook for another 5 minutes.
5. Again, remove the pan and add kale and sprinkle cheese.
6. Return the pan to the air fryer and cook for 4 more minutes.
7. Garnish with cilantro before serving!

Veggie Hash

Preparation Time: 10 minutes | Cooking Time: 25 minutes | Servings: 4

Ingredients:
- 4 beaten eggs
- ½ teaspoon kosher salt
- 2 minced garlic cloves
- ½ cup chopped red onion
- 2 cups diced green bell peppers
- ½ teaspoon ground black pepper
- 6 slices of cooked & chopped bacon
- 2 cups quartered Brussels sprouts

Directions:
1. Preheat the air fryer to 350 degrees Fahrenheit.
2. Mix bacon, onion, garlic, Brussels, bell peppers, salt, and pepper in a bowl.
3. Transfer the mixture to a 7-inch baking pan and place it in the air fryer.
4. Make sure the pan fits inside and cook the ingredients for 15 minutes.
5. Add the whisked eggs to the mixture and return the pan to the air fryer to cook for an additional 10 minutes.
6. Combine thoroughly to break up the hash before serving.

Cheesy Pancake

Preparation Time: 10 minutes | Cooking Time: 9 minutes | Servings: 2

Ingredients:
- 2 eggs
- ⅛ teaspoon salt
- ½ cup almond milk
- 1 ¼ cup almond flour
- 1 teaspoon vanilla extract
- 1 teaspoon baking powder
- Parchment paper as needed
- 2 tablespoons melted butter
- Round baking pan as needed
- ½ cup grated mozzarella cheese
- 2 tablespoons granulated erythritol

Directions:
1. Make sure the round baking pan you pick fits into your air fryer — 7 inches is the standard.
2. Preheat the air fryer to 400 degrees Fahrenheit.
3. Line your baking pan with parchment paper.
4. Puree eggs, milk, butter, and vanilla extract in a blender for a minute.
5. Follow with the remaining ingredients except for cheese and blend until smooth.
6. Pour the mixture into the pan, mix in the cheese, and transfer it to the air fryer.
7. Cook for 9 minutes or until puffed and golden brown from the top.
8. Slice before serving with a syrup of choice.

Strawberry Cheese Pancake

Preparation Time: 10 minutes | Cooking Time: 9 minutes | Servings: 2

Ingredients:
- 2 eggs
- ⅛ teaspoon salt

- ½ cup whole milk
- ¼ cup feta cheese
- 1 ¼ cup all-purpose flour
- 1 teaspoon vanilla extract
- 1 teaspoon baking soda
- 2 tablespoons melted butter
- ¼ cup chopped strawberries
- Round baking pan as needed
- Parchment paper as needed
- 2 tablespoons granulated erythritol

Directions:
1. Make sure the round baking pan you pick fits into your air fryer — 7 inches is the standard.
2. Preheat the air fryer to 400 degrees Fahrenheit.
3. Line your baking pan with parchment paper.
4. Puree eggs, milk, butter, and vanilla extract in a blender for a minute.
5. Follow the remaining ingredients except for cheese and strawberries and blend until smooth.
6. Pour the mixture into the pan, mix in the cheese and strawberries, and transfer it to the air fryer.
7. Cook for 9 minutes or until puffed and golden brown from the top.
8. Slice before serving with a syrup of choice.

Breakfast Egg Bowls

Preparation Time: 10 minutes | Cooking Time: 20 minutes | Servings: 4

Ingredients:
- 4 eggs
- 4 tablespoons cooking cream
- Salt & black pepper as needed
- Baking sheet or pan as needed
- 4 tablespoons grated mozzarella
- 4 tablespoons mixed chives & parsley
- 4 tops off and insides cut out dinner rolls

Directions:
1. Use a baking sheet that fits inside the air fryer.
2. Place dinner rolls on it and cracks an egg in each.
3. Fill each dinner roll with cooking cream, mixed herbs, salt, and pepper.
4. Top with mozzarella and place the sheet in the air fryer.
5. Cook for 20 minutes at 350 degrees Fahrenheit.
6. Serve on plates and enjoy!

Air Fried Sandwich Muffins

Preparation Time: 10 minutes | Cooking Time: 6 minutes | Servings: 2

Ingredients:
- 2 eggs
- 2 bacon strips
- 2 halved English muffins
- Salt & black pepper as needed

Directions:
1. Add cracked eggs to the air fryer with bacon.
2. Close the lid and cook for 6 minutes at 392 degrees Fahrenheit.
3. Warm up the muffins in the microwave for thirty seconds.
4. Divide the contents of the air fryer on each halved muffin and season with salt and pepper.
5. Serve and enjoy hot!

Polenta Bites

Preparation Time: 10 minutes | Cooking Time: 20 minutes | Servings: 4

Ingredients:
- 3 cups water
- 1 cup cornmeal
- 1 tablespoon butter
- Cooking spray as needed
- Salt & black pepper as needed
- 2 tablespoons brown sugar

Directions:
1. Stir in all the ingredients except sugar in a pan over medium heat.
2. Let it boil before removing heat, stir it, and store it in the fridge to cool.
3. Shape 1 tablespoon of polenta into a ball and do the same with the remaining mixture.
4. Grease the air fryer basket with cooking spray and place the polenta balls.
5. Cover and cook for 8 minutes at 380 degrees Fahrenheit.
6. Serve on plates with a sprinkling of sugar on top.

Tasty Cinnamon Toast

Preparation Time: 10 minutes | Cooking Time: 5 minutes | Servings: 6

Ingredients:
- ½ cup brown sugar
- 12 whole-wheat bread slices
- 1 soft stick of butter
- 1 ½ teaspoon vanilla extract
- 1 ½ teaspoon cinnamon powder

Directions:
1. Combine all the ingredients except bread in a bowl.
2. Spread the mixture on bread slices and arrange them in the air fryer.
3. Cover and cook for 5 minutes at 400 degrees Fahrenheit.
4. Serve immediately and enjoy!

Yummy Breakfast Soufflé

Preparation Time: 10 minutes | Cooking Time: 8 minutes | Servings: 4

Ingredients:
- 4 beaten eggs
- Souffle dishes as needed
- 4 tablespoons cooking cream
- 2 tablespoons chopped cilantro
- 2 tablespoons chopped chives
- Salt & black pepper as needed
- A pinch of crushed red chili pepper

Directions:
1. Combine all the ingredients in a bowl and transfer them to the souffle dishes.
2. Place the dishes in the air fryer and cover them.
3. Cook for 8 minutes at 350 degrees Fahrenheit.
4. Remove and eat straight from the souffle dishes.

Yummy Potato Hash

Preparation Time: 10 minutes | Cooking Time: 25 minutes | Servings: 4

Ingredients:
- 2 eggs
- 1 ½ cubed potatoes
- 2 teaspoons canola oil
- 1 chopped yellow onion
- ½ teaspoon dried oregano
- 1 chopped green bell pepper
- Salt & black pepper as needed

Directions:
1. Preheat the air fryer to 350 degrees Fahrenheit.
2. Stir in oil, onion, bell pepper, salt, and pepper, and cover to cook for 5 minutes.

3. Next, add the remaining ingredients and cook for another 20 minutes at 360 degrees Fahrenheit.
4. Serve and enjoy hot!

Biscuits Casserole

Preparation Time: 10 minutes | Cooking Time: 15 minutes | Servings: 8

Ingredients:
- 2 ½ cups almond milk
- 3 tablespoons almond flour
- ½ oz. chopped sausage
- 12 oz. quartered biscuits
- Cooking spray as needed
- Salt & black pepper as needed

Directions:
1. Use cooking spray to grease the air fryer and preheat at 350 degrees Fahrenheit.
2. Place biscuits on the bottom and combine with chopped sausage.
3. Toss in the remaining ingredients and cover to cook for 15 minutes.
4. Serve and enjoy hot!

Eggs Casserole

Preparation Time: 10 minutes | Cooking Time: 25 minutes | Servings: 6

Ingredients:
- 12 eggs
- 1 cup kale
- 1 oz. ground turkey
- 1 cubed sweet potato
- 1 tablespoon olive oil
- ½ teaspoon paprika
- Salt & black pepper as needed
- 2 chopped tomatoes as needed

Directions:
1. Whisk eggs in a bowl with the rest of the ingredients except oil and tomatoes.
2. Preheat the oven to 350 degrees Fahrenheit.
3. Add oil to the egg mixture, and cover to cook for 25 minutes.
4. Serve hot with chopped tomatoes, and enjoy!

Cheese Air Fried Bake

Preparation Time: 10 minutes | Cooking Time: 20 minutes | Servings: 4

Ingredients:
- 2 eggs
- 2 cups milk
- Cooking spray as needed
- ½ teaspoon onion powder
- Salt & black pepper as needed
- 3 tablespoons chopped cilantro
- 4 cooked & crumbled bacon slices
- 2 ½ cups shredded mozzarella cheese
- 1 oz. casings removed & chopped breakfast sausage

Directions:
1. Whisk eggs in a bowl with the rest of the ingredients except bacon and sausage.
2. Preheat the oven to 320 degrees Fahrenheit.
3. Grease the air fryer with cooking spray. Add bacon, sausage, and the egg mixture and cover to cook for 20 minutes.
4. Serve hot and enjoy!

Oatmeal Casserole

Preparation Time: 10 minutes | Cooking Time: 20 minutes | Servings: 8

Ingredients:
- 1 egg
- 2 cups milk
- ⅔ cup blueberries
- 2 cups steel-cut oats
- ⅓ cup brown sugar
- 2 tablespoons butter
- ½ cup chocolate chips
- 1 teaspoon vanilla extract
- Cooking spray as needed
- 1 teaspoon baking soda
- 1 peeled & mashed banana
- 1 teaspoon cinnamon powder

Directions:
1. Combine sugar, baking soda, cinnamon, chocolate chips, blueberries, and banana in a bowl.
2. Combine eggs, vanilla extract, and butter in a separate bowl.
3. Preheat the air fryer to 320 degrees Fahrenheit.
4. Use cooking spray to grease the air fryer and spread oats in it.
5. Toss in both the bowl mixes, cinnamon first, egg mix second.
6. Cover and cook for 20 minutes.
7. Stir before serving and enjoy hot!

Tomato Bacon Breakfast

Preparation Time: 10 minutes | Cooking Time: 30 minutes | Servings: 6

Ingredients:
- 8 beaten eggs
- ¼ cup olive oil
- 2 tablespoons chicken broth
- 1 oz. cubed white bread
- 1 chopped yellow onion
- ½ oz. shredded cheddar
- 2 tablespoons chopped chives
- ½ oz. shredded mozzarella jack
- Salt & black pepper as needed
- ½ teaspoon crushed red pepper
- 28 oz. chopped canned tomatoes
- 1 oz. cooked & chopped smoked bacon

Directions:
1. Add oil to the air fryer and preheat at 350 degrees Fahrenheit.
2. Stir in all the ingredients and cover to cook for 20 minutes.
3. Serve with a sprinkling of chives, and enjoy!

Raspberry French Toast

Preparation Time: 10 minutes | Cooking Time: 20 minutes | Servings: 6

Ingredients:
- 4 eggs
- 2 cups half and half
- ½ cup powdered sugar
- 12 oz. cubed bread loaf
- Cooking spray as needed
- 8 oz. cubed cream cheese
- 1 teaspoon vanilla extract
- 1 cup warm raspberry jam
- 1 teaspoon cinnamon powder

Directions:

1. Use cooking spray to grease the air fryer and preheat at 300 degrees.
2. Spread raspberry on the bottom of the air fryer and add half of the bread cubes.
3. Add cream cheese and cover with the remaining half of the bread.
4. Combine eggs with half and half, cinnamon, powdered sugar, and vanilla extract in a bowl and pour on the contents in the air fryer.
5. Cover and cook for 20 minutes.
6. Serve immediately and enjoy!

Asparagus Frittata

Preparation Time: 10 minutes | Cooking Time: 5 minutes | Servings: 2

Ingredients:

- 4 beaten eggs
- 4 tablespoons whole milk
- Cooking spray as needed
- 10 steamed asparagus tips
- Salt & black pepper as needed
- 2 tablespoons grated mozzarella

Directions:

1. Combine all the ingredients in a bowl except asparagus.
2. Preheat the air fryer to 400 degrees and use cooking spray to grease the inside.
3. Toss in asparagus the egg mixture and cover to cook for 5 minutes.
4. Serve immediately and enjoy!

Oatmeal Flax Muffins

Preparation Time: 15 minutes | Cooking Time: 15 minutes | Servings: 4

Ingredients
Dry Ingredients

- 2.5 cups of wheat flour
- 2.5 cups of oats
- ½ cup of brown sugar
- 2tablespoons of flaxseed powder
- 2 teaspoons of cinnamon
- 1teaspoon of baking powder
- Salt according to taste

Wet Ingredients

- 1 cup of almond milk
- 2 eggs
- 1/4 cup of olive oil
- 1 teaspoon of vanilla extract
- 4 bananas (ripened & peeled)

Directions

1. Take a bowl and beat together all the wet ingredients.
2. Now take another bowl and thoroughly stir the dry ingredients.
3. Now mix both the wet and dry ingredients.
4. Take a muffin cup lined with muffin papers, and pour the mixture into it.
5. Add the muffin cups to the air fryer basket.
6. Add the basket to the unit.
7. Set the temperature of the air fryer to 400 degrees f.
8. Set the time to 15 minutes.
9. Once done, serve the baked muffins!

Turkey Filled Omelets

Preparation Time: 15 minutes | Cooking Time: minutes | Servings: 4

Ingredients

- 2 tablespoons of olive oil

- 4 tablespoons of champignon mushroom
- 4 chopped shallot
- 2 sage leaves
- 2 teaspoons of chili flakes (crushed)
- ¼ teaspoon of white pepper
- Salt, to taste
- 1 .5 cup of turkey (cooked & shredded)
- 6 eggs, whisked

For toppings

- 2 tablespoons of crème Fraiche

Directions

1. Ignite the flame on medium heat, put a frying pan over it, and add olive oil.
2. Cook for 5 minutes all the ingredients in the frying pan except the egg and turkey, and toppings.
3. Now put in the turkey, cook for 3 minutes, and put it aside.
4. Take a medium-sized bowl and beat the egg with salt and pepper.
5. Now add the cooked turkey once it has cooled into the egg mixture.
6. Take a cake pan and mist it with oil. And pour in the egg-turkey mixture in it.
7. Add the cake pan to the air fryer basket.
8. Add the basket to the unit.
9. Set the temperature of the air fryer to 400 degrees f.
10. Set the time to 6-8 minutes.
11. Once cooked, put the seasoning over the omelets and serve!

Air Fryer Egg Cups

Preparation Time: 12 minutes | Cooking Time: 10 minutes | Servings: 4

Ingredients

- 6 eggs
- 4 tablespoons of cream
- 4 tablespoons of mozzarella cheese
- 4 ounces of sausages
- 2 cloves of garlic minced
- ½ cup of kale
- Olive oil, as needed

Directions

1. Cook the sausages over medium heat in a frying pan for 5 minutes and put them aside.
2. Add some olive oil and sauté the garlic paste in the same frying pan.
3. Add the kale to the frying pan and wilt the kale.
4. Mix the sausages, cream, mozzarella, and eggs in a bowl.
5. Brush some oil in muffin cups and pour in the egg mixture.
6. Add the muffins to the air fryer basket or air fryer tray.
7. Add the basket to the unit.
8. Set the temperature of the air fryer to 350 degrees F.
9. Set the time to 10 minutes.
10. Serve once done!

Mediterranean Frittata

Preparation Time: 12 minutes | Cooking Time: 12 minutes | Servings: 4

Ingredients

- 8 eggs
- 1 /2 cup of cooking cream
- ½ ounces of cheddar
- 2 bell peppers
- 2 cups of mushrooms diced into cubes
- 10 slices of bacon (cooked and diced)

- 2 tablespoons of dill, chopped
- Salt and Pepper according to taste

Directions
1. Whisk eggs and cream in a bowl.
2. Pour in the sliced mushrooms, bell pepper, cooked bacon, and cheddar.
3. Put the mixture into a round pan greased with oil spray.
4. Add the salt and pepper according to taste as well.
5. Put the pan in the air fryer basket and bake in the air fryer for 12 minutes at 350 degrees F.
6. Use the dill to serve with the frittata once cooked!

Air Fryer Breakfast Cottage Pizza

Preparation Time: 12 minutes | Cooking Time: 8 minutes | Servings: 4

Ingredients
- 1 pizza dough made from wheat
- 5 eggs (scrambled)
- ½ cup Italian sausages
- 1 /3 cup chopped red bell peppers
- 1 cup of cottage cheese

Directions
1. Use some cooking spray or olive oil to brush over a pizza pan.
2. Put the dough in the pan and cook in the air fryer at 350 degrees F for 5 minutes.
3. Then take out the dough and add eggs, sausage, bell pepper, and cheese
4. Cook in an air fryer until cheese melts.
5. Serve.

Prosciutto & Kale Egg Cups

Preparation Time: 15 minutes | Cooking Time: 10 minutes | Servings: 1-3

Ingredients
- 3 slices of prosciuttos
- 4 eggs, whisked
- ¼ cup of kale leaves
- Oil spray, for greasing

Directions
1. Mist the three muffin cups with oil.
2. Distribute equally the prosciutto in muffin cups
3. Put in the kale and add whisked eggs equally.
4. Season with salt and pepper according to taste.
5. Bake the mixture in the air fryer basket at 350 degrees F for 10 minutes.
6. Serve once done!

Greek-Style Frittata

Preparation Time: 12 minutes | Cooking Time: 12 minutes | Servings: 2

Ingredients
- 2 eggs
- 1 ½ tablespoon of cooking cream
- ½ cup of baby spinach
- 4 tablespoons of feta cheese
- ½ cup of cherry tomatoes
- 4 tablespoons of thinly sliced onions
- ½ teaspoon of dried thyme
- Salt and pepper according to taste

Directions
1. Take a cake pan and grease it with some oil.
2. Whisk the cream and egg in a bowl.
3. Add the remaining ingredients and mix.
4. Pour the mixture into the cake pan and use aluminum foil to cover it.

5. Put it in the air fryer and cook for 12 minutes at 350 degrees f.
6. Once it's done, serve!

Green Casserole

Preparation Time: 12 minutes | Cooking Time: 22 minutes | Servings: 4

Ingredients
- 20 eggs
- 1 yellow onion
- 1 red pepper bell thinly sliced
- 4 teaspoons of kosher salt
- 12 ounces of spinach leaves
- 4 garlic cloves minced
- 4 tablespoons of dill
- 2 tablespoons of olive oil
- 4 cups of cooking cream
- 2 tablespoons of Dijon mustard
- ½ teaspoon of black pepper
- 10 ounces of cottage cheese

Directions
1. Take a frying pan and sauté some pepper, onion, salt, and oil.
2. Put in the minced garlic and the baby spinach and fry for 3 more minutes till the spinach becomes wilted.
3. Add the dill and shift the mixture into a baking dish greased with some oil.
4. Whisk eggs, cream, and mustard in a bowl with salt and pepper.
5. Drizzle it over the spinach and sprinkle it on top of the cottage cheese.
6. Transfer the mixture to the air fryer, bake at 350 degrees F, and cook for 18-22 minutes.
7. Once it's done, serve!

Kale, Feta, and Peppers Omelet

Preparation Time: 12 minutes | Cooking Time: 8 minutes | Servings: 1

Ingredients
- 2 eggs
- ½ tablespoon of olive oil
- 1 clove of minced onion
- 4 tablespoons of diced bell peppers
- ½ cup of kale
- 4 tablespoons of feta cheese
- Salt and pepper according to taste

Directions
1. Whisk egg with salt and pepper.
2. Fry bell peppers in olive oil in a pan for 2 minutes.
3. Add in some salt, pepper, minced onion, and kale, and cook for 2 more minutes.
4. Pour the mixture into a dish and let it cool.
5. Once it's cooled, pour the mixture and the egg into a cake pan and put it in the air fryer basket.
6. Put the basket inside the air fryer and cook it at 400 degrees F for 8 minutes.
7. Once it's done, season with some feta cheese and serve!

Air Fryer Vegetable Omelet

Preparation Time: 12 minutes | Cooking Time: 8-10 minutes | Servings: 1

Ingredients
- 1 egg
- 2 tablespoons of whole milk
- Salt to taste
- 4 tablespoons of mixed vegetables, chopped (personal preferences)

- 4 tablespoons of parmesan cheese (grated)
- Oil spray, for greasing

Directions
1. Beat the egg and milk in a bowl.
2. Pour in the salt and vegetables.
3. Take a round pan and grease it with some oil.
4. Pour the egg mixture into the round pan and add it to the air fryer basket.
5. Add the basket to the air fryer.
6. Cook it for 10 minutes at 350 degrees F.
7. Once 6 minutes pass, takes out the pan and top it with cheese.
8. Cook for 2 more minutes, and then serve.

Air Fryer Egg Bites

Preparation Time: 12 minutes | Cooking Time: 10 minutes | Servings: 1

Ingredients
- 2 eggs
- 1 tablespoon of heavy cream
- 1 tablespoon of scallions
- 4 tablespoons of grated cheese
- Salt and pepper according to taste

Directions
1. Brush some oil over the ramekins molds.
2. Add the scallions and shift the ramekins mold to the air fryer.
3. Set the temperature to 340 degrees F and cook for 5 minutes.
4. Simultaneously, whisk the eggs with cream, salt, and pepper.
5. Now take out the ramekins mold once the scallions are cooked, pour the egg mixture, and top it with cheese.
6. Add it back to the air fryer.
7. Set the time to 8 minutes and cook at 360 degrees F.
8. Once it's done, serve!

Sweet Potato Fritters

Preparation Time: 18 minutes | Cooking Time: 12 minutes | Servings: 3

Ingredients
- 1 cup of grated sweet potatoes
- ½ cup of all-purpose flour
- 4 tablespoons of red onions sliced
- 1/8 tablespoons of turmeric powder
- Olive oil
- Salt and pepper according to taste

Directions
1. Thoroughly mix all the ingredients in a medium-size bowl.
2. Use your hands to make patties from the mixture.
3. Grease the air fryer basket and line it with parchment paper.
4. According to capacity, add patties keeping the space between the air fryer basket.
5. Add it to the air fryer and cook at 350 degrees f for 12 minutes.
6. Make sure to flip the patties after halftime, tor evenly on both sides.
7. Once it's done, serve!

Crispy Quinoa Cakes

Preparation Time: 16 minutes | Cooking Time: 8 minutes | Servings: 2

Ingredients
- 1 1/2 cups of quinoa (cooked & chilled)
- ½ cup of shredded carrots

- ½ cup of shredded mozzarella cheese
- 1 tablespoon of oregano
- 1 clove of garlic minced
- 2 eggs
- 1/3 cup of breadcrumbs
- 1 ½ tablespoon of olive oil
- Salt and pepper according to taste

Directions
1. Thoroughly mix all the ingredients in a bowl except the breadcrumbs and basil.
2. Pour in the breadcrumbs and use your hands to make patties from the marinade.
3. Take a baking tray and brush over some oil.
4. Put in the patties and keep in the refrigerator for 2 hours.
5. Defrost the patties.
6. Shift the patties to an air fryer basket lined with parchment paper.
7. Mist patties with oil spray.
8. Set the temperature of the air fryer to 350 degrees F and cook for 8 minutes.
9. Flip the patties after halftime to cook evenly on both sides.
10. Once it's done, season with oregano and serve!

Mustard, Bacon, and Cheese Sandwich

Preparation Time: 12 minutes | Cooking Time: 12-14 minutes | Servings: 4

Ingredients
- 4 slices of sourdough bread (thick in size)
- 2 tablespoons of yellow mustard
- 2 slices of parmesan cheese
- 4 slices of bacon
- 2 tablespoons of butter

Directions
1. Take the butter and brush it over the bread slices.
2. Glaze the butter side with mustard.
3. Top with cheese, bacon, and butter slice.
4. Make a proper sandwich.
5. Put it in the air fryer basket with the butter side facing upwards and transfer it to the air fryer.
6. Cook for 12-14 minutes at 310 degrees F.
7. Flip the sandwich after 6-7 minutes to cook evenly on both sides.
8. Once it's done, serve!

Strawberries Jam Filled Toasts

Preparation Time: 12 minutes | Cooking Time: 15 minutes | Servings: 1

Ingredients
- 2 ounces of Greek yogurt
- 1 egg
- 2 bread slices
- 4 tablespoons of cooking cream
- 2 sliced strawberry
- 2 tablespoons of whipped cream
- 1 tablespoon of strawberry jam
- ½ teaspoon of vanilla extract

Directions
1. Take a bowl and mix strawberries, yogurt, and jam.
2. Cut a bread slice in half, lay the mixture over it, and cover with the other slice.
3. Beat heavy cream, egg, and vanilla extract and dip in the sandwich.
4. Now take a cake pan and line it with parchment paper.

5. Shift the sandwich to the cake pan and transfer it to the air fryer basket.
6. Put it in the air fryer and cook at 310 degrees F for 15 minutes.
7. Once cooked, season with some whipped cream, and serve!

Bacon-Wrapped Croquettes

Preparation Time: 10 minutes | Cooking Time: 12 minutes | Servings: 1

Ingredients
- 4 potato croquettes
- 4 strips of bacon
- 4 tablespoons of Greek yogurt
- Oil spray, for greasing

Directions
1. Place the potato croquette on a dish and use the bacon strips to wrap it.
2. Put it on the air fryer basket, and mist it with oil spray.
3. Transfer the basket to the air fryer and cook at 350 degrees F for 12 minutes.
4. Make sure to flip after 6 minutes to cook evenly on both sides.
5. Once it's done, serve with yogurt!

Cinnamon-Cake Doughnut Holes

Preparation Time: 12 minutes | Cooking Time: 12 minutes | Servings: 2

Ingredients
- 1 cup flour (whole wheat)
- 2 tablespoons of brown sugar
- ½ teaspoon of baking soda
- 2 tablespoons of butter
- 2 tablespoons of milk
- 1 teaspoon of cinnamon
- Salt according to taste

Directions
1. Take a bowl and mix all the ingredients except cinnamon and make dough.
2. Knead the dough, and using your hands, make balls from it.
3. Use the cinnamon and some additional sugar mixture to roll over the doughnut holes.
4. Shift it to an air fryer basket lined with parchment paper and transfer it to the air fryer.
5. Make for 12 minutes at 350 degrees F and serve!

Air Fryer Chocolate Croissants

Preparation Time: 10 minutes | Cooking Time: 6 minutes | Servings: 2

Ingredients
- 2 packets of whole wheat crescent rolls
- ½ cup of dark chocolate
- ¼ cup of avocado oil
- Some sugar (powdered)

Directions
1. Take a pan and heat avocado oil and chocolate in it to melt them.
2. Take the crescent rolls, slice them into a triangle shape, and add the chocolate-coco syrup.
3. Seal the triangles and transfer them to the air fryer.
4. Bake in the air fryer at 350 degrees F for 5-6 minutes or until baked properly.
5. Dust with some sugar and enjoy.

Cheese Stuffed Crescent Rolls

Preparation Time: 10 minutes | Cooking Time: 6 minutes | Servings: 2

Ingredients
- 2 whole wheat crescent doughs
- 8 slices of cheddar cheese
- 1 cup of oil
- 2 teaspoons of garlic paste
- 2 teaspoons of onion powder
- Cilantro leaves for garnish
- Salt according to taste

Directions
1. Take a knife and slice the crescent dough into triangles.
2. Put on the cheese slices and roll them.
3. Mix all the ingredients in a bowl except the rolls and cilantro.
4. Coat the dough with the marinade.
5. Shift the rolls to the air fryer basket and put them in the air fryer.
6. Bake in the air fryer for 6 minutes at 350 degrees F.
7. Once it's done, season with some chopped cilantro.

Morning Glory Muffins

Preparation Time: 12 minutes | Cooking Time: 18 minutes | Servings: 4

Ingredients
- 1 cup of almond flour
- 1 teaspoon of baking powder
- 1 teaspoon of cinnamon
- ½ teaspoon of ginger
- 2 tablespoons of apple sauce
- ½ cup of plain yogurt
- 1/3 cup of maple syrup
- 1 teaspoon of vanilla extract
- 1 small egg
- ½ cup of carrots
- ½ cup of apples
- 4 tablespoons of raisins
- Salt according to taste
- 4 tablespoons of pecans for topping

Directions
1. Take a bowl and add apples, raisins, and carrots.
2. Mix all the wet and dry ingredients separately in two bowls.
3. Add in the shredded ingredients and mix all the ingredients in the two bowls.
4. Brush muffin cups with oil, put in the mixture, and top with pecans.
5. Transfer to the air fryer and bake for 12-18 minutes at 350 degrees F.
6. Once it's done, serve!

Carrot Raisin Muffins

Preparation Time: 22 minutes | Cooking Time: 20 minutes | Servings: 2-4

Ingredients
- ½ cup of almond flour
- ½ cup of oats
- 1 teaspoon of baking soda
- ½ teaspoon of cinnamon
- 1/8 teaspoon of nutmeg
- 2 eggs
- 1 teaspoon of vanilla extract
- 2 tablespoons of maple syrup
- ½ cup of apple sauce

- 1 cup of carrots shredded
- 2 tablespoons of raisins
- Salt according to taste

Directions
1. Mix carrots, raisins, and applesauce in a small bowl.
2. Take two bowls and mix all the remaining dry and wet ingredients separately.
3. Combine the ingredients of the two bowls and beat them well.
4. Add in the carrot mixture and mix well.
5. Brush some oil on muffin tins and pour in the mixture.
6. Transfer it to the air fryer, and bake for 20 minutes at 400 degrees F.
7. Serve once done!

Pita Bread Cheese Pizza

Preparation Time: 12 minutes | Cooking Time: 8 minutes | Servings: 4

Ingredients
- 1 pita Bread
- 2 tablespoons of pizza sauce
- 2 tablespoons of mozzarella cheese
- 2 teaspoons of olive oil

For toppings
- 4 slices of spicy salumi
- 2-3 tablespoons of Italian sausages
- ½ tablespoon of onions diced thinly
- 2 cloves of garlic minced

Directions
1. Place the pita bread in a dish and coat it with pizza sauce.
2. Spread all the toppings over it and sprinkle cheese at the end
3. Drizzle a little olive oil.
4. Add the pita bread to the air fryer tray
5. Add the tray to the unit.
6. Close the unit.
7. Transfer to air fryer and cook at 360 degrees F for 6-8 minutes.
8. Once it's done, serve!

Loaded Hash Browns

Preparation Time: 12 minutes | Cooking Time: 18 minutes | Servings: 4

Ingredients
- 2 russet potatoes, shredded
- 4 tablespoons of scallions, diced
- 4 tablespoons of onions thinly sliced
- 1 clove of garlic minced
- ½ teaspoon of chili powder
- Salt and pepper according to taste
- 1 teaspoon of olive oil

Directions
1. Soak shredded potatoes in water for half an hour.
2. Dry the potatoes using a paper towel and mix them with all the remaining ingredients in a bowl.
3. Make hash shapes out of the mixture and transfer them to the basket lined with parchment paper.
4. Add a basket to the unit and air fry at 390 degrees F for 18 minutes.
5. Once it's done, serve!

Walnut and Cornmeal Muffins

Preparation Time: 10 minutes | Cooking Time: 16 minutes | Servings: 2

Ingredients
- 1 cup of cornmeal

- 4 tablespoons of almond flour
- ½ teaspoon of baking soda
- 6 tablespoons of white sugar
- ½ teaspoon orange zest
- 2 tablespoons of orange juice
- 4 tablespoons of softened butter
- 1 small organic egg
- 2 tablespoons of almond milk
- 4 tablespoons of diced walnuts
- Salt according to taste

Directions
1. Take two bowls and mix all the wet and dry ingredients separately except the walnut.
2. Combine the Ingredients of the two bowls and add walnuts.
3. Brush some muffin cups with olive oil and pour in the mixture.
4. Transfer them to an air fryer basket and cook at 350 degrees F for 16 minutes.
5. Once it's done, serve!

Healthy Banana and Chocolate Chip Muffins

Preparation Time: 12 minutes | Cooking Time: 16 minutes | Servings: 1

Ingredients
- 1 egg
- 1 tablespoon of vegan butter
- 2 tablespoons of almond milk
- ¼ teaspoon of baking soda
- ¾ cup of almond flour
- ½ cup of bananas mashed
- 2 tablespoons chocolate chips

Directions
1. Take two bowls and mix all the dry and wet ingredients chips separately.
2. Mix all the contents of the two bowls.
3. Grease muffin cups with some oil and pour in the batter.
4. Transfer to the air fryer basket and bake in the air fryer at 350 degrees for 16 minutes.
5. Once it's done, serve!

Savory and Salty Breakfast Muffins

Preparation Time: 22 minutes | Cooking Time: 15 minutes | Servings: 2

Ingredients
- 2 eggs
- 1 tablespoon of olive oil
- 3 tablespoons of whole milk
- ¾ cup of all-purpose flour
- ½ tablespoon of baking soda
- 1/8 teaspoon of yellow mustard
- 3 oz. of shredded cheddar cheese
- ¼ teaspoon of Worcestershire sauce.

Directions
1. Beat the egg in a bowl, add milk and oil, and mix well.
2. Now add all the remaining ingredients and thoroughly mix.
3. Brush oil over ramekins and pour in the mixture.
4. Transfer the ramekins to the air fryer basket and put them in the air fryer.
5. Bake in the air fryer at 350 degrees F for 15 minutes.
6. Serve and Enjoy!

Blueberries Oats Muffin

Preparation Time: 12 minutes | Cooking Time: 15 minutes | Servings: 2

Ingredients

- 4 tablespoons of sugar
- 2 small egg
- 3 tablespoons of softened butter
- Salt according to taste
- 1/4 cup almond milk
- ½ teaspoon of lime zest
- 1/8 teaspoon of vanilla extract
- ¼ teaspoon of baking soda
- 1 cup all-purpose flour
- 6 tablespoons of oats
- ½ cup of blueberries

Directions

1. Take a bowl and mix all the dry ingredients except the blueberries.
2. Now take another bowl and thoroughly whisk all the wet ingredients.
3. Combine the two mixtures and put them in the blueberries.
4. Grease ramekins with some oil and pour in the batter.
5. Transfer to air fryer and cook at 375 degrees F for 15 minutes.
6. Serve and Relax!

English Muffins Pizza

Preparation Time: 12 minutes | Cooking Time: 7 minutes | Servings: 4

Ingredients

- 2 scrambled eggs
- 2 Italian sausages crumbled
- 2 sliced English muffins
- 5 ½ tablespoons of grated pepper jack cheese

Directions

1. First, cook the English muffins in greased ramekins molds for 4 minutes at 350 degrees F inside an air fryer.
2. Once it's cooked, top with scrambled eggs and cooked sausages.
3. Top with some pepper jack cheese and air fry for another 3 minutes at 350 degrees F.
4. Serve and enjoy!

Bacon, Spinach, and Eggs Casserole

Preparation Time: 14 minutes | Cooking Time: 15-18 minutes | Servings: 2

Ingredients

- 1 cup of egg whites
- ½ cup of baby spinach
- 2 slices of baked and crushed bacon
- ½ cup of diced mushrooms
- ½ white onion thinly sliced
- 1 green pepper diced
- ¾ cup of mozzarella cheese grated
- Salt and pepper according to taste
- 2 teaspoons of olive oil

Directions

1. Except for the spinach, fry the vegetables in a pan and sauté for 2 minutes in oil.
2. Shift the vegetables to a cake pan greased with some oil and lay them out evenly.
3. Cook the spinach over the veggies.
4. Beat egg white with salt and pepper and drizzle over the veggies.
5. Now season with the crumbled bacon and mozzarella cheese.

6. Transfer to the air fryer basket and cook in the air fryer at 375 degrees for 15-18 minutes.
7. Once it's done, serve!

Classic Scrambled Eggs

Preparation Time: 12 minutes | Cooking Time: 5-6 minutes | Servings:

Ingredients

- 4 eggs
- 2 tablespoons of unsalted butter
- 3 tablespoons of cheddar cheese
- 3 tablespoons of whole milk
- 1 tablespoon of diced dill
- Salt and pepper according to taste

Directions

1. Melt butter in the air fryer in a pan for 1 minute at 300 degrees F.
2. Beat eggs in a bowl and add softened butter to it,
3. Pour in the salt and pepper and shift to the air fryer.
4. Cook for another 2 minutes, beat the eggs once again, and add the milk and cheddar.
5. Cook for 3 more minutes, and you are done.
6. Top with some dill before serving.

Kale, Eggs, and Cheese Frittata

Preparation Time: 14 minutes | Cooking Time: 12-15 minutes | Servings: 2

Ingredients

- 4 eggs
- 2 tablespoons of cooking cream
- 4 tablespoons of diced kale
- 4 tablespoons of cottage cheese
- 2tablespoons of cherry tomatoes sliced in two
- 2 tablespoons of scallions thinly sliced
- ½ teaspoon of thyme
- 1/4 teaspoon of rosemary
- Salt and pepper according to taste

Directions

1. Take a bowl and thoroughly beat all the ingredients in it.
2. Now pour them into the cake pan greased with oil.
3. Use aluminum foil to seal the cake pan.
4. Transfer to the air fryer basket and put it in the air fryer.
5. Bake for about 12-15 minutes at 250 degrees F.
6. Once it's done, serve!

Tortillas with Avocado Dipping Sauce

Preparation Time: 14 minutes | Cooking Time: 25 minutes | Servings: 2

Ingredients

- 2 tablespoons of butter
- 6 eggs
- 2 tortillas (large size)
- 3 oz. of cream cheese
- 5 slices of cooked bacon
- 4 tablespoons of grated mozzarella cheese.
- Salt and pepper according to taste

For Avocado Dipper

- 1 avocado
- 3 tablespoons of cooking cream
- 2 tablespoons of sour cream
- ½ teaspoon of lime juice
- ½ dill of chopped pickle
- Salt and pepper according to taste

Directions

1. Take a bowl and thoroughly mix all the ingredients for the avocado dipper and put it aside.

2. Make scrambled eggs in butter and cook on medium heat.
3. Sprinkle with salt, pepper, and the two powders.
4. Place tortilla in a dish, coat with cream cheese, and put a bacon slice.
5. Do this for both tortillas.
6. Now add equal proportions of egg scramble over the tortillas.
7. Sprinkle over some grated mozzarella and put it in the air fryer.
8. Cook for 15 minutes at 400 degrees F.
9. Serve with the tasty avocado dipper!

Breakfast Hardboiled Eggs

Preparation Time: 12 minutes | Cooking Time: 10 minutes | Servings: 2

Ingredients
- 4 large organic eggs

Directions
1. Put the eggs in the air fryer on a wire rack.
2. Add it to the unit.
3. Cook for 10 minutes at 260 degrees F.
4. Remove the eggs and put them in water.
5. Peel them after 5 minutes.
6. Serve!

Classic Cinnamon and Nutmeg Toast

Preparation Time: 14 minutes | Cooking Time: 4 minutes | Servings: 2

Ingredients
- 4 slices of sourdough
- 2 teaspoons of cinnamon
- 4 teaspoons of brown sugar
- ¼ teaspoon of nutmeg
- 2 tablespoons of granulated white sugar
- 4 teaspoons of butter

Directions
1. Combine all the ingredients in a bowl except the sourdough slices and butter.
2. Place the bread on a dish and coat it with softened butter.
3. Season it over the cinnamon mixture.
4. Transfer to air fryer basket greased with some oil and put in the air fryer.
5. Cook in the air fryer at 400 degrees F for 4 minutes.
6. Make sure to flip after 2 minutes to cook evenly on both sides.
7. Once it's done, serve!

Simple Chicken and Cheese Muffin Quiche

Preparation Time: 15 minutes | Cooking Time: 15 minutes | Servings: 4

Ingredients
- 8 eggs
- 2/3 cups of grated mozzarella cheese
- ½ cup of boiled and shredded chicken
- Salt and pepper according to taste

Directions
1. Beat the eggs in a bowl with salt and pepper.
2. Add in the cheese and the shredded chicken.
3. Pour the mixture into ramekins molds brushed with oil.
4. Put in the air fryer basket and transfer to the air fryer.
5. Cook for 15 minutes at 350 degrees.
6. Serve and Enjoy!

Frozen Sausage Links

Preparation Time: 6 minutes | Cooking Time: 8 minutes | Servings: 4

Ingredients
- 8 links breakfast sausages uncooked

Directions
1. Arrange the sausages in an air fryer basket lined with parchment paper
2. Transfer to the air fryer and cook at 400 degrees F for 8 minutes or until properly cooked.
3. Make sure to flip after half time to cook evenly on both sides.
4. Once it's done, serve!

Breakfast Frozen Hash Browns

Preparation Time: 12 minutes | Cooking Time: 16 minutes | Servings: 2

Ingredients
- 6 hash browns frozen
- Salt and pepper according to taste
- 2 tablespoons of canola oil for greasing

Directions
1. Take an air fryer basket and line it with parchment paper.
2. Arrange the hash in the air fryer basket.
3. Season it with some salt and pepper according to your liking.
4. Brush the hash browns with some oil.
5. Transfer to the air fryer and cook at 350 degrees F for 16 minutes.
6. Serve!

Cinnamon Rolls

Preparation Time: 14 minutes | Cooking Time: 15 minutes | Servings: 2

Ingredients
- 6 ready-to-bake cinnamon rolls
- Icing sugar for topping
- Olive oil spray for greasing

Directions
1. Take the air fryer basket, line it with parchment paper, and spray some oil.
2. Now place the cinnamon rolls and transfer them to the air fryer.
3. Cook in the air fryer at 340 degrees F for 15 minutes.
4. Sprinkle with some icing sugar once done and Serve!

Make-Ahead Air Fryer Breakfast Burritos

Preparation Time: 10 minutes | Cooking Time: 15 minutes | Servings: 1

Ingredients:
- 1 pound mild country bulk sausage
- 12 large eggs, beaten
- salt and ground black pepper to taste
- 1 cup shredded Cheddar cheese
- 15 (8-inch) flour tortillas

Directions:
1. In a large pan over medium-high heat, crumble sausage. Cook until the meat is no longer pink, about 10 minutes. Using a slotted spoon, transfer to a large mixing basin.
2. Turn the heat down to medium. Season the beaten eggs in the skillet with salt and pepper. Three minutes in the oven. Cook for another 2 minutes, stirring occasionally. Turn off the heat. One last time, stir to break up bigger parts. Pour into the bowl with the meat, then whisk in the cheese.

3. One tortilla should be placed in a clean work area. Place 1/4 cup of the sausage-egg mixture on the tortilla's bottom third, closest to you. Fold the tortilla end over the mixture. Fold both sides of the tortilla over the filling to form an envelope. Tuck, roll and arrange seam side down on a baking pan. Continue with the remaining tortillas and filling.
4. Refrigerate the baking sheet for 2 hours. Burritos should be stored in a covered freezer-safe container until ready to serve.
5. Preheat the air fryer to 400 degrees F when ready to cook (200 degrees C).
6. Cook for 5 minutes with the burrito seam-side down in the preheated air fryer.

Spicy Homemade Breakfast Sausage in the Air Fryer

Preparation Time: 10 minutes | Cooking Time: 15 minutes | Servings: 1

Ingredients:
- 1 pound ground pork
- One teaspoon of sea salt
- One teaspoon of rubbed sage
- One teaspoon of crushed red pepper
- ½ teaspoon dried marjoram
- ½ teaspoon onion powder
- ½ teaspoon ground black pepper
- ¼ teaspoon dried thyme

Directions:
1. Preheat an air fryer to 400°F (200 degrees C).
2. In a large mixing bowl, combine ground pork, sea salt, sage, red pepper, marjoram, onion powder, pepper, and thyme. Mix well with your hands until equally blended. Make eight patties out of the mixture.
3. Cook for 5 minutes with four patties in the air fryer basket. Cook for 5 minutes longer after carefully flipping the burgers. Repeat with the remaining patties on a plate lined with paper towels.

Hasselback Air Fryer Potatoes

Preparation Time: 10 minutes | Cooking Time: 15 minutes | Servings: 1

Ingredients:
- 4 (6 ounces) russet potatoes, scrubbed and dried
- Two chopsticks
- Four tablespoons olive oil, or as needed
- salt and ground black pepper to taste
- ½ teaspoon chopped fresh chives (optional)

Directions:
1. Preheat the air fryer to 350°F (180 degrees C).
2. Cut a very thin slice lengthwise from the flattest side for one potato. Place the potato cut-side down on a chopping board, so it lays uniformly without rolling—place chopsticks along the top and bottom sides of the potato lengthwise. Slice the potato lengthwise into 1/4-inch slices, ensuring the knife rests on the chopsticks each time to keep the bottom of the potato intact. Rep with the remaining potatoes. Brush oil on the outsides and between the slices. Season with salt and pepper to taste.
3. Place the potatoes in the air fryer dish and cook for 15 minutes. Brush with oil and cook for another 15 minutes until the edges are crispy and the centers are soft. Serve garnished with chives.

Air Fryer Salmon Nuggets

Preparation Time: 10 minutes | Cooking Time: 15 minutes | Servings: 1

Ingredients:
- ⅓ cup maple syrup
- ¼ teaspoon ground dried chipotle pepper
- One pinch of sea salt
- 1 ½ cups butter- and garlic-flavored croutons
- One large egg
- 1 (1 pound) skinless, center-cut salmon fillet, cut into one 1/2-inch chunk
- cooking spray

Directions:
1. In a saucepan, combine maple syrup, chipotle powder, and salt and bring to a simmer over medium heat. Reduce the heat to low to stay warm.
2. Place the croutons in the bowl of a tiny food processor and pulse until fine crumbs form—place in a small basin. In a separate dish, whisk the egg.
3. Preheat the air fryer to 390°F (200 degrees C).
4. Lightly season the fish with sea salt. Dip fish in egg mixture lightly, allowing excess to fall out. Coat fish with crouton breading, shaking off excess. Place on a dish and lightly coat with cooking spray.
5. Coat the air fryer basket with cooking spray. Place salmon nuggets within, working in batches as necessary to minimize congestion.
6. Cook for 3 minutes in a hot air fryer. Turn the salmon pieces gently, spritz generously with oil, and heat until the salmon is cooked through, 3 to 4 minutes more. Drizzle with heated chipotle-maple syrup and arrange on a serving plate. Serve right away.

Air Fryer Hasselback Potatoes

Preparation Time: 10 minutes | Cooking Time: 15 minutes | Servings: 1

Ingredients:
- Four medium Yukon Gold potatoes
- Three tablespoons of melted butter
- One tablespoon of olive oil
- Three cloves of garlic, crushed
- ½ teaspoon ground paprika
- salt and ground black pepper to taste
- One tablespoon of chopped fresh parsley

Directions:
1. Preheat an air fryer to 350°F (175 degrees C).
2. Make 1/4-inch or 1/2-inch slices across each potato's full length, ensuring the knife only cuts through to the bottom 1/2-inch, leaving the bottom of the potato intact.
3. Mix the butter, olive oil, garlic, and paprika in a small bowl. Brush some of the mixtures into the slits of each potato—season with salt and pepper to taste.
4. Cook the potatoes in the air fryer basket for 15 minutes. Brush the potatoes with the butter mixture again, carefully getting them down into the fanned-out slices to prevent them from drying. Cook for another 15 minutes, or until the potatoes are tender.
5. Remove the potatoes from the basket and brush them with any leftover butter mixture. Serve immediately with chopped parsley on top.

Tasty Baked Eggs

Preparation Time: 10 minutes | Cooking Time: 15 minutes | Servings: 1

Ingredients:
- 4 eggs

- 1-pound of torn baby spinach
- 7 ounces of chopped ham
- 4 tablespoons of milk
- 1 tablespoon of olive oil
- Cooking spray
- Salt and black pepper to the taste

Directions:
1. Cook and boil baby spinach in a skillet of oil over medium heat for a few minutes.
2. Spray four ramekins with cooking spray, then add the baby spinach, ham, and an egg to each.
3. Season with salt and pepper to taste. Fill each ramekin with bread. Place ramekins in a preheated Air Fryer at 350° F for 20 minutes.
4. Enjoy!

Breakfast Egg Bowls

Preparation Time: 10 minutes | Cooking Time: 15 minutes | Servings: 1

Ingredients:
- 4 dinner rolls, chopped the tops off, and scooped out the insides
- 4 tablespoons of heavy cream
- 4 eggs
- 4 teaspoons of chives mixed with parsley
- Salt and black pepper to taste
- 4 teaspoons of Parmesan

Directions:
1. Place dinner rolls on a baking sheet and breaks an egg into each.
2. Dividing heavy cream and mixed herbs in each roll, and season with salt and pepper.
3. Sprinkle Parmesan on the rolls, place them in your air bowl, and bake for 20 minutes at 350° F.
4. Divide the bread bowls among the plates.
5. Enjoy!

Delicious Breakfast Soufflé

Preparation Time: 10 minutes | Cooking Time: 15 minutes | Servings: 1

Ingredients:
- 4 eggs, whisked
- 4 tablespoons of heavy cream
- A pinch of red chili pepper, crushed
- 2 tablespoons of parsley, chopped
- 2 tablespoons of chives, chopped
- Salt and black pepper to the taste

Directions:
1. Whisk together the eggs, salt, pepper, heavy cream, red chili pepper, parsley, and chives in a saucepan, then divide among four soufflé plates.
2. Place the soufflés in the air Fryer and cook for 8 minutes at 350° F.
3. They should be served.
4. Enjoy!

Air Fried Sandwich

Preparation Time: 10 minutes | Cooking Time: 15 minutes | Servings: 1

Ingredients:
- 2 English muffins halved
- 2 eggs
- 2 bacon strips
- Salt and black pepper to the taste

Directions:

1. Crack the eggs into your air Fryer, top with bacon, cover, and cook at 392° F for 6 minutes.
2. Warm the English muffin halves in the microwave for a few seconds, then split the eggs into two halves, top with bacon, season with salt and pepper, and serve breakfast.
3. Enjoy!

Rustic Breakfast

Preparation Time: 10 minutes | Cooking Time: 15 minutes | Servings: 1

Ingredients:
- 7 ounces of baby spinach
- 8 chestnuts mushrooms, halved
- 8 tomatoes, halved
- 1 garlic clove, minced
- 4 chipolatas
- 4 bacon slices, chopped
- Salt and black pepper to the taste
- 4 eggs
- Cooking spray

Directions:
1. Spray a pan with cooking spray and add the onions, garlic, and mushrooms.
2. Finish with spinach and cracked eggs after adding bacon and chipolatas.
3. Season with salt and pepper, place the pan in the cooking basket of your air Fryer, and cook for 13 minutes at 350° F.
4. Breakfast is served.
5. Enjoy!

Egg Muffins

Preparation Time: 10 minutes | Cooking Time: 15 minutes | Servings: 1

Ingredients:
- 1 egg
- 2 tablespoons of olive oil
- 3 tablespoons of milk
- 3.5 ounces of white flour
- 1 tablespoon of baking powder
- 2 ounces of Parmesan, grated
- A splash of Worcestershire sauce
- 1 tablespoon of starch
- 2 tablespoons of butter

Directions:
1. In a saucepan, combine the egg and starch, butter, baking powder, cheese, and Parmesan, stir well, and divide among 4 silicon muffin cups.
2. Place the cups in the cooking basket of your air Fryer, cover them, and cook for 15 minutes at 392° F.
3. Serve hot.
4. Enjoy!

Polenta Bites

Preparation Time: 10 minutes | Cooking Time: 15 minutes | Servings: 1

Ingredients:
- For the polenta:
- 1 tablespoon of butter
- 1 cup of cornmeal
- 3 cups of water
- Salt and black pepper to the taste
- For the polenta bites:
- 2 tablespoons of powdered sugar
- Cooking spray

Directions:

1. In a saucepan, combine water, cornmeal, sugar, salt, and pepper, mix, and bring to a boil over medium heat, simmer for 10 minutes, remove from heat, whisk again, and place in the refrigerator until cold.
2. 1 scoop polenta, shaped into a ball, placed on a working surface
3. Repeat with the remaining polenta balls, then set them all in the cooking basket of your Air Fryer, drizzle with cooking oil, and cover and steam for 8 minutes at 380° F.
4. Arrange polenta in dishes, sprinkle with sugar, and serve as toast.
5. Enjoy!

Delicious Breakfast Potatoes

Preparation Time: 10 minutes | Cooking Time: 15 minutes | Servings: 1

Ingredients:

- 2 tablespoons of olive oil
- 3 potatoes, cubed
- 1 yellow onion, chopped
- 1 red bell pepper, chopped
- Salt and black pepper to taste
- 1 teaspoon of garlic powder
- 1 teaspoon of sweet paprika
- 1 teaspoon of onion powder

Directions:

1. Grease the basket of your Air Fryer with olive oil, then add the potatoes and season with salt & pepper.
2. Mix the onion, bell pepper, garlic powder, paprika, and onion powder, then cover and cook for 30 minutes at 370° F.
3. Serve the potatoes as a snack on plates.

Tasty Cinnamon Toast

Preparation Time: 10 minutes | Cooking Time: 15 minutes | Servings: 1

Ingredients:

- 1 stick of butter, soft
- 12 bread slices
- ½ cup of sugar
- 1½ teaspoon of vanilla extract
- 1 ½ teaspoon of cinnamon powder

Directions:

1. Mix the soft butter, honey, and cinnamon in a cup.
2. Spread this over the bread pieces and place them in the fryer for 5 minutes at 400° F.
3. Divide among plates and serve for breakfast.
4. Enjoy!

Delicious Potato Hash

Preparation Time: 10 minutes | Cooking Time: 15 minutes | Servings: 1

Ingredients:

- 1 ½ potato, cubed
- 1 yellow onion, chopped
- 2 teaspoons of olive oil
- 1 green bell pepper, chopped
- Salt and black pepper to the taste
- ½ teaspoon of dried thyme
- 2 eggs

Directions:

1. Heat the oil in the Air Fryer to 350° F, add bell pepper, salt, and black pepper, mix, and fry for 5 minutes.
2. Combine the onions, thyme, and peas in a mixing bowl. Stir, cover, and cook for 20 minutes at 360° F.

3. Breakfast is served.
4. Enjoy!

Sweet Breakfast Casserole

Preparation Time: 10 minutes | Cooking Time: 15 minutes | Servings: 1

Ingredients:

- 3 tablespoons of brown sugar
- 4 tablespoons of butter
- 2 tablespoons of white sugar
- ½ teaspoon cinnamon powder
- ½ cup flour
- For the casserole:
- 2 eggs
- 2 tablespoons of white sugar
- 2 ½ cups white flour
- 1 teaspoon of baking soda
- 1 teaspoon of baking powder
- 2 eggs
- ½ cup of milk
- 2 cups of buttermilk
- 4 tablespoons of butter
- Zest from 1 lemon, grated
- 1 2/3 cup blueberries

Directions:

1. Mix the beans with 2 teaspoons of white sugar, 2 and 12 cups of white flour, baking powder, baking soda, 2 potatoes, milk, buttermilk, 4 tablespoons of butter, lemon zest, and blueberries in a saucepan suitable for the fryer, stir, and place in a saucepan that fits the fryer.
2. In a separate dish, combine 3 tablespoons of brown sugar, 2 tablespoons white sugar, 4 tablespoons butter, 12 cups flour, and cinnamon to make a crumble, then pour over the blueberries. Add 12 glasses of milk.
3. Bake at 300° F for 30 minutes in a preheated Air Fryer.
4. Serve for breakfast on separate plates. Seasoning should be done using olive oil.
5. Enjoy!

Eggs Casserole

Preparation Time: 10 minutes | Cooking Time: 15 minutes | Servings: 1

Ingredients:

- 1-pound turkey, ground
- 1 tablespoon of olive oil
- ½ teaspoon of chili powder
- 12 eggs
- 1 sweet potato, cubed
- 1 cup of baby spinach
- Salt and black pepper to the taste
- 2 tomatoes, chopped for serving

Directions:

1. Whisk the eggs in a bowl with salt, pepper, chili powder, spinach, sweet potato, and turkey.
2. Heat your Air Fryer to 350° F, add oil, and heat it again.
3. Attach a mixture of eggs to your Air Fryer, distribute over the top, and cover and steam for 25 minutes.
4. Serve for breakfast on separate plates.
5. Enjoy!

CHAPTER 2:
Snacks & Appetizers

Mexican Apple Snack

Preparation Time: 10 minutes | Cooking Time: 5 minutes | Servings: 4

Ingredients:
- ¼ cup chopped almond
- Baking pan as needed
- 2 teaspoons lime juice
- ½ cup dark chocolate chips
- ½ cup clean caramel sauce
- 3 cored, peeled & cubed big apples

Directions:
1. Combine apples with lime juice in a bowl and transfer to a pan that fits in the air fryer.
2. Toss in the remaining ingredients and add the pan inside the air fryer.
3. Cover and cook for 5 minutes at 320 degrees Fahrenheit.
4. Toss with care and serve immediately!

Quick Banana Snack

Preparation Time: 10 minutes | Cooking Time: 5 minutes | Servings: 8

Ingredients:
- 16 baking cups crust
- ¼ cup almond butter
- ¾ cup dark chocolate chips
- 1 tablespoon coconut oil
- Baking pan as needed
- 1 peeled & sliced into 16 pieces banana

Directions:
1. Stir chocolate chips in a pan over medium heat until they melt, and then turn off the heat.
2. Whisk almond butter and coconut oil in a bowl.
3. Scoop a teaspoon of melted dark chocolate into the cup, throw in a slice of banana and cover with a teaspoon of peanut butter mix on top.
4. Follow the same steps with other cups and place the prepared cups in a baking pan that fits the air fryer.
5. Place the baking pan in the air fryer and cover to cook for 5 minutes at 320 degrees Fahrenheit.
6. Freeze before serving!

Coconut Chicken Bites

Preparation Time: 10 minutes | Cooking Time: 13 minutes | Servings: 4

Ingredients:
- 2 eggs
- 8 chicken tenders
- ¾ cup shredded coconut
- Cooking spray as needed
- 2 teaspoons minced garlic
- ¾ cup panko bread crumbs
- Salt & black pepper as needed

Directions:
1. Whisk eggs, garlic, salt, and pepper in a bowl.
2. Stir coconut and panko in a separate bowl.
3. First coat chicken tenders with egg mixture then coconut mixture properly.
4. Once all coated, grease them with cooking spray and transfer them to the air fryer.
5. Cover and cook for 10 minutes at 350 degrees Fahrenheit.
6. Serve on a platter and enjoy!

Simple Zucchini Cakes

Preparation Time: 10 minutes | Cooking Time: 12 minutes | Servings: 12

Ingredients:
- 1 egg
- 3 grated zucchinis
- ½ cup chopped chives
- 2 minced garlic cloves
- 1 chopped yellow onion
- ½ cup almond flour
- Cooking spray as needed
- Salt & black pepper as needed

Directions:
1. Mix all the ingredients in a bowl.
2. Shape into small patties and grease with cooking spray.
3. Place them in the air fryer and cook for 6 minutes at 370 degrees Fahrenheit.
4. Serve immediately and enjoy!

Pesto Crackers

Preparation Time: 10 minutes | Cooking Time: 17 minutes | Servings: 6

Ingredients:
- 1 ¼ cups almond flour
- 1 minced garlic clove
- 3 tablespoons butter
- Baking sheet as needed
- ¼ teaspoon dried oregano
- 2 tablespoons basil pesto
- ½ teaspoon baking powder
- Salt & black pepper as needed

Directions:
1. Combine all the ingredients in a bowl until you get dough.
2. Take a baking sheet that fits the air fryer and line it with parchment paper.
3. Spread the dough on the baking sheet and fit the sheet in the air fryer.
4. Cover and cook for 17 minutes at 325 degrees Fahrenheit.
5. Remove to cool and cut into crackers before serving!

Beef Jerky Quick Snack

Preparation Time: 2 hours | Cooking Time: 1 hour 30 minutes | Servings: 6

Ingredients:
- 2 cups tamari sauce
- 2 oz. sliced beef round
- 2 tablespoons black pepper
- ½ cup Worcestershire sauce
- 2 tablespoons red pepper flakes

Directions:
1. Whisk all the ingredients except beef in a bowl.
2. Toss in the beef slices to coat and refrigerate for 6 hours.
3. Add the beef slices to the air fryer and cover to cook for 1 hour 30 minutes at 370 degrees Fahrenheit.
4. Remove to cool and serve cold.

Tasty Banana Chips

Preparation Time: 10 minutes | Cooking Time: 15 minutes | Servings: 4

Ingredients:
- A pinch of sea salt
- 1 teaspoon canola oil
- ½ teaspoon chaat masala
- 4 peeled & sliced bananas
- ½ teaspoon turmeric powder

Directions:
1. Combine banana slices with the remaining ingredients.
2. Preheat the air fryer to 360 degrees Fahrenheit and add the banana slices.
3. Cover and cook for 15 minutes, flipping them once.

4. Serve immediately and enjoy!

Quick Zucchini Chips

Preparation Time: 10 minutes | Cooking Time: 1 hour | Servings: 6

Ingredients:
- 2 tablespoons canola oil
- 3 thinly sliced zucchinis
- Salt & black pepper as needed
- 2 tablespoons red wine vinegar

Directions:
1. Combine all the ingredients except zucchini in a bowl.
2. Add zucchini slices to coat and transfer into the air fryer.
3. Cover and cook for an hour at 200 degrees Fahrenheit.
4. Serve cold and enjoy!

Delicious Spring Rolls

Preparation Time: 10 minutes | Cooking Time: 25 minutes | Servings: 8

Ingredients:
- 1 grated carrot
- 1 teaspoon sugar
- 10 spring roll sheets
- 2 tablespoons water
- 1 teaspoon tamari sauce
- 3 minced garlic cloves
- 2 tablespoons canola oil
- ½ minced chili pepper
- 2 tablespoons corn flour
- 2 chopped yellow onions
- 1 tablespoon grated ginger
- Salt & black pepper as needed
- 2 cups shredded green cabbage

Directions:
1. Heat all the ingredients except corn flour, roll sheets, and water in a pan over medium heat.
2. Stir thoroughly, cook for a minute or two, and remove from the heat to cool.
3. Cut the sheets into squares, divide the cabbage mix between them and make a roll with each.
4. Mix corn flour with water to create a medium-consistency paste and seal the rolls closed.
5. Transfer the rolls to the air fryer and cover to cook for 10 minutes at 360 degrees Fahrenheit.
6. Flip to the other side to cook for another 10 minutes.
7. Serve hot with ketchup or any sauce!

Crispy Fish Sticks

Preparation Time: 10 minutes | Cooking Time: 12 minutes | Servings: 2

Ingredients:
- 1 beaten egg
- 4 oz. panko bread crumbs
- 4 tablespoons canola oil
- Salt & black pepper as needed
- 4 boneless, skinless & cut in medium sticks white fish fillets

Directions:
1. Combine bread crumbs with oil in a bowl.
2. Whisk egg and season with salt and pepper in a separate bowl.
3. Take each fish stick, dip first in the egg, and then coat the crumbs properly.
4. Lastly, transfer all the fish sticks to the air fryer after following the above procedure.
5. Cover and cook for 12 minutes at 360 degrees Fahrenheit.
6. Serve hot with any sauce!

Air Fried Crab Sticks

Preparation Time: 10 minutes | Cooking Time: 12 minutes | Servings: 4

Ingredients:
- 15 halved crab sticks
- 3 teaspoons sesame oil
- 4 teaspoons of Cajun seasoning

Directions:
1. Marinate crab sticks with sesame oil and Cajun seasoning.
2. Add to the air fryer and cover to cook for 12 minutes at 350 degrees Fahrenheit.
3. Serve hot with a sauce of your choice!

Simple Chickpea Snack

Preparation Time: 10 minutes | Cooking Time: 10 minutes | Servings: 4

Ingredients:
- 1 tablespoon canola oil
- ½ teaspoon ground coriander
- 1 teaspoon smoked paprika
- Salt & black pepper as needed
- 15 oz. drained canned chickpeas

Directions:
1. Combine all the ingredients in a bowl.
2. Transfer to the air fryer and cover to cook for 10 minutes at 390 degrees Fahrenheit.
3. Serve in bowls and enjoy!

Fun Sweet Popcorn

Preparation Time: 5 minutes | Cooking Time: 10 minutes | Servings: 4

Ingredients:
- 4 oz. brown sugar
- 4 tablespoons butter
- 4 tablespoons corn kernels

Directions:
1. Cook corn kernels by adding them to the air fryer at 400 degrees Fahrenheit for 6 minutes.
2. Remove to a tray and let it cool.
3. Melt sugar and butter in a pan over low heat, stirring until everything dissolves.
4. Add in the corn kernels and toss to coat while removing from heat.
5. Spread it on a tray and allow it to cool before serving!

Cajun Shrimp Appetizer

Preparation Time: 10 minutes | Cooking Time: 5 minutes | Servings: 2

Ingredients:
- 1 tablespoon canola oil
- ¼ teaspoon chipotle powder
- Salt & black pepper as needed
- ½ teaspoon old bay seasoning
- 20 peeled & deveined tiger shrimp

Directions:
1. Combine all the ingredients in a bowl.
2. Add the marinated shrimp to the air fryer and cover to cook for 5 minutes at 390 degrees Fahrenheit.
3. Serve on a platter with a sauce of choice.

Seafood Appetizer

Preparation Time: 10 minutes | Cooking Time: 25 minutes | Servings: 4

Ingredients:
- 1 tablespoon butter

- 1 cup chopped celery
- 1 cup flaked crab meat
- 1 teaspoon sweet paprika
- 2 tablespoons panko bread crumbs
- ½ cup chopped red onion
- 1 cup mayonnaise
- Salt & black pepper as needed
- 1 cup chopped green bell pepper
- 1 teaspoon Worcestershire sauce
- 1 cup peeled & deveined baby shrimp

Directions:
1. Add all the ingredients except breadcrumbs, butter, and paprika to a bowl.
2. Transfer into a dish that fits in the air fryer and set the dish in there.
3. Top with bread crumbs and butter and cover to cook for 25 minutes at 320 degrees, giving a toss halfway.
4. Serve in bowls and enjoy with a sprinkling of paprika on top.

Chicken Breast Rolls

Preparation Time: 10 minutes | Cooking Time: 22 minutes | Servings: 4

Ingredients:
- 4 mozzarella slices
- A drizzle of canola oil
- 2 cups kale
- Salt & black pepper as needed
- 1 cup chopped sun-dried tomatoes
- 1 ½ tablespoon Italian seasoning
- 4 boneless & skinless chicken breasts

Directions:
1. Use a meat tenderizer to flatten chicken breasts.
2. Combine the rest of the ingredients and divide the chicken breasts to create rolls and seal them.
3. Grease the air fryer basket with oil and arrange the rolls.
4. Cover and cook for 17 minutes at 375 degrees Fahrenheit, flipping once.
5. Serve on a platter and enjoy!

Greek Lamb Meatballs

Preparation Time: 10 minutes | Cooking Time: 8 minutes | Servings: 10

Ingredients:
- 4 oz. minced lamb meat
- Salt & black pepper as needed
- 1 tablespoon chopped thyme
- 1 slice of toasted & crumbled bread
- ½ tablespoon grated lime peel
- 2 tablespoons crumbled feta cheese

Directions:
1. Combine meat with all the remaining ingredients in a bowl.
2. Shape 10 meatballs out of the mixture and arrange them in the air fryer.
3. Cover and cook for 8 minutes at 400 degrees Fahrenheit.
4. Serve on a platter with a sauce of choice.

Jalapeno Balls

Preparation Time: 10 minutes | Cooking Time: 4 minutes | Servings: 3

Ingredients:
- 3 oz. cream cheese
- ½ teaspoon dried cilantro
- ¼ teaspoon onion powder
- 1 chopped jalapeno pepper
- ¼ teaspoon minced garlic
- Salt & black pepper as needed

- 3 cooked & crumbled bacon slices

Directions:
1. Combine all the ingredients in a bowl.
2. Shape small meatballs out of the mixture and add them to the air fryer.
3. Cover and cook for 4 minutes at 350 degrees Fahrenheit.
4. Serve on a platter with a sauce of choice.

Beef Patties

Preparation Time: 10 minutes | Cooking Time: 8 minutes | Servings: 4

Ingredients:
- 1 chopped leek
- 14 oz. minced beef
- 2 tablespoons strip-cut ham
- 3 tablespoons panko bread crumbs
- ½ teaspoon ground coriander
- Salt & black pepper as needed

Directions:
1. Combine all the ingredients and shape small patties out of the mixture.
2. Add them to the air fryer basket and cover to cook for 8 minutes at 400 degrees Fahrenheit.
3. Serve on a platter with a sauce of choice.

Black Olive Balls

Preparation Time: 10 minutes | Cooking Time: 4 minutes | Servings: 6

Ingredients:
- 4 oz. cream cheese
- 1 tablespoon chopped oregano
- 14 chopped salami slices
- 8 pitted & minced black olives
- Salt & black pepper as needed
- 2 tablespoons sun-dried tomato pesto

Directions:
1. Combine all the ingredients in a bowl and shape small balls out of them.
2. Add the balls to the air fryer basket and cover to cook for 4 minutes at 350 degrees Fahrenheit.
3. Serve on a platter of a sauce of choice!

Spinach Balls

Preparation Time: 10 minutes | Cooking Time: 7 minutes | Servings: 30

Ingredients:
- 2 eggs
- 1 cup flour
- 16 oz. spinach
- ⅓ cup grated parmesan
- 1 teaspoon garlic powder
- 1 tablespoon onion powder
- 4 tablespoons melted butter
- ⅓ cup crumbled cottage cheese
- ¼ teaspoon ground nutmeg
- Salt & black pepper as needed
- 3 tablespoons cooking cream

Directions:
1. Blend all the ingredients in the blender thoroughly and freeze the mixture for 10 minutes.
2. Shape 30 balls out of the mixture and add to the air fryer basket.
3. Cover and cook for 7 minutes at 300 degrees Fahrenheit.
4. Serve immediately and enjoy!

Kale & Celery Crackers

Preparation time: 10 minutes | Cooking time: 20 minutes | Servings: 6

Ingredients:
- ⅓ cup canola oil
- 1 bunch chopped oregano
- 4 minced garlic cloves
- 2 cups ground flaxseed
- 4 bunches of chopped kale
- ½ bunch chopped celery
- 2 cups soaked overnight & drained flaxseed

Directions:
1. Blend ground flaxseed, garlic, kale, celery, and oregano in a food processor.
2. Add oil and soaked flaxseed in the end and process thoroughly.
3. Spread the mixture in the air fryer.
4. Cut into crackers and cover to cook for 20 minutes at 380 degrees Fahrenheit.
5. Serve immediately and enjoy!

Tasty Tuna Cakes

Preparation Time: 10 minutes | Cooking Time: 10 minutes | Servings: 12

Ingredients:
- 3 eggs
- ½ teaspoon dried chives
- 1 teaspoon dried cilantro
- Cooking spray as needed
- 1 teaspoon garlic powder
- ½ cup chopped red onion
- Salt & black pepper as needed
- 15 oz. drained & flaked canned tuna

Directions:
1. Combine all the ingredients in a bowl and shape medium-size cakes out of them.
2. Add them to the air fryer basket and grease them with cooking spray.
3. Cover and cook for 10 minutes at 350 degrees Fahrenheit, flipping once after 5 minutes.
4. Serve on a platter with any sauce.

Egg White Chips

Preparation Time: 5 minutes | Cooking Time: 8 minutes | Servings: 2

Ingredients:
- 4 eggs whites
- ½ tablespoon water
- Salt & black pepper as needed
- 2 tablespoons shredded mozzarella

Directions:
1. Whisk all the ingredients in a bowl.
2. Spoon the mixture into a muffin pan compatible with your air fryer size.
3. Transfer the pan to the air fryer and cover to cook for 8 minutes at 350 degrees Fahrenheit.
4. Serve with any sauce you like.

Turkey Pepper Nachos

Preparation Time: 10 minutes | Cooking Time: 7 minutes | Servings: 6

Ingredients:
- 1 teaspoon salt
- 1 oz. ground turkey
- Baking pan as needed
- 1 tablespoon chili powder
- 1 teaspoon ground coriander
- 1 teaspoon garlic powder
- 1 oz. strip-cut red bell peppers
- 1 ½ cups grated cheddar cheese
- ½ teaspoon ground black pepper
- ½ teaspoon fresh chopped parsley

Directions:
1. Preheat the air fryer to 400 degrees Fahrenheit.
2. Combine all the spices in a bowl and cook the turkey in a skillet until browned.
3. Add the spices to the turkey and stir.
4. Arrange the bell pepper strips on a greased baking pan that fits inside the air fryer.
5. Add cooked turkey and cheese on top.
6. Transfer the pan to the air fryer and cook for 8 minutes or until the cheese is melted.
7. Serve immediately and enjoy!

Chicken Pepper Nachos

Preparation Time: 10 minutes | Cooking Time: 7 minutes | Servings: 6

Ingredients:
- 1 teaspoon salt
- 1 oz. ground chicken
- 1 tablespoon paprika
- 1 teaspoon ground coriander
- 1 teaspoon garlic powder
- 1 oz. strip-cut red bell peppers
- 1 ½ cups grated cheddar cheese
- ½ teaspoon ground black pepper
- ½ teaspoon fresh chopped cilantro

Directions:
1. Preheat the air fryer to 400 degrees Fahrenheit.
2. Combine all the spices in a bowl and cook the chicken in a skillet until tender.
3. Add the spices to the chicken and stir.
4. Arrange the bell pepper strips on a greased baking pan that fits inside the air fryer.
5. Add cooked chicken and cheese on top.
6. Transfer the pan to the air fryer and cover to cook for 8 minutes or until the cheese is melted.
7. Serve immediately and enjoy!

Tasty Chicharrones

Preparation Time: 30 minutes | Cooking Time: 3 hours | Servings: 10

Ingredients:
- 1 teaspoon kosher salt
- 2 tablespoons canola oil
- 4 oz. pork back fat with skin
- Parchment paper as needed
- ½ teaspoon ground black pepper

Directions:
1. Preheat the air fryer to 225 degrees and line the tray with parchment paper.
2. Remove the fat and cut the pork into one-inch by two-inch strips.
3. Arrange the strips on the air fryer tray and transfer the fat to a big pot
4. Drizzle the strips with canola oil and cook for 3 hours in the air fryer to dry out the skin.
5. Meanwhile, heat the pot of pork fat over medium heat.
6. Once strips are dry, throw them in the melted pork fat and fry until they bubble up, for at least 2-3 minutes.
7. Serve in a large bowl and season with salt and pepper.

Cheesy Chicharrones

Preparation Time: 30 minutes | Cooking Time: 3 hours | Servings: 10

Ingredients:
- 1 teaspoon salt
- 2 tablespoons canola oil
- 4 oz. pork back fat with skin
- Parchment paper as needed
- ½ teaspoon ground black pepper
- 2 tablespoons grated mozzarella cheese

Directions:
1. Preheat the air fryer to 225 degrees and line the tray with parchment paper.
2. Remove the fat and cut the pork into one-inch by two-inch strips.
3. Arrange the strips on the air fryer tray and transfer the fat to a big pot
4. Drizzle the strips with olive oil and cook for 3 hours in the air fryer to dry out the skin.
5. Meanwhile, heat the pot of pork fat over medium heat.
6. Once strips are dry, throw them in the melted pork fat and fry until they bubble up, for at least 2-3 minutes.
7. Serve in a large bowl and season with salt, and pepper, and top with cheese.

Parmesan Garlic Bread Muffins

Preparation Time: 20 minutes | Cooking Time: 25 minutes | Servings: 12

Ingredients:
- 4 eggs
- ½ cup greek yogurt
- 1 cup coconut flour
- 2 cups almond flour
- ¼ cup minced garlic
- ¼ cup chopped cilantro
- Cooking spray as needed
- 2 teaspoons baking powder
- 6 tablespoons melted butter
- ¼ cup fresh grated parmesan
- 1 cup shredded cheddar cheese
- Muffin tin or muffin cups as needed

Directions:
1. Preheat the air fryer to 325 degrees Fahrenheit and grease the muffin tin with cooking spray.
2. Put greek yogurt, 1 tablespoon garlic, eggs, and salt in a food processor.
3. Next, toss in all the flour, baking powder, cheddar cheese, and cilantro, and pulse until you get a smooth dough.
4. Divide half of the batter between the cups, divide the grated parmesan between the cups, and top with the remaining batter.
5. Mix melted butter and garlic and brush the surface of the muffins with this mixture.
6. Transfer the muffin tin or cups to the air fryer and cover to cook for 25 minutes or until golden brown from the top.
7. Let it cool before serving!

Herby Cheesy Muffins

Preparation Time: 20 minutes | Cooking Time: 25 minutes | Servings: 12

Ingredients:
- 4 eggs
- ½ cup sour cream
- 2 cups almond flour
- 1 cup coconut flour
- 2 tsp baking powder
- ¼ cup minced garlic
- ¼ cup chopped cilantro
- ½ teaspoon dried oregano
- Cooking spray as needed
- 6 tablespoons melted butter
- 1 cup shredded cheddar cheese
- Muffin tin or muffin cups as needed
- ½ teaspoon dried chopped rosemary

Directions:
1. Preheat the air fryer to 325 degrees Fahrenheit and grease the muffin tin with cooking spray.
2. Put sour cream, 1 tablespoon of garlic, eggs, and salt in a food processor.
3. Next, toss in all the flour, baking powder, cheddar cheese, and herbs, and pulse until you get a smooth dough.
4. Divide the batter between the cups or tin.
5. Mix melted butter and garlic and brush the surface of the muffins with this mixture.
6. Transfer the muffin tin or cups to the air fryer and cover to cook for 25 minutes or until golden brown from the top.
7. Let it cool before serving!

Brussel Sprout Chips

Preparation Time: 10 minutes | Cooking Time: 15 minutes | Servings: 4

Ingredients:
- 1 teaspoon kosher salt
- 2 tablespoons avocado oil
- Parchment paper as needed
- 1 oz. ends removed Brussel Sprouts

Directions:
1. Preheat the air fryer to 240 degrees Fahrenheit and line the tray with parchment paper.
2. Remove the skin from Brussel sprouts one leaf at a time and put the leaves in a large bowl while you peel.
3. Drizzle avocado oil on the leaves, season with salt, and toss before spreading on the air fryer tray.
4. Cover and cook for 15 minutes, tossing halfway to ensure even cooking.
5. Serve immediately and enjoy!

Asian Style Brussel Sprout Chips

Preparation Time: 10 minutes | Cooking Time: 15 minutes | Servings: 4

Ingredients:
- 1 teaspoon sea salt
- 1 tablespoon canola oil
- Parchment paper as needed
- 1 tablespoon tamari sauce
- 1 oz. ends removed Brussel sprouts

Directions:
1. Preheat the air fryer to 240 degrees Fahrenheit and line the tray with parchment paper.
2. Remove the skin from Brussel sprouts one leaf at a time and put the leaves in a large bowl while you peel.
3. Drizzle olive oil on the leaves, add tamari sauce, season with salt, and toss before spreading on the air fryer tray.
4. Cover and cook for 15 minutes, tossing halfway to ensure even cooking.
5. Serve immediately and enjoy!

Honey Brussel Sprout Chips

Preparation Time: 10 minutes | Cooking Time: 15 minutes | Servings: 4

Ingredients:
- 1 teaspoon sea salt
- 2 tablespoons canola oil
- 1 teaspoon honey

- Parchment paper as needed
- 1 oz. ends removed Brussel sprouts

Directions:
1. Preheat the air fryer to 240 degrees Fahrenheit and line the tray with parchment paper.
2. Remove the skin from Brussel sprouts one leaf at a time and put the leaves in a large bowl while you peel.
3. Drizzle canola oil and honey on the leaves, season with salt, and toss before spreading on the air fryer tray.
4. Cover and cook for 15 minutes, tossing halfway to ensure even cooking.
5. Serve immediately and enjoy!

Easy Cauliflower Crunch

Preparation Time: 5 minutes | Cooking Time: 6 hours | Servings: 4

Ingredients:
1. 1 teaspoon kosher salt
2. 1 tablespoon sunflower oil
3. 4 cups bite-sized cut cauliflower florets

Directions:
1. Preheat the air fryer to 135 degrees Fahrenheit.
2. Wash and dry the florets and toss olive oil and sea salt in a bowl.
3. Transfer to the air fryer basket in a flat layer and cover to cook for 6 hours.
4. Toss after every hour for proper dehydration.
5. Let it cool as it will turn crispy.
6. Store in an airtight jar for over a month or have it immediately.

Easy Broccoli Crunch

Preparation Time: 5 minutes | Cooking Time: 6 hours | Servings: 4

Ingredients:
- 1 teaspoon kosher salt
- 1 tablespoon avocado oil
- 4 cups bite-sized cut broccoli florets

Directions:
1. Preheat the air fryer to 135 degrees Fahrenheit.
2. Wash and dry the broccoli florets and toss them in a bowl with avocado oil and sea salt.
3. Transfer to the air fryer basket in a flat layer and cover to cook for 6 hours.
4. Toss after every hour for proper dehydration.
5. Let it cool as it will turn crispy.
6. Store in an airtight jar for over a month or have it immediately.

Lemon Pepper Broccoli Crunch

Preparation Time: 5 minutes | Cooking Time: 6 hours | Servings: 4

Ingredients:
- 1 teaspoon kosher salt
- 1 tablespoon avocado oil
- 1 teaspoon lemon pepper seasoning
- 4 cups bite-sized cut broccoli florets

Directions:
1. Preheat the air fryer to 135 degrees Fahrenheit.
2. Wash and dry the broccoli florets and toss them in a bowl with avocado oil and sea salt.
3. Transfer to the air fryer basket in a flat layer and cover to cook for 6 hours.
4. Toss after every hour for proper dehydration.
5. Let it cool to turn crispy, and toss the lemon pepper seasoning.

6. Store in an airtight jar for over a month or have it immediately.

Cayenne Zucchini Chips

Preparation Time: 15 minutes | Cooking Time: 4 hours | Servings: 8

Ingredients:
- 2 teaspoons kosher salt
- 2 tablespoons canola oil
- 1 teaspoon cayenne pepper
- 4 cups of very thinly-sliced zucchini

Directions:
1. Preheat the air fryer to 135 degrees Fahrenheit.
2. Toss the zucchini slices in a bowl with olive oil, cayenne, and kosher salt.
3. Transfer the zucchini slices to the air fryer basket and cover to cook for 4 hours.
4. Toss occasionally for proper dehydration.
5. Remove from the air fryer once crispy and enjoy!

Tasty Cucumber Chips

Preparation Time: 15 minutes | Cooking Time: 3 hours | Servings: 4

Ingredients:
- 2 teaspoons kosher salt
- Baking tray as needed
- Parchment paper as needed
- 2 tablespoons white wine vinegar
- 4 cups of very thinly-sliced cucumber

Directions:
1. Preheat the air fryer to 200 degrees Fahrenheit.
2. Dry the cucumber slices with paper towels.
3. Toss the slices in a bowl with vinegar and kosher salt.
4. Transfer the zucchini slices to a tray lined with parchment paper that fits inside the air fryer.
5. Add the tray to the air fryer and cover to cook for 3 hours.
6. The slices will start curling and getting brown.
7. Let them cool to make them crispier.
8. Once properly crispy, enjoy right away or store in an airtight jar for over a month.

Roasted Paprika Potatoes with Sour Cream

Preparation Time: 14 minutes | Cooking Time: 22 minutes | Servings: 2

Ingredients
- 2 sweet potatoes diced into cubes
- ½ tablespoon of chili powder
- Black pepper according to desire
- 1 cup of sour cream
- 1 tablespoon of olive oil

Directions
1. Soak the sweet potatoes for half an hour.
2. Use a paper towel to dry the potatoes.
3. Put half tablespoon of olive oil and chili powder in a bowl and stir in the potatoes.
4. Transfer the potatoes to the air fryer basket and put them in the air fryer.
5. Cook in the air fryer at 350 degrees F for 22 minutes.
6. Once it's done, drizzle some salt and pepper.
7. Use the sour cream while serving the potatoes!

Air Fryer Chicken Alfredo Quinoa Balls

Preparation Time: 14 minutes | Cooking Time: 12 minutes | Servings: 2

Ingredients
- 3 tablespoons of grated parmesan cheese
- 1 cup of quinoa (boiled)

- ½ cup of boiled chicken
- ½ teaspoon of garlic paste
- ½ teaspoon of onion powder
- ½ cup of Italian breadcrumbs
- Salt and pepper according to taste
- ½ tablespoon of cilantro for garnish

Directions
1. Mix all the ingredients in a bowl except chicken, quinoa, breadcrumbs, and cilantro.
2. Once they are thoroughly mixed, toss in the chicken and quinoa and mix thoroughly.
3. Use your hands to make a ball shape from the batter.
4. Coat the balls with the breadcrumbs and line them in the air fryer.
5. Cook them in the air fryer for 12 minutes at 400 degrees F.
6. Flipping halfway through.
7. Drizzle over some cilantro and serve once done.

Three Cheese Stuffed Mushrooms

Preparation Time: 14 minutes | Cooking Time: 8 minutes | Servings: 2

Ingredients
- 4 ounces of mushrooms
- 3 ounces. of cream cheese
- 2 tablespoons of parmesan cheese
- 1 tablespoon of sharp cheddar cheese
- 1 tablespoon of mozzarella cheese
- ½ teaspoon of Worcestershire sauce
- 2cloves of minced garlic clove
- Salt and pepper according to taste

Directions
1. Remove the stems of the mushrooms and wash with water.
2. Thoroughly mix all the remaining ingredients in a bowl.
3. Fill the mushroom caps with this batter.
4. Transfer to the air fryer in an air fryer basket.
5. Add the basket to the unit.
6. Cook the mushrooms for 8 minutes at 350 degrees f.
7. Once it's done, serve!

Air Fried Cheesy Spinach Crostini

Preparation Time: 12 minutes | Cooking Time: 8 minutes | Servings: 2

Ingredients
- 2 baguette rounds (whole-wheat)
- ½ cup of olive oil
- 1 cup of pecorino cheese, shredded
- 2 cups of spinach dip

Directions
1. Use a knife to dice the baguette into round shapes.
2. Grease olive oil over it and put it in an air fryer basket.
3. Transfer to the air fryer basket and toast it at 400 degrees F for 4 minutes.
4. Mix the spinach dip and the grated cheese in a separate bowl.
5. Coat the toasted crostini with the spinach-cheese mixture and shift it again to the air fryer.
6. Bake the crostini at 400 degrees for 4 minutes.
7. Serve!

Ricotta Fig Crostini

Preparation Time: 12 minutes | Cooking Time: 8 minutes | Servings: 1

Ingredients
- 2 baguette slices (whole-wheat)
- 2 figs

- 2 tablespoons of olive oil
- 1 oz. of ricotta
- 2 sprigs of chopped oregano

Directions
1. Place the baguette on a plain dish and grease it with olive oil.
2. Top with the remaining ingredients.
3. Put in the air fryer and bake it for 8 minutes at 340 degrees F.
4. Serve when done!

Cream Cheese Salmon with Strawberry Mint Bruschetta

Preparation Time: 14 minutes | Cooking Time: 12 minutes | Servings: 2

Ingredients
- 6 ounces of salmon fillet
- 1 ½ tablespoon of cream cheese
- 1 ½ tablespoon of Italian nut crumbs

For the Strawberry Mint Bruschetta
- 1 cup of sliced strawberries
- 2 tablespoons of chopped mint
- 1 tablespoon of olive oil
- ½ tablespoon of kosher salt
- ½ tablespoon of red wine vinegar

Directions
1. Take a bowl and mix all the ingredients of strawberry mint bruschetta and marinate in the refrigerator for half an hour.
2. Place the salmon on a plain dish and grease with some oil.
3. Coat with cream cheese and drizzle over some Italian nut crumbs.
4. Transfer it to the air fryer and cook for 12 minutes at 380 degrees F.
5. Once done, serve with the strawberry mint bruschetta!

Air Fryer Bacon-Wrapped Shrimp Tapas on Avocado Toast

Preparation Time: 20 minutes | Cooking Time10-15 minutes | Servings: 2

Ingredients
- 8 shrimps
- 4 slices of bacon
- 8 baguette slices (whole-wheat)
- 1/3 of an avocado
- 1/3 teaspoon of minced garlic
- 2 teaspoons of lemon juice
- Salt and pepper according to taste

Directions
1. Place the baguette in a plain dish and use a knife to make slices.
2. Brush with some oil and rub over salt and pepper.
3. Toast the baguette for 4 minutes in the air fryer.
4. Now rub over the garlic paste.
5. Put garlic and lemon juice in a bowl and mix with crushed avocado.
6. Use a paper towel to dry the shrimps to extract excessive moisture.
7. Use the bacon slices to wrap the shrimp and brush with some oil.
8. Transfer the shrimps to the air fryer and cook for 6 minutes at 380 degrees F.
9. Sprinkle some salt and pepper over the toast and avocado.
10. Once it's done, put the shrimp on the toast and Serve!

Perfect Crostini

Preparation Time: 14 minutes | Cooking Time: 15 minutes | Servings: 3

Ingredients
- 1 baguette, sliced
- 2 cloves of minced garlic.
- 8 ½ ounces of ricotta cheese
- 2 tablespoons of oregano
- 2 red chilies
- 7 ounces of black olives
- ½ cup cherry tomatoes

Directions
1. Brush some oil over the sliced baguette.
2. Put the slices in the air fryer basket and transfer them to the air fryer.
3. Bake in the air fryer at 400 degrees for 15 minutes.
4. Rub the garlic paste over the baked crostini.
5. Now mix all the remaining ingredients except the tomatoes in a separate bowl.
6. Season this batter over the baked crostini topped with diced tomatoes and a little oil.
7. Perfect crostini is ready to be served!

Cannoli Stuffed French toast

Preparation Time: 15 minutes | Cooking Time: 18 minutes | Servings: 4

Ingredients
For Cannoli Filling
- 2 cups of cottage cheese
- ¼ cup of powdered sugar
- 1 teaspoon of vanilla extract
- 1/3 cup of mini chocolate chips

For French toast
- 8 brioche bread slices
- 4 eggs
- ¼ cup of softened butter
- 2 cups of half & half
- ¼ cup of powdered sugar
- ¼ cup of vanilla extract
- 1 teaspoon of cinnamon
- Honey

Directions
1. Stir the sugar and cottage cheese in a bowl and pour the vanilla extract and chocolate chips.
2. Now beat butter and eggs, add all the French toast ingredients except the brioche slices, and mix.
3. Meanwhile, brush some oil over the air fryer basket.
4. Dip the brioche slices in the mixture.
5. Top the brioche slices with the cottage cheese mixture.
6. Put inside the air fryer and bake at 350 degrees F for 12-18 minutes.
7. Make sure to flip after half time to cook evenly on both sides.
8. Drizzle some honey on top once cooked and serve.

Classic Smashed Potatoes

Preparation Time: 14 minutes | Cooking Time: 20-40 minutes | Servings: 2

Ingredients
- 1 pound of potatoes (small size)
- 2 tablespoons of olive oil
- ½ teaspoon of dried thyme
- ½ lime zest
- Salt and pepper according to taste

Directions
1. Boil the potatoes in hot water for about 15 minutes and drain.
2. Now take a bowl and mix all the remaining ingredients in it.
3. Stir the potatoes in the marinade and put them on the baking tray.
4. Use a masher to crush the potatoes and roast them in the air fryer at 350 degrees F for 20 minutes.
5. Once it's done, serve!

Air Fryer Lemon Potatoes

Preparation Time: 14 minutes | Cooking Time: 22 minutes | Servings: 2

Ingredients
- 1 ½ cups of potato wedges
- 1 tablespoon of olive oil
- ½ teaspoon of basil (dried)
- 1 tablespoon of lemon juice
- Salt according to taste

Directions
1. Mix all the ingredients in a bowl except the potatoes.
2. Once the ingredients are thoroughly mixed, toss in the potato wedges and stir well.
3. Transfer the potatoes to the air fryer basket lined with parchment paper, and cook at 380 degrees F for 22 minutes.
4. Make sure to flip the potatoes after 10-11 minutes to cook evenly on all sides.
5. Once it's done, drop some lemon juice over it and serve!

Greek Feta Fries in an Air-Fryer

Preparation Time: 15 minutes | Cooking Time: 16-17 minutes | Servings: 4

Ingredients
- Oil spray
- 4 Yukon Gold potatoes
- 2 tablespoons of olive oil
- 4 teaspoon of lime zest
- 1 teaspoon of thyme
- 1 teaspoon of kosher salt
- ½ teaspoon of garlic paste
- ½ teaspoon of onion powder
- ½ teaspoon of chili powder
- 1 teaspoon of black pepper
- 1 cup of feta cheese grated
- 4 ounces of grated chicken breast
- ½ cup of tzatziki sauce
- ½ cup of plum tomatoes
- ¼ cup of red onions thinly sliced
- 2 tablespoons of parsley
- 2 tablespoons of oregano

Directions
1. Slice the Yukon potatoes in a fries shape.
2. Mix onion powder, lime zest, garlic paste, and oregano with salt and pepper in a bowl and stir thoroughly.
3. Add some oil to the mixture, put in the potatoes, and stir.
4. Brush some cooking spray on the air fryer basket.
5. Set the temperature of the air fryer to 400 degrees F.
6. Cook in the air fryer for 17 minutes.
7. Top the potatoes with all the remaining ingredients.
8. Greek Feta Fries are ready to be served!

Air Fryer Chicken with Saucy Quinoa Salad

Preparation Time: 15 minutes | Cooking Time: 15-25 minutes | Servings: 4

Ingredients
- 2 cups of quinoa
- 4 teaspoons olive oil
- 4 teaspoons of cumin powder
- 4 teaspoons coriander powder
- 4 teaspoons chili powder
- 4 chicken breast fillets
- 7 ounces of broad beans unfrozen
- 4 tomatoes, medium-sized
- 8 spring onions
- 8.5 ounces of kale & baby spinach
- 1 cup of mint leaves
- ½ cup of almonds diced
- 1 cup of yogurt
- ¼ cup of lime juice
- 2 tablespoons of tahini
- 2 cloves of garlic minced

Directions
1. Add a cup of water to a saucepan and pour in the washed quinoa for 10 minutes of high flame.
2. Put it aside once cooked to let it cool.
3. Now pour the chicken into a bowl and season with some cumin, chili powder, and coriander, and stir well.
4. Take an air fryer basket and line it with parchment paper.
5. Spray with some oil and align the chicken in the air fryer basket.
6. Transfer to the air fryer and set the temperature at 400 degrees F.
7. Cook for 15 minutes and put aside once done.
8. Now take a pan and pour in water.
9. Pour the beans into it and cook on medium heat for 2 minutes.
10. Meanwhile, take a bowl and mix up the lemon juice and yogurt with the garlic paste and tahini.
11. Take the lightly cooked beans from the water and mix them with quinoa and other unused ingredients.
12. Mix the quinoa and lime juice mixture.
13. Chicken is all set to be served with this sauce!

Buffalo Quinoa Bites

Preparation Time: 15 minutes | Cooking Time: 7-10 minutes | Servings: 4

Ingredients
- 1 cup of quinoa (cooked)
- ½ cup of cannellini beans
- ½ cup of panko breadcrumbs
- 1 egg
- 4 tablespoons of buffalo wing sauce for seasoning
- 1 ounce of cheddar cheese grated
- Salt and pepper according to taste

Directions
1. Take a bowl and mix all the listed ingredients, excluding cheese.
2. Mix thoroughly and make a batter from it.
3. Now use your hands to make 8 balls from the batter.
4. Press the balls with your hands to flat them and pour cheese into the center.
5. Seal from all ends and put in a cooking tray lined with parchment paper.
6. Transfer the cooking tray to the air fryer unit.
7. Set the temperature to 400 degrees F and the time to 7-10 minutes.
8. Once cooked, drizzle some buffalo sauce on the top.

9. Buffalo quinoa is ready to be served!

Tofu Coated with Quinoa Flakes

Preparation Time: 15 minutes | Cooking Time: 12 minutes | Servings: 4

Ingredients
- 2 blocks of tofu, diced into cubes
- 1 cup of cornstarch
- 1 cup of soy milk, unsweetened

Quinoa Flakes Mix Ingredients:
- 1 cup of quinoa flakes
- 1/4 cup of nutritional yeast
- 2 tablespoons of thyme
- 2 tablespoons of cilantro
- 2 tablespoons of sage leaves
- 4 tablespoons of rosemary
- 2 teaspoons of black pepper

Directions
1. Combine all the quinoa flakes mixture in a bowl and set aside for further use.
2. Take two bowls and pour cornstarch in one and soy milk in the other.
3. Now place the tofu in a dish and use a knife to slice it.
4. Dip the slices in cornstarch and then into the soy milk.
5. Give the tofu slices the third dip in the quinoa flakes mixture.
6. Line an air fryer basket with parchment paper and put the tofu.
7. Put in the air fryer unit.
8. Set the time of the air fryer to 12 minutes.
9. Adjust the temperature to 400 degrees F.
10. Serve once cooked!

Air Fryer Zucchini Fries with Tzatziki Dip

Preparation Time: 15 minutes | Cooking Time: 10-12 minutes | Servings: 4

Ingredients
- 2 zucchinis
- 10.5 ounces of oat bran
- 7 ounces of almond flour
- 4 eggs
- 1 teaspoon minced garlic
- Salt and pepper according to taste

For the Tzatziki Dip
- ½ cup of Greek yogurt
- 2 cucumbers
- 2 lemons juiced
- Mint
- Dill

Directions
1. Take a bowl, mix all the Tzatziki dip ingredients, and put it aside.
2. Take two medium-sized bowls and whisk eggs in one while pouring the baking flour into the other.
3. Now take a third bowl and mix oat bran with salt and pepper.
4. Dip zucchini in flour, then in egg wash, and at the end in oat bran.
5. Put the zucchini in a cooking tray lined with parchment paper.
6. Transfer the zucchini to the air fryer unit.
7. Adjust the temperature of the air fryer to 10-12 minutes.
8. Set the temperature to 400 degrees F.
9. Once cooked, serve with the Tzatziki dip!

Air Fryer Pita Pockets

Preparation Time: 15 minutes | Cooking Time: 7 minutes | Servings: 4

Ingredients
- 6 pita pockets
- ¼ cup melted butter
- 1 teaspoon of garlic paste
- 1 teaspoon of minced onion
- 1 teaspoon of cilantro
- Salt and pepper according to taste

Directions
1. Place the pita pockets on a dish and use a knife or a stencil to make them into triangles shapes.
2. Now take a bowl and thoroughly mix all the ingredients.
3. Brush the mixture over triangles.
4. Take a cooking tray and line it with parchment paper.
5. Arrange the pita triangles in the cooking tray.
6. Put them in the air fryer unit.
7. Adjust the temperature of the air fryer to 350 degrees F
8. Set the time to 7 minutes.
9. Serve the Pita Pockets once cooked!

Air Fryer Feta Cheese Appetizer

Preparation Time: 15 minutes | Cooking Time: 12 minutes | Servings: 4

Ingredients
- 16-20 ounces of feta cheese
- 4 tablespoons of olive oil
- 4 tablespoons of maple syrup
- 2 teaspoons of dried thyme
- 2 teaspoons of chili flakes

Directions
1. Put the feta cheese on a cooking tray lined with parchment paper.
2. Drizzle with olive oil and maple syrup.
3. Evenly scatter the thyme and chili flake over it.
4. Put the cooking tray in the air fryer unit.
5. Set the temperature of the air fryer to 400 degrees F.
6. Adjust the time between 10-12 minutes.
7. Serve once the cheese softens!

Air-Fryer Fish Cakes

Preparation Time: 15 minutes | Cooking Time: 10 minutes | Servings: 2

Ingredients
- 8 ounces of white fish
- 4 tablespoons of panko breadcrumbs
- 1.5 tablespoons of parsley
- 1 teaspoon of Thai sweet chili sauce
- 1 tablespoon of canola mayonnaise
- 2 small egg
- 1 lemon wedge
- Salt and pepper according to taste

Directions
1. Combine all the ingredients in a mixing bowl and mix thoroughly.
2. Transform the batter into a cake-shaped slab and spray some oil.
3. Take an air fryer basket and grease it with cooking oil.
4. Put the fish cake in it and put it inside the air fryer unit.
5. Adjust the temperature of the air fryer to 400 degrees F.
6. Set the time to 10 minutes.
7. Once cooked, served with the lemon wedge!

Air Fryer Olives, Garlic & Tomatoes

Preparation Time: 15 minutes | Cooking Time: 15 minutes | Servings: 4

Ingredients
- 2 cups of Kalamata olives
- 2 cups of green olives
- 2 cups of cherry tomatoes
- ½ cup of garlic cloves, minced
- ¼ cup of olive oil
- ¼ cup of mixed herbs

Directions
1. Toss all the ingredients in a mixing bowl and stir.
2. Take an air fryer basket and line it with parchment paper.
3. Transfer the basket to the air fryer.
4. Adjust the temperature of the air fryer to 360 degrees F.
5. Set the time of the air fryer between 5-7 minutes.
6. Once it's cooked, serve with pasta!

Mixed Veggies Pancakes

Preparation Time: 15 minutes | Cooking Time: 15 minutes | Servings: 2

Ingredients
- 2 tablespoons of ground flaxseed
- ¼ cup of water
- 3-4 medium russet potatoes, chopped and squeezed
- 1/2 onion thinly diced
- Salt and pepper according to taste
- ½ cup of carrots, sliced thinly
- ¼ cup of peas
- 4 tablespoons of drained corn
- 4 tablespoons of fresh parsley, thinly sliced
- 1/3 cup of almond flour
- Cooking oil spray

Directions
1. Toss all the ingredients in a bowl except the parsley, flour, salt & pepper.
2. Thoroughly mix the ingredients and add in the flour and other unused ingredients.
3. Mix it well and stir it to form the dough for pancakes.
4. Take an air fryer basket and line it with parchment paper.
5. Mist pancakes with oil spray.
6. Pour in all the mixture on the basket in patties form.
7. Set the temperature of the air fryer to 400 degrees F.
8. Adjust the time to 15 minutes and put the basket in the air fryer.
9. Once it's cooked, serve!

Vegan Coconut French Toasts

Preparation Time: 15 minutes | Cooking Time: 5 minutes | Servings: 2

Ingredients
- 4 slices of gluten-free bread
- 2 cups of coconut milk
- 1 teaspoon of baking soda
- 2 cups of unsweetened and grated coconut
- ¼ cup of honey

Directions
1. Take a plain dish and evenly lay the coconut shaving.
2. Take a medium-sized bowl, add coconut milk and baking soda, and mix thoroughly.
3. Now take the bread slices and dip them in coconut milk and then in the coconut flakes.
4. Please put them in a basket lined with parchment paper.
5. Add the basket to the unit.
6. Set the temperature of the air fryer to 400 degrees F.
7. Adjust the time between 4-5 minutes.
8. Make sure to flip halfway to let the bread slices cook evenly on both sides.

9. Trickle honey on top and serve!

Delicious Lime Tofu

Preparation Time: 15 minutes | Cooking Time: 17-20 minutes | Servings: 4

Ingredients
- 2 pounds of super-firm tofu's, drained and pressed
- 4 teaspoons soy sauce
- 4 teaspoons arrowroot powder

For the lemon juice
- 2 teaspoons of lime zest
- ½ cup of lime juice
- 1 cup of water
- 1/3 cup of sugar
- 4 teaspoons of arrowroot powder

Directions
1. Take a bowl, thoroughly mix all the ingredients under lime juice, and put it aside.
2. Place the tofu on a cutting dish and use a knife to slice them into cubes.
3. Pour them into a zip lock bag along with the soy sauce and arrowroot powder and shake it well.
4. Marinate it at room temperature for 20-30 minutes.
5. Take the air fryer basket and spray with cooking oil spray.
6. Set the temperature of the air fryer to 400 degrees.
7. Adjust the time between 15-17 minutes.
8. Put the tofu in the air fryer basket and transfer it to the unit.
9. Once cooked, pour the lime sauce and the tofu into a pan and cook again for 2 minutes.
10. Once it's done, serve!

Crispy Potato Nuggets

Preparation Time: 15 minutes| Cooking Time: 15 minutes | Servings: 4

Ingredients
- 2 cups of potatoes, diced
- ½ teaspoon of olive oil
- ¼ teaspoon of garlic powder
- 2 cups of cooked baby spinach, chopped
- 4 tablespoons of almond milk
- Salt and pepper according to taste
- Cooking spray

Directions
1. Boil the potatoes for 30 minutes, drain and use a paper towel to pat fry them.
2. Meanwhile, put garlic powder in a pan, add some oil and fry for 1 minute.
3. Pour in the baby spinach and cook for 2 minutes.
4. Now take the boiled potatoes and mash them in a bowl with milk, salt, and pepper.
5. Pour in the spinach mixture and stir thoroughly.
6. Carve out nuggets shape from this batter using your hands.
7. Now, set the temperature of the air fryer to 400 degrees F.
8. Adjust the time between 14-15 minutes.
9. Take a basket and line it with parchment paper.
10. Align the nuggets in the air fryer basket and put them inside the air fryer unit.
11. Once it's done, serve!

Vegan Corn Fritters

Preparation Time: 25 minutes | Cooking Time: 15 minutes | Servings: 3

Ingredients
- 2 tablespoons of grounded cornmeal
- 3 tablespoons of all-purpose flour
- ¼ teaspoon of baking soda
- Garlic and onion powder according to taste
- A pinch of chili powder
- 1 teaspoon of Green Chiles with juice
- 2 tablespoons of finely diced cilantro

Cream corn mixture Ingredients
- ½ cup of corn
- 2 tablespoons of almond milk
- Salt and pepper according to taste

Other Ingredients
- 1 cup of grilled corn kernels
- 3 tablespoons of yellow mustard, for dipping only

Directions
1. Thoroughly mix all the main ingredients in a bowl.
2. Now pour the cream corn mixture ingredients into a blender.
3. Blend them and pour them into the mixed main ingredients.
4. Pour out the grilled kernels into the mixture and thoroughly mix.
5. Take an air fryer basket and line it with parchment paper.
6. Put the mixture into the air fryer basket using a cookie scoop.
7. Adjust the temperature of the air fryer to 400 degrees F.
8. Set the time to 15 minutes and put the basket in the air fryer unit.
9. Make sure to flip them halfway to let them cook evenly on both sides.
10. Once it's done, serve with the yellow mustard!

Herbed and Spiced Baked Tofu Fries

Preparation Time: 15 minutes | Cooking Time: 15 minutes | Servings: 2

Ingredients
- 8 ounces of extra-firm tofu, drained and pressed
- 1 tablespoon of olive oil
- A pinch of thyme
- A pinch of basil
- A pinch of chili powder
- 1/5 teaspoon of cayenne pepper
- 1/5 teaspoon of onion powder
- A pinch of garlic powder
- Salt and pepper according to taste

Directions
1. Mix all the ingredients in a bowl except the tofu and olive oil.
2. Put the tofu on a cutting tray and slice them.
3. Coat them with the mixture and put them in the air fryer basket lined with parchment paper.
4. Set the temperature of the air fryer to 400 degrees F and the time to 15 minutes.
5. Put the air fryer basket in the air fryer unit and let it be cooked.
6. Once it's done, serve!

Mushroom Pizzas with Hummus Drizzle

Preparation Time: 14 minutes | Cooking Time: 6 minutes | Servings: 2

Ingredients
- 4-6 portobello mushrooms, large
- ¼ tablespoon red wine vinegar
- Salt and pepper according to taste
- 1 clove of minced garlic

- 2 ounces of zucchini, julienned
- 1.5 tablespoons of sweet red pepper, sliced
- 1 olive kalamata olive, diced
- ¼ teaspoon of dried oregano
- 4 tablespoons of hummus

Directions
1. De-stem the mushrooms and press them.
2. Pour the red wine vinegar, salt, and pepper on the mushrooms.
3. Put them in the air fryer unit and cook at 400 degrees F for 4 minutes.
4. Meanwhile, take a separate bowl and mix all the remaining ingredients except hummus.
5. Pour an equal proportion of the mixture over each cooked mushroom.
6. Now put the mushrooms back into the air fryer.
7. Cook again at 400 degrees F for 6 minutes.
8. Once it is done, trickle over the hummus.
9. Mushroom pizza is ready to be served!

Delicious Vegan Pasta Chips
Preparation Time: 10 minutes | Cooking Time: 5-8 minutes | Servings: 2

Ingredients
- 2 cups of farfalle pasta, boiled and drained
- 2 tablespoons of Aquafaba
- 2 tablespoons of nutritional yeast
- 2 teaspoons of Italian seasoning
- Salt and pepper according to taste

Directions
1. Toss all the ingredients in a bowl and stir.
2. Line an air fryer basket with parchment paper.
3. Pour the pasta mixture into the basket.
4. Set the temperature of the air fryer to 400 degrees and the time to 5 minutes.
5. Put the air fryer basket in the unit and let it be cooked.
6. After 2-3 minutes, shake the basket and put it again in the unit.
7. Once it's cooked, serve!

Buffalo Turkey Pizza
Preparation Time: 15 minutes | Cooking Time: 15 minutes | Servings: 4

Ingredients
- 5 inches of pizza crust (whole wheat)
- ¼ cup of pizza sauce
- ¾ cup of boiled turkey
- ½ red onion, chopped finely
- ¼ large green bell pepper seeded, finely diced
- 1 cup of mozzarella cheese
- 2 tablespoons of parmesan cheese
- 2 tablespoons of buffalo wing sauce
- 2 cups of ranch sauce

Directions
1. Spray some cooking oil on the pizza pan and layout the pizza dough on it.
2. Layer it with pizza sauce, turkey, onions, and bell peppers.
3. Top with grated mozzarella and parmesan cheese.
4. Change the function of the air fryer to Pizza.
5. Set the temperature to 400 degrees F and the time to 12 minutes.
6. Put the pizza pan on the fourth rack of the air fryer unit and let it be cooked.
7. Once it's done, pour some Buffalo wings sauce and ranch sauce on top.
8. Serve!

Basil Pesto Pizza
Preparation Time: 15 minutes | Cooking Time: 15 minutes | Servings: 4

Ingredients
- 5 inches pizza crust (whole-wheat)
- 4 tablespoons of pesto
- 2 tablespoons of basil leaves, sliced
- ½ red onion chopped finely
- ½ cup of mozzarella cheese
- ¼ cup olive oil

Directions
1. Spray some cooking oil on the pizza pan and layout the pizza dough on it.
2. Lay pesto sauce all over and top with mozzarella, onion, and basil.
3. Now change the function of the air fryer to pizza.
4. Set the temperature of the unit to 400 degrees F.
5. Put the pizza pan on the fourth rack of the unit and bake it for 12 minutes.
6. Once it's done, serve!
7. Drizzle olive oil on top if liked.

BBQ Turkey Pizza
Preparation Time: 15 minutes | Cooking Time: 12 minutes | Servings: 2

Ingredients
- 6 inches classic crust pizza
- 2 tablespoons of ranch dressing
- 2 tablespoons of BBQ sauce
- ¾ cup of boiled turkey, sliced
- ½ cup of kale leaves
- ½ cup of plum, diced
- 1 tablespoon of onion, finely chopped
- ½ teaspoon of Italian seasoning
- ½ cup of mozzarella cheese, grated

Directions
1. Spray some cooking oil on the pizza pan and spread the pizza crust on it.
2. Evenly spread all the ingredients on the pizza crust, starting with BBQ sauce and ranch dressing.
3. Then top with the remaining listed ingredients one by one.
4. Now change the function of the air fryer to pizza.
5. Set the temperature of the unit to 400 degrees F.
6. Put the pizza pan inside the unit and bake it for 12 minutes.
7. Once it's done, serve!

Christmas Pizza
Preparation Time: 25 minutes | Cooking Time: 12-24 minutes | Servings: 2-4

Ingredients
- 6 teaspoons of olive oil
- 8 bacon, fat trimmed, sliced thinly
- 4 red onions, chopped finely
- 2/3 cup of cranberries
- 2/3 cup of white wine vinegar
- 2/3 cup of brown sugar
- 4 cups of pizza sauce
- 4 cups of sweet potatoes, finely chopped
- 4 cups of mozzarella, grated
- 4 cups of turkey, grated
- ½ cup of fresh sage leaves
- 2 pizza crusts, size 13 inches

Directions

1. Spray some cooking oil on the pizza pan and spread the pizza crust on it.
2. Now take a saucepan and cook the bacon with vinegar, sugar, and cranberries for 2 minutes.
3. Now divide the mixture into 2 equal proportions and spread it on each pizza crust.
4. Drizzle with the remaining ingredients and put it in the air fryer.
5. Now change the function of the air fryer to Pizza.
6. Set the temperature of the unit to 400 degrees F.
7. Adjust the temperature to 12 minutes.
8. Do this for the second pizza as well.
9. Cook the pizza in batches.
10. Once it's done, serve!

Simple and Classic Marinara Pizza

Preparation Time: 15 minutes | Cooking Time: 12 minutes | Servings: 1

Ingredients
- 1 pizza crust (12 inches in size)
- ½ cup of marinara sauce
- ½ cup of oregano leaves
- 2 red onions, finely chopped
- ½ cup of mozzarella cheese
- ¼ cup of olive oil

Directions
1. Spray some cooking oil on two round pans and spread the pizza crusts on them.
2. Top both the pizza crust with all the listed ingredients in equal proportions.
3. Sprinkle olive oil in the end.
4. Now change the function of the air fryer to pizza.
5. Set the temperature of the unit to 400 degrees F.
6. Put the pan inside the basket, and bake it for 12 minutes.
7. Once it's done, serve!

Sweet Cinnamon Plantains

Preparation Time: 15 minutes | Cooking Time: 12 hours | Servings: 4

Ingredients
- 4-6 plantains, peeled
- 2/3 teaspoon of cinnamon
- 4 teaspoons brown sugar
- 1/6 teaspoon of nutmeg

Directions
1. Place the plantains on a cutting board and use a knife to cut them into a round shape.
2. Pour it into a bowl and drizzle the cinnamon, nutmeg, and brown sugar.
3. Take a dehydrating basket and put the plantains over it.
4. Put the basket in the air fryer.
5. Change the mode to "dehydrate".
6. Adjust the temperature to 125 degrees F and set the time to super convection 12 hours.
7. Serve once it gets crispy!

Dehydrated Toasted BBQ Almonds

Preparation Time: 15 minutes | Cooking Time: 20 hours | Servings: 2

Ingredients
- 1 pound of almonds
- 3 tablespoons of BBQ dry rub spice

Directions
1. Soak the almonds in water for a day.
2. Drain them and use a paper towel to pat them dry.
3. Take a dehydrating basket and put the almonds over it.

4. Put the basket in the air fryer.
5. Change the mode to "dehydrate".
6. Adjust the temperature to 125 degrees F and set the time to super convection 20 hours.
7. Serve once the almonds get crispy!
8. serve with a sprinkle of BBQ dry rub

Dehydrated Cashews

Preparation Time: 15 minutes | Cooking Time: 24 minutes | Servings: 4

Ingredients
- 1-pound cashews
- Salt according to taste

Directions
1. Soak the cashews in water for a day.
2. Drain them and use a paper towel to pat them dry.
3. Take a dehydrating basket and put the cashews over it.
4. Put the basket inside the air fryer.
5. Change the mode to "dehydrate".
6. Adjust the temperature to 125 degrees F and set the time to super convection 24 hours.
7. Serve once the cashews once they get crispy!
8. Season it with salt if liked.

Maple Glazed Dehydrated Toasted Almonds

Preparation Time: 15 minutes | Cooking Time: 20 hours 5 minutes | Servings: 4

Ingredients
- 1-pound almonds, raw
- ¼ cup maple syrup
- 2 teaspoons rosemary
- 4 teaspoons brown sugar
- Salt according to taste

Directions
1. Soak the almonds in water for a day.
2. Drain them and use a paper towel to pat them dry.
3. Take a dehydrating basket and put the almonds over it.
4. Put the basket inside the air fryer.
5. Change the mode to "dehydrate".
6. Adjust the temperature to 120 degrees F and set the time to super convection 20 hours.
7. Once the almonds are done, put a frying pan on medium flame.
8. Add all the remaining ingredients to it and heat.
9. Add the dehydrated almonds to this mixture and remove them from the flame.
10. Take a baking tray and line it with parchment paper.
11. Scatter the almonds mixture over it and put it on the fourth rack of the air fryer.
12. Change the mode to "bake" and adjust the temperature to 350 degrees F.
13. Set the time to 5 minutes.
14. Once it's done, serve!

Dehydrated Sweet Potatoes

Preparation Time: 15 minutes | Cooking Time: 12 Hours | Servings: 4

Ingredients
- 4 sweet potatoes, medium-sized

For the spices
- 2 teaspoons rosemary
- 2 teaspoons garlic paste
- 2 teaspoons onion powder
- Salt and pepper according to taste

Directions
1. Peel the sweet potatoes and dice them finely.

2. Sprinkle all the spices and other ingredients and toss them.
3. Put the potatoes in a dehydrating basket.
4. Put the basket in the fourth rack of the air fryer.
5. Change the mode to "dehydrate".
6. Adjust the temperature to 125 degrees F and set the super convection for 12-14 hours.
7. Make sure to check the potatoes after every 4-5 hours.
8. Serve once dehydrated!

Prosciutto And Cheese Puff Pastry Pinwheels

Preparation Time: 10 minutes | Cooking Time: 15 minutes | Servings: 1

Ingredients:
- One sheet (8.65 ounces) of store-bought puff pastry
- Two tablespoons of Dijon mustard
- Two tablespoons mayonnaise
- One teaspoon of finely chopped fresh basil leaves, plus more for garnish
- One teaspoon of finely chopped fresh oregano leaves, plus more for garnish
- 1/2 teaspoon finely chopped fresh thyme leaves, plus more for garnish
- 1/2 teaspoon finely chopped fresh rosemary leaves, plus more for garnish
- 1 large egg
- 1 tablespoon water
- All-purpose flour for rolling the puff pastry
- Four slices prosciutto
- 1/2 cup grated parmesan cheese

Directions:
1. Thaw the puff pastry in the fridge overnight. You may also defrost it on the counter: Remove the frozen puff pastry from its box and thaw it on a baking sheet set on the kitchen counter for 40 minutes, or until cold yet flexible.
2. Preheat the oven as follows:
3. Place the oven rack in the center position. Preheat the oven to 400 0F. Set aside two baking sheets lined with parchment paper.
4. Combine the mustard, mayonnaise, basil, oregano, thyme, and rosemary in a small bowl. Set it aside for now.
5. Before baking, brush crispy prosciutto and parmesan pinwheels with egg wash.
6. Bake the pinwheels for 14 to 16 minutes, one baking sheet at a time, until golden brown.
7. The second baking sheet should be baked.
8. Crispy prosciutto and parmesan pinwheels on a baking sheet.
9. If preferred, garnish with herbs and serve warm or at room temperature.

Pizza Roll

Preparation Time: 10 minutes | Cooking Time: 15 minutes | Servings: 1

Ingredients:
- Refrigerated pizza crust tubes
- Garlic salt
- Italian seasoning
- Shredded Mozzarella cheese
- Parmesan cheese
- Pepperoni
- Marinara sauce

Directions:

1. Preparing the pizza dough is the first stage in producing pizza rolls. Although you may prepare homemade pizza dough, we usually use refrigerated.
2. This food may be found in the refrigerated case beside the biscuits and crescent rolls. It comes in a long tube and is frequently seen with the brand and generic labels.
3. Now it's time to cut your pizza rolls into bite-sized pieces.
4. Use a serrated knife or a sharp pizza cutter when cutting through the dough. A normal kitchen knife tends to compress the dough rather than see it through.
5. Place each piece, face side up, on a rimmed baking sheet that has been gently oiled. Bake in a preheated oven for 10 minutes or until light golden brown.
6. Remove the rolls from the oven and place them on a big dish, surrounded by a small bowl of marinara sauce.

Bread Cutlet

Preparation Time: 10 minutes | Cooking Time: 15 minutes | Servings: 1

Ingredients:
- 4 White Bread Slices (or brown bread)
- One large Potato, boiled, peeled, and mashed
- 1/3 cup Green Peas (fresh or frozen), boiled
- 1/3 cup grated Cabbage
- 1/3 cup grated Carrot
- Two tablespoons + 1/3 cup Dry Breadcrumbs
- One medium Onion, finely chopped
- 1-2 Green Chilies, seeded and finely chopped
- 1/2 teaspoon grated Ginger
- 1/4 teaspoon Garam Masala Powder
- 1 teaspoon Lemon Juice
- 1 tablespoon + 3 tablespoons Oil
- Water
- Salt to taste
- Two grated Cheese Cubes and Tomato Ketchup for garnishing

Directions:
1. In a pan, heat one tablespoon of oil over medium heat. Sauté the finely chopped onion till lightly brown, about 1-2 minutes. Sauté for 30 seconds with the grated ginger and green chilies.
2. Garam masala powder, grated carrot, grated cabbage, boiling peas
3. Cook for 1-2 minutes. Turn off the heat and transfer the prepared mixture to a mixing bowl. Allow it to cool at ambient temperature for 4-5 minutes.
4. Heat a nonstick shallow frying pan over medium heat with 2-3 tablespoons of oil. Place 2-3 cutlets on it and shallow fried over medium heat until the bottom surface gets light golden brown.
5. Flip them carefully, drizzle with one tablespoon of oil, and lightly fry the second side until golden brown. Flip and heat until both sides are golden brown. Each side will take around 2 minutes to cook on medium heat. Place the shallow-fried cutlet on a platter.
6. Prepare for serving by shallow-frying the remaining ones. Garnish with shredded cheese and tomato ketchup on each.

Pepperoni Calzones

Preparation Time: 10 minutes | Cooking Time: 15 minutes | Servings: 1

Ingredients:
- 2 pounds (32 ounces) of prepared pizza dough
- 4-6 tablespoons marinara sauce, plus more for dipping

- 8 ounces ricotta cheese
- 4 ounces pepperoni, sliced
- 8 ounces mozzarella cheese, grated
- Two tablespoons of fresh oregano, chopped
- For the egg wash:
- 1 large egg
- 1 tablespoon water

Directions:
1. Preheat the oven to 375 degrees Fahrenheit.
2. Divide the prepared pizza dough into four evenly sized balls for big calzones or six for smaller ones. Working with one dough ball at a time, keep the remaining dough balls covered to prevent them from drying out.
3. Turn the dough ball out onto a lightly floured board. Roll it out with a rolling pin until you get a circle 6-8 inches in diameter, depending on your size. I will aim for around 8 inches if you're preparing four bigger calzones. Choose 6-inches for the smaller version.
4. Make the egg wash once your calzones have been sealed. Mix the egg and one tablespoon of water in a small dish using a fork. Brush the egg wash over the tops of the calzones using a pastry brush.
5. Using parchment paper, line a baking sheet. Bake the calzones for 35 to 40 minutes until the calzones are a deep golden brown all over.
6. Calzones Baked Serve the calzones warm with additional marinara for dipping.

Rice Cake with Dulce de Leche and Dark Chocolate

Preparation Time: 10 minutes | Cooking Time: 15 minutes | Servings: 1

Ingredients:
- Four plain unsalted rice cakes
- 1/2 cup store-bought dulce de leche
- 1/4 teaspoon flaky sea salt, plus more for garnish
- 1/2 cup dark chocolate chips
- One tablespoon of coconut oil (any kind)

Directions:
1. Line a small baking sheet with wax or parchment paper. 2 teaspoons dulce de leche on each rice cake, leaving a 1/4-inch border around the outside borders. Place them on the baking sheet and season with a touch of salt.
2. Dulce de Leche Rice Cake Dipped in Dark Chocolate
3. Freeze the rice cakes for about 10 minutes or until the chocolate solidifies. Then, scarf it down right away!
4. These goodies are best consumed on the day they are made, but you may make extra and freeze them for your future joyful self! Simply wrap them in plastic and stack them in a freezer-safe bag for up to 1 week in the freezer.

Cheeseburger Empanadas

Preparation Time: 10 minutes | Cooking Time: 15 minutes | Servings: 1

Ingredients:
- Two tablespoons of canola oil, divided
- One green bell pepper, seeded and diced
- 1 Spanish onion, finely diced
- Six cloves of garlic, minced
- 1 1/2 teaspoons kosher salt, divided
- Freshly ground black pepper, to taste
- 1 pound ground beef (preferably 80/20 lean to fat ratio)
- Two tablespoons recent or sofrito (homemade or store-bought)
- Two teaspoons of garlic powder
- 1 teaspoon onion powder
- 1/2 teaspoon ground cumin

- Two teaspoons paprika
- One tablespoon of dried oregano
- 1 packet sazòn con achiote
- One tablespoon of tomato paste
- 2 (14-ounce) packages of Goya discos empanada dough for frying, thawed
- 10 ounces mild cheddar cheese, shredded
- For frying
- 1 1/2 cups canola oil
- Dipping sauces for serving
- Sour cream
- Thousand island dressing
- Barbeque sauce
- Chimichurri

Directions:
1. Warm the oil in a large skillet over medium-high heat. Cook, occasionally stirring, until the bell peppers and onions are softened, about 4 minutes. Season with 1/2 teaspoon salt and freshly ground black pepper to taste. Cook for 30 to 1 minute, or until the garlic is aromatic.
2. Aromatics are being prepared for cheeseburger empanadas.
3. Place the empanadas on a dish lined with paper towels to drain any excess oil. Rep with the rest of the empanadas.
4. Immediately serve the empanadas with your favorite burger dipping sauce, barbecue sauce, or crema.
5. Empanadas are best when cooked fresh, but if you have any leftovers, wrap them in plastic or store them in an airtight container in the refrigerator for up to 5 days. Then, reheat in a 400°F oven for 6 minutes or until well warmed.

Lotus, Purple Sweet Potato, and Coconut Rice Pudding

Preparation Time: 10 minutes | Cooking Time: 15 minutes | Servings: 1

Ingredients:
- 1 cup white glutinous rice
- 9 ounces purple sweet potatoes, peeled and cut into 3/4-inch cubes
- One small lotus root (about 6 ounces), peeled and cut into 1/8-inch rounds
- 3 cups cocònut water
- 2 ounces palm sugar
- 1 (15-ounce) can dream of lotus seeds, drained
- 1 1/4 cups coconut cream

Directions:
1. Add the sticky rice to a small bowl and cover with water by at least 2 inches. Allow at least 30 minutes for the rice to soak. Drain the rice well in a fine mesh sieve and put it over a sink.
2. Add liquid to a saucepan of rice to soak, with ingredients for lotus seed, lotus root, and sweet potato rice pudding nearby.
3. Make the rice pudding as follows:
4. In a saucepan, combine sliced lotus and diced sweet potato to make a quick coconut rice pudding with lotus and sweet potato.
5. Adding coconut milk to a saucepan of lotus and sweet potato coconut rice pudding
6. Serve the rice pudding warm in dishes with more coconut cream drizzled on top.

Crash Hot Potatoes with Smoked Salmon

Preparation Time: 10 minutes | Cooking Time: 15 minutes | Servings: 1

Ingredients:

- For the potatoes
- 1 1/2 pounds of petite gold potatoes
- Two tablespoons of olive oil
- 1/2 teaspoon salt
- 1/4 teaspoon freshly ground black pepper
- For the toppings
- 6 ounces whipped cream cheese
- 5 ounces hot- or cold-smoked salmon
- 1/4 cup red onion, finely diced
- Two tablespoons of capers, drained

Directions:

1. Put the potatoes in a medium saucepan with enough water to cover them by at least 1 inch. Place the saucepan over high heat on the stove.
2. When the water begins to boil, decrease the heat to medium and cook, uncovered, for 15 to 20 minutes, or until the potatoes can be easily pierced with a fork or paring knife.
3. Remove the potatoes from the heat and place them in a colander over a sink to drain.
4. Making crispy potatoes with smoked salmon, red onions, and capers by boiling potatoes
5. Allow the potatoes to cool on the baking pan for about 15 minutes.
6. Place a heaping spoonful of whipped cream cheese on top of each potato. Add a tiny slice of smoked salmon, a sprinkling of red onion, and a few capers to the cream cheese.
7. On a baking pan, combine simple potatoes and smoked salmon.
8. Transfer the potatoes to a serving plate to serve. Serve immediately.

Homemade Rye Bread

Preparation Time: 10 minutes | Cooking Time: 15 minutes | Servings: 1

Ingredients:

- Two packages of active dry yeast (4 1/2 teaspoons or 16 grams)
- 2 1/2 cups warm water (just barely warm to the touch)
- 2/3 cup molasses (regular, NOT blackstrap)
- Two tablespoons of caraway seeds (optional)
- 1 tablespoon salt
- 1/4 cup vegetable oil
- 1/4 cup cocoa powder (unsweetened)
- 2 cups rye flour
- 5 cups of bread flour

Directions:

1. In a small bowl, dissolve the yeast and molasses in warm water. Pour the yeast mixture into a large metal mixing basin.
2. Add the caraway seeds, salt, vegetable oil, cocoa powder, 2 cups rye flour, and 2 cups bread flour, stirring with a wooden spoon after each addition.
3. Add additional bread flour, a cup at a time, until the dough is no longer sticky and difficult to combine with a wooden spoon. Then, distribute half a cup of flour on a broad, clean, flat surface and place the dough on top.
4. Place the baking stone in the oven if you're using one. Preheat the oven to 350°F for at least 30 minutes before baking.
5. If baking on a stone rather than in a pan, score the loaves on top a few times just before placing them in the oven.
6. Place the loaves in the oven. Mist the dough with water for the first 10 minutes of baking if you have a mister.

Bake for 40-50 minutes, or until golden brown. When tapped, the bread should sound hollow.

Pan con Tomate

Preparation Time: 10 minutes | Cooking Time: 15 minutes | Servings: 1

Ingredients:

- One loaf of ciabatta bread, approximately 1 pound
- 1/4 cup olive oil, plus more for drizzling
- 1 to 2 garlic cloves, peeled
- 2 to 3 large ripe tomatoes (about 2 pounds), cored and halved crosswise
- 1/2 teaspoon kosher salt, or to taste
- Flaky sea salt, for garnish

Directions:

1. Set an oven rack 7 to 8 inches away from the broiler element and preheat the broiler to high.
2. To make slicing the ciabatta bread simpler, cut it in half. Place the loaf's flat sides on a cutting board and cut each into 1/2-inch slices. Cut the slices in half, depending on the size of the bread. You want slices approximately 4 inches long, which are easy to pick up with your hands and bite into.
3. 2 tablespoons tomato mixture, spooned over each slice of bread. Drizzle with additional oil and season with flaky salt before serving.

Quick Pickled Radishes

Preparation Time: 10 minutes | Cooking Time: 15 minutes | Servings: 1

Ingredients:

- 1 cup white vinegar
- 1/2 cup sugar
- 1 teaspoon kosher salt
- Two bay leaves
- Two teaspoons of pickling spice
- Four small sprigs of fresh dill, divided
- Four bunches (about 2 pounds with leaves) of radishes
- Special Equipment
- 2-pint jars

Directions:

1. In a 1-cup liquid measuring cup, place 3 to 4 ice cubes. Fill the measuring cup halfway with cold water.
2. Vinegar Measuring Cup for Quick Pickled Radishes
3. Combine the vinegar, sugar, salt, bay leaves, pickling spice, and two dill sprigs in a small saucepan. Bring to a boil, stirring for 1 minute, or until the sugar dissolves.
4. Brine for Pickling Poured into Radishes Jar
5. Refrigerate for at least 12 hours before eating, after sealing the jar with a cover.

Easy Whipped Ricotta Toast

Preparation Time: 10 minutes | Cooking Time: 15 minutes | Servings: 1

Ingredients:

- 10 (1/2-inch) slices of crusty sourdough bread
- Two tablespoons of extra virgin olive oil, plus more for bread
- 1 1/2 teaspoons kosher salt
- Freshly ground black pepper
- 15 ounces whole milk ricotta
- Finely grated zest of 1 lemon
- One tablespoon of fresh lemon juice
- 1/3 cup honey
- One teaspoon of fresh thyme leaves
- Flaky sea salt for serving (optional)

Directions:

1. Preheat the oven to 425 degrees Fahrenheit.
2. Arrange the bread on a large baking sheet. Lightly brush both sides with olive oil. Season the tops with one teaspoon of salt and a few black pepper grinds. Bake for 10 minutes, or until the tops are golden and toasted. It is not necessary to flip them halfway through.
3. Bread for Whipped Ricotta Toast on a Baking Sheet
4. Meanwhile, combine the ricotta, lemon zest, olive oil, the remaining 1/2 teaspoon salt, and a few grinds of black pepper in a food processor. 1 minute, or until the ricotta is extremely creamy and frothy. With a rubber spatula, scrape the sides and bottom of the bowl and process for 30 seconds more.

Pepperoni Rolls

Preparation Time: 10 minutes | Cooking Time: 15 minutes | Servings: 1

Ingredients:

- 1/4 cup warm water
- 1 (.25-ounce) package (2 1/4 teaspoons) active dry yeast
- 3 1/2 cups (451g) all-purpose flour, divided, plus more if needed
- 1 teaspoon salt
- Eight tablespoons (113g) of unsalted butter, divided
- Two tablespoons honey
- 3/4 cup buttermilk
- 1 large egg
- 8 to 9 ounces (about 144 slices) thinly sliced pepperoni

Directions:

1. Put 1/4 cup warm water in a small basin, sprinkling yeast on top. Allow it to settle for 5 minutes, or until dissolved and creamy.
2. Meanwhile, combine 3 cups (387g) of flour and salt in a large mixing basin.
3. Activated Yeast Bowl for Pepperoni Rolls
4. Melt the butter, then combine it with the milk, honey, and egg:
5. Divide the dough into 12 equal pieces and set aside for 10 minutes on a gently floured board.
6. Melt the remaining four tablespoons of butter in a small saucepan. Make 12 nearly equal stacks of pepperoni.

Smoked Chicken Wings

Preparation Time: 10 minutes | Cooking Time: 15 minutes | Servings: 1

Ingredients:

- Cherry wood chips for gas grill or chunks for smoker or charcoal grill
- 1 tablespoon kosher salt
- One tablespoon of garlic powder
- One tablespoon of light brown sugar, tightly packed
- 1 tablespoon paprika
- Two teaspoons of freshly ground black pepper
- Two teaspoons of onion powder
- One teaspoon of ancho chili powder
- 5 pounds of chicken wings
- Extra virgin olive oil for brushing the wings

Directions:

1. You don't need a heavy smoker! To provide indirect, low heat, 225oF to 275oF, use a grill, either gas or charcoal.
2. Switch one burner to high heat to get low indirect heat on a gas grill. The wings will be grilled over the unlit burners. Place a smoker box or a perforated aluminum foil bag filled with wood chips on top of the lighted burner to make smoke.

3. Shift unlit coals to one side to get low indirect heat on a charcoal barbecue. Light some coal and stack it on top of unlit coals. Reduce airflow by closing the vents. For smoke, add wood pieces straight to the ignited coals.
4. Add 3 to 4 wood pieces to the smoker for a dedicated smoker. Place the pieces directly on the embers using a water pan or kamado grill. Use cherry wood pellets in a pellet smoker.

Homemade French Fries

Preparation Time: 10 minutes | Cooking Time: 15 minutes | Servings: 1

Ingredients:

- 2 1/2 pounds Russet potatoes (4 medium potatoes)
- Two tablespoons of distilled vinegar
- 1 to 2 quarts of peanut oil
- Kosher salt

Directions:

1. Fill a big basin halfway with cold water and place it aside. Peel the potatoes with a vegetable peeler if preferred. Cut the fries into 1/4-inch to 3/8-inch thick slices with a mandolin or a knife, depending on your choice. I like 1/4-inch because it keeps the crispiest.
2. Cut the potato by hand, and take the edge off one side to produce a flat surface.
3. Replace the fries in the basin and cover with cold water until completely immersed. Incorporate the white vinegar. Allow the fries to soak for at least 2 hours at room temperature, preferably overnight (if soaking lasts 2 hours, store in the fridge).

Soy Sauce Eggs

Preparation Time: 10 minutes | Cooking Time: 15 minutes | Servings: 1

Ingredients:

- 1 cup water
- 1/2 cup soy sauce
- 1 tablespoon sugar
- Six tablespoons mirin
- Two cloves of garlic smashed
- 1/4-inch piece unpeeled ginger smashed
- Six large eggs, cold straight from the fridge
- Ice, for chilling the eggs

Directions:

1. Bring the water, soy sauce, sugar, mirin, garlic, and ginger to a boil in a small saucepan over medium-high heat. Reduce the heat to medium-low and keep the saucepan simmering for 3 to 5 minutes until the sugar dissolves and the marinade somewhat decreases.
2. Place the marinade in a heatproof jar with a tight-fitting cover that can accommodate six eggs in a single layer. Place aside to cool.
3. If you don't have a steamer basket, do the following: Over medium-high heat, bring a medium pot of water to a boil. There should be enough water to immerse the eggs completely. When it begins to boil, carefully add the eggs and simmer for 7 minutes.

Indian Okra in the Air Fryer

Preparation Time: 10 minutes | Cooking Time: 15 minutes | Servings: 1

Ingredients:

- 2 cups frozen cut okra, thawed
- 2 tablespoons oil
- 2 tablespoons gram flour (besan)
- 1 teaspoon salt, or to taste

- 1 teaspoon red chili powder
- 1 teaspoon ground coriander
- 1 teaspoon chaat masala
- ½ teaspoon ground cumin
- ½ teaspoon amchoor (dried mango powder) (Optional)

Directions:
1. In a dish, place the thawed okra. Preheat an air fryer for 5 minutes at 400 degrees F (200 degrees C).
2. In the meantime, heat the oil in a pan over medium heat. Combine the gram flour, salt, chili powder, coriander, chaat masala, cumin, and anchor in a mixing bowl. Stir to blend and continue stirring for 2 minutes, or until aromatic. Remove from the fire and toss with the okra to coat. Place the okra in the air fryer basket.
3. Cook for 5 minutes in a hot air fryer. Flip the okra and air-fry for 5 to 10 minutes, flipping every 5 minutes, until cooked through and crispy.

Perfect Turkey Breast Roast in the Air Fryer

Preparation Time: 10 minutes | Cooking Time: 15 minutes | Servings: 1

Ingredients:
- 1 (3 pounds) frozen turkey breast roast
- 2 cups water
- ⅓ cup kosher salt
- ⅓ cup brown sugar
- ground black pepper to taste
- 2 tablespoons butter, or as needed
- 1 seasoned pinch of salt, or to taste (such as Texas Roadhouse®)

Directions:
1. Refrigerate frozen turkey breast for 24 hours to thaw.
2. Bring the water to a boil, then add the kosher salt, brown sugar, and pepper. Remove brine from heat and let aside for 30 minutes to cool fully. Remove the turkey breast from the wrapping, leaving the netting in place if feasible. Cover turkey with cooled brine; add more water if required to completely cover, stirring to ensure brine is blended with water. Allow the turkey to brine in the refrigerator for 8 hours or overnight.
3. Preheat an air fryer to 390°F (200°C) according to the manufacturer's instructions.
4. Remove the turkey from the brine and set it aside. Pat the turkey dry. Rub with butter and season with salt and pepper.
5. Cook turkey for 15 minutes in a hot air fryer; flip, remove the netting, and season again. Reduce the temperature to 360°F (182 degrees C). Cook for another 20 minutes, rotating after 15 minutes. Increase the temperature to 390°F (200°C), flip, and cook until the middle is no longer pink, about 15 minutes more. Remove the turkey and set it aside for 5 minutes before carving and serving.

Air Fryer Tajin® Apple Chips

Preparation Time: 10 minutes | Cooking Time: 15 minutes | Servings: 1

Ingredients:
- ½ tablespoon chile-lime seasoning (such as Tajin®), or more to taste

Directions:
1. Preheat the air fryer to 180°F (82 degrees C).
2. Using a mandolin, thinly slice the apple.
3. Place as many apple slices as possible in the air fryer basket, ensuring they don't touch.
4. Cook for 12 minutes in the air fryer, working in batches as required. Remove the basket and heat until the apple slices are gently browned on the other side, 8 to 12

minutes longer. Sprinkle with chile-lime seasoning right away.

Air Fryer Salmon with Spicy Peach Glaze

Preparation Time: 10 minutes | Cooking Time: 15 minutes | Servings: 1

Ingredients:
- ¼ cup all fruit, no sugar added peach preserves
- 1 clove of garlic, minced
- ¼ teaspoon ground ginger
- ½ teaspoon Asian chili garlic sauce, or to taste
- 2 teaspoons lemon juice
- aluminum foil
- cooking spray
- 2 (6 ounces) fillets of salmon (1-inch thick)
- salt and freshly ground black pepper
- ½ teaspoon sesame seeds
- 1 medium green onion, thinly sliced
- lemon juice (optional)

Directions:
1. In a microwave-safe bowl, combine peach preserves, minced garlic, powdered ginger, chili garlic sauce, and lemon juice. Microwave for 30 to 35 seconds on high or until boiling. Remove from the microwave and whisk one more; leave aside.
2. Make an air fryer foil sling by cutting a sheet of foil large enough to cover the bottom of the air fryer basket and extend it up to two sides, approximately 2" inches. Place the foil in the basket and spray it with cooking spray. To facilitate ventilation, poke a few holes in the foil that line up with the holes in the basket.
3. Season the salmon fillets with salt and pepper on both sides and set them on the foil sling. Spray lightly with cooking spray.
4. Air fried for 8 minutes at 390 degrees F (198 degrees C). Use an instant-read thermometer to check for doneness. Farmed salmon is "medium" at 125 degrees Fahrenheit (51 degrees Celsius), whereas wild salmon is "medium" at 120 degrees Fahrenheit (51 degrees Celsius) (48 degrees C). If necessary, increase air frying time in 3-minute increments until salmon is done to preference.
5. Using the edges of the foil sling, remove the salmon filets from the air fryer.
6. Pour prepared glaze over fillets and serve with the remaining glaze as a sauce. Drizzle lemon juice over the fillets and sprinkle with sesame seeds and green onions.

Air Fryer Salmon with Maple-Bourbon Glaze

Preparation Time: 10 minutes | Cooking Time: 15 minutes | Servings: 1

Ingredients:
- 4 (4 ounce) fillets frozen salmon fillets
- salt and freshly ground black pepper
- Glaze:
- 2 tablespoons unsalted butter
- ⅓ cup bourbon
- 3 tablespoons pure maple syrup
- 1 teaspoon Sriracha sauce
- 1 pinch salt

Directions:
1. Preheat an air fryer for 5 minutes at 400 degrees F (200 degrees C).
2. Season the salmon fillets with salt and pepper before placing them in the air fryer basket.
3. Cook for 6 minutes in the air fryer, or 8 minutes if the fillets are thick.

4. In the meantime, melt the butter in a saucepan over medium heat. Combine the bourbon, maple syrup, Sriracha, and salt in a mixing bowl. Continue to whisk until the glaze comes to a boil. As soon as it begins to boil, reduce the heat to medium-low and continue to simmer until the glaze has thickened, about 10 minutes.
5. Using a silicon brush, apply glaze to salmon fillets. Reduce the air fryer temperature to 370°F (187°C) and continue to air fry for 6 or 8 minutes if the fillets are thick.

Mini Air Fryer Cherry Hand Pies

Preparation Time: 10 minutes | Cooking Time: 15 minutes | Servings: 1

Ingredients:
- 1 (14.1 ounces) package of refrigerated pie dough
- ½ (21 ounces) can of cherry pie filling
- butter-flavored cooking spray
- 1 teaspoon coarse sugar crystals for sprinkling

Directions:
1. Roll out each pie dough circle to 1/8-inch thickness. Cut 16 circles out of the dough with a 3-inch round cookie cutter (8 from each dough round).
2. Wet the perimeter of a circle, then place 1 tablespoon of cherry pie filling in the center. Fold the round and squeeze the dough's sides together to seal it. Crimp the edges with a fork to seal them even further. Cut a slit in the top of the crust with a sharp knife. Repeat with the rest of the dough circles.
3. Preheat an air fryer to 350°F (175°C) and coat the air fryer bucket with cooking spray. Arrange the pies in a single layer in the basket (you may need to work in batches). Coat the pies' tops with additional cooking spray and sprinkle with coarse sugar.
4. Cook until golden brown in the air fryer, about 9 minutes.

Air Fryer Garlic-Parmesan Potato Wedges

Preparation Time: 10 minutes | Cooking Time: 15 minutes | Servings: 1

Ingredients:
- 1 large russet potato, scrubbed
- 1 tablespoon vegetable oil
- 1 tablespoon finely grated Parmesan cheese
- ¼ teaspoon garlic powder
- ¼ teaspoon Italian seasoning

Directions:
1. Preheat an air fryer to 425°F (220°C) according to the manufacturer's instructions. Nonstick foil should be used to line the basket.
2. With a paring knife, pierce the potato many times. Microwave on high for 7 to 10 minutes, or until very soft, rotating halfway through to ensure equal cooking. Remove from the oven and set aside until cool enough to handle.
3. Cut the potato in half lengthwise with a sharp knife. Cut each half into four wedges, then cut each wedge in half. Drizzle with oil and coat with a brush.
4. Place the potatoes in the air fryer close together, with the skin on the foil and the cut-sides exposed to the air. Sprinkle with Parmesan cheese, garlic powder, and Italian seasoning before separating the pieces. (Beginning them together allows you to get more cheese and spice on the potatoes.)
5. Cook for about 20 minutes, monitoring every 5 minutes, until golden brown. Reduce the temperature of the air fryer to 350 degrees F. (175 degrees C). Continue to air-fry for another 5 minutes until nicely browned and crispy.

Salmon with Skin en Papillote in the Air Fryer

Preparation Time: 10 minutes | Cooking Time: 15 minutes | Servings: 1

Ingredients:
- 2 pieces of parchment paper (13x15 inches)
- 1 medium zucchini, cut into 1/3-inch rounds
- 1 medium yellow squash, cut on the diagonal 1/3-inch wide
- 1 teaspoon sazonador total (from Goya)
- 2 (4 ounces) fillets of skin-on salmon
- 2 tablespoons butter

Directions:
1. Preheat an air fryer for 10 minutes at 400 degrees F (200 degrees C).
2. Place two pieces of parchment paper side by side and fold each in half. Sprinkle with sazonador spice and place equal portions of zucchini and squash along the seam. Place the salmon fillets on the veggies and sprinkle with the remaining spice. 1 tbsp butter on each fillet
3. Fold each parchment square by folding the rectangles in half over the fish first. Then, beginning at one corner, create a series of straight folds on the squares' outside rims to seal the edge together.
4. Air-fried, the salmon for 10 minutes or until it flakes easily with a fork. When thoroughly cooked, the packets should be puffed up and slightly browned.

Seasoned Crunchy Cod Fillets in the Air Fryer

Preparation Time: 10 minutes | Cooking Time: 15 minutes | Servings: 1

Ingredients:
- avocado oil cooking spray
- ⅓ cup unseasoned panko bread crumbs
- ⅓ cup stone-ground yellow cornmeal
- 2 teaspoons seasoning mix (such as Trader Joe's® 21 Seasoning Salute Blend)
- 1 teaspoon paprika
- ½ teaspoon salt, or to taste
- ½ cup buttermilk
- 3 (5 ounces) cod fillets
- 1 tablespoon all-purpose flour

Directions:
1. Make a 3-inch foil sling in the bottom of a basket-style air fryer, going across the bottom and up the sides. To match the holes in the basket, poke a few holes in the bottom of the foil sling. Avocado oil should be sprayed on the sling. Omit this step if using a shelf-style air fryer.
2. Preheat the air fryer to 400°F (200 degrees C).
3. In a small mixing bowl, combine panko crumbs, yellow cornmeal, spice blend, paprika, and salt. Pour the buttermilk into a separate basin.
4. Dry the cod fillets with paper towels and gently flour on both sides. Each flour-coated fillet should be dipped into the buttermilk, then into the crumb mixture. Place each fillet on the foil sling, if using, or on the rack of a shelf-style air fryer, and pat the crumb mixture over both sides. Avocado oil should be sprayed on each fish fillet.
5. Cook in the air fryer for 10 to 12 minutes, or until the salmon flakes easily. Remove the cod fillets from the air fryer using the sling and serve immediately.

Air Fryer Bay Scallops, Asparagus, and Mushrooms

Preparation Time: 10 minutes | Cooking Time: 15 minutes | Servings: 1

Ingredients:
- ½ pound bay scallops rinsed and patted dry
- 8 spears of asparagus
- 4 medium mushrooms, sliced
- 1 tablespoon olive oil
- 1 teaspoon lemon-pepper seasoning
- 1 teaspoon parsley flakes
- ½ teaspoon ground paprika
- 2 wedges lemon

Directions:
1. Preheat an air fryer to 400°F (200 degrees C).
2. In a large mixing bowl, combine the scallops, asparagus, mushrooms, olive oil, lemon-pepper seasoning, parsley, and paprika. Stir until everything is well blended. Place in the air fryer basket.
3. Cook for 8 minutes in a hot air fryer, shaking halfway through.
4. With lemon slices, serve.

Air Fryer Buffalo-Ranch Potato Wedges

Preparation Time: 10 minutes | Cooking Time: 15 minutes | Servings: 1

Ingredients:
- 2 medium Russet potatoes, cut into wedges
- ¼ cup cayenne pepper sauce (such as Frank's® RedHot®)
- 2 tablespoons olive oil
- 2 tablespoons ranch dressing mix
- 1 teaspoon salt

Directions:
1. Preheat an air fryer to 400°F (200 degrees C).
2. In a large mixing basin, combine potatoes, pepper sauce, olive oil, ranch dressing mix, and salt; whisk until potatoes are equally covered.
3. Cook for 8 minutes with 8 wedges in the air fryer basket. Return the wedges to the sauce-filled dish with tongs and give them another swirl. Return to the basket and cook for another 10 minutes, shaking halfway through. Continue with the remaining 8 potato wedges.

Air Fryer Salt and Vinegar Fries for One

Preparation Time: 10 minutes | Cooking Time: 15 minutes | Servings: 1

Ingredients:
- 1 large Yukon Gold potato
- 1 cup distilled white vinegar
- ½ tablespoon light vegetable oil
- salt and ground black pepper to taste

Directions:
1. Peel the potato and cut it into 1/2-inch sticks lengthwise. For a few seconds, rinse potato sticks under cold running water. Transfer to a large mixing bowl. Pour in just enough water to cover the potatoes with vinegar. Allow soaking for 30 minutes.
2. Preheat the air fryer to 320°F (160 degrees C).
3. Drain and pat dry the potatoes. Toss in a bowl with the oil, salt, and pepper and place in the air fryer basket.
4. Cook for 16 minutes in a hot air fryer until soft but not browned. Shake the basket and heat it to 355 degrees Fahrenheit (180 degrees C). 6 minutes in the air, shake, and check for doneness. Cook for another 6 minutes, or until the outsides of the fries are crispy and golden. Before serving, taste and adjust the salt.

Air Fryer Ramen Bun Burger for One

Preparation Time: 10 minutes | Cooking Time: 15 minutes | Servings: 1

Ingredients:
- 2 cups water
- 1 (3 ounces) package beef-flavored ramen noodles, seasoning packet reserved
- 1 small egg
- cooking spray
- 4 ounces ground beef

Directions:
1. Bring water to a boil in a large saucepan over high heat. Pour in the noodles and cook for 3 minutes. Allow it cool for 2 minutes after removing it from the heat. Drain.
2. Preheat an air fryer to 400°F (200 degrees C).
3. Meanwhile, mix the egg and 1/2 of the leftover spice packet in a separate dish. Gently fold in the noodles until uniformly covered. Divide the noodles into two small circular containers to produce more consistent buns.
4. Spray the air fryer basket with nonstick cooking spray. Place one piece of the noodles in the basket. To make the bun, flatten the noodle mixture with a spatula. For 4 minutes in the oven. Cook until the bun is golden brown on the other side, about 4 minutes more. Repeat with the remaining noodles on a dish.
5. Form the meat into a patty with the remaining spices. For 4 minutes in the air fryer. Cook for another 4 minutes on the other side. Place the burger between two ramen rolls.

Air Fryer Italian Sausages, Peppers, and Onions

Preparation Time: 10 minutes | Cooking Time: 15 minutes | Servings: 1

Ingredients:
- 2 small onions
- 1 small red bell pepper, thinly sliced
- 1 small yellow bell pepper, thinly sliced
- 1 small orange bell pepper, thinly sliced
- 2 tablespoons olive oil
- 1 teaspoon Italian seasoning
- ¾ teaspoon salt
- ½ teaspoon ground black pepper
- 1 pound sweet Italian sausage links
- 4 each lightly toasted buns
- 4 slices provolone cheese

Directions:
1. Preheat the air fryer to 350°F (180 degrees C).
2. Cut the onions in half from root to stem, then into thirds. In a medium mixing dish, combine the onions and bell peppers. Toss in the olive oil, Italian seasoning, salt, and pepper. Place the veggies in the air fryer basket, and the sausage links on top, not touching.
3. 15 minutes in the air fryer Air fried the sausages for another 10 minutes.
4. Top each sausage with veggies and provolone cheese in a bun.

Air Fryer Teriyaki Snap Peas and Mushrooms

Preparation Time: 10 minutes | Cooking Time: 15 minutes | Servings: 1

Ingredients:
- 1 (8 ounces) package of fresh sugar snap peas
- ½ (8 ounces) package of mushrooms, sliced

- 3 tablespoons teriyaki sauce
- 2 teaspoons olive oil

Directions:
1. Preheat an air fryer to 400°F (200 degrees C).
2. In a large mixing basin, add snap peas, mushrooms, teriyaki sauce, and olive oil; toss until equally mixed. Fill the air fryer basket halfway with the veggie mixture. Cook for 12 minutes in an air fryer, shaking halfway through.

Air Fryer Sweet Potato Fries

Preparation Time: 10 minutes | Cooking Time: 15 minutes | Servings: 1

Ingredients:
- 1 medium sweet potato, peeled
- 1 tablespoon canola oil
- ½ teaspoon kosher salt
- ¼ teaspoon pepper
- ⅛ teaspoon garlic powder
- ⅛ teaspoon ground sweet paprika

Directions:
1. Preheat the air fryer to 400°F (200 degrees C).
2. Cut the sweet potato into half-width fries. Toss in a bowl with canola oil to coat. Season with salt, pepper, garlic powder, and paprika, and toss until evenly coated.
3. Place a uniform layer of fries in the air fryer basket, working in batches if required.
4. Cook for 10 minutes in a hot air fryer until browned. Cook the remaining fries in the same manner.

Air Fryer Beignets

Preparation Time: 10 minutes | Cooking Time: 15 minutes | Servings: 1

Ingredients:
- cooking spray
- ½ cup all-purpose flour
- ¼ cup white sugar
- ⅛ cup water
- One large egg, separated
- 1 ½ teaspoon melted butter
- ½ teaspoon baking powder
- ½ teaspoon vanilla extract
- One pinch salt
- Two tablespoons of confectioners' sugar, or to taste

Directions:
1. Preheat the air fryer to 370°F (185 degrees C). Nonstick cooking sprays a silicone egg-bite mold.
2. In a large mixing basin, combine the flour, sugar, water, egg yolk, butter, baking powder, vanilla extract, and salt. To blend, stir everything together.
3. In a small bowl, beat the egg white with an electric hand mixer on medium speed until soft peaks form. Fold into the batter. Transfer the batter to the prepared mold using a tiny hinged ice cream scoop.
4. Fill the silicone mold and place it in the air fryer basket.
5. Fry for 10 minutes in a hot air fryer. Carefully remove the mold from the basket; pop the beignets and flip them onto a parchment paper circle.
6. Return the parchment circle containing the beignets to the air fryer basket. Cook for another 4 minutes. Take the beignets out of the air fryer basket and sprinkle them with confectioners' sugar.

Air Fryer Burgers

Preparation Time: 10 minutes | Cooking Time: 15 minutes | Servings: 1

Ingredients:
- 1 (16 ounces) package of ground beef
- ½ red onion, diced
- One teaspoon of minced garlic
- One teaspoon salt
- One teaspoon of ground black pepper
- One teaspoon of Worcestershire sauce
- One teaspoon of hot English mustard

Directions:
1. Preheat an air fryer to 350°F (175 degrees C).
2. In a mixing bowl, combine the meat, red onion, garlic, salt, pepper, Worcestershire sauce, and English mustard.
3. Patties may be made by flattening a ball of ground beef with your hand and rounding the sides to the appropriate size.
4. Cook the burgers in the preheated air fryer for about 10 minutes, or until firm and no longer pink in the middle. In the middle, an instant-read thermometer should read at least 160 degrees F. (70 degrees C).

Air Fryer Sausage

Preparation Time: 10 minutes | Cooking Time: 15 minutes | Servings: 1

Ingredients:
- 1 (12 ounces) package of pork link sausages (such as Farmer John®)

Directions:
1. Preheat the oven to 400° F. (200 degrees C).
2. Arrange the sausage links in a single layer in the air fryer basket. Depending on the size of your air fryer, you may need to work in batches.
3. Cook until the sausages begin to brown, 4 to 6 minutes. Air-fry the sausages for 3 to 5 minutes more, or until they are no longer pink in the middle. In the center, an instant-read thermometer should read 160 degrees F. (70 degrees C).

Air Fryer Mushrooms

Preparation Time: 10 minutes | Cooking Time: 15 minutes | Servings: 1

Ingredients:
- 1 (8 ounces) package of cremini mushrooms, halved or quartered
- Two tablespoons of avocado oil
- One teaspoon of low-sodium soy sauce (such as Bragg®)
- ½ teaspoon garlic granules
- salt and ground black pepper to taste

Directions:
1. Preheat the air fryer to 375°F (190 degrees C).
2. In a mixing basin, combine the mushrooms, avocado oil, soy sauce, garlic granules, salt, and pepper; toss to coat—place in the air fryer bowl.
3. Cook the mushrooms for 10 minutes in the air fryer, shaking periodically.

Tasty Balls

Preparation Time: 10 minutes | Cooking Time: 15 minutes | Servings: 1

Ingredients:
- Two cloves of garlic, minced
- 16 ounces lean ground beef
- 4 ounces ground pork
- ½ cup grated Parmesan cheese
- ⅓ cup Italian seasoned bread crumbs
- One egg
- One teaspoon of Italian seasoning

- ½ teaspoon salt

Directions:
1. Preheat an air fryer to 350°F (175 degrees C).
2. In a large mixing bowl, combine the meat, pork, Parmesan cheese, bread crumbs, egg, garlic, Italian seasoning, and salt. Mix until everything is well blended. Place 16 equal meatballs on a baking sheet (a tiny ice cream scoop is useful).
3. Cook for 8 minutes with half of the meatballs in the air fryer basket. Cook for another 2 minutes after shaking the basket. Transfer to a serving platter and let aside for 5 minutes to rest. Rep with the remaining meatballs.

Lumpia in the Air Fryer

Preparation Time: 10 minutes | Cooking Time: 15 minutes | Servings: 1

Ingredients:
- 1 pound Italian hot sausage links
- ½ cup finely sliced green onions
- ¼ cup diced onions
- ½ cup finely chopped carrots
- ½ cup finely chopped water chestnuts
- Two cloves of garlic, minced
- Two tablespoons of soy sauce
- ½ teaspoon salt
- ¼ teaspoon ground ginger
- 16 spring roll wrappers
- avocado oil cooking spray

Directions:
1. Remove the casing from the sausage and cook it in a pan over medium heat for 4 to 5 minutes, or until slightly browned. Combine the green onions, carrots, and water chestnuts in a mixing bowl. Cook and stir for 5 to 7 minutes until the onions are tender and transparent. Cook for 1 to 2 minutes after adding the garlic. Soy sauce, salt, and ginger to taste. Remove from heat after stirring until the filing is fully mixed.
2. Make an angle using a spring roll wrapper. Fill the wrapper with a scant 1/4 cup of the filling. To construct a roll, fold the bottom corner over the filling and tuck in the edges. Wet your finger and softly wet the edges. Continue with the remaining wrappers and filling. Spray avocado oil on each roll.
3. Preheat an air fryer to 390°F (198 degrees C). Place the lumpia rolls in the basket, not touching; cook in batches as required. Fry for 4 minutes, then turn and cook for another 4 minutes, or until the skins are crispy.

Air Fryer Lumpia

Preparation Time: 10 minutes | Cooking Time: 15 minutes | Servings: 1

Ingredients:
- One tablespoon of sesame oil
- 1 pound ground pork
- ⅓ cup chopped water chestnuts
- Three green onions, chopped
- Four tablespoons of reduced-sodium soy sauce
- Two tablespoons of rice vinegar
- 3 cups shredded cabbage
- Two large carrots, grated
- 18 lumpia wrappers
- olive oil cooking spray

Directions:
1. In a large skillet over medium-high heat, heat the oil. Cook until the pork is browned, approximately 5 minutes, breaking it up into tiny pieces. Cook for 5

minutes further after adding the water chestnuts, green onion, soy sauce, and vinegar.
2. Turn the heat up to high and add the cabbage—Cook for 2 minutes, or until the cabbage is tender and the liquid has gone. Remove from heat and whisk in shredded carrots. Allow the mixture to cool for 3 minutes.
3. Preheat the air fryer to 400°F (200 degrees C).
4. Meanwhile, arrange a lumpia wrapper in a diamond form on a clean surface, with one corner at the bottom. Fill the wrapper with two teaspoons of filling. Fold in the bottom half and then the sides securely. Roll gently and seal with a few droplets of water. Continue with the remaining wrappers and filling.
5. Mist each roll lightly with olive oil. Arrange as many lumpia as possible in the air fryer basket without touching them. Cook for 5 minutes in a hot air fryer. Cook for 3 minutes more on the other side. Transfer to a plate lined with paper towels. Rep with the leftover lumpia.

Air Fryer Churros

Preparation Time: 10 minutes | Cooking Time: 15 minutes | Servings: 1

Ingredients:
- ¼ cup butter
- ½ cup milk
- One pinch salt
- ½ cup all-purpose flour
- Two eggs
- ¼ cup white sugar
- ½ teaspoon ground cinnamon

Directions:
1. In a saucepan over medium-high heat, melt the butter. Pour in the milk and season with salt. Reduce the heat to medium and bring it to a boil, constantly stirring with a wooden spoon. Add the flour all at once. Continue to whisk until the dough comes together.
2. Remove from the fire and set aside 5 to 7 minutes to cool. With a wooden spoon, mix in the eggs until the pastry comes together. Fill a pastry bag with a big star tip with the dough. Pipe dough strips directly into the air fryer basket.
3. Five minutes in an air fryer at 340 degrees F (175 degrees C).
4. Meanwhile, mix the sugar and cinnamon in a separate dish and spread it out on a shallow plate.
5. Take the cooked churros out of the air fryer and roll them in the cinnamon-sugar mixture.

Air Fryer Pakoras

Preparation Time: 10 minutes | Cooking Time: 15 minutes | Servings: 1

Ingredients:
- 2 cups chopped cauliflower
- 1 cup diced yellow potatoes
- One ¼ cups chickpea flour (besan)
- ¾ cup water
- ½ red onion, chopped
- One tablespoon salt
- One clove of garlic, minced
- One teaspoon of curry powder
- One teaspoon coriander
- ½ teaspoon ground cayenne pepper, or more to taste
- ½ teaspoon cumin
- One serving of cooking spray

Directions:

1. Combine cauliflower, potatoes, chickpea flour, water, red onion, salt, garlic, curry powder, coriander, cayenne pepper, and cumin in a large mixing basin. Set aside 10 minutes to relax.
2. Preheat the air fryer to 350°F (175 degrees C).
3. Coat the air fryer basket with cooking spray. 2 tablespoons cauliflower mixture, flattened in the basket Repeat as many times as the space in your basket permits without the pakoras touching. Spray the top of each pakora with nonstick cooking spray.
4. Eight minutes in the oven. Cook for an additional 8 minutes on the other side. Transfer to a plate lined with paper towels. Rep with the remaining batter.

Air Fryer Tostones

Preparation Time: 10 minutes | Cooking Time: 15 minutes | Servings: 1

Ingredients:

- Two green (unripe) plantains
- olive oil cooking spray
- 3 cups water, or as needed
- salt to taste

Directions:

1. Preheat an air fryer to 400°F (200 degrees C).
2. Remove the plantain tips. Make a vertical cut from end to end in the skin, careful not to cut through the thick skin and into the plantain flesh. Plantain, still in its peel, should be cut into 1-inch segments. Starting at the slit, peel the skin off each portion.
3. Spray the plantain pieces with olive oil spray and place them in the air fryer basket. Five minutes in the air fryer. Prepare a dish of salted water in the meantime.
4. Using tongs, remove the plantain pieces from the air fryer. Using a Costanera, pound to roughly 1/2-inch thickness (plantain smasher). While the remainder of the tostones is broken, soak them in a dish of salted water.
5. After removing the tostones from the salted water, blot them dry using a paper towel.
6. Return to the air fryer in batches, filling the basket with a single layer each time. Season the tops with salt and coat with olive oil spray; air fry for 5 minutes. With tongs, flip over and coat the opposite side with olive oil spray. Season with salt and pepper. For 4 to 5 minutes, air fry until golden brown and crunchy.

Air Fryer Bacon

Preparation Time: 10 minutes | Cooking Time: 15 minutes | Servings: 1

Ingredients:

- ½ (16 ounces) package of bacon

Directions:

1. Preheat an air fryer to 390 degrees F (200 degrees C).
2. Lay bacon in the air fryer basket in a single layer; some overlap is okay.
3. Fry for 8 minutes. Flip and continue cooking until bacon is crisp, about 7 minutes more. Transfer cooked bacon to a plate lined with paper towels to soak up excess grease.

Air Fryer Meatloaf

Preparation Time: 10 minutes | Cooking Time: 15 minutes | Servings: 1

Ingredients:

- 1 pound lean ground beef
- One small onion, finely chopped
- One large egg, lightly beaten
- Three tablespoons of dry bread crumbs
- One tablespoon of chopped fresh thyme
- One teaspoon salt
- ground black pepper to taste
- Two mushrooms, thickly sliced
- One tablespoon olive oil, or as needed

Directions:

1. Preheat an air fryer to 392°F (200 degrees C).
2. In a mixing bowl, combine ground beef, onion, bread crumbs, thyme, egg, salt, and pepper. Knead and completely combine. Place the mixture in a small loaf pan. Smooth the top, push the mushrooms, and drizzle with olive oil.
3. Cook the meatloaf in the preheated air fryer for about 25 minutes or until well browned. In the middle, an instant-read thermometer should read at least 165 degrees F. (72 degrees C).
4. Allow the meatloaf to rest for at least 10 minutes before cutting it into wedges and serving.

Air Fryer Falafel

Preparation Time: 10 minutes | Cooking Time: 15 minutes | Servings: 1

Ingredients:

- 1 cup dry garbanzo beans
- 1 ½ cups fresh cilantro, stems removed
- ¾ cup fresh flat-leafed parsley stems removed
- One small red onion, quartered
- One clove garlic
- Two tablespoons of chickpea flour
- One tablespoon of ground coriander
- One tablespoon of ground cumin
- One tablespoon sriracha sauce
- salt and ground black pepper to taste
- ½ teaspoon baking powder
- ¼ teaspoon baking soda
- cooking spray

Directions:

1. Soak chickpeas for 24 hours in a big amount of cold water. Rub your fingers through the wet chickpeas to help loosen and remove the skins. Rinse and drain well. To dry, spread chickpeas on a wide clean dish towel.
2. In a food processor, combine chickpeas, cilantro, parsley, onion, and garlic until rough paste forms. Transfer the mixture to a large mixing basin. Mix in the chickpea flour, coriander, cumin, sriracha, salt, and pepper. Allow the mixture to rest for 1 hour, covered.
3. Preheat an air fryer to 375°F (190 degrees C).
4. To the chickpea mixture, add baking powder and baking soda. Using your hands, mix until just blended. Create 15 equal-sized balls and softly press to form patties. Coat the falafel patties in frying spray.
5. Cook for 10 minutes in a preheated air fryer with seven falafel patties. Cook for 10 to 12 minutes, then transfer cooked falafel to a platter and repeat with the remaining eight falafel.

CHAPTER 3:
Vegetables & Sides

Quick Glazed Beets

Preparation Time: 10 minutes | Cooking Time: 40 minutes | Servings: 8

Ingredients:
- 1 tablespoon bacon fat
- 3 oz. trimmed small beets
- 4 tablespoons honey

Directions:
1. Preheat the air fryer to 360 degrees Fahrenheit.
2. Add in the ingredients, stir and cover to cook for 40 minutes.
3. Serve immediately and enjoy as a side!

Stuffed Portobello Mushrooms

Preparation Time: 10 minutes | Cooking Time: 20 minutes | Servings: 4

Ingredients:
- 1 cup torn spinach
- ⅓ cup bread crumbs
- 1 tablespoon olive oil
- ¼ cup mascarpone cheese
- 5 tablespoons grated parmesan
- ¼ teaspoon chopped thyme
- 4 big portobello mushroom caps

Directions:
1. Marinate mushroom caps with oil and transfer them to the air fryer basket.
2. Cover and cook for 2 minutes at 350 degrees Fahrenheit.
3. Meanwhile, combine the remaining ingredients in a bowl but only half parmesan.
4. Fill the mushroom caps with the mixture and top with the remaining parmesan.
5. Cover and cook again in the air fryer basket for 10 minutes at the previous temperature.
6. Serve immediately and enjoy as a side.

Lunch Special Pancake

Preparation Time: 10 minutes | Cooking Time: 10 minutes | Servings: 2

Ingredients:
- 1 cup salsa
- ½ cup almond flour
- ½ cup almond milk
- 3 beaten eggs
- 1 tablespoon butter
- 1 cup peeled & deveined small shrimp

Directions:
1. Preheat the air fryer to 400 degrees Fahrenheit.
2. Add butter and melt in the air fryer.
3. Whisk eggs, flour, and milk in a bowl and pour into the air fryer as a pancake.
4. Cover and cook for 12 minutes at 350 degrees Fahrenheit.
5. Combine shrimp and salsa in a bowl and serve the pancake on a plate.

Asian Style Lentil Fritters

Preparation Time: 10 minutes | Cooking Time: 10 minutes | Servings: 2

Ingredients:
- ⅓ cup water
- 2 teaspoons olive oil
- 4 minced garlic cloves
- Mint chutney as needed
- ½ cup chopped parsley
- 1 ½ cup chopped spinach
- 1 chopped hot chili pepper
- 1 teaspoon baking soda
- ¾ cup chopped red onion
- 1-inch grated ginger piece
- 1 teaspoon garam masala
- ½ teaspoon turmeric powder
- Salt & black pepper as needed
- 1 cup soaked for an hour and drained yellow lentils

Directions:
1. Blend all the ingredients in a blender and shape medium balls out of the mixture.
2. Preheat the air fryer to 400 degrees Fahrenheit and add the balls inside once preheated.
3. Cover and cook for 10 minutes.
4. Remove and serve with any sauce you like.

Tasty Potato Wedges

Preparation Time: 10 minutes | Cooking Time: 25 minutes | Servings: 4

Ingredients:
- 1 tablespoon sesame oil
- 2 wedgie-cut potatoes
- 3 tablespoons sour cream
- Salt & black pepper as needed
- 2 tablespoons sweet and sour sauce

Directions:
1. Marinate potato wedges with sesame oil and season with salt and pepper.
2. Toss them in the air fryer basket and cover to cook for 25 minutes at 25 minutes.
3. Flip them once after 15 minutes.
4. Serve with sour cream and sweet and sour sauce!

Corn, Lemon & Cheese

Preparation Time: 10 minutes | Cooking Time: 15 minutes | Servings: 2

Ingredients:
- 2 lemon juice
- Olive oil as needed
- ½ cup grated cottage cheese
- 2 teaspoons sweet paprika
- 2 husks removed corns on the cob

Directions:
1. Marinate corn with a drizzle of olive oil and paprika.
2. Add to the air fryer and cover to cook for 14 minutes at 400 degrees Fahrenheit.
3. Flip them once after 7 minutes.
4. Serve with a sprinkling of lemon juice and cheese on top.

Brussel Sprouts Dish

Preparation Time: 10 minutes | Cooking Time: 15 minutes | Servings: 4

Ingredients:
- ½ cup mayonnaise
- 6 teaspoons canola oil
- ½ teaspoon chopped oregano
- Salt & black pepper as needed
- 2 tablespoons crushed roasted garlic
- 1 oz. trimmed & halved brussels sprouts

Directions:
1. Marinate Brussel sprouts with canola oil, salt, and pepper.
2. Toss in the air fryer and cover to cook for 15 minutes at 390 degrees Fahrenheit.
3. Meanwhile, combine mayonnaise with oregano and garlic thoroughly.
4. Serve Brussels sprouts with mayo sauce on top.

String Beans Dish

Preparation Time: 10 minutes | Cooking Time: 25 minutes | Servings: 4

Ingredients:
- 2 tablespoons olive oil
- ½ oz. chopped shallots
- ¼ cup toasted pecans
- Salt & black pepper as needed
- 1 ½ oz. trimmed & steamed for 2 minutes string beans

Directions:
1. Combine all the ingredients thoroughly in a bowl.
2. Add to the air fryer basket and cook for 25 minutes at 400 degrees Fahrenheit.
3. Serve as a side and enjoy!

Pecorino Button Mushrooms

Preparation Time: 10 minutes | Cooking Time: 15 minutes | Servings: 3

Ingredients:
- 1 egg white
- 9 button mushroom caps
- 1 tablespoon melted butter
- 1 teaspoon Italian seasoning
- A pinch of salt & black pepper
- 2 tablespoons grated pecorino
- 3 crumbled cream cracker slices

Directions:
1. Combine all the ingredients except mushrooms in a bowl.
2. Fill the mushrooms with this mixture and transfer them neatly to the air fryer.
3. Cover and cook for 15 minutes at 360 degrees Fahrenheit.
4. Serve as a side and enjoy!

Tasty Garlic Potatoes

Preparation Time: 10 minutes | Cooking Time: 20 minutes | Servings: 6

Ingredients:
- 2 tablespoons butter
- 5 minced garlic cloves
- 2 tablespoons canola oil
- ½ teaspoon dried basil
- 1 teaspoon dried thyme
- ⅓ cup grated parmesan
- 3 oz. halved red potatoes
- ½ teaspoon dried oregano
- Salt & black pepper as needed
- 2 tablespoons chopped cilantro

Directions:
1. Combine all the ingredients thoroughly except parmesan in a bowl.
2. Transfer to the air fryer basket and cover to cook for 20 minutes at 400 degrees Fahrenheit.
3. Flip once after 10 minutes to ensure even baking.
4. Serve the potatoes with parmesan on top.

Vermouth Mushrooms

Preparation Time: 10 minutes | Cooking Time: 25 minutes | Servings: 4

Ingredients:
- 1 tablespoon canola oil
- 2 minced garlic cloves
- 2 oz. white mushrooms
- 2 tablespoons white vermouth
- 2 teaspoons herbs de Provence

Directions:
1. Combine all the vermouth in a bowl and transfer to the air fryer.
2. Cover and cook the mushrooms for 20 minutes at 350 degrees Fahrenheit.
3. Toss with vermouth and cook for an additional 5 minutes.
4. Serve as a side and enjoy!

Quick Eggplant Fries

Preparation Time: 10 minutes | Cooking Time: 5 minutes | Servings: 4

Ingredients:
- 1 beaten egg
- 2 tablespoons whole milk
- Cooking spray as needed
- 2 cups Italian bread crumbs
- ½ cup shredded Italian cheese
- Salt and black pepper as needed
- 1 peeled & cut into medium-sized fries eggplant

Directions:
1. Whisk egg, milk, salt, and pepper in a bowl.
2. Combine Italian bread crumbs with cheese in a separate bowl.
3. Dip the eggplant fries first in the egg mixture, then in the bread crumbs mixture.
4. Grease the air fryer with cooking spray and place the coated eggplant fries.
5. Cover and cook for 5 minutes at 400 degrees Fahrenheit.
6. Serve as a side and enjoy!

Tasty Roasted Carrots

Preparation Time: 10 minutes | Cooking Time: 20 minutes | Servings: 4

Ingredients:
- 1 oz. baby carrots
- 2 teaspoons canola oil
- 4 tablespoons lemon juice
- 1 teaspoon herbs de Provence

Directions:
1. Combine all the ingredients in a bowl and add to the air fryer.
2. Toss, cover, and cook for 20 minutes at 320 degrees Fahrenheit.
3. Serve as a side and enjoy!

Tasty Roasted Parsnips

Preparation Time: 10 minutes | Cooking Time: 40 minutes | Servings: 6

Ingredients:
- 1 tablespoon avocado oil
- 2 tablespoons honey
- 1 tablespoon dried parsley flakes
- 2 oz. peeled & cut into medium-sized chunks parsnips

Directions:
1. Grease the air fryer with oil and preheat it to 360 degrees Fahrenheit.
2. Toss in the remaining ingredients and cover to cook for 40 minutes.
3. Serve as a side and enjoy!

Quick Creamy Endives

Preparation Time: 10 minutes | Cooking Time: 10 minutes | Servings: 6

Ingredients:
- ½ cup Greek yogurt
- 1 teaspoon minced garlic

- ½ teaspoon curry powder
- 3 tablespoons lime juice
- 6 trimmed & halved endives
- Salt & black pepper as needed

Directions:
1. Toss all the ingredients in a bowl and set aside for 10 minutes.
2. Meanwhile, preheat the air fryer to 350 degrees Fahrenheit and add the bowl contents to the air fryer.
3. Cover and cook for 10 minutes.
4. Serve as a side and enjoy!

Roasted Peppers Dish

Preparation Time: 10 minutes | Cooking Time: 20 minutes | Servings: 4

Ingredients:
- 1 tablespoon canola oil
- 1 chopped red onion
- 1 tablespoon sweet paprika
- Salt & black pepper as needed
- 4 medium-cut strips of red bell peppers
- 4 medium-cut strips of green bell peppers
- 4 medium-cut strips of yellow bell peppers

Directions:
1. Add all the peppers to the air fryer and season with the remaining ingredients.
2. Cover and cook for 20 minutes at 350 degrees Fahrenheit.
3. Serve as a side and enjoy!

Creamy Brussels Sprouts

Preparation Time: 10 minutes | Cooking Time: 25 minutes | Servings: 8

Ingredients:
- 1 cup milk
- ½ cup chopped onion
- 2 cups cooking cream
- Olive oil as needed
- 1 oz. chopped bacon
- 4 tablespoons butter
- 3 oz. halved brussels sprouts
- ¼ teaspoon ground nutmeg
- 3 oz. halved brussels sprouts
- Salt & black pepper as needed
- 3 tablespoons prepared horseradish

Directions:
1. Preheat the air fryer to 370 degrees Fahrenheit.
2. Toss in oil, bacon, Brussels sprouts, salt, and pepper.
3. Add the remaining ingredients and toss well.
4. Cover and cook for 25 minutes.
5. Serve as a side and enjoy!

Delicious Herbed Tomatoes

Preparation Time: 10 minutes | Cooking Time: 15 minutes | Servings: 4

Ingredients:
- 1 tablespoon sesame oil
- 2 minced garlic cloves
- ½ chopped teaspoon oregano
- Salt & black pepper as needed
- 4 halved & insides scooped out big tomatoes

Directions:
1. Toss all the ingredients in the air fryer.
2. Cover and cook for 15 minutes at 390 degrees Fahrenheit.
3. Serve as a side and enjoy!

Delicious Barley Risotto

Preparation Time: 10 minutes | Cooking Time: 30 minutes | Servings: 8

Ingredients:
- ¾ oz. barley
- 2 oz. skim milk
- 5 cups vegetable broth
- 3 tablespoons olive oil
- 2 minced garlic cloves
- 1 teaspoon dried oregano
- 3 oz. sliced mushrooms
- 2 chopped yellow onions
- 1 teaspoon dried tarragon
- Salt & black pepper as needed
- 2 oz. peeled & chopped sweet potato

Directions:
1. Bring broth and barley to a boil over medium heat and cook for 15 minutes.
2. Preheat the air fryer to 350 degrees Fahrenheit.
3. Grease the air fryer with oil and add all the remaining ingredients, including barley.
4. Stir and cover to cook for 15 minutes.
5. Serve as a side and enjoy!

Cheesy Artichokes

Preparation Time: 10 minutes | Cooking Time: 6 minutes | Servings: 6

Ingredients:
- 10 oz. kale
- ½ cup sour cream
- 8 oz. cream cheese
- ½ cup mayonnaise
- ½ cup chicken broth
- 3 minced garlic cloves
- Baking pan as needed
- 1 teaspoon onion powder
- 8 oz. shredded mozzarella
- 14 oz. canned artichoke hearts
- 16 oz. grated parmesan cheese

Directions:
1. Add all the ingredients except mozzarella and parmesan to a pan that fits in the air fryer.
2. Stir and cover to cook for 6 minutes at 350 degrees Fahrenheit.
3. Lastly, stir in mozzarella and parmesan before serving!

Beet Salad & Cilantro Dressing

Preparation Time: 10 minutes | Cooking Time: 14 minutes | Servings: 4

Ingredients:
- 4 beets
- 1 chopped garlic clove
- 2 tablespoons capers
- Chopped bunch of cilantro
- Salt & black pepper as needed
- 2 tablespoons red wine vinegar
- 1 tablespoon olive oil

Directions:
1. Cook the beets in the air fryer for 14 minutes at 360 degrees Fahrenheit.
2. Meanwhile, combine the remaining ingredients except for vinegar in a bowl thoroughly.
3. Remove beets to a cutting board and allow to cool.
4. Put them in a salad bowl after peeling and slicing them.
5. Drizzle the beets with vinegar and the bowl mixture and serve.

Yummy Broccoli Salad

Preparation Time: 10 minutes | Cooking Time: 8 minutes |
Servings: 4

Ingredients:
- 6 minced garlic cloves
- 1 tablespoon sesame oil
- Salt & black pepper as needed
- 1 floret separated broccoli head
- 1 tablespoon Chinese rice wine vinegar

Directions:
1. Add half of the peanut oil and season broccoli with salt and pepper in a bowl.
2. Toss well and transfer to the air fryer.
3. Cover and cook for 8 minutes at 350 degrees Fahrenheit, shaking it once after 4 minutes.
4. Remove the broccoli to a salad bowl and toss with the remaining ingredients.
5. Serve and enjoy!

Beets Arugula Salad

Preparation Time: 10 minutes | Cooking Time: 10 minutes |
Servings: 4

Ingredients:
- 2 cups arugula
- Olive oil as needed
- ½ cup orange juice
- 2 chopped green onion
- 2 teaspoons dijon mustard
- 2 tablespoons brown sugar
- 2 teaspoons grated orange zest
- 1 ½ oz. peeled & quartered beets
- 2 tablespoons apple cider vinegar

Directions:
1. Marinate beets with olive oil and orange juice in a bowl.
2. Add them to the air fryer and cover to cook for 10 minutes at 350 degrees Fahrenheit.
3. Remove the beets to a bowl and toss green onion, arugula, and orange zest.
4. Whisk sugar, mustard, and vinegar in a bowl and add to the beets mixture.
5. Give a toss and serve immediately.

Artichokes With Special Sauce

Preparation Time: 10 minutes | Cooking Time: 6 minutes |
Servings: 2

Ingredients:
- 3 garlic cloves
- 3 anchovy fillets
- ¼ cup sesame oil
- Olive oil as needed
- 2 trimmed artichokes
- 2 minced garlic cloves
- 1 tablespoon lime juice
- ¼ cup olive oil

Directions:
1. Combine artichokes with sesame oil, two minced garlic cloves, and lime juice.
2. Toss well and add to the air fryer to cook for 6 minutes at 350 degrees.
3. Meanwhile, thoroughly blend sesame oil, anchovy, three garlic cloves, and olive oil in a food processor.
4. Drizzle it over the artichokes on a plate or bowl and serve!

Brussel Sprouts & Tomatoes Mix

Preparation Time: 5 minutes | Cooking Time: 10 minutes |
Servings: 4

Ingredients:
- 1 tablespoon olive oil

- 6 halved grape tomatoes
- 1 oz. trimmed Brussels sprouts
- Salt & black pepper as needed
- ¼ cup chopped scallions

Directions:
1. Sprinkle Brussels sprouts with salt and pepper and transfer to the air fryer.
2. Cook for 10 minutes at 350 degrees Fahrenheit.
3. Remove to a bowl and toss with the remaining ingredients.
4. Serve immediately and enjoy!

Spicy Cabbage

Preparation Time: 10 minutes | Cooking Time: 8 minutes |
Servings: 4

Ingredients:
- 1 grated carrot
- ¼ cups apple juice
- ¼ cup apple cider vinegar
- 1 cut into 8 wedges cabbage
- 1 tablespoon sesame seed oil
- ½ teaspoon cayenne pepper
- 1 teaspoon crushed red pepper flakes

Directions:
1. Combine all the ingredients in a pan that fits in the air fryer.
2. Preheat the air fryer to 350 degrees Fahrenheit and add the pan inside.
3. Cook for 8 minutes at the selected temperature.
4. Serve the cabbage mix and enjoy!

Quick Air Fried Leeks

Preparation Time: 10 minutes | Cooking Time: 7 minutes |
Servings: 4

Ingredients:
- 1 tablespoon lime juice
- 1 tablespoon melted butter
- Salt & black pepper as needed
- 4 washed, ends-cut & halved leeks

Directions:
1. Combine leeks with butter, salt, and pepper.
2. Add to the air fryer and cook for 7 minutes at 350 degrees Fahrenheit.
3. Serve on a platter with a drizzle of lime juice.

Collard Greens & Turkey Wings

Preparation Time: 10 minutes | Cooking Time: 20 minutes |
Servings: 6

Ingredients:
- 1 chopped sweet onion
- 2 smoked turkey wings
- 2 tablespoons olive oil
- 3 minced garlic cloves
- 1 tablespoon brown sugar
- Salt & black pepper as needed
- 2 ½ oz. chopped collard greens
- ½ teaspoon chili flakes
- 2 tablespoons white wine vinegar

Directions:
1. Use a pan that fits the air fryer and heat oil over medium heat.
2. Stir in onions for 2 minutes and add the remaining ingredients.
3. Preheat the air fryer to 350 degrees Fahrenheit and transfer the pan with the contents.
4. Cook for 15 minutes in the air fryer and serve once done!

Okra Corn Salad

Preparation Time: 10 minutes | Cooking Time: 12 minutes | Servings: 6

Ingredients:
- 1 cup sweet corn kernels
- 1 teaspoon sugar
- 1 oz. trimmed okra
- 6 chopped green onion
- 2 tablespoons olive oil
- 3 chopped green bell peppers
- Salt & black pepper as needed
- 28 oz. chopped canned tomatoes

Directions:
1. Use a pan that fits the air fryer and heat oil over medium heat.
2. Stir in green onion and bell peppers and cook for 5 minutes.
3. Add the remaining ingredients and stir.
4. Transfer the pan with the contents to the air fryer.
5. Cook for 7 minutes at 360 degrees Fahrenheit in the air fryer and serve once done!

Collard Greens & Bacon

Preparation Time: 10 minutes | Cooking Time: 12 minutes | Servings: 4

Ingredients:
- 1 oz. collard greens
- 3 chopped bacon strips
- 2 tablespoons chicken broth
- Salt & black pepper as needed
- ¼ cup halved grape tomatoes
- 1 tablespoon apple cider vinegar

Directions:
1. Use a pan that fits the air fryer and cook bacon in it over medium heat for a minute or two.
2. Add the remaining ingredients and stir.
3. Transfer the pan with the contents to the air fryer.
4. Cook for 10 minutes at 320 degrees Fahrenheit in the air fryer and serve once done!

Fantastic Radish Hash

Preparation Time: 10 minutes | Cooking Time: 7 minutes | Servings: 4

Ingredients:
- 4 eggs
- 1 oz. sliced radishes
- ⅓ cup grated parmesan
- ½ teaspoon minced onion
- ½ teaspoon minced garlic
- Salt & black pepper as needed

Directions:
1. Combine all the ingredients in a bowl thoroughly.
2. Transfer the contents to a pan that fits the air fryer.
3. Cook for 7 minutes at 350 degrees Fahrenheit.
4. Serve once done, and enjoy!

Swiss Chard Salad

Preparation Time: 10 minutes | Cooking Time: 13 minutes | Servings: 4

Ingredients:
- ¼ cup raisins
- 2 tablespoons olive oil
- ¼ cup toasted pine nuts
- 1 bunch of torn Swiss chard
- A pinch of chili flakes
- 1 chopped small yellow onion
- 1 tablespoon red wine vinegar
- Salt & black pepper as needed

Directions:
1. Use a pan that fits the air fryer and heat oil over medium heat.
2. Add, stir and cook chard and onions for 5 minutes.
3. Add the remaining ingredients and stir.
4. Transfer the pan with the contents to the air fryer.
5. Cook for 8 minutes at 350 degrees Fahrenheit in the air fryer and serve once done!

Flavored Air Fried Tomatoes

Preparation Time: 10 minutes | Cooking Time: 15 | Servings: 8

Ingredients:
- ¼ cup olive oil
- ¼ cup chopped basil
- 4 minced garlic cloves
- ½ cup grated parmesan
- ½ teaspoon dried thyme
- 1 chopped jalapeno pepper
- 2 oz. halved grape tomatoes
- Salt & black pepper as needed

Directions:
1. Combine all the ingredients except thyme and parmesan in a bowl thoroughly.
2. Transfer the contents to the air fryer.
3. Cook for 15 minutes at 390 degrees Fahrenheit.
4. Remove to a bowl and toss with basil and parmesan before serving.

Garlic Tomatoes

Preparation Time: 10 minutes | Cooking Time: 15 minutes | Servings: 4

Ingredients:
- ¼ cup avocado oil
- 4 crushed garlic cloves
- 3 chopped rosemary springs
- 1 oz. cherry tomatoes
- Salt & black pepper as needed

Directions:
1. Toss all the ingredients in a bowl well.
2. Add to the air fryer and cook for 15 minutes at 360 degrees Fahrenheit.
3. Serve once done, and enjoy!

Stuffed Poblano Peppers

Preparation Time: 10 minutes | Cooking Time: 15 minutes | Servings: 4

Ingredients:
- 1 tablespoon canola oil
- 1 chopped white onion
- ½ cup chopped parsley
- 2 teaspoons minced garlic
- 8 oz. chopped mushrooms
- Salt & black pepper as needed
- 10 tops cut off & deseeded poblano peppers

Directions:
1. Heat oil in a pan over medium heat and stir and cook onions and mushrooms for 5 minutes.
2. Add the remaining ingredients except for poblano and stir for 2 minutes.
3. Divide this mixture between poblano peppers and transfer to the air fryer.
4. Cook for 15 minutes at 350 degrees Fahrenheit.
5. Serve once done, and enjoy!

Eggplant With Garlic Sauce

Preparation Time: 10 minutes | Cooking Time: 10 minutes | Servings: 4

Ingredients:
- 2 tablespoons olive oil
- 2 minced garlic cloves
- 1 tablespoon tamari sauce
- 1 chopped red chili pepper
- 1 tablespoon grated ginger
- 3 halved & sliced eggplants
- 1 chopped green onion stalk
- 1 tablespoon red wine vinegar

Directions:
1. Use a pan that fits the air fryer and heat oil over medium heat.
2. Add, stir and cook eggplant slices for 2 minutes.
3. Add the remaining ingredients and stir.
4. Transfer the pan with the contents to the air fryer.
5. Cook for 7 minutes at 320 degrees Fahrenheit in the air fryer and serve once done!

Greek Potato Mix

Preparation Time: 10 minutes | Cooking Time: 20 minutes | Servings: 2

Ingredients:
- 1 bay leaf
- 2 tablespoons butter
- 1 ½ tablespoon flour
- ½ cup chicken broth
- 1 chopped red onions
- 2 tablespoons Greek yogurt
- Salt & black pepper as needed
- 1 roughly-chopped small carrot
- 2 wedgie-cut medium potatoes

Directions:
1. Use a pan that fits the air fryer and melt butter over medium heat.
2. Add, stir and cook onion and carrot for 3 minutes.
3. Add the remaining ingredients except for Greek yogurt and stir.
4. Transfer the pan with the contents to the air fryer.
5. Cook for 16 minutes at 320 degrees Fahrenheit in the air fryer
6. Add the yogurt, stir and serve!

Air Fried Asparagus

Preparation Time: 10 minutes | Cooking Time: 15 minutes | Servings: 4

Ingredients:
- 1 lemon juice
- ¼ cup olive oil
- 1 teaspoon lemon zest
- 4 minced garlic cloves
- 4 oz. crumbled cottage cheese
- ½ teaspoon dried thyme
- ¼ teaspoon red pepper flakes
- Salt & black pepper as needed
- 2 oz. trimmed fresh asparagus
- 2 tablespoons finely chopped parsley

Directions:
1. Whisk oil, lemon zest, garlic, thyme, and pepper flakes in a bowl.
2. Toss in the remaining ingredients except for lemon juice and parsley and transfer to the air fryer basket.
3. Cook for 8 minutes at 350 degrees F.
4. Serve with a drizzle of lemon juice and a sprinkling of parsley on top!

Tasty Creamy String Beans

Preparation Time: 10 minutes | Cooking Time: 15 minutes | Servings: 4

Ingredients:
- 2 oz. string beans
- ½ cup cooking cream
- ⅔ cup grated parmesan
- 1 cup shredded mozzarella
- A pinch of red pepper flakes
- Salt & black pepper as needed
- 2 teaspoons grated lemon zest

Directions:
1. Add beans to a dish that fits in the air fryer.
2. Add the remaining ingredients and toss.
3. Transfer the dish to the air fryer and cook for 15 minutes at 350 degrees Fahrenheit.
4. Serve once done, and enjoy!

Air Fryer Spanish Spicy Potatoes

Preparation Time: 15 minutes | Cooking Time: 30 minutes | Servings: 2

Ingredients
- 4 large potatoes, sliced into wedges
- 2 tablespoons of olive oil
- 1 teaspoon of chili powder
- 1 teaspoon of garlic, dried
- 1 teaspoon of barbacoa seasoning
- Salt and pepper according to taste

For the sauce
- 1 chopped onion
- ½ cup of tomato puree
- 1 fresh tomato
- 1 tablespoon of red wine vinegar
- ½ teaspoon of chili powder
- 1 teaspoon of coriander
- 1 teaspoon of thyme
- 1/2 teaspoon of mixed spice
- ½ teaspoon of oregano
- 1 teaspoon of rosemary

Directions
1. Take a bowl, mix all the sauce ingredients, and put it aside.
2. Take a bowl, add potatoes, and season with all the main ingredients.
3. Stir them and put them into an air fryer basket lined with parchment paper.
4. Transfer them to the air fryer unit and set the temperature to 350 degrees F.
5. Set the time to 30 minutes.
6. Once it's done, serve with the sauce!

Spinach Croquettes

Preparation Time: 15 minutes | Cooking Time: 10 minutes | Servings: 2

Ingredients
- 1 cup of whole milk
- 1 pound of spinach
- 1/3 cup vegetable broth
- 4 cups of panko breadcrumbs
- 4 onions
- Salt and pepper according to taste
- 6 garlic cloves
- 1 cup tapioca flour
- 1/3 cup of olive oil
- 2 cups coriander leaves

Directions
1. Boil spinach in water for 3 minutes.

2. Drain it and put it aside.
3. Take a frying pan and add the vegetable broth and milk.
4. Boil it for 4 minutes and then add oil and garlic paste and fry for 2 minutes.
5. Pour in the onions and cook them a little.
6. Now add all the ingredients (except bread crumbs) to the pan, including the boiled and chopped spinach.
7. Thoroughly mix and drizzle salt and pepper according to your liking.
8. Put the mixture in the refrigerator for 4-6 hours.
9. Make round croquettes from the mixture and coat with bread crumbs
10. Put them in an air fryer basket sprayed with cooking oil.
11. Set the temperature of the air fryer to 360 degrees F.
12. Adjust the time to 10 minutes.
13. Transfer the basket to the air fryer unit and let it be baked.
14. Serve once done!

Roasted Savory Carrots

Preparation Time: 15 minutes | Cooking Time: 20 minutes | Servings: 2

Ingredients
- 2 cups of carrots
- ¼ cup of olive oil
- 1 teaspoon garlic paste
- 1 teaspoon chili powder
- 1/2 cup of grated pecorino cheese
- Salt and pepper according to taste

Directions
1. Use a peeler to peel the carrots and wash them.
2. Toss the carrots with oil, chili powder, and garlic paste in a bowl.
3. Put it in an air fryer basket lined with parchment paper.
4. Set the timer to 20 minutes and bake the carrots at 380 degrees F.
5. Once done, drizzle the grated cheese, salt & pepper on top of it.
6. Serve!

Smoky Cauliflower

Preparation Time: 14 minutes | Cooking Time: 10 minutes | Servings: 2-4

Ingredients
- 2 cauliflowers sliced to florets
- ¼ cup of olive oil
- 2 teaspoons chipotle powder
- 1.5 teaspoon salt or according to taste
- 4 garlic cloves, minced
- ¼ cup of cilantro

Directions
1. Mix all the ingredients in a bowl except the cilantro.
2. Toss the cauliflower in the mixture.
3. Put in an air fryer basket sprayed with cooking spray.
4. Transfer to the air fryer unit.
5. Cook the cauliflower for 10 minutes at 450 degrees F.
6. Drizzle cilantro once cooked and serve!

Garlic Parmesan Air Fryer Roasted Radishes

Preparation Time: 15 minutes | Cooking Time: 14 minutes | Servings: 2

Ingredients
- 1 pound of radishes
- 2 tablespoons of olive oil
- 2 garlic cloves, minced
- ¼ teaspoon of sea salt
- ¼ cup of grated parmesan cheese

- Chili flakes

Directions
1. Put some olive oil over chopped radishes.
2. Transfer to the air fryer basket lined with parchment paper.
3. Cook in the air fryer for 8 minutes at 350 degrees.
4. Simultaneously, thoroughly mix all the remaining ingredients in a bowl except the cheese.
5. Now take the cooked radishes and rub them with the olive oil mixture and cheese.
6. Transfer it back to the air fryer and cook at 400 degrees F for 6 more minutes.
7. Once it's done, serve!

Air Fryer Spinach

Preparation Time: 15 minutes | Cooking Time: 8 minutes | Servings: 2

Ingredients
- 2 cups of baby spinach
- 2 tablespoons of butter
- 2 teaspoons of garlic paste
- Salt and pepper according to taste

Directions
1. Wash the baby spinach with water to clean any debris.
2. Put the baby spinach in an air fryer basket lined with parchment paper.
3. Season with salt, pepper, garlic paste, and butter.
4. Transfer to the air fryer unit.
5. Set the temperature of the air fryer to 400 degrees F and the time to 8 minutes.
6. Once it's done, serve!

Orange-Cranberry Butternut Squash with Ginger

Preparation Time: 15 minutes | Cooking Time: 14 minutes | Servings: 4

Ingredients
- 2.5 pounds of butternut squash
- ½ cup of cranberries
- ½ cup of orange juice
- 1/6 cup of maple syrup
- 1/6 cup of butter
- ¼ cup of ginger, shredded
- Salt according to taste
- 1 orange, sliced
- 2 tablespoons of cilantro

Directions
1. Take an air fryer basket and line it with aluminum foil.
2. Now put the butternut squash on a cutting board and slice it.
3. Now mix all the remaining ingredients in a bowl except the orange and parsley.
4. pour this marinade over the butternut squash
5. Put it in the air fryer basket.
6. Transfer to the air fryer unit and adjust the temperature to 350 degrees F.
7. Cook the squash for 10-14 minutes till the butternut is browned.
8. Serve with the juicy orange slices and cilantro!

Air Fryer Garlic Aioli Artichokes

Preparation Time: 10 minutes | Cooking Time: 8 minutes | Servings: 2

Ingredients
- 24 ounces of artichoke hearts
- ¼ cup of olive oil
- ¼ cup of parmesan cheese, grated
- 1 teaspoon of Italian seasoning

- 1 teaspoon of sea salt
- 1 teaspoon lime pepper
- 1 teaspoon garlic powder

Garlic Aioli:
- 1 cup of mayonnaise
- 4 cloves of minced garlic
- 2 tablespoons of lime juice
- 1 teaspoon of sea salt
- ½ teaspoon of black pepper or according to taste

Directions
1. Mix all the ingredients for garlic aioli in a separate bowl and set it aside for further use.
2. Marinate in the refrigerator for at least 30 minutes.
3. Now place the artichoke hearts on a plain dish and use a paper towel to pat them dry.
4. Toss the artichoke in a bowl with all the main ingredients listed above.
5. Now put the artichokes in the air fryer lined with parchment paper.
6. Transfer to air fryer unit and cook for 8 minutes at 400 degrees F.
7. Once it's crispy, serve with the garlic aioli sauce!

Herb Air Fryer Butternut Squash

Preparation Time: 10 minutes | Cooking Time: 8 minutes | Servings: 2

Ingredients
- 2-pounds of butternut squash
- ¼ cup of avocado oil
- 1.5 teaspoon of Himalayan salt
- 2 teaspoons of garlic powder
- 1 teaspoon of onion powered
- 1 teaspoon of granulated sugar
- 4 teaspoons of Italian seasoning

Directions
1. Place the butter squash on a cutting board and dice it into cubes.
2. Drizzle all the ingredients over it and toss in a bowl.
3. Put the squash in an air fryer basket lined with parchment paper
4. Transfer to the air fryer unit and cook at 400 degrees for 8 minutes.
5. Serve once crispy!

Curried Carrots with Dates & Almonds

Preparation Time: 25 minutes
Cooking Time: 25 minutes
Servings: 3

Ingredients
- 2/3 cup almonds
- 8 carrots
- 4 teaspoons avocado oil
- 2 teaspoon curry powder
- Salt and pepper according to taste
- 8 dates
- ¼ cup olive oil
- ¼ cup of lime juice

Directions
1. Roast the almonds on a baking sheet for 10-11 minutes.
2. Meanwhile, toss all the remaining ingredients in a bowl except the dates, oil, and lime juice.
3. Now put this mixture in an air fryer basket lined with parchment paper.
4. Transfer to the air fryer and cook at 390 degrees F for 15 minutes.
5. Take it out, put it on a dish, and garnish with the roasted almonds and the dates.

6. Drizzle over the lime juice and sprinkle some avocado oil.
7. Serve!

Air Fryer Vegetable Kabobs

Preparation Time: 15 minutes | Cooking Time: 10 minutes | Servings: 2

Ingredients
- 2 cups of button mushrooms, cubed
- 2 cups of grape tomatoes, cubed
- 2 zucchinis, cubed
- 1 teaspoon ground coriander
- 1 sliced bell pepper, cubed
- 2 onions, cubed
- Salt according to taste

Directions
1. Take some skewers and skew them across the vegetables.
2. Drizzle it with salt and coriander.
3. Transfer the skewers to the air fryer and rotate at intervals.
4. Toast in the air fryer unit at 400 degrees F for 10 minutes.
5. Once it's done, serve!
6. Cook in batches according to the capacity of your air fryer.

Air Fryer Pineapple Teriyaki Veggie Kabobs

Preparation Time: 15 minutes | Cooking Time: 8-12 minutes | Servings: 3

Ingredients
- 8 pineapple chunks
- Salt and pepper according to taste
- 8 vegetable kabobs
- 1 cup teriyaki sauce

Directions
1. Poke the skewers in the pineapple chunks in an alternate combination with vegetable kabobs.
2. Put the skewers in the air fryer rack and dribble with the teriyaki sauce.
3. Drizzle salt and pepper on top of it and transfer to the air fryer unit.
4. Cook for 8-12 minutes at 350 degrees F or until cooked.
5. Once it's done, serve!

Mixed Veggies

Preparation Time: 25 minutes | Cooking Time: 22 minutes | Servings: 4

Ingredients
- 1 cup of carrots
- 1 cup of sweet potatoes
- 1 cup of shallots
- 1 cup of zucchini
- 1 cup of butternut squash
- Salt and black pepper according to taste
- ½ tablespoon Italian seasoning
- 1 tablespoon of ranch seasoning
- 2 tablespoons of olive oil

Directions
1. Place the vegetables on a cutting board and dice them into cubes.
2. Take a bowl, add all the vegetables, and drizzle oil and the listed seasoning.
3. Thoroughly toss the vegetables and put them in an air fryer basket sprayed with oil.
4. Transfer the basket to the air fryer and cook at 356 degrees for 22 minutes.

5. Once it's done, serve!

Vegetable Medley

Preparation Time: 25 minutes | Cooking Time: 12 minutes | Servings: 4

Ingredients
- 2 eggplants, diced into cubes
- 2 zucchinis, diced into cubes
- 2 summer squash, diced into cubes
- 2 cups shiitake mushrooms, diced into cubes
- 2 cups whole grape tomatoes, diced into cubes
- ¼ cup of olive oil
- 4 cloves garlic
- 1 teaspoon of dried thyme
- 1 teaspoon of kosher salt
- 2 teaspoons of lime zest
- 2 teaspoons of lime juice

Directions
1. Place the vegetables on a cutting board and slice them into cubes.
2. Put the veggies in a bowl and season with all the listed ingredients except the lime juice and zest.
3. Toss it thoroughly and put it in the air fryer basket sprayed with cooking spray.
4. Transfer it to the air fryer and cook at 360 degrees F for 12 minutes.
5. Season with some lemon zest and juice once cooked.
6. Mediterranean vegetable medley is ready to be served!

Roasted Vegetables

Preparation Time: 25 minutes | Cooking Time: 10-15 minutes | Servings: 2

Ingredients
Firm vegetables
- 2 sweet potatoes
- 2 potatoes
- 2 cups butternut squash
- 2 carrots
- 1 head broccoli
- 2 red onions

Seasoning
- 1/3 cup of olive oil
- 2 teaspoons of sea salt

Directions
1. Use a peeler to peel the vegetables and slice them into pieces.
2. Wash the vegetables with water, drain and use a paper towel to pat dry.
3. Now put the firm vegetables in a bowl and stir them with oil and salt.
4. Put these veggies in an air fryer basket lined with parchment paper.
5. Transfer to the air fryer and cook it at 350 degrees F for 5 minutes.
6. Simultaneously, pour the other vegetables into a bowl and toss them well with oil and salt.
7. Now, put these veggies in an air fryer basket lined with parchment paper.
8. Transfer to the air fryer and cook it at 350 degrees F for 5 minutes.
9. Serve the veggies!

Vegetables with Halloumi Cheese

Preparation Time: 22 minutes | Cooking Time: 18 minutes | Servings: 3

Ingredients
- 2 onion wedges
- 2 sliced red pepper sliced
- 4 sliced courgettes
- 2 tablespoons of canola oil
- 12 cherry tomatoes
- 2 blocks of sliced halloumi cheese

Directions
1. Take an air fryer basket and line it with parchment paper.
2. Put in the onion wedges, red peppers, and sliced courgettes.
3. Drizzle with some oil and transfer to the air fryer unit.
4. Cook in the air fryer at 400 degrees F for 10 minutes.
5. Afterward, add the tomatoes to the cooked veggies and drizzle with salt and pepper.
6. Cook the vegetables for another 5 minutes at 400 degrees F.
7. Finally, put in the halloumi slices and put them back into the air fryer.
8. Cook it at 392 degrees F for 3 minutes.
9. Once it's done, serve!

Feta Cheese with Roast Vegetables

Preparation Time: 25 minutes | Cooking Time: 25 minutes | Servings: 2

Ingredients
- 1 sliced eggplant
- 2 quartered zucchinis
- 2 sliced red pepper
- 2 yellow peppers
- 2 chopped red onion
- 8 cloves garlic
- 1 teaspoon chili powder
- 2 teaspoon mixed herbs
- Salt and black pepper, to taste
- 1/3 cup of olive oil
- Crumbled cottage cheese
- Cilantro, as required

Directions
1. Put all the vegetables on a cutting board and slice them into cubes.
2. Pour in the olive oil and all the seasoning and stir them well.
3. Put all the vegetables except the tomatoes into the air fryer basket and
4. Put in the air fryer and cook at 366 degrees for 15 minutes.
5. Put the tomatoes with these vegetables after 7-8 minutes.
6. Once it's done, season with the cheese and herbs.
7. Serve!

Brined Vegetables

Preparation Time: 25 minutes | Cooking Time: 22 minutes | Servings: 2

Ingredients
- 2 sliced potatoes
- 2 eggplants, round
- 2 zucchinis, round
- 2 red onion circles
- 2 large tomato rounds
- 2 cups of canola oil
- 2 cloves garlic
- 2 teaspoon basil
- Salt and pepper according to taste
- 2 cans of diced tomatoes
- 4 sprigs thyme

For the Topping
- 1 cup feta cheese
- 6 slices of crusty whole wheat bread
- Few olives

Directions
1. Wash the vegetables and slice them on a cutting board.
2. Put them in a bowl and drizzle some oil.
3. Season with garlic, basil, salt & pepper, and thoroughly stir.
4. Pour in a cup of water and add the tomatoes.
5. Take around the cooking dish and line it with aluminum foil.
6. Put the veggies in the dish and transfer them to the air fryer unit.
7. Set the temperature to 390 degrees F and cook for 22 minutes.
8. Once it's done, season with the toppings and serve with thyme!

Simple Jicama Chip
Preparation Time: 25 minutes | Cooking Time: 15 minutes | Servings: 2

Ingredients
- 20 ounces jicama, peeled and diced into small sticks
- 3 tablespoons of olive oil
- 1 tablespoon chili powder
- 1 tablespoon garlic powder
- 1 tablespoon salt
- ¼ tablespoon of cayenne pepper
- Few drops of lemon

Directions
1. Clean the jicama by putting it under running water.
2. Slice the jicama into quarter-inch thick sticks.
3. Put them in a bowl and toss them with all the ingredients.
4. Take an air fryer and line it with parchment paper.
5. Put the Jicama sticks in the basket and transfer them to the air fryer basket.
6. Cook in the air fryer for 12-15 minutes at 400 degrees F.
7. Make sure to flip the sticks halfway.
8. Once it's done, serve!

Easy Ratatouille Vegetable Mix
Preparation Time: 25 minutes | Cooking Time: 10 minutes | Servings: 2

Ingredients
- 1 medium eggplant
- 1 zucchini, small size
- 1 tomato, medium size
- 1 yellow bell pepper
- 1 red bell pepper
- 1 medium-sized onion
- 2 fresh cayenne pepper (sliced)
- 12 sprigs of fresh basil (sliced)
- 6 sprigs of fresh rosemary (cut)
- 4 clove garlic (crushed)
- Salt according to taste
- 1 teaspoon ground black pepper
- 2 tablespoon olive oil
- 3 tablespoons white wine
- 3 teaspoons of balsamic vinegar

Directions
1. Put all the ingredients in a bowl and mix them thoroughly.
2. Now take an air fryer basket and grease it with oil.
3. Put the veggie mixture into the basket and put it in the air fryer unit.

4. Set the unit's temperature to 400 degrees F and cook for 10 minutes.
5. Let the veggies rest in the air fryer for about 5 minutes before serving.

Crunchy Vegetable Nuggets
Preparation Time: 25 minutes | Cooking Time: 12 minutes | Servings: 2

Ingredients
- 8 potatoes mashed after boiling
- 2 cups of peas (crumpled)
- 2 cups of cauliflower (shredded)
- 2 cups of soy nuggets (drenched and crumpled)
- 3 cups panko breadcrumbs
- 1/2 cup parsley leaves (sliced)
- ½ cup walnuts, (chop up)
- 2 green chilis (chopped)
- 2 teaspoons Italian mixed herbs seasoning
- Cooking oil spray
- Salt and black pepper according to taste

Directions
1. Put all the ingredients in a bowl and mix them into a dough form.
2. Shape the batter into round shapes and put it into an air fryer basket greased with cooking spray.
3. Do this for all the batter.
4. Spray some cooking spray over the shaped nuggets in the basket.
5. Transfer the air fryer basket to the unit.
6. Set the temperature to 400 degrees F and cook for 12 minutes.
7. Flip the nuggets halfway to cook evenly on both sides.
8. Serve once done!

Veggie Tortillas Wraps
Preparation Time: 25 minutes | Cooking Time: 20 minutes | Servings: 2

Ingredients
- 2 cups of portobello mushrooms
- 4 sweet peppers, yellow, diced
- 2 medium-sized onions, diced

Ingredients for Fajita Sauce
- 12 teaspoon sweet chili sauce
- 4 teaspoon tamari sauce
- 1 teaspoon smoked paprika
- Paprika according to taste
- 1 teaspoon ground coriander
- Salt according to taste

Side Servings
- 16 tortillas

Toppings of the choice
- Guacamole
- Salsa
- Sour cream

Directions
1. Pour all the ingredients of Fajita sauce into a large bowl and thoroughly mix them.
2. Now slice the portobello, sweet peppers, and mid-size onions on a cutting board.
3. Put them in a bowl and pour in the fajita sauce.
4. Take an air fryer basket and line it with parchment paper.
5. Put the basket in the air fryer unit.
6. Cook it for 20 minutes at 400 degrees F.
7. Make sure to shake the air fryer basket after 10 minutes.
8. Season with toppings of choice and serve with tortillas!

Garlic Parmesan String Beans

Preparation Time: 25 minutes | Cooking Time: 12 minutes | Servings: 2

Ingredients

- 3 cups of string beans
- ¼ cup garlic oil
- Salt and black pepper according to taste
- 2/3 teaspoon garlic powder
- 2/3 teaspoon onion powder
- 1 cup of grated parmesan cheese
- Cooking oil spray

Directions

1. Thoroughly mix all the ingredients in a large bowl except cheese.
2. Put them in an air fryer basket sprayed with cooking oil.
3. Transfer the air fryer basket to the air fryer.
4. Set the time to 10-12 minutes and adjust the temperature to 400 degrees F.
5. Once it's done, season with parmesan cheese and serve!

Crispy Avocado Fries

Preparation Time: 10 minutes | Cooking Time: 5 minutes | Servings: 2

Ingredients

- 4 cups of kale, grated
- 1/2 cup of parsley
- 1/2 cup of plain Greek yogurt
- ¼ cup of lemon juice
- 2 teaspoons maple syrup
- ½ teaspoon ground chipotle pepper

Other Ingredients

- ½ cup of cornmeal
- 2 organic eggs, whisked
- 1 teaspoon garlic paste
- 1 teaspoon ground chipotle pepper
- 2 medium avocados, peeled and diced
- Cooking spray
- Salt and pepper according to taste

Directions

1. Pour the eggs into a bowl, beat them, and put them aside.
2. Now put the main ingredients and mix them in a separate bowl.
3. Similarly, mix the garlic paste, chipotle pepper, salt, and cornmeal.
4. Now dip the avocado slices in the egg mixture and the cornmeal mixture.
5. Put them in an air fryer basket greased with cooking spray.
6. Transfer to the air fryer and set the temperature to 400 degrees F.
7. Set the time to 5 minutes and let it cook.
8. Make sure to flip the avocados halfway.
9. Drizzle with some salt and pepper and stir.
10. Once the avocados are done, serve with the yogurt mixture!

Sesame and Vinegar String Beans

Preparation Time: 12 minutes | Cooking Time: 10-12 minutes | Servings: 3

Ingredients

- 4 cups string beans
- ¼ cup sesame oil
- 2 teaspoons sesame seeds
- Salt and black pepper according to taste
- 2 teaspoon red wine vinegar
- Cooking spray

Directions

1. Thoroughly mix all the ingredients in a bowl.
2. Put them in an air fryer basket sprayed with cooking oil.
3. Set the temperature of the air fryer to 400 degrees F.
4. Set the timer to 10-12 minutes and put the basket in the air fryer.
5. Make sure to flip the green beans after 5-6 minutes.
6. Serve once done!

Spicy Herbed Yellow Squash

Preparation Time: 10 minutes | Cooking Time: 15 minutes | Servings: 2

Ingredients

- 6 cups of yellow squash, slashed to two pieces
- 2 tablespoons of olive oil
- 2 cloves of garlic, crushed
- Salt and black pepper according to taste
- ½ teaspoon basil, dried
- ½ teaspoon rosemary, dried
- 2 tablespoons of parsley, diced

Directions

1. Take a large bowl and stir all the ingredients.
2. Thoroughly rub the ingredients over the squash.
3. Put them in an air fryer basket sprayed with cooking oil.
4. Set the temperature of the air fryer to 400 degrees f.
5. Set the time to 15 minutes and put the basket in the air fryer.
6. Make sure to flip the green beans after 7-minutes.
7. Serve once done!

Coated Carrots Fries

Preparation Time: 10 minutes | Cooking Time: 12 minutes | Servings: 3

Ingredients

- 3 cups of carrots, diced to half-inch thickness
- 2 cups panko breadcrumbs
- 4 organic eggs
- 2/3 cup pecorino cheese
- 1 teaspoon garlic paste
- Salt and black pepper according to taste

Directions

1. Whisk the eggs in a bowl and add salt, pepper, and garlic.
2. Beat it thoroughly and dunk the carrot sticks in it.
3. Coat the carrot sticks with breadcrumbs.
4. Now take an air fryer basket and line it with parchment paper.
5. Align it to the air fryer and basket and transfer it to the unit.
6. Adjust the temperature to 400 degrees F and cook for 10-12 minutes.
7. Drizzle grated cheese over the top once it's cooked and Serve!

Nuts and Vegetables with Rice

Preparation Time: 10 minutes | Cooking Time: 8 minutes | Servings: 2

Ingredients

- 2 cups string beans
- 2 cups of pine nuts
- 2 teaspoons garlic paste
- Salt and black pepper according to taste
- 2 teaspoons sesame oil
- 1 cup of boiled rice, drained

Directions

1. Take a medium-sized bowl and thoroughly mix all the ingredients except the rice.
2. Lay them in an air fryer basket lined with parchment paper.
3. Set the temperature of the air fryer to 400 degrees F.
4. Adjust the timer to 8 minutes and put the basket in the air fryer.
5. Serve along with the rice once it's done!

Roasted Asparagus with Tahini Sauce

Preparation Time: 20 minutes | Cooking Time: 12 minutes | Servings: 2

Ingredients
- 2s cup fresh asparagus, chopped
- 2 tablespoons of sesame oil
- 1 teaspoon of soy sauce
- 1 teaspoon of chili powder
- Salt according to taste

Tahini sauce Ingredients
- 2 teaspoons of garlic paste
- 2/3 cup of lemon juice
- 2/3 cup of tahini
- 1/4 teaspoon of sea salt
- 1/2 teaspoon ground cumin
- 2/3 cup of water, or as needed

Topping Ingredients
- Sliced sparsely

Directions
1. Put the tahini sauce ingredients in a blender, blend until it smooths out, and put it aside.
2. Now mix all the main ingredients in a large bowl.
3. Now take an air fryer basket and line it with parchment paper.
4. Align the asparagus mixture in the air fryer basket and transfer it to the unit.
5. Adjust the temperature to 400 degrees F and cook for 10-12 minutes.
6. Once it's done, sprinkle some sparse tahini sauce on it!

Perfect Stack of Tomatoes

Preparation Time: 10 minutes | Cooking Time: 7-10 minutes | Servings: 4

Ingredients
- 2/3 cup of fat-free mayo
- 1/2 teaspoon of lime zest, shredded
- ¼ cup of lime juice
- 2 teaspoons of thyme, dried
- 2/3 cup of almond flour
- 4 egg whites
- 1.5 cups of cornmeal
- Salt and black pepper according to taste
- 2medium green tomatoes, diced into cubes
- 4 medium red tomatoes, diced into cubes

Directions
1. Put the egg whites in a bowl and beat them gently.
2. Take a bowl, add the cornmeal, and mix with salt, pepper, and flour.
3. Now take another bowl and mix all the remaining ingredients except the tomatoes.
4. Dice the tomatoes into four pieces and dunk them in the egg.
5. Dip it into the cornmeal mixture and put them in the air fryer basket lined with parchment paper.
6. Cook at 400 degrees F for 7 minutes in the air fryer unit.
7. Once it's done, serve!

Pumpkin Fries with Sweet Greek Yogurt Sauce

Preparation Time: 10 minutes | Cooking Time: 8 minutes | Servings: 2

Ingredients
- 2/3 cup of plain Greek yogurt
- 2 tablespoons of honey
- 3 tablespoons of chipotle peppers in adobo sauce
- Salt according to taste
- 2 pumpkins, medium-sized sliced to an inch thickness
- 2/3 teaspoon of garlic paste
- 1/2 teaspoon of ground coriander
- 1/2 teaspoon of chili powder

Directions
1. Pour the yogurt into a bowl and drizzle with salt and chipotle pepper.
2. Pour in the honey, mix and marinate in the refrigerator for 20-30 minutes.
3. Now take a knife and slice the pumpkin along its length.
4. Clean the seeds and put them in a bowl.
5. Drizzle the salt and garlic paste and mix with chili and ground coriander.
6. Stir it thoroughly and put it in an air fryer basket greased with cooking oil.
7. Transfer the pumpkin to the air fryer and set the temperature to 400 degrees F.
8. Cook for 8 minutes and flip the pumpkin fries after 4 minutes.
9. Once it's done, serve with the chipotle sauce!

Lemon Glazed Mushrooms

Preparation Time: 15 Minutes | Cooking Time: 12-14 Minutes | Servings: 4

Ingredients
- 2 cups of mushrooms, cut
- 4 teaspoons of garlic paste
- 1/3 cup of softened butter
- ¼ cup pecorino cheese
- 2 teaspoons lemon juice
- 1 teaspoons lemon zest, grated

Directions
1. Thoroughly mix all the main ingredients in a large bowl except the butter and cheese.
2. Now take an air fryer basket and line it with parchment paper.
3. Align the mushrooms in the air fryer basket and transfer them to the unit.
4. Adjust the temperature to 400 degrees F and cook for 12-14 minutes.
5. Once it's done, sprinkle some grated cheese and softened butter!

Poppers Peppers

Preparation Time: 12 minutes | Cooking Time: 15-20 minutes | Servings: 4

Ingredients
- 20 ounces cream cheese, melted
- 1.5 cups of cheddar cheese, grated
- 1.5 cups of Monterey Jack cheese, grated
- 8 bacon slices, boiled and crushed
- 1/2 teaspoon of garlic paste
- 1/2 teaspoon of paprika
- Salt according to taste
- 1/2 teaspoon smoked paprika
- 2-pounds of fresh jalapenos, cut in two and seeded
- 1 cup of Italian breadcrumbs
- 4 organic eggs
- Sour cream for serving

Directions

1. Take a bowl and beat the eggs in it.
2. Now take a dish and pour in the panko breadcrumbs.
3. Thoroughly mix all the remaining ingredients in a bowl.
4. Use a knife to slice open the peppers and stuff them with the cheese mixture.
5. Dip the peppers in the egg mixture and then in the Panko.
6. Now take an air fryer basket and line it with parchment paper.
7. Align the peppers in the air fryer basket and transfer them to the unit.
8. Adjust the temperature to 350 degrees F and cook for 15-20 minutes.
9. Once it's done, serve with the sour cream!

Pickle Fries

Preparation Time: 10 minutes | Cooking Time: 10 minutes | Servings: 2

Ingredients

- 6 dill pickle slices
- 2 tablespoons of all-purpose flour
- Salt according to taste
- 1 egg
- 1/4 tablespoon dill pickle juice
- A pinch of paprika
- A pinch of garlic powder
- 1 cup panko breadcrumbs
- Cooking spray
- Ranch salad dressing, for serving

Directions

1. Place the pickles on a plain dish and use a paper towel to extract excessive moisture.
2. Now take 3 separate bowls.
3. Beat the egg in the first bowl with the garlic, cayenne, and pickle juice.
4. Pour breadcrumbs into the second one.
5. Now mix all the remaining ingredients in the third bowl except the ranch salad seasoning.
6. Pick the pickles and dunk them in the flour mixture's third bowl.
7. Then dunk them in the egg mixture before coating them with the breadcrumbs.
8. Now take an air fryer basket and line it with parchment paper.
9. Align the pickles in the air fryer basket and transfer them to the unit.
10. Adjust the temperature to 400 degrees F and cook for 10 minutes.
11. Once it's done, serve with the ranch salad!

Fried Eggplants Chips

Preparation Time: 10 minutes | Cooking Time: 8 minutes | Servings: 2

Ingredients

- 4 eggs
- 1 cup cheddar cheese, shredded
- 1 cup of wheat germ, toasted
- 2 teaspoons of Italian seasoning
- 1.5 teaspoons of garlic salt
- 2 eggplant, medium-sized
- Oil for greasing

Directions

1. Beat the egg in a bowl and put it aside.
2. Now mix all the ingredients in another bowl except the eggplants.

3. Place the eggplants on a cutting board and use a knife to slice them into half-inch thickness.
4. Dunk the eggplant in the egg wash and then in the wheat germ mixture.
5. Now take an air fryer basket and grease it with cooking oil.
6. Align the eggplants in the air fryer basket and transfer them to it.
7. Adjust the temperature to 400 degrees F and cook for 8 minutes.
8. Serve once done!

Whole Baked Potatoes with Creamy Filling

Preparation Time: 10 minutes | Cooking Time: 45 minutes | Servings: 2

Ingredients

- 4 baking potatoes, big
- 3 tablespoons olive oil
- Salt and pepper, to taste

Filling Ingredients

- 4 cups of sour cream
- 4 teaspoon garlic paste
- 2 teaspoon fresh scallions
- 1 teaspoon sliced chives
- Salt and black pepper according to taste
- 2 teaspoons of Worcestershire sauce

Directions

1. Use a peeler to peel the potatoes and drizzle them with olive oil, salt, and pepper according to desire.
2. Now take a large bowl and toss well all the filling ingredients.
3. Place the potatoes in an air fryer basket greased with cooking oil.
4. Put the potatoes in the air fryer basket and transfer them to the air fryer.
5. Adjust the temperature to 350 degrees F and cook for 45 minutes.
6. Once done, use a knife to slice the potatoes to create a hollow space and fill it with the filling mixture.
7. Serve!

Beets in Air Fryer

Preparation Time: 10 minutes | Cooking Time: 15 minutes | Servings: 4

Ingredients

- 4 cups beets, skinned and finely diced
- Salt according to taste
- Cooking spray

Directions

1. Take an air fryer basket and brush it with cooking spray.
2. Line up the beets in the air fryer basket and transfer them to the air fryer.
3. Adjust the temperature to 400 degrees F and cook for 15 minutes.
4. Flip after 7-8 minutes to cook evenly on both sides.
5. Drizzle with salt once it's crisp and served!

BBQ Coated Cauliflower

Preparation Time: 10 minutes | Cooking Time: 12 minutes | Servings: 4

Ingredients

- 2 cups of cauliflower florets
- 2 tablespoons olive oil
- Salt according to taste
- ¼ teaspoon of chili powder
- 1 tablespoon sriracha sauce
- ¼ cup BBQ sauce

Directions
1. Put the cauliflower in a bowl and mix thoroughly with all the listed ingredients.
2. Let it marinate at room temperature for 5-10 minutes.
3. Take an air fryer basket and line it with parchment paper.
4. Put the florets in the air fryer basket.
5. Adjust the timer of the air fryer to 12 minutes.
6. Set the temperature to 400 degrees F and transfer the florets to the air fryer

Masala Galette
Preparation Time: 10 minutes | Cooking Time: 15 minutes | Servings: 1

Ingredients:
- 2 tbsp. of garam masala
- 2 medium potatoes boiled and mashed
- 1 ½ cup of coarsely crushed peanuts
- 3 tsp. of ginger finely chopped
- 1-2 tbsp. of fresh coriander leaves
- 2 or 3 green chilies finely chopped
- 1 ½ tbsp. of lemon juice
- Salt and pepper to taste

Directions:
1. In a sterile basin, combine the components.
2. Make flat and round galettes out of this mixture.
3. Gently wet the galettes with water. On each galette, top with crumbled peanuts.
4. Preheat the Air Fryer to 160° F for 5 minutes. Place the Fry Basket galettes in the lower oven for another 25 minutes.
5. The same temperature. Turn them over to get them to cook. With ketchup or mint chutney, serve.

Potato Samosa
Preparation Time: 10 minutes | Cooking Time: 15 minutes | Servings: 1

Ingredients:
- 2 tbsp. of unsalted butter
- 1 ½ cup of all-purpose flour
- A pinch of salt to taste
- Add as much water as required to make the dough stiff and firm
- For filling:
- 2-3 big potatoes boiled and mashed
- ¼ cup of boiled peas
- 1 tsp. of powdered ginger
- 1 or 2 green chilies that are finely chopped or mashed
- ½ tsp. of cumin
- 1 tsp. of coarsely crushed coriander
- 1 dry red chili broken into pieces
- A small amount of salt (to the taste)
- ½ tsp. of dried mango powder
- ½ tsp. of red chili powder.
- 1-2 tbsp. Of coriander.

Directions:
1. Rub the dough to make it stiff and flat for wrapping. Allow it to sit in a jar until the filling is complete.
2. In a saucepan, combine the ingredients and stir thoroughly to make a sticky paste. Make a copy of the bread.
3. Form the dough into balls and flatten them. Divide them in half and fill them with the filling. Use water to assist you in folding the rims and forming a cone shape.

4. Preheat the Air Fryer for 5-6 minutes at 300 degrees Fahrenheit. Place all samosas in the fry basket and properly shut the basket. Keep the Air Fryer at 200° for another 20 to 25 minutes.
5. Open the basket halfway through and flip the samosas for normal preparation. After that, cook for around 10 minutes at 250° to achieve the correct golden-brown color. Serve dripping wet. Chutney with tamarind or mint is recommended as a side dish.

Vegetable Kebab
Preparation Time: 10 minutes | Cooking Time: 15 minutes | Servings: 1

Ingredients:
- 2 cups of mixed vegetables
- 3 onions chopped
- 5 green chilies-roughly chopped
- 1 ½ tbsp. of ginger paste
- 1 ½ tsp. of garlic paste
- 1 ½ tsp. of salt
- 3 tsp. of lemon juice
- 2 tsp. of garam masala
- 4 tbsp. of chopped coriander
- 3 tbsp. of cream
- 3 tbsp. of chopped capsicum
- 3 eggs
- 2 ½ tbsp. Of white sesame seeds

Directions:
1. Grind the ingredients, except the egg, into a smooth paste. Cover the meals with paste. Now, beat the eggs and season with salt.
2. Scatter the coated veggies in the egg mixture, then add the sesame seeds and herbs. Place the veggies on a skewer.
3. Preheat the Air Fryer for roughly 5 minutes at 160° F. Cook for another 25 minutes with the sticks in the basket.
4. During the cooking procedure, swap the clamps to the cook's suit at the same temperature.

Sago Galette
Preparation Time: 10 minutes | Cooking Time: 15 minutes | Servings: 1

Ingredients:
- 2 cups of sago soaked
- 1 ½ cup of coarsely crushed peanuts
- 3 tsp. of ginger finely chopped
- 1-2 tbsp. of fresh coriander leaves
- 2 or 3 green chilies finely chopped
- 1 ½ tbsp. of lemon juice
- Salt and pepper to the taste

Directions:
1. Wash the soaking sago, then combine it with the remaining ingredients in a clean basin. Make flat and round galettes out of this mixture.
2. Gently wet the galettes with water on each galette, top with crumbled peanuts.
3. Preheat the air Fryer to 160° F for 5 minutes. Place the fry basket galettes in the bottom oven for another 25 minutes at the same temperature. Turn them over to get them to cook. Serve with chutney, basil, or ketchup on the side.

Stuffed Capsicum Baskets
Preparation Time: 10 minutes | Cooking Time: 15 minutes | Servings: 1

Ingredients:

- 3-4 long capsicum
- ½ tsp. of salt
- ½ tsp. of pepper powder
- For filling:
- 1 medium onion finely chopped
- 1 green chili finely chopped
- 2 or 3 large potatoes boiled and mashed
- 1 ½ tbsp. of chopped coriander leaves
- 1 tsp. of fenugreek
- 1 tsp. of dried mango powder
- 1 tsp. of cumin powder
- Salt and pepper to the taste
- For topping:
- 3 tbsp. of grated cheese
- 1 tsp. of red chili flakes
- ½ tsp. of oregano
- ½ tsp. of basil
- ½ tsp. of parsley

Directions:
1. Take all of the ingredients and combine them in a bowl labeled "Filling."
2. Remove the capsicum stem. Remove the caps. Remove the seeds as well.
3. Season the interior of the capsicum with salt and pepper. Turn on after they've been separated for a while.
4. Fill in the empty capsicums with the intended filling. Sprinkle the grated cheese on top, followed by the seasoning.
5. Preheat the air Fryer to 140°F for 5 minutes. Put the capsicums in and around the fry basket. Allow them to cook for another 20 minutes at the same temperature. To avoid overcooking, alternate them.

Baked Macaroni Pasta

Preparation Time: 10 minutes | Cooking Time: 15 minutes | Servings: 1

Ingredients:
- 1 cup of pasta
- 7 cups of boiling water
- 1 ½ tbsp. of olive oil
- A pinch of salt
- For tossing pasta:
- 1 ½ tbsp. of olive oil
- ½ cup of small carrot pieces
- Salt and pepper to the taste
- ½ tsp. of oregano
- ½ tsp. of basil
- For the white sauce:
- 2 tbsp. of olive oil
- 2 tbsp. of all-purpose flour
- 2 cups of milk
- 1 tsp. of dried oregano
- ½ tsp. of dried basil
- ½ tsp. of dried parsley
- Salt and pepper to the taste

Directions:
1. Cook the pasta and filter when finished. Toss the pasta with the other ingredients and set away. To make the sauce, combine all of the ingredients in a pan and bring it to a boil.
2. Drop the sauce and continue to simmer to thicken it. Apply the pasta to the sauce and place it in a glass dish decorated with cheese.
3. Preheat the air Fryer to 160°F for 5 minutes. Place it in the bowl basket and secure it. Allow it to cook for another

10 minutes at the same temperature. Continue to whisk the sauce.

Macaroni Samosa

Preparation Time: 10 minutes | Cooking Time: 15 minutes | Servings: 1

Ingredients:
- 1 cup of all-purpose flour
- 2 tbsp. of unsalted butter
- A pinch of salt to the taste
- Take the amount of water sufficient enough to make a stiff dough
- For filling:
- 3 cups of boiled macaroni
- 2 onion sliced
- 2 capsicum sliced
- 2 carrot sliced
- 2 cabbage sliced
- 2 tbsp. of soya sauce
- 2 tsp. of vinegar
- 2 tbsp. of ginger finely chopped
- 2 tbsp. of garlic finely chopped
- 2 tbsp. of green chilies finely chopped
- 2 tbsp. of ginger-garlic paste
- Some salt and pepper to taste
- 2 tbsp. of olive oil
- ½ tsp. of Ajinomoto

Directions:
1. Rub the dough to make it stiff and flat for wrapping. Set it aside to rest in a bowl while you prepare the filling.
2. In a saucepan, combine the ingredients and stir thoroughly to make a sticky paste. Work the paint out.
3. Form the dough into balls and flatten them. Split in half, then add the filling. Use water to assist you in folding the rims and forming a cone shape.
4. Preheat the air Fryer for 5-6 minutes at 300 degrees Fahrenheit. Place everything in the fry basket samosas, then properly seal the basket. Keep the air Fryer at 200° for another 20 to 25 minutes.
5. To ensure that the samosas cook evenly, open the bowl and turn them over. After that, cook for around 10 minutes at 250° to achieve the golden tan color. Serve dripping wet. Tamarinds or green chutney are suggested side dishes.

Burritos

Preparation Time: 10 minutes | Cooking Time: 15 minutes | Servings: 1

Ingredients:
- ½ cup of red kidney beans (soaked overnight)
- ½ small onion chopped
- 1 tbsp. of olive oil
- 2 tbsp. of tomato puree
- ¼ tsp. of red chili powder
- 1 tsp. of salt to the taste
- 4-5 flour tortillas
- Vegetable Filling:
- 1 tbsp. of olive oil
- 1 medium onion finely sliced
- 3 flakes of garlic crushed
- ½ cup of French beans (Slice them lengthwise into thin and long slices)
- ½ cup of mushrooms thinly sliced
- 1 cup of cottage cheese cut in too long and slightly thick fingers

- ½ cup of shredded cabbage
- 1 tbsp. of coriander, chopped
- 1 tbsp. of vinegar
- 1 tsp. of white wine
- A pinch of salt to the taste
- ½ tsp. of red chili flakes
- 1 tsp. of freshly ground peppercorns
- ½ cup of pickled jalapenos (Chop them up finely)
- 2 carrots (Cut into long thin slices)
- 1-2 lettuce leaves shredded.
- 1 or 2 spring onions chopped finely. Also, cut the greens.
- 1 tomato. Remove the seeds and chop them into small pieces.
- 1 green chili chopped.
- 1 cup of cheddar cheese, grated.

Directions:
1. Cook the beans with the onion and garlic until soft, then mash them coarsely. Make the sauce you'll need for the burrito now. Make sure the sauce is somewhat thick.
2. Cook the ingredients well in a skillet for the filling, ensuring the veggies are browned on the exterior.
3. To create the salad, combine all ingredients in a mixing bowl. Place the tortilla on top of a sauce layer, then the beans and stuffing in the center. Before rolling, add the salad on top of the filling.
4. Preheat the air Fryer for 5 minutes at 200 degrees Fahrenheit. Keep the burritos inside the fry basket. Close the basket completely. Allow the air Fryer to continue at 200°F for another 15 minutes.
5. Remove the basket halfway through and turn the burritos over to ensure even cooking.

Cheese and Bean Enchiladas

Preparation Time: 10 minutes | Cooking Time: 15 minutes | Servings: 1

Ingredients:
- Flour tortillas (as many as required)
- 4 tbsp. of olive oil
- 1 ½ tsp. of garlic that has been chopped
- 1 ½ cups of readymade tomato puree
- 3 medium tomatoes. Puree them in a mixer
- 1 tsp. of sugar
- A pinch of salt or to the taste
- A few red chili flakes to sprinkle
- 1 tsp. of oregano
- 2 tbsp. of oil
- 2 onions chopped finely
- 2 capsicums chopped finely
- 2 cups of readymade baked beans
- A few drops of Tabasco sauce
- 1 cup of crumbled or roughly mashed cottage cheese (cottage cheese)
- 1 cup of grated cheddar cheese
- A pinch of salt
- 1 tsp. of oregano
- ½ tsp. of pepper
- 1 ½ tsp. of red chili flakes or to taste
- 1 tbsp. of finely chopped jalapenos
- 1 cup of grated pizza cheese (mix mozzarella and cheddar cheese)

Directions:
1. Prepare the tortillas for cooking.
2. Now it's time to make the red sauce. 2 tbsp in a saucepan, heated and stirred in the garlic Fill in the blanks with the

remaining ingredients for the sauce. Continue your journey. Cook before the sauce droplets get too thick.
3. In a separate pot, heat 1 tablespoon of oil for the filling. Fry onions and garlic until caramelized or golden brown in hue. Cook for two minutes after adding the other ingredients to the filling.
4. Remove the pot from the heat and grate some cheese over it. Mix thoroughly and allow it to rest for a few minutes.
5. Let's get the plate ready. Take a tortilla and top it with some of the surface sauce. The filling should now be placed in a line at the bottom. Turn the tortilla carefully upwards. The same goes for tortillas in general.
6. Place all the tortillas on a platter and top with the shredded cheese. Cover this with an aluminum sheet.
7. Preheat the air Fryer to 160° C for 4-5 minutes. Break the bowl and place it into the tray. Continue to run the fryer for another 15 minutes. A normal cook should turn the tortillas over in between.

Veg Momos

Preparation Time: 10 minutes | Cooking Time: 15 minutes | Servings: 1

Ingredients:
- 1 ½ cup of all-purpose flour
- ½ tsp. of salt or to taste
- 5 tbsp. of water
- For filling:
- 2 cups of carrots grated
- 2 cups of cabbage grated
- 2 tbsp. of oil
- 2 tsp. of ginger-garlic paste
- 2 tsp. of soy sauce
- 2 tsp. of vinegar

Directions:
1. Knead the dough and leave it aside, covered with plastic wrap. Then, prepare the filling components, covering the veggies properly with the sauce.
2. Print and cut the dough into a rectangle. Insert the middle filling. To preserve the filling, fold the dough in half and crimp the edges.
3. Preheat the air Fryer to 200° F for 5 minutes. Close the fry box after adding the gnocchi. Allow them to simmer for another 20 minutes together. Chili or ketchup sauce are suggested side dishes.

Cornflakes French Toast

Preparation Time: 10 minutes | Cooking Time: 15 minutes | Servings: 1

Ingredients:
- Bread slices (brown or white)
- 1 egg white for every 2 slices
- 1 tsp. of sugar for every 2 slices
- Crushed cornflakes

Directions:
1. Combine two slices and cut them on the diagonal. In a mixing dish, whisk the egg whites with a little sugar.
2. Dip the bread triangles in the mixture and top with the crushed cornflowers.
3. Preheat the air Fryer to 180°C. Close the fry box and place the coated bread triangles inside for 4 minutes. Allow them to cook at the same temperature for at least another 20 minutes.
4. To ensure an even cook, flip the triangles. Serve these pieces with chocolate sauce.

Mint Galette

Preparation Time: 10 minutes | Cooking Time: 15 minutes | Servings: 1

Ingredients:

- 2 cups of mint leaves (Sliced fine)
- 2 medium potatoes boiled and mashed
- 1 ½ cup of coarsely crushed peanuts
- 3 tsp. of ginger finely chopped
- 1-2 tbsp. of fresh coriander leaves
- 2 or 3 green chilies finely chopped
- 1 ½ tbsp. of lemon juice
- Salt and pepper to the taste

Directions:

1. Combine the cut mint leaves and the remaining ingredients in a clean dish. Make flat and spherical galettes out of this mixture.
2. Gently wet the galettes with water. Each peanut should be covered with a smashed galette.
3. Preheat the air Fryer to 160 degrees Fahrenheit. Cook the galettes in a frying pan for 5 minutes. Allow for another 25 minutes of steaming at the same temperature.
4. Continue flipping them around until you have an even cook. Serve with chutney, basil, or ketchup on the side.

Cottage Cheese Sticks

Preparation Time: 10 minutes | Cooking Time: 15 minutes | Servings: 1

Ingredients:

- 2 cups of cottage cheese
- 1 big lemon-juiced
- 1 tbsp. of ginger-garlic paste
- For seasoning, use salt and red chili powder in small amounts
- ½ tsp. of carom
- One or two papadums
- 4 or 5 tbsp. of corn flour
- 1 cup of water

Directions:

1. Cut the cheese into long, thin slices. Currently, make a marinade using lemon juice, red chili powder, spices, ginger garlic paste, and carom.
2. Allow the cottage cheese slices to marinade in the sauce for around 20 minutes before rolling them in dry corn flour to set them behind.
3. Put the papadum in a pot and toast it. Crush them into extremely little pieces and fry them. Take another bottle and fill it with around 100 ml of water.
4. In this water, dissolve 2 tbsp corn flour. Dip the cottage cheese parts in the corn flour solution and roll them onto the smashed papadum bits so that the papadum adheres to the curd cheese.
5. Preheat the air Fryer for 10 minutes at 290 degrees Fahrenheit. Then, open the fryer basket and place the cottage cheese chunks inside. Close the basin tightly. Allow the fryer to rest at 160° for another 20 minutes.
6. Halfway through, open the basket and scatter some cottage cheese to allow for typical cooking. You should eat them with ketchup or mint chutney until they're cooked.

Palak Galette

Preparation Time: 10 minutes | Cooking Time: 15 minutes | Servings: 1

Ingredients:

- 2 tbsp. of garam masala
- 2 cups of palak leaves

- 1 ½ cup of coarsely crushed peanuts
- 3 tsp. of ginger finely chopped
- 1-2 tbsp. of fresh coriander leaves
- 2 or 3 green chilies finely chopped
- 1 ½ tbsp. of lemon juice
- Salt and pepper to the taste

Directions:

1. In a sterile basin, combine the components. Make flat and round galettes out of this mixture. Gently wet the galettes with water. On each galette, coat with crushed peanuts.
2. Preheat the air Fryer to 160° F for 5 minutes. Place the galettes in the fry basket and cook for another 25 minutes at the same temperature. Turn them over to get them to cook. With ketchup or mint chutney, serve.

Spinach Pie

Preparation Time: 10 minutes | Cooking Time: 15 minutes | Servings: 1

Ingredients:

- 7 ounces of flour
- 2 tablespoons of butter
- 7 ounces of spinach
- 1 tablespoon of olive oil
- 2 eggs
- 2 tablespoons of milk
- 3 ounces of cottage cheese
- Salt and black pepper to the taste
- 1 yellow onion, chopped

Directions:

1. In a food processor, combine the flour and butter, 1 egg, milk, salt, and pepper, and pulse well. Transfer to a basin, knead, cover, and set aside for 10 minutes.
2. Heat the oil in a skillet over medium heat, then add the onion and spinach, constantly stirring for 2 minutes.
3. Stir in the salt, pepper, leftover egg, and cottage cheese, and heat through.
4. Divide the dough into four pieces, roll each slice, lay it on the bottom of a ramekin, spread the spinach filling over the dough, and cook for 15 minutes at 360° F in the basket of your air Fryer.
5. Serve hot.
6. Enjoy!

Balsamic Artichokes

Preparation Time: 10 minutes | Cooking Time: 15 minutes | Servings: 1

Ingredients:

- 4 big artichokes, trimmed
- Salt and black pepper to the taste
- 2 tablespoons of lemon juice
- ¼ cup of extra virgin olive oil
- 2 teaspoons of balsamic vinegar
- 1 teaspoon of oregano, dried
- 2 garlic cloves, minced

Directions:

1. Season the artichokes with salt and pepper, rub with half the oil and half the lemon juice, and cook for 7 minutes at 360° F in an air Fryer.
2. Meanwhile, combine the remaining lemon juice, vinegar, oil, salt, pepper, garlic, and oregano in a mixing bowl.
3. Arrange the artichokes on a platter, drizzle with the balsamic vinaigrette, and serve.
4. Enjoy!

CHAPTER 4:
Poultry

Sticky Chicken Wings

Preparation Time: 2 hours | Cooking Time: 15 minutes | Servings: 6

Ingredients:
- 16 chicken wings
- 2 tablespoons maple syrup
- 2 tablespoons tamari sauce
- 3 tablespoons lime juice
- ¼ teaspoon white pepper
- Salt & black pepper as needed

Directions:
1. Whisk all the ingredients, add chicken last and toss to coat.
2. Keep in the fridge for 2 hours and transfer the chicken to the air fryer.
3. Cook for 6 minutes at 370 degrees Fahrenheit.
4. Increase the temperature to 400 degrees Fahrenheit and cook the chicken for 3 minutes.
5. Serve once done, and enjoy!

Chicken & Apricot Sauce

Preparation time: 10 minutes | Cooking time: 20 minutes | Servings: 4

Ingredients:
- ¼ cup white wine
- ¼ cup chicken broth
- 2 tablespoons maple syrup
- 1 tablespoon olive oil
- ¼ cup apricot preserves
- 1 ½ teaspoon grated ginger
- 2 tablespoons white vinegar
- ½ teaspoon dried marjoram
- ½ teaspoon smoked paprika
- Salt & black pepper as needed
- 1 medium-cut piece of whole chicken

Directions:
1. Marinate chicken with marjoram, paprika, oil, salt, and pepper.
2. Add to the air fryer and cook for 10 minutes at 360 degrees Fahrenheit.
3. Transfer chicken into a pan that fits the air fryer and adds the remaining ingredients.
4. Stir and add the pan with the contents to the air fryer and cook for an additional 10 minutes at the same temperature.
5. Serve once done, and enjoy!

Chicken With Coconut Sauce

Preparation time: 10 minutes | Cooking time: 12 minutes | Servings: 6

Ingredients:
- 1 cup chicken broth
- ¼ cup coconut milk
- 1 tablespoon olive oil
- 3 ½ oz chicken breasts
- 1 tablespoon lime juice
- 2 teaspoons sweet paprika
- 1 teaspoon red pepper flakes
- Salt & black pepper as needed
- 1 ¼ cups chopped yellow onion
- 2 tablespoons chopped scallions

Directions:
1. Heat oil in a pan over medium heat that fits the air fryer.
2. Stir and cook onions in it for 4 minutes.
3. Add the remaining ingredients and toss the chicken last with salt & pepper.
4. Stir and transfer to the air fryer to cook for 12 minutes at 360 degrees Fahrenheit.

5. Serve once done, and enjoy!

Chicken With Cilantro Sauce

Preparation Time: 30 minutes | Cooking Time: 25 minutes | Servings: 6

Ingredients:
- 4 garlic cloves
- A pinch of salt
- ½ cup olive oil
- ¼ cup red wine
- 12 chicken thighs
- 1 cup chopped cilantro
- Honey as needed
- 1 teaspoon dried oregano

Directions:
1. Pulse all the ingredients except chicken in a food processor.
2. Combine the chicken with the mixture thoroughly and refrigerate for half an hour.
3. Drain the chicken and add to the air fryer basket.
4. Cook for 25 minutes at 380 degrees Fahrenheit, flipping once after 15 minutes.
5. Serve once done, and enjoy!

Mexican Chicken

Preparation Time: 10 minutes | Cooking Time: 20 minutes | Servings: 4

Ingredients:
- 16 oz. salsa verde
- 1 tablespoon olive oil
- ¼ cup chopped parsley
- 1 teaspoon garlic powder
- Salt & black pepper as needed
- 1 ½ cup grated Mexican cheese
- 1 oz. skinless & boneless chicken breast

Directions:
1. Use a baking dish that fits the air fryer and marinate the chicken breasts with all the ingredients except cheese.
2. Add to the air fryer and cook for 20 minutes at 380 degrees Fahrenheit.
3. Top with cheese and cook for an additional 2 minutes.
4. Serve once done, and enjoy!

Chicken & Black Olives Sauce

Preparation Time: 10 minutes | Cooking Time: 8 minutes | Servings: 2

Ingredients:
- 2 tablespoons olive oil
- 3 minced garlic cloves
- 1 cup pitted black olives
- ¼ cup chopped cilantro
- 1 tablespoon lime juice
- Salt & black pepper as needed
- 1 cut into 4 pieces chicken breast

Directions:
1. Blend a tablespoon of olive oil, lime juice, cilantro, olives, salt, and pepper in a food processor and put it in a bowl.
2. Marinate the chicken with a tablespoon of olive oil, garlic, salt, and pepper and transfer to a preheated air fryer.
3. Cook for 8 minutes at 370 Fahrenheit.
4. Serve with a topping of olives blend on top!

Maple Duck Breasts

Preparation Time: 10 minutes | Cooking Time: 22 minutes | Servings: 2

Ingredients:
- 1 teaspoon maple syrup

- 1 tablespoon mustard
- 1 teaspoon tomato puree
- ½ teaspoon apple vinegar
- 1 halved smoked duck breast

Directions:
1. Whisk all the ingredients except duck breasts well in a bowl
2. Toss in the duck breasts to coat properly.
3. Add the duck breasts to the air fryer and cook for 15 minutes at 370 degrees Fahrenheit.
4. Remove the cooked duck breasts, toss them in the same bowl of maple mixture and return the duck pieces to the air fryer.
5. Cook for an additional 6 minutes and serve once done.

Creamy Coconut Chicken

Preparation Time: 2 hours | Cooking Time: 25 minutes | Servings: 4

Ingredients:
- 4 big chicken legs
- 2 tablespoons grated ginger
- 5 teaspoons turmeric powder
- 4 tablespoons coconut milk
- Salt & black pepper as needed

Directions:
1. Whisk all the ingredients except chicken in a bowl.
2. Toss in the chicken to coat properly and set aside for 2 hours.
3. Add the coated chicken to a preheated air fryer and cook for 25 minutes at 370 degrees Fahrenheit.
4. Serve once done, and enjoy!

Chicken & Asparagus

Preparation Time: 10 minutes | Cooking Time: 20 minutes | Servings: 4

Ingredients:
- 8 asparagus spears
- 8 halved chicken wings
- 1 teaspoon ground coriander
- Salt & black pepper as needed
- 1 tablespoon chopped oregano

Directions:
1. Use a kitchen towel to dry chicken wings and season with coriander, oregano, salt, and pepper.
2. Transfer to the air fryer basket and cook for 20 minutes at 360 degrees Fahrenheit.
3. Meanwhile, add asparagus to a heated pan over medium heat.
4. Add water and let steam for a few minutes.
5. Remove the asparagus to a bowl filled with ice water.
6. Drain the asparagus and place neatly on plates.
7. Serve with chicken wings on the side.

Delicious Herbed Chicken

Preparation Time: 30 minutes | Cooking Time: 40 minutes | Servings: 4

Ingredients:
- 1 whole chicken
- 2 tablespoons olive oil
- 1 tablespoon lime juice
- 1 teaspoon garlic powder
- 1 teaspoon onion powder
- ½ teaspoon dried oregano
- 1 teaspoon dried rosemary
- Salt & black pepper as needed

Directions:
1. Marinate the chicken with all the ingredients and set aside for half an hour.

2. Transfer to the air fryer and cook for 20 minutes from both sides at 360 degrees Fahrenheit.
3. Remove chicken to cool once done, slice, and serve.

Chinese Stuffed Chicken

Preparation Time: 10 minutes | Cooking Time: 35 minutes | Servings: 8

Ingredients:
- 1 cubed yam
- 10 wolfberries
- 4 ginger slices
- 1 whole chicken
- 1 teaspoon tamari sauce
- 2 chopped red pepper
- 3 teaspoons sesame oil
- Salt & white pepper as needed

Directions:
1. Marinate chicken with tamari sauce, sesame oil, salt, and pepper, and stuff it with yam, wolfberries, ginger, and pepper.
2. Transfer the chicken to the air fryer and cook for 20 minutes at 400 degrees Fahrenheit.
3. Slice once done and serve!

Chicken With Capers

Preparation Time: 10 minutes | Cooking Time: 20 minutes | Servings: 2

Ingredients:
- 4 chicken thighs
- 1 sliced lemon
- ½ cup chicken broth
- 3 tablespoons capers
- 4 minced garlic cloves
- 4 chopped scallions
- 3 tablespoons melted butter
- Salt & black pepper as needed

Directions:
1. Rub chicken with butter and season with salt and pepper.
2. Transfer it to a baking dish that fits in the air fryer.
3. Toss the remaining ingredients except for scallions in the chicken and combine them properly.
4. Add the baking dish with contents to the air fryer and cook for 20 minutes at 370 degrees Fahrenheit, shaking after 10 minutes.
5. Serve the chicken with scallions and enjoy!

Easy Duck Breasts

Preparation Time: 10 minutes | Cooking Time: 40 minutes | Servings: 6

Ingredients:
- ½ cup white wine
- 3 tablespoons flour
- 2 cups chicken broth
- 6 halved duck breasts
- ¼ cup chopped cilantro
- 6 tablespoons melted butter
- 2 cups chopped mushrooms
- Salt & black pepper as needed

Directions:
1. Marinate duck breasts with salt and pepper and three tablespoons of butter in a bowl.
2. Combine remaining melted butter with the remaining ingredients except for mushrooms and parsley in a separate bowl and stir well.
3. Place duck breasts in a baking dish that fits in the air fryer and add the melted butter sauce with mushrooms and cilantro on top.

68

4. Cook for 40 minutes in the air fryer at 350 degrees Fahrenheit.
5. Serve once done, and enjoy!

Chicken Breasts In Tomatoes Sauce

Preparation Time: 10 minutes | Cooking Time: 20 minutes | Servings: 4

Ingredients:
- 1 chopped red onion
- ¼ cup red wine vinegar
- ¼ cup grated cheddar
- Cooking spray as needed
- ¼ teaspoon garlic powder
- Salt & black pepper as needed
- 14 oz. chopped canned tomatoes
- 4 skinless & boneless chicken breasts

Directions:
1. Grease a baking dish that fits the air fryer with cooking spray.
2. Add chicken and the remaining ingredients, combine well, and transfer the dish to the air fryer.
3. Cook for 20 minutes at 400 degrees Fahrenheit.
4. Serve once done, and enjoy!

Chicken Thighs With Apple Mix

Preparation Time: 12 hours | Cooking Time: 30 minutes | Servings: 4

Ingredients:
- ¾ cup apple juice
- ½ cup honey
- ½ teaspoon dried rosemary
- 1 tablespoon grated ginger
- 3 cored & quartered apples
- 3 tablespoons chopped onion
- Salt & black pepper as needed
- 1 tablespoon apple cider vinegar
- 8 bone and skin-on chicken thighs

Directions:
1. Marinate chicken with all the ingredients except apple pieces.
2. Toss, cover, and refrigerate for 12 hours.
3. Add the mixture to a baking dish that fits the air fryer and toss in apple pieces.
4. Transfer the dish to the air fryer and cook for half an hour at 350 degrees Fahrenheit.
5. Serve once done, and enjoy!

Chicken Creamy Veggie Mix

Preparation Time: 10 minutes | Cooking Time: 30 minutes | Servings: 6

Ingredients:
- 1 bay leaf
- 2 cups whipping cream
- 29 ounces of chicken broth
- 8 oz. chopped mushrooms
- 17 oz. trimmed asparagus
- 3 tablespoons melted butter
- ½ cup chopped yellow onion
- ¾ cup chopped red peppers
- 3 teaspoons chopped oregano
- Salt & black pepper as needed
- 40 oz. boneless & skinless chicken pieces

Directions:
1. Heat butter in a pan over medium heat.
2. Stir in onion and peppers and cook for 3 minutes.
3. Add bay leaf, stock, salt, and pepper, let it come to a boil, and simmer for 10 minutes.

4. Stir in the remaining ingredients and transfer to the air fryer to cook for 15 minutes at 360 degrees Fahrenheit.
5. Serve once done, and enjoy!

Air Fried Chicken Mix

Preparation Time: 10 minutes | Cooking Time: 20 minutes | Servings: 8

Ingredients:
- 1 green bell pepper
- 1 minced garlic clove
- 1 tablespoon canola oil
- 1 chopped red onion
- Cooking spray as needed
- 1 chopped red bell pepper
- 10 halved white mushrooms
- Salt & black pepper as needed
- 2 tablespoons shredded mozzarella cheese
- 3 oz. skinless & boneless chicken breasts

Directions:
1. Marinate chicken with garlic, salt, and pepper and grease with cooking spray.
2. Transfer to a preheated air fryer and cook for 12 minutes at 390 degrees Fahrenheit.
3. Meanwhile, heat oil in a pan over medium heat and sauté onions for 2 minutes.
4. Add the remaining ingredients except for cheese and cook for 8 minutes while stirring occasionally.
5. Serve chicken on a plate with the pan mixture with cheese on top!

Chicken Cacciatore

Preparation Time: 10 minutes | Cooking Time: 20 minutes | Servings: 4

Ingredients:
- 1 bay leaf
- 1 teaspoon minced garlic
- 1 chopped yellow onion
- 1 teaspoon dried thyme
- 8 bone-in chicken drumsticks
- Salt and black pepper as needed
- ½ cup pitted & sliced black olives
- 28 oz. crushed canned tomatoes and juice

Directions:
1. Combine all the ingredients in a heatproof dish that fits the air fryer.
2. Add the dish to a preheated air fryer and cook for 20 minutes at 365 degrees Fahrenheit.
3. Serve once done, and enjoy!

Turkey With Veggies

Preparation Time: 10 minutes | Cooking Time: 34 minutes | Servings: 4

Ingredients:
- 2 bay leaves
- 1 chopped carrot
- 1 cup chicken broth
- 2 oz. turkey quarters
- 3 minced garlic cloves
- 1 chopped celery stalk
- 2 tablespoons olive oil
- ½ teaspoon dried sage
- 1 chopped yellow onion
- ½ teaspoon dried thyme
- ½ teaspoon dried oregano
- Salt & black pepper as needed

Directions:
1. Marinate turkey quarters with a tablespoon of oil, herbs, salt, and pepper.

2. Add to the air fryer and cook for 20 minutes at 360 degrees Fahrenheit.
3. Mix the remaining ingredients in a pan that fits in the air fryer.
4. Add the turkey to the pan, add the pan to the air fryer and cook for an additional 14 minutes.
5. Serve once done, and enjoy!

Lemon Chicken

Preparation Time: 10 minutes | Cooking Time: 30 minutes | Servings: 6

Ingredients:
- 2 lemon juice
- 2 grated lemon zest
- 1 tablespoon canola oil
- Salt & black pepper as needed
- 1 medium-cut piece of whole chicken

Directions:
1. Marinate chicken with all the ingredients.
2. Add to the air fryer and cook for half an hour at 350 degrees Fahrenheit, flipping pieces after 15 minutes.
3. Serve once done, and enjoy!

Cheese Crusted Chicken

Preparation Time: 10 minutes | Cooking Time: 15 minutes | Servings: 4

Ingredients:
- 1 beaten egg
- 1 tablespoon water
- ½ cup avocado oil
- ¼ teaspoon minced garlic
- Salt & black pepper as needed
- 1 cup shredded asiago cheese
- 1 cup grated mozzarella cheese
- 4 cooked & crumbled bacon slices
- 4 skinless & boneless chicken breasts

Directions:
1. Combine garlic, mozzarella, salt, and pepper in a bowl.
2. Whisk eggs with water in a separate bowl.
3. Sprinkle salt and pepper over the chicken and coat each piece first in egg mixture, then in cheese mixture.
4. Place the pieces in the air fryer and cook for 15 minutes at 320 degrees Fahrenheit.
5. Serve by topping with bacon and asiago cheese.

Chicken With Garlic Sauce

Preparation Time: 10 minutes | Cooking Time: 20 minutes | Servings: 4

Ingredients:
- 2 thyme sprigs
- 1 tablespoon olive oil
- ¼ cup chicken broth
- ¼ cup dry white wine
- 1 tablespoon melted butter
- Salt & black pepper as needed
- 2 tablespoons chopped cilantro
- 4 skin-on & bone-in chicken breasts
- 40 peeled & chopped garlic cloves

Directions:
1. Marinate chicken breasts with oil, salt, and pepper.
2. Transfer to the air fryer to cook for 4 minutes from both sides at 360 degrees Fahrenheit.
3. Remove the chicken to a dish that fits the air fryer and toss in the remaining ingredients.
4. Add the dish to the air fryer and cook for an additional 15 minutes at 350 degrees Fahrenheit.
5. Serve once done, and enjoy!

Pepperoni Chicken

Preparation Time: 10 minutes | Cooking Time: 22 minutes | Servings: 6

Ingredients:
- 14 oz. tomato puree
- 1 tablespoon olive oil
- 6 oz. sliced mozzarella
- 2 oz. sliced pepperoni
- 1 teaspoon garlic powder
- 1 teaspoon dried thyme
- Salt & black pepper as needed
- 4 medium skinless & boneless chicken breasts

Directions:
1. Combine chicken with garlic powder, thyme, salt, and pepper.
2. Add the chicken to the air fryer to cook for 6 minutes at 350 degrees Fahrenheit.
3. Remove the chicken to a dish that fits in the air fryer and top with mozzarella slices, tomato puree, and pepperoni slices.
4. Add the dish to the air fryer to cook for an additional 15 minutes at the same temperature.
5. Serve once done, and enjoy!

Turkey, Peas & Mushrooms Casserole

Preparation Time: 10 minutes | Cooking Time: 20 minutes | Servings: 4

Ingredients:
- ½ cup peas
- 1 cup bread cubes
- 1 cup chicken broth
- 1 chopped celery stalk
- 1 chopped red onion
- 1 cup mushrooms soup cream
- Salt & black pepper as needed
- 2 oz. skinless & boneless turkey breasts

Directions:
1. Combine turkey with all the ingredients except bread cubes and mushroom cream in a pan that fits in the air fryer.
2. Add to the air fryer for 15 minutes at 360 degrees Fahrenheit.
3. Stir in bread cubes and mushroom soup cream and cook for an additional 5 minutes at the same temperature.
4. Serve once done, and enjoy!

Duck & Veggies

Preparation Time: 10 minutes | Cooking Time: 20 minutes | Servings: 8

Ingredients:
- 2 chopped carrots
- 1 cup chicken broth
- 2 chopped zucchini
- 3 tablespoon white wine
- 1 small grated ginger piece
- Salt & black pepper as needed
- 1 chopped in medium pieces duck

Directions:
1. Combine all the ingredients in a pan that fits in the air fryer.
2. Cook for 20 minutes at 370 degrees Fahrenheit.
3. Serve once done, and enjoy!

Tasty Greek Chicken

Preparation Time: 10 minutes | Cooking Time: 15 minutes | Servings: 4

Ingredients:
- 1 lime juice
- 1 lime sliced
- 1 oz. chicken thighs
- 2 tablespoons olive oil
- 3 minced garlic cloves
- 1 teaspoon dried thyme
- ½ oz. trimmed asparagus
- 1 roughly-chopped zucchini
- Salt & black pepper as needed

Directions:
1. Combine all the ingredients in a heatproof pan that fits the air fryer.
2. Cook for 15 minutes at 380 degrees Fahrenheit in a preheated air fryer.
3. Serve once done, and enjoy!

Chicken Chestnuts Mix

Preparation Time: 10 minutes | Cooking Time: 12 minutes | Servings: 2

Ingredients:
- ½ oz. chicken pieces
- 2 tortillas for serving
- 2 tablespoons tamari sauce
- A pinch of grated ginger
- 2 teaspoons minced garlic
- A pinch of ground allspice
- 2 tablespoons chicken broth
- 1 chopped small yellow onion
- 4 tablespoons water chestnuts
- 2 tablespoons balsamic vinegar

Directions:
1. Combine all the ingredients in a heatproof pan that fits the air fryer.
2. Cook for 12 minutes at 360 degrees Fahrenheit in the air fryer.
3. Serve once done, and enjoy!

Veggie Stuffed Chicken Breasts

Preparation Time: 10 minutes | Cooking Time: 15 minutes | Servings: 4

Ingredients:
- 1 chopped zucchini
- 3 chopped tomatoes
- 1 chopped red onion
- 2 tablespoons canola oil
- 1 cup shredded parmesan
- 1 teaspoon Italian seasoning
- 2 chopped yellow bell peppers
- Salt & black pepper as needed
- 4 skinless & boneless chicken breasts

Directions:
1. Create a slit mimicking a pocket on each chicken breast.
2. Rub it with canola oil, salt, and pepper.
3. Combine the remaining ingredients except for parmesan in a bowl, fill chicken breasts with this mixture, and sprinkle parmesan cheese on top.
4. Transfer to the air fryer basket and cook for 15 minutes at 350 degrees Fahrenheit.
5. Serve once done, and enjoy!

Duck Breasts & Raspberry Sauce

Preparation Time: 10 minutes | Cooking Time: 15 minutes | Servings: 4

Ingredients:
- ½ cup water
- ½ cup raspberries
- 1 tablespoon brown sugar
- Cooking spray as needed
- 1 teaspoon balsamic vinegar
- Salt & black pepper as needed
- ½ teaspoon cinnamon powder
- 2 skin-on & scored duck breasts

Directions:
1. Sprinkle duck breasts with salt and pepper and grease with cooking spray.
2. Transfer to a preheated air fryer and cook for 10 minutes at 350 degrees Fahrenheit.
3. Meanwhile, heat water over medium and add the remaining ingredients to a pan.
4. Stir and let it simmer and blend in a blender to puree and return to the pan
5. Add the cooked duck breasts to the sauce in the pan, combine and serve.

Simple Duck Breasts

Preparation Time: 10 minutes | Cooking Time: 15 minutes | Servings: 4

Ingredients:
- 1 ½ tablespoon olive oil
- 2 tablespoons lime juice
- ½ teaspoon lime pepper
- Salt & black pepper as needed
- 4 skinless & boneless duck breasts
- 4 peeled, tops cut off & quartered garlic heads

Directions:
1. Marinate duck breasts with all the ingredients in a bowl.
2. Transfer to the air fryer and cook for 15 minutes at 350 degrees Fahrenheit.
3. Serve once done, and enjoy!

Chicken Breasts & Passion Fruit Sauce

Preparation Time: 10 minutes | Cooking Time: 10 minutes | Servings: 4

Ingredients:
- 2-star anise
- 2 oz. honey
- 4 chicken breasts
- 1 tablespoon whiskey
- 1 bunch chopped dill
- Salt & black pepper as needed
- 4 halved, deseeded & pulp reserved passion fruits

Directions:
1. Add the passion fruit pulp with the remaining ingredients except chicken in a heated pan over medium heat.
2. Stir and let it simmer for 5 minutes before removing it from heat.
3. Meanwhile, season chicken with salt and pepper and add a preheated air fryer.
4. Cook it for 10 minutes at 360 degrees Fahrenheit.
5. Serve chicken with the sauce in the pan on top!

Quick Creamy Chicken Casserole

Preparation Time: 10 minutes | Cooking Time: 12 minutes | Servings: 4

Ingredients:
1. 1 ½ cups milk
2. 3 tablespoons flour
3. 1 cup bread crumbs
4. ½ cup cooking cream
5. 4 tablespoons butter

6. 10 oz. chopped spinach
7. ½ cup grated mozzarella
8. Salt & black pepper as needed
9. 2 cup skinless, boneless & cubed chicken breasts

Directions:
1. Melt butter in a pan over medium and stir in flour as well.
2. Stir in milk, cooking cream, and mozzarella for 2 minutes and remove from heat.
3. Add chicken and spinach to a pan that fits in the air fryer.
4. Season with salt and pepper spread the cream mixture and top with bread crumbs.
5. Add to the air fryer and cook for 12 minutes at 350 degrees Fahrenheit.
6. Serve once done, and enjoy!

Chicken & Radish Mix

Preparation Time: 10 minutes | Cooking Time: 30 minutes | Servings: 4

Ingredients:
- 1 teaspoon sugar
- 6 halved radishes
- 1 cup chicken broth
- 1 tablespoon olive oil
- 4 bone-in chicken thighs
- 3 thinly-cut sticks of carrots
- 2 tablespoons chopped dill
- Salt & black pepper as needed

Directions:
1. Add broth, dill, carrots, sugar, and radishes to a heated pan over medium heat.
2. Strictly use a pan that fits in the air fryer. Let the mixture simmer for 20 minutes, covered partly.
3. Meanwhile, marinate the chicken with olive oil, salt, and pepper, and add to the air fryer.
4. Cook for 4 minutes at 350 degrees Fahrenheit.
5. Remove the chicken to the radish mixture, toss and transfer everything to the air fryer to cook for an additional 4 minutes.
6. Serve once done, and enjoy!

Turkey Burgers

Preparation Time: 10 minutes | Cooking Time: 8 minutes | Servings: 4

Ingredients:
- 1 minced shallot
- 1 grated lemon zest
- A drizzle of olive oil
- 2 teaspoons lemon juice
- Guacamole as needed
- Burger buns as needed
- 1 oz. ground turkey meat
- 1 teaspoon ground coriander
- 1 teaspoon sweet paprika
- Salt & black pepper as needed
- 1 minced small jalapeno pepper

Directions:
1. Combine all the ingredients in a bowl and shape burger patties out of the mixture.
2. Place the patties in a preheated air fryer with a drizzle of oil.
3. Cook for 8 minutes from both sides at 370 degrees Fahrenheit.
4. Add the patties to slightly toasted buns and enjoy with guacamole.

Simple Chicken Lunch

Preparation Time: 10 minutes | Cooking Time: 20 minutes | Servings: 6

Ingredients:
- 3 chopped carrots
- ¼ cup chicken broth
- 1 chopped bunch of baby spinach
- 1 cup shredded chicken
- Salt & black pepper as needed
- 1 cup roughly-sliced shiitake mushrooms

Directions:
1. Blend broth with baby spinach in a blender and transfer to a pan that fits in the air fryer.
2. Toss in the remaining ingredients and add to the air fryer
3. Cook for 18 minutes at 350 degrees Fahrenheit.
4. Serve once done, and enjoy!

Chicken Mix Casserole

Preparation Time: 10 minutes | Cooking Time: 30 minutes | Servings: 8

Ingredients:
- 12 oz. corn
- 1 cup clean salsa
- 6 chopped kale leaves
- ½ cup chopped parsley
- 1 cup clean tomato puree
- Cooking spray as needed
- 2 teaspoons chili powder
- 2 teaspoons ground cumin
- 1 tablespoon garlic powder
- 14 oz. canned black beans
- 2 chopped jalapeno peppers
- 1 cup already-cooked quinoa
- ½ cup chopped green onions
- 3 cups shredded mozzarella cheese
- 3 cups cooked & shredded chicken breast

Directions:
1. Grease a baking dish that fits in the air fryer with cooking spray.
2. Add all the ingredients, toss and transfer the dish to the air fryer.
3. Cook for 17 minutes at 350 degrees Fahrenheit.
4. Slice, serve warm, and enjoy!

Duck & Cherries

Preparation Time: 10 minutes | Cooking Time: 20 minutes | Servings: 4

Ingredients:
- ½ cup sugar
- ¼ cup maple syrup
- 1 chopped jalapeno
- 4 chopped sage leaves
- 2 cups pitted cherries
- 2 cups sliced rhubarb
- ⅓ cup balsamic vinegar
- 1 teaspoon minced garlic
- 1 teaspoon ground cumin
- ½ teaspoon ground clove
- 1 tablespoon grated ginger
- ½ cup chopped red onion
- ½ teaspoon cinnamon powder
- Salt & black pepper as needed
- 4 boneless, skin-on & scored duck breasts

Directions:
1. Season duck with salt and pepper and add to the air fryer to cook for 5 minutes from both sides at 350 degrees Fahrenheit.

2. Meanwhile, add all the ingredients to a heated pan over medium heat.
3. Stir, let it come to a simmer, and cook for 10 minutes.
4. Remove the air-fried duck breasts to the mixture pan, stir and serve warm.

Dijon Baked Chicken Breast

Preparation Time: 5 minutes | Cooking Time: 24 minutes | Servings: 5

Ingredients:
- ¼ teaspoon salt
- 1 tablespoon olive oil
- ¼ cup Dijon mustard
- 1 tablespoon minced garlic
- Parchment paper as needed
- ¼ cup freshly-chopped cilantro
- ¼ teaspoon ground black pepper
- 1 ½ oz. thinly-sliced chicken breast
- 1 tablespoon fresh-squeezed lime juice

Directions:
1. Preheat the air fryer to 375 degrees and line your air fryer tray with parchment paper.
2. Arrange the chicken breasts on the tray.
3. Combine all the ingredients in a bowl and add them to the chicken breasts.
4. Add the tray to the air fryer and cook for 18 minutes.
5. Slice before serving hot!

Air Fried Chicken Quesadilla

Preparation Time: 10 minutes | Cooking Time: 12 minutes | Servings: 2

Ingredients
- 4 corn tortillas (gluten-free)
- 3-4 tablespoons of shredded cheddar cheese
- 12 ounces chicken breast, diced into cubes
- 1 cup guacamole

Directions
1. Brush some oil over an air fryer basket.
2. Layout the tortillas in it.
3. Drizzle with shredded cheese and chicken.
4. Put the other tortilla over it and do this for other tortillas.
5. Put in the air fryer and cook at 350 degrees F for 12 minutes.
6. Serve with guacamole

Cosmic Wings

Preparation Time: 10 minutes | Cooking Time: 12 minutes | Servings: 2

Ingredients
- 12 ounces of chicken wings
- ½ tablespoon of garlic paste
- ¼ tablespoon of onion powder
- ¼ tablespoon of paprika
- ½ tablespoon of dried cilantro
- A pinch of oregano
- 4 ounces Jerry Sauce
- 1/2 lemon, juiced
- Salt and pepper according to taste

Directions
1. Mix all the ingredients in a bowl except the chicken, lemon juice, and cosmic jerry sauce.
2. Now use this marinade to coat the chicken.
3. Put the chicken in an air fryer basket sprayed with cooking spray.
4. Transfer it to the air fryer and cook the chicken at 375 degrees F for 12 minutes.

5. Make sure to flip the chicken after 6 minutes.
6. Once it's done, drizzle cosmic jerry sauce and lemon juice on it and serve!

Air Fryer Chicken Meatballs with Pasta

Preparation Time: 10 minutes | Cooking Time: 12 minutes | Servings: 3

Ingredients
- 3 pounds of ground chicken breast
- 2 cups Italian breadcrumbs
- 2 organic eggs
- 2 tablespoons of Italian seasoning
- Salt and black pepper according to taste
- 1 cup of marinara sauce
- 2/3 cup of grated mozzarella cheese
- 4 cups of pasta, boiled and drained

Directions
1. Cook the pasta according to package instructions.
2. Mix all the listed ingredients in a bowl except the mozzarella and marinara sauce.
3. Thoroughly stir the grounded chicken breasts in it.
4. Use your hands to make meatballs out of the batter.
5. Brush the meatballs with cooking oil.
6. Align it in the air fryer basket brushed with cooking spray.
7. Let it cook in the air fryer at 375 degrees F for 12 minutes.
8. Open the air fryer and drizzle the meatballs with marinara sauce and mozzarella.
9. Close the door and cook for another 4 minutes.
10. Once it's done, serve with the cooked pasta!

Delicious Turkey Meatballs

Preparation Time: 10 minutes | Cooking Time: 12 minutes | Servings: 4

Ingredients
- 2 pounds of ground turkey
- 1 cup of breadcrumbs
- 2 whisked eggs
- ½ cup of fresh cilantro
- 2 tablespoons tamari sauce
- Black pepper according to taste
- Cooking oil spray

Directions
1. Mix all the ingredients in a bowl.
2. Thoroughly mix them until the batter becomes even.
3. Use your hands to make meatballs from the mixture.
4. Grease the meatballs with cooking spray.
5. Put the meatballs in the air fryer basket lined with parchment paper.
6. Transfer to the air fryer and cook at 400 degrees F for 12 minutes.
7. Make sure to flip the meatballs after 6 minutes.
8. Serve once done!

Saucy Asian Chicken Wings

Preparation Time: 10 minutes | Cooking Time: 12 minutes | Servings: 4

Ingredients
- 16 chicken wings, hot wings cut
- Salt and pepper according to taste
- 3 teaspoons of garlic paste
- Cooking spray
- 2/3 cup of chicken stock
- 2/3 teaspoon of garlic powder
- 2 tablespoons of tamari sauce
- 1.5 cups of sugar

- 1/2 cup of vinegar
- ¼ cup cornstarch
- 1/3 cup of water

Directions
1. Add the water to the cornstarch, mix, and put it aside.
2. Place the chicken wings in a bowl and drizzle with oil, salt & pepper.
3. Put it in an air fryer basket and transfer it to the air fryer.
4. Set the time of the air fryer to 12 minutes.
5. Adjust the temperature to 400 degrees F.
6. Simultaneously, simmer the broth in a frying pan for some time.
7. Then add all the remaining ingredients, including the cornstarch mixture.
8. Half cook these ingredients and then add the air-fried chicken wings from the air fryer.
9. Let all the ingredients cook for 2 minutes.
10. Once it's done, serve!

Greek Chicken Meatballs

Preparation Time: 20 minutes | Cooking Time: 14 minutes | Servings: 4

Ingredients
- 2 pounds of ground chicken
- 2 organic eggs
- 3 tablespoons of garlic paste
- 2 tablespoons of dried thyme
- 2 teaspoons of lime zest
- 2 teaspoons of dried onion powder
- 1.5 teaspoons of kosher salt
- ¼ teaspoon fresh ground black pepper
- Cooking spray
- 4 servings of rice
- 2 cups of mixed vegetables, cooked

Directions
1. Mix all the main ingredients in a bowl and thoroughly stir.
2. Knead the batter and use your hands to make meatballs.
3. Spray cooking spray over the meatballs.
4. Put the meatballs in an air fryer basket greased with cooking oil.
5. Adjust the temperature of the air fryer to 350 degrees F and set the time to 14 minutes.
6. Transfer the basket to the air fryer unit.
7. Once the meatballs are done, serve with the side servings!

Air Fryer Chicken Nuggets

Preparation Time: 10 minutes | Cooking Time: 10 minutes | Servings: 2

Ingredients
- 4 pounds of chicken breasts, sliced into half-inch cubes
- 2/3 cup of pickle juice
- 2/3 cup of milk
- 4 eggs

Breading Ingredients
- 2 cups of all-purpose flour
- ¼ cup of powdered sugar
- ½ teaspoon smoked paprika
- ¼ teaspoon chili powder
- Salt and black pepper according to taste
- 1 teaspoon of baking soda
- 4 teaspoons of cayenne pepper

Directions
1. Drizzle the chicken with pickle juice in a bowl.
2. Marinate at room temperature for 10 minutes.

3. Whisk egg with milk in a separate bowl and put aside.
4. Now take another bowl and mix all the remaining ingredients in it.
5. Take the marinated chicken and dip it in the egg mixture.
6. Then coat it with the flour mixture and shed off any surplus flour.
7. Put it in the air fryer basket and brush with oil.
8. Transfer the basket to the air fryer and set the temperature to 400 degrees F.
9. Cook in it for 10 minutes and turn the chicken after 5 minutes.
10. Serve once it's done!

Perfect Alfredo Chicken

Preparation Time: 10 minutes | Cooking Time: 12 minutes | Servings: 2

Ingredients
- 1 tablespoon of lime juice
- 4 chicken breasts, cut into two pieces
- 2 teaspoons of chicken seasoning
- 1 teaspoon of minced garlic
- Salt and black pepper according to taste
- 4 slices provolone cheese
- 1 cup of blue cheese, grated
- 1 cup of alfredo sauce

Directions
1. Mix the two kinds of cheese and the alfredo sauce and put it aside.
2. To make the marinade for the chicken, thoroughly mix all the remaining ingredients.
3. Put the chicken on a plain dish and coat it with the marinade.
4. Spray cooking spray on an air fryer basket and put it in the chicken.
5. Cook in the air fryer at 400 degrees F for 12 minutes.
6. Serve the chicken with the alfredo-cheese mix!

Greek Baked Chicken Wings

Preparation Time: 20 minutes | Cooking Time: 25-30 minutes | Servings: 2

Ingredients
- 1 cup of extra virgin olive oil
- 4 lemons juiced and zest
- 3 tablespoons of garlic paste
- 3 tablespoons of dried thyme
- Salt and pepper according to taste
- 2 teaspoons of sweet pepper
- 2 teaspoons of smoked paprika

For the chicken wings
- 6 pounds of chicken wings
- Feta cheese grated
- Lemon wedges

Directions
1. Stir the olive oil and the lemon juice and pour in all the marinade ingredients.
2. Coat the chicken with the marinade and refrigerate it for 24 hours.
3. When ready to cook, take an air fryer basket and line it with parchment paper.
4. Transfer it to the air fryer and cook at 400 degrees F for 25 minutes.
5. Air Fry them for another 5 minutes to get a crispy texture.
6. Serve with lemon wedges and add some feta to it.

Shake 'N Bake' Style Chicken

Preparation Time: 10 minutes | Cooking Time: 25 minutes | Servings: 2

Ingredients

- 2 pounds of chicken thighs or drumsticks
- 2 eggs
- 1 cup Shake 'n bake' Seasoned coating mix
- Oil spray

Directions

1. Whisk the eggs in a bowl and pour the seasoning into the other bowl.
2. Now dip the chicken in the egg mixture and then coat it with the seasoning.
3. Take an air fryer basket and brush it with oil.
4. Put the chicken in the basket and transfer it to the air fryer unit.
5. Cook in the air fryer for 25 minutes at 360 degrees.
6. Make sure to flip the chicken halfway to cook evenly on both sides.
7. Once it's done, serve!

Air Fryer Green Chili Chicken Bake

Preparation Time: 10 minutes | Cooking Time: 16 minutes | Servings: 4

Ingredients

- 8 flour tortillas
- 2 pounds of chicken grated
- 2 cups of Green Chile Salsa
- 1 cup of sour cream
- 1 pound of Monterey Jack and Habanero cheese grated

Directions

1. Mix the sour cream and green Chile salsa in a bowl.
2. Layout the tortilla on a cooking tray lined with parchment paper.
3. Pour the chicken over it, followed by the salsa mixture.
4. Drizzle the Monterey Jack and Habanero in the ends and cover with another tortilla.
5. Top with additional salsa mix and cheese.
6. Do this for all the tortillas.
7. Transfer the cooking tray to the air fryer unit.
8. Cook in the air fryer at 375 degrees F for 16 minutes.
9. Once it's done, serve with any season of your liking.
10. Note: work in batches.

Air Fried Loaded Chicken with Potatoes

Preparation Time: 10 minutes | Cooking Time: 12 minutes | Servings: 2

Ingredients

- 2 pounds of chicken breasts
- 2 onions
- ¼ cup of oil
- 2 teaspoon garlic powder
- 3 cup mozzarella cheese, grated
- 6 chopped scallions
- 4 potatoes, peeled
- Salt and pepper according to taste
- Bacon for topping

Directions

1. Place the potatoes on a cutting board and use a knife to cut the potato into big pieces.
2. Now slice the chicken into inch-thick slices.
3. Toss the potatoes and chicken in a zip lock bag with all the ingredients except the green onions.
4. Make sure that they are well coated and marinate them at room temperature for 30 minutes.
5. Now put them in an air fryer basket lined with parchment paper.

6. Transfer to the air fryer and cook at 400 degrees F for 20 minutes.
7. Shake the air fryer basket after every 12 minutes.
8. Open the air fryer and add some more cheese with the topping ingredient.
9. Let it broil in the air fryer for 5 minutes.
10. Drizzle with the scallions and serve!

Creamy Air Fried Chicken Broccoli Rice

Preparation Time: 10 minutes | Cooking Time: 20 minutes | Servings: 6

Ingredients

- 3 pounds of chicken breasts, diced into cubes
- 2cups instant rice
- 1 cup of cream soup
- 2 cups Broccoli Florets
- 2 tablespoons of garlic paste
- 2 tablespoons of onion powder
- 1/3 cup of dried cilantro
- 1 teaspoon paprika

Directions

1. Thoroughly mix all the ingredients in a bowl except the rice, broccoli, and cream soup.
2. Make sure that the chicken is properly glazed in it.
3. Now take 12 pieces of foil on a plain surface.
4. Pour in rice, then chicken and drizzle with cream soup and broccoli in equal portions on each one of them.
5. Pour half cup of water into each foil before tightly sealing it.
6. Put it in a round tray and transfer it to the air fryer.
7. Cook in the air fryer at 370 degrees F for 20 minutes.
8. Once it's done, serve!

Chicken Stuffing Casserole

Preparation Time: 10 minutes | Cooking Time: 15 minutes | Servings: 3

Ingredients

- 3 cups of rotisserie chicken, grated
- ¼ cup olive oil
- 20 ounces of condensed bacon soup cream
- 2/3 cup of heavy cream
- 2 box stove top stuffing, cooked

Directions

1. Take a casserole dish and brush it with olive oil.
2. Now whisk the bacon soup with cream.
3. Pour chicken into the casserole dish and pour the bacon mixture over it.
4. Top with the cooked stovetop stuffing and transfer it to the air fryer.
5. Set the temperature of the air fryer to 350 degrees F and cook for 30 minutes.
6. Make sure to flip the chicken after 15 minutes.
7. Once it's done, serve!

Garlicky Lemon Chicken Drumsticks

Preparation Time: 10 minutes | Cooking Time: 20 minutes | Servings: 4

Ingredients

- 10 chicken drumsticks
- 4 lemons, medium
- 4 teaspoons of black pepper
- 1 tablespoon of chipotle powder
- 1 tablespoon of garlic paste
- 2 teaspoons of onion powder
- 2 teaspoons of thyme
- 2 tablespoons of lemon zest

Directions

1. Place the chicken in a dish and pour the lemon juice over it.
2. Rub the chicken thoroughly with the lemon juice and add all the ingredients except the lemon zest.
3. Thoroughly coat the chicken drumsticks with spices.
4. Marinate the drumsticks at room temperature for at least half an hour.
5. When ready to cook, put the drumsticks in an air fryer basket sprayed with cooking spray.
6. Transfer it to the air fryer and cook at 400 degrees F for 20 minutes.
7. Serve with lemon zest!

Air Fried Chicken Shawarma

Preparation Time: 20 minutes | Cooking Time: 12-20 minutes | Servings: 4

Ingredients

- 3 pounds of chicken breasts (boneless)
- 8 loaves of pita bread, whole wheat

Spices

- ¼ cup of olive oil
- 1 tablespoon of garlic powder
- 2 lemons, juiced
- 2 teaspoons of ground coriander
- 1 teaspoon chili powder
- teaspoon allspice (crushed)
- ½ teaspoon turmeric, crushed
- ½ teaspoon cinnamon crushed
- Salt according to taste
- 1 teaspoon black pepper, ground

Tahini Sauce

- 1 cup tahini sesame paste
- 1 lemon's juiced
- ½ cup warm water
- ½ teaspoon of ground coriander
- 1 teaspoon of garlic paste
- Salt to taste
- 4 teaspoons of parsley

Tomato Cucumber Salad

- 2 cups of tomatoes sliced
- 2 English cucumbers
- ¼ cup of onion, minced
- 1 lemon, juiced
- 2 teaspoons of red wine
- 4 teaspoons of olive oil
- ¼ cup of parsley
- Salt and pepper according to taste

Directions

1. Pour all the spices of the main ingredients into a bowl and mix with the garlic powder, olive oil, and lemon juice.
2. Now place the chicken on a slicing board and use a knife to cut it along the length.
3. Put the slices in a zip lock bag and pour in the marinade.
4. Thoroughly coat the chicken with the marinade and marinate it in the refrigerator for 24 hours.
5. Now put the chicken in an air fryer basket lined with parchment paper.
6. Set the temperature of the air fryer to 380 degrees F and put the basket in the cooking unit.
7. Adjust the temperature of the air fryer between 8-10 minutes.
8. Turn the chicken after 4-5 minutes and let it cook.
9. Meanwhile, prepare the tahini sauce by blending all the ingredients in a high-speed blender.
10. Similarly, mix the cucumber salad ingredients in another bowl.
11. Now lay the pita bread on a plain surface and brush it with olive oil.
12. Bake it in the air fryer for 2 minutes on each side at 400 degrees F.
13. Now lay it on a plain surface and pour the tahini sauce and the salad.
14. Fill it with the cooked chicken and wrap it like shawarma.
15. Once it's done, serve!

Air Fried Lemon Pepper Drumsticks

Preparation Time: 10 minutes | Cooking Time: 25 minutes | Servings: 2

Ingredients

- 16 chicken drumsticks
- 2 tablespoons of lemon pepper seasoning
- 1 teaspoon of garlic paste
- 4 teaspoons of baking soda
- 1 teaspoon chili powder
- 3 tablespoons lemon juice
- ½ cup of olive oil

Directions

1. Take a bowl and add the olive oil to it.
2. Mix with lemon juice and the lemon pepper seasoning and put it aside.
3. Now take another bowl and mix all the remaining ingredients in it.
4. Coat the chicken with the marinade from the second bowl and put it in the air fryer basket.
5. Transfer to the cooking unit and cook at 375 degrees F for 25 minutes.
6. Now take out the drumsticks and pour them in lemon pepper seasoning mix.
7. Rub the drumsticks thoroughly with the mix and serve!

Chicken Legs

Preparation Time: 20 minutes | Cooking Time: 15 minutes | Servings: 3

Ingredients

- 16 chicken drumsticks
- ¼ cup of olive oil

Spices Ingredients

- 2 teaspoons of kosher salt
- 1 teaspoon of black pepper
- 2 teaspoons of garlic paste
- 1 tablespoon of cayenne pepper
- ½ teaspoon of chili powder
- 2 teaspoons of onion powder

Directions

1. Prepare the marinade for the chicken by pouring all the spices into a bowl and mixing it with all the listed herbs.
2. Take a zip lock bag, pour in the chicken and olive oil, and rub thoroughly.
3. Now pour in the herbs, mix and coat the chicken with the marinade.
4. Let it marinate at room temperature for 15 minutes.
5. Prepare an air fryer basket by lining it with parchment paper.
6. Put the marinated chicken in the basket and transfer it to the air fryer.
7. Let it cook at 400 degrees F for 10 minutes.
8. Once it's done, serve!

Air Fried Lemon Feta Chicken

Preparation Time: 10 minutes | Cooking Time: 20-25 minutes | Servings: 2

Ingredients
- 4 chicken breasts, cut into two
- 2 tablespoons of lemon juice
- ¼ cup of crumbled feta cheese
- ½ teaspoon of pepper

Directions
1. Spray a cooking pan with oil and pour in the chicken.
2. Drizzle it with all the listed ingredients and thoroughly coat it.
3. Put the chicken in the air fryer.
4. Set the temperature of the air fryer to 165 degrees F.
5. Adjust the time between 20-25 minutes and close the door.
6. Once it's cooked, serve!

Air Fired Greek Chicken

Preparation Time: 10 minutes | Cooking Time: 15 minutes | Servings: 2

Ingredients
- 2 chicken breasts
- 1 onion, sliced
- 1 bell pepper, sliced
- 1 zucchini, sliced
- 2 teaspoons of dried oregano
- 1 teaspoon of cilantro
- 1 teaspoon garlic paste
- ½ teaspoon of oregano
- Salt and pepper according to taste
- 3 tablespoons of olive oil
- ¼ cup of feta cheese, crumbled

Directions
1. Take a large bowl and mix all the listed ingredients except the feta cheese
2. Stir it thoroughly and put it in an air fryer basket lined with parchment paper.
3. Put the basket in the air fryer unit.
4. Adjust the temperature of the air fryer to 380 degrees F.
5. Set the time to 15 minutes and let it cook.
6. Once it's done, drizzle some feta on the top and serve!

Stuffed Chicken Breasts

Preparation Time: 10 minutes | Cooking Time: 30-25 minutes | Servings: 4

Ingredients:
- ¼ cup of olive oil
- 1 cup of onion, sliced thinly
- 1 cup bell pepper, cut into cubes
- 1 cup mushrooms, cut into cubes
- 2 teaspoon garlic paste
- 1 cup spinach, diced thinly
- 1 teaspoon Italian seasoning (dried)
- Salt and pepper according to taste
- 1 cup cottage cheese, shredded
- 8 chicken breasts
- 8 prosciutto slices
- 24 toothpicks
- 1.5 cups of parmesan cheese, shredded
- 1.5 cups of panko breadcrumbs
- 2 teaspoon cilantro, dried
- 1 whisked egg
- Oil spray

Directions:
1. Take a frying pan and heat the olive oil in it.
2. Add the onions and sauté for 3 minutes.
3. Pour in the veggies and sauté for another 3 minutes before drizzling all the spices.
4. Sprinkle the cottage cheese when spinach starts to wilt and cook till the veggies break into cubes.
5. Take the chicken breast and use a knife to make cavities in it.
6. Take the prosciutto and pour two tablespoons of vegetable mixture over it, and roll around the prosciutto.
7. Stuff it in the prosciutto rolls in the chicken cavities which you created.
8. Now take a bowl, mix all the remaining ingredients except the eggs, and add salt and pepper.
9. Take another bowl and whisk the egg in it.
10. Dip the chicken in the panko mix and then in the egg wash.
11. Coat it again with the breadcrumbs and put it in the air fryer basket lined with parchment paper.
12. Transfer the chicken to the air fryer cooking unit and set the temperature to 370 degrees F.
13. Cook the chicken for 22 minutes in the air fryer.
14. Once it's crispy, serve!

Greek Chicken Skewers with Feta Cheese Sauce

Preparation Time: 10 minutes | Cooking Time: 8 minutes | Servings: 2

Ingredients:
- 6 chicken breasts, sliced into cubes
- 4 lemons, wedges
- 1 tablespoon of garlic paste
- ¼ cup of Greek yogurt
- ¼ cup of olive oil
- 2 tablespoons of dried basil
- 2 teaspoons of dried thyme
- Salt and Pepper according to taste

For Feta Sauce
- 6 ounces of feta cheese, grated
- 1/3 cup of Greek yogurt
- 1 lemon, zest, and juice
- 1 teaspoon of garlic paste
- 2 teaspoons of basil, diced
- 1 teaspoon chili flakes
- Black pepper according to taste

Directions:
1. Mix all the main ingredients, veggies and spices, and juices in a bowl and stir well.
2. Marinate the chicken in the mixture for 24 hours and refrigerate.
3. Meanwhile, put all the feta sauce ingredients in a blender and blend until smooth.
4. Take lemon wedges and skew them on a skewer alternatively to chicken bites when ready to cook.
5. Do this for all the chicken.
6. Transfer it to the air fryer in an air fryer basket.
7. Set the temperature of the air fryer to 350 degrees F.
8. Adjust the time to 8 minutes and close the door.
9. Once it's cooked, serve with the feta sauce!

Grilled Chicken Kabobs

Preparation Time: 10 minutes | Cooking Time: 15 minutes | Servings: 4

Ingredients
- 2 pounds of chicken breasts
- 4 teaspoons of garlic puree
- 2 limes, zest, and juice
- 4 teaspoons of olive oil
- 4 teaspoons of thyme

- 4 teaspoons of basil
- Salt and pepper according to taste

Directions

1. Place the kabobs on a plain surface and use a knife to slice them into medium-size cubes.
2. Take a large bowl and mix all the ingredients in it.
3. Toss the chicken in it and seal using a cling film.
4. marinate it at room temperature for at least 4-6 hours
5. When ready to cook, put the chicken slices in an air fryer basket sprayed with cooking spray.
6. Adjust the temperature of the air fryer to 375 degrees F and set the time to 15 minutes.
7. Transfer the basket to the air fryer and let it cook.
8. Once it's done, serve!

Greek Chicken and Orzo Pasta Salad

Preparation Time: 10 minutes | Cooking Time: 18 -20 minutes | Servings: 4

Ingredients

- 4 tablespoons of olive oil
- 2 teaspoons of kosher Salt
- 1 teaspoon of oregano (or to taste)
- 1 teaspoon of garlic paste
- ½ teaspoon of black pepper
- 2 lemons, juiced
- 2-pound boneless chicken tenderloins
- ¼ cup of unsalted butter
- 2 tablespoons of extra-virgin olive oil
- 2 cloves of minced garlic
- 1 cup Italian breadcrumbs

For the Dressing:

- 1 cup extra virgin olive oil
- ½ cup of red wine vinegar
- 2 teaspoons of kosher salt
- 1 teaspoon of dried oregano
- 1 teaspoon of black pepper, crushed
- 2 garlic cloves, minced
- 1 lemon, juiced

For the Salad:

- Kosher salt
- 2 pounds of orzo
- 20 ounces of cherry tomatoes, cut into two pieces
- 2 English cucumbers, sliced
- ¼ cup of cilantro
- 3 cups feta cheese, grated

Directions

1. Thoroughly mix all the ingredients for the dressing and put it aside.
2. Now, cook the orzo in boiling water and drain it for the salad.
3. Take a dish, pour the breadcrumbs, and stir it with garlic, oil, and butter.
4. Bake the crumbs in the air fryer at 400 degrees f for 3 minutes and afterward put them aside.
5. Once the orzo has cooled, pour in all the remaining salad ingredients and stir.
6. To cook the chicken, mix all the spices in the main ingredients in a bowl and coat the chicken.
7. Let it marinate at room temperature for 1-4 hours.
8. Now align the chicken in an air fryer basket lined with parchment paper.
9. Transfer the basket to the air fryer unit.
10. Cook the chicken at 400 degrees f for 15 minutes.
11. Take out the chicken after 15 minutes and slice it into slices an inch thick.
12. Now lay down the salad on a dish and drizzle the grated cheese.

13. Put the chicken on the top, and lastly, season with the baked breadcrumbs.
14. Serve!

Kale and Feta Stuffed Chicken Breasts

Preparation Time: 25 minutes | Cooking Time: 20 minutes | Servings: 4

Ingredients

- 4 chicken breasts
- 12 ounces of kale
- 1 cup of feta cheese, grated
- 1 teaspoon of garlic paste
- Salt and pepper according to taste
- ¼ cup of olive oil
- ½ cup of red onions, diced finely

Directions

1. Heat some oil in a skillet and sauté the kale for 3 minutes.
2. Pour salt, red onions, and garlic paste into the skillet and stir.
3. Cook for 3 minutes and remove from the flame.
4. Drizzle some feta over the top and stir.
5. Place the chicken breasts on a plain surface and make 4-inch cuts to make cavities for stuffing.
6. Stuff each chicken breast with half a tablespoon of the kale mix.
7. Use toothpicks to seal the slits and drizzle salt and garlic powder over them.
8. Brush the chicken with olive oil and put it in the air fryer basket greased with oil.
9. Put in the air fryer and cook at 350 degrees F for 20 minutes.
10. Serve once cooked!

Mediterranean Chicken Thighs

Preparation Time: 20 minutes | Cooking Time: 25 minutes | Servings: 2

Ingredients:

- 1 pound chicken thighs, with bone
- ¼ cup extra virgin olive oil
- 1 tablespoon red wine vinegar
- ½ lemon's juice and zest
- 3 tablespoons of garlic paste
- 1 teaspoon oregano
- ¼ teaspoon thyme
- ½ teaspoon chili powder
- ½ teaspoon ground coriander
- A pinch of cayenne pepper
- Salt and pepper according to taste
- Parsley, for seasoning
- Feta cheese, for seasoning

For Salad

- 2 small tomatoes (seeded, diced)
- ¼ English cucumber (diced)
- 3 green onions
- 2 tablespoons of cilantro (chopped)
- 2 tablespoons feta cheese (crumbled)
- 2 tablespoons of extra virgin olive oil
- 1 tablespoon of lemon juice
- 1 minced garlic clove (minced)
- ½ teaspoon of sumac
- Salt and Pepper according to taste

Directions:

1. Place the chicken on a plain surface and use a paper towel to dry them.
2. Drizzle with the listed spices and toss everything in a bowl.

3. Put the chicken in a zip lock bag with the spices.
4. Marinate in the refrigerator for a minimum of 2 hours.
5. Once you are ready to cook, brush the air fryer basket with some oil.
6. Arrange the chicken thighs' skin side down and transfer them to the air fryer.
7. Set the temperature of the air fryer to 380 degrees F.
8. Adjust the temperature to 25 minutes.
9. Open the air fryer after 10 minutes, flip the chicken, and close it again.
10. In the meantime, take a large bowl and stir all the ingredients for the salad.
11. Layer it on a dish and place the cooked chicken over the salad.
12. Drizzle with feta and cilantro.
13. Serve hot!

Greek Chicken Bowl

Preparation Time: 10 minutes | Cooking Time: 8 minutes | Servings: 2

Ingredients
- 2 recipe air-fried chicken breasts
- 2 recipe instant pot quinoa, cooked
- 2 servings of cucumber tomato salad
- ½ cup of feta cheese
- 1 cup of black olives
- 2 lemon vinaigrette dressing recipes

Directions
1. Take an air fryer basket and spray some cooking spray over it.
2. Arrange the chicken in the air fryer basket and put it inside the unit.
3. Let it cook at 400 degrees F for 12 minutes.
4. Turn the chicken after 6 minutes to cook evenly.
5. Once the chicken is cooked, place it on a dish and drizzle all listed ingredients.
6. Serve!

Turkey Panini

Preparation Time: 20 minutes | Cooking Time: 25 minutes | Servings: 2

Ingredients
- 10 bacon strips
- 4 sourdough slices
- ½ cup of ranch dressing
- 1 Ounce of turkey breasts
- 5 slices of American cheese
- 4 teaspoons of salted butter

Directions
1. Take an air fryer rack and layer the bacon over it.
2. Spray with some cooking spray and transfer the rack into the air fryer.
3. Cook at 400 degrees F for 15 minutes.
4. Once it's done, let it cool for a while.
5. Now butter the sourdough on one side and put it in the air fryer basket.
6. Top with the turkey, American cheese, and bacon.
7. Place another bread slice on the top and transfer the basket to the air fryer.
8. Cook the sandwiches for 10 minutes at 400 degrees F.
9. Once it's done, serve with any sauce of desire!

Glazed Chicken Breast with Basil Corn Salad

Preparation Time: 22 minutes | Cooking Time: 22 minutes | Servings: 3

Ingredients for Marinade
- ½ cup of olive oil

- 1 tablespoon of garlic paste
- 1 cup white wine vinegar
- 1 cup tamari sauce
- ½ cup of Worcestershire sauce
- 2 teaspoons of lemon juice
- Salt and black pepper according to taste
- ¼ cup of Italian seasoning
- 4 teaspoons of smoked paprika
- ½ cup of mustard
- 1 cup of honey

Chicken Ingredient
- Cooking spray
- 14-16 chicken breasts

Salad Ingredients
- 4 cups of fresh corn
- 2 cups of cherry tomatoes, cut into two
- 2 cups grated feta
- 1/2 red onion, thinly sliced
- 1 cup basil, diced finely
- ¼ tablespoon of extra-virgin olive oil
- 1 lemon, juiced
- Salt and black pepper according to taste

Directions
1. Thoroughly mix all the salad ingredients in a bowl and put them aside.
2. Mix all the ingredients for the marinade in a separate bowl and stir it thoroughly.
3. Take a zip-lock bag and pour in the chicken along with the marinade.
4. Coat the chicken thoroughly with the marinade and marinate it for 2 hours at room temperature.
5. Take an air fryer basket and line it with parchment paper.
6. Align the chicken breasts in the air fryer basket and transfer them to the air fryer.
7. Adjust the time to 22 minutes and fix the temperature at 350 degrees F.
8. Turn the chicken breasts after 12 minutes to cook the chicken evenly.
9. Serve with the salad once it's cooked!

Thanksgiving Turkey

Preparation Time: 10 minutes | Cooking Time: 20 minutes | Servings: 4

Ingredients
- Salt and black pepper according to taste
- 1 teaspoon of dried oregano
- 4 teaspoons of crushed rosemary
- 2/3 teaspoons of dried sage
- 2/3 teaspoon of garlic paste
- 2/3 teaspoons of chili powder
- 2 teaspoons of dark brown sugar
- 4 pounds turkey breast, with bone
- Cooking spray

Directions
1. Mix all the ingredients in a bowl except the turkey,
2. Place the turkey on a plain dish and rub it with the spice mix.
3. Put the turkey in the air fryer sprayed with cooking spray.
4. Set the temperature of the air fryer to 400 degrees F.
5. Put the basket in the air fryer,
6. Cook the turkey for 20 minutes skin side down.
7. Turn the turkey and cook for 15 minutes with the skin side facing up.
8. Once it's done, slice and serve!

Air Fryer Cheesy Chicken Sausage Rolls

Preparation Time: 10 minutes | Cooking Time: 14 minutes |
Servings: 2

Ingredients

- 8 cups of minced chicken
- 2 cups of corn kernels, drained, cut
- 2 cups of zucchini, shredded
- 4 small carrots, shredded
- 1.5 cup mozzarella cheese
- 2 cups of dried panko breadcrumbs
- 4 teaspoons Vegemite squeeze
- 2 green onions, sliced thinly
- 1 tablespoon of garlic paste
- 2 sheets of frozen puff pastry, soft and cut into two
- 2 gently whisked organic eggs
- Sweet chili sauce for the serving

Directions

1. Mix chicken with breadcrumbs, corn, and grated cheese.
2. Add the vegetables and all the remaining ingredients except the pastry and stir.
3. Drizzle with salt and pepper and thoroughly mix.
4. Layout the pastry on a dish and pour one-third cup of the chicken mixture over the pastry.
5. Roll up the pastries and slice them into three pieces.
6. Follow the same procedure for all the pastries.
7. Take an air fryer basket and brush it with oil.
8. Arrange the pastries in the basket and transfer them to the air fryer,
9. Cook in the air fryer at 400 degrees F for 14 minutes.
10. Once it's done, serve with the sauce of desire!

Air Fryer Crumbed Chicken Schnitzel

Preparation Time: 20 minutes | Cooking Time: 16 minutes |
Servings: 4

Ingredients

- 16 chicken thigh fillets
- 2 cups of panko breadcrumbs
- 2 teaspoons of herb seasoning
- 3 eggs, mildly beaten
- 2/3 cup almond flour
- 4 cups of coleslaw
- Salt and pepper according to taste

Directions

1. Layout two sheets of siren wrap on a plain surface and put half chicken on it.
2. Ground the chicken with a rolling pin.
3. Follow the same procedure for all the chicken halves.
4. Pour the breadcrumbs into a bowl and stir it thoroughly with the herb seasoning.
5. Lightly beat the eggs in a separate bowl.
6. Now pour flour on a dish and drizzle with salt and pepper.
7. Take the chicken pieces and drench them in the flour, then dip in the egg wash and lastly in the breadcrumbs.
8. Let it marinate in the refrigerator for at least half an hour.
9. Put it in the air fryer basket when ready to cook.
10. Grease it with cooking spray and transfer it to the air fryer.
11. Set the temperature to 400 degrees F and let it cook for 16 minutes.
12. Once it's done, serve it with coleslaw!

Air Fryer Japanese Chicken Tenders

Preparation Time: 10 minutes | Cooking Time: 14 minutes |
Servings: 4

Ingredient

- 2.5 pounds of chicken thigh
- ¼ cup of sachet McCormick kits crumb seasoning
- Cooking spray
- 1 cup of kewpie mayonnaise
- 4 teaspoons of pickled ginger
- 2 teaspoons of pickling liquid

Directions

1. Place the chicken in a plain dish and rub it with all the ingredients except the pickling liquid and mayo.
2. Place it in an air fryer basket brushed with cooking oil.
3. Transfer to the air fryer and unit and set the temperature to 400 degrees F.
4. Close the door and let it cook for 14 minutes.
5. In the meantime, mix the pickling liquid with mayo in a bowl.
6. Once it's cooked, serve with the mayo sauce!

Air Fryer Whole Turkey with Gravy

Preparation Time: 20 minutes | Cooking Time: 25 minutes |
Servings: 5

Ingredients

- 2.5 pounds of the whole turkey
- 2tablespoons of butter, sliced
- 2 cloves of garlic, minced
- Cooking oil
- Salt and black pepper according to taste
- ¾ cup of chicken stock
- 1/3 cup of almond flour
- 1 cup of potato salad, side serving

Directions

1. Lift the skin of the turkey and tuck the garlic and butter.
2. Drizzle salt, pepper, and oil over the turkey.
3. Transfer it to the air fryer basket along with half of the stock.
4. Cook in the air fryer for 2 hours at 350 degrees F.
5. Open the air fryer after 20 minutes and pour in some more stock.
6. Once the turkey is cooked, let it cool for half an hour.
7. In the meantime, take a pan and add air fryer liquid in it along with flour and beat until it's smooth.
8. Transfer this mixture to the air fryer and cook at 400 degrees for 10 minutes.
9. Once the mixture becomes gel-like, pour it over the turkey and serve with potato salad!

Classic Hawaiian Pineapple Chicken

Preparation Time: 10 minutes | Cooking Time: 25 minutes |
Servings: 4

Ingredients

- 2/3 cup of tamari sauce
- 2/3 cup of pineapple juice
- 2/3 cup of brown sugar, packed
- 1 tablespoon of garlic paste
- 1 tablespoon of freshly shredded ginger
- 4 teaspoons of sesame oil
- 4 teaspoons of hot sauce
- 12 boneless chicken breasts
- ½ cup of fresh cilantro leaves, finely chopped

For The Pineapple

- 2 large pineapples, sliced to wedges
- ½ cup of brown sugar

Directions

1. Add the pineapple juice and stir it with tamari sauce, brown sugar, and hot sauce.
2. Pour in the sesame oil, ginger, and garlic and mix thoroughly.

3. Keep the fourth portion of this mixture for later use.
4. Put the remaining mixture into a zip lock bag and add the chicken.
5. Coat the chicken in the sauce and marinate it in the refrigerator for 24 hours.
6. Place the chicken in the air fryer basket with brown sugar and pineapple when ready to cook.
7. Set the temperature of the air fryer to 400 degrees F and cook for 25 minutes.
8. Turn the chicken halfway and brush the reserved Sriracha sauce every 10 minutes.
9. Serve with toppings.

Air Fryer Whole BBQ Chicken With Baked Potatoes

Preparation Time: 10 minutes | Cooking Time: 8 minutes | Servings: 2

Ingredients
- 1 pound of chicken, whole
- 4 teaspoons of BBQ dry rub
- Cooking spray
- 1 large baked potato

Directions
1. Take the chicken and wash it under running water.
2. Drain it and use a paper towel to pat it dry.
3. Place the chicken on a plain dish and rub over the BBQ dry rub.
4. Spray it with cooking spray and transfer it to the air fryer basket.
5. Adjust baked potato alongside.
6. Set the temperature of the air fryer to 400 degrees F.
7. Adjust the time to 45 minutes and put the basket in the unit.
8. Turn the chicken after halftime to cook evenly on both sides.
9. Once it's done, serve!

Nashville Hot Chicken

Preparation Time: 20 minutes | Cooking Time: 10-15 minutes | Servings: 2

Ingredients
- 1 tablespoon of dill pickle juice, cut into two
- 1 tablespoon of hot pepper sauce, cut into two
- 1 pound of chicken tenderloins
- 3/4 cup of almond flour
- 1 organic egg
- ½ cup buttermilk
- Cooking spray
- ¼ cup of olive oil
- ¼ tablespoon of cayenne pepper
- 1 tablespoon of dark brown sugar
- ¼ teaspoon of chipotle powder
- ½ teaspoon of chili powder
- ¼ teaspoon of garlic powder
- Salt and black pepper according to taste
- Dill pickle slices for sides

Directions
1. Mix the pickle juice with half of the hot sauce and salt in a bowl.
2. Rub it over the chicken and marinate it in the refrigerator for at least 2 hours.
3. Mix the flour, salt, and pepper in another bowl.
4. Likewise, beat another bowl and beat the eggs with buttermilk, the left pickle juice, and hot sauce.
5. Take the marinated chicken, drench it in the flour, then dip it in the egg wash and then the flour mixture once more.

6. Place it in the air fryer basket sprayed with cooking spray.
7. Transfer it to the air fryer and set the temperature to 375 degrees F.
8. Set the time to 12 minutes and close the door.
9. Turn the chicken after 6 minutes to cook evenly.
10. In the meantime, stir the sugar in a bowl with garlic powder, oil, and other remaining spices.
11. Once the chicken is cooked, pour it over it and shake it to layer it thoroughly with the sauce.
12. Serve along with the pickle dills!

Air Fryer Pistachio Crusted Chicken

Preparation Time: 20 minutes | Cooking Time: 18 minutes | Servings: 2

Ingredients
- 4 boneless chicken thigh fillet
- Salt and black pepper according to taste
- ½ cup of kewpie mayonnaise
- 1 cup of roasted pistachios, grounded
- Cooking spray

Directions
1. Take the chicken and wash it under running water.
2. Place it on a plain dish and use a paper towel to dry it.
3. Rub over the salt and pepper and coat with the mayonnaise.
4. Put the chicken in the air fryer basket with a layer of pistachios beneath.
5. Drizzle another layer of pistachios over the top of the chicken.
6. Spray with cooking spray and transfer to the air fryer.
7. Set the temperature of the air fryer to 375 degrees F and adjust the temperature to 18 minutes.
8. Turn the chicken breasts after halftime in the air fryer,
9. Once it's done, serve!

Air Fryer Buttermilk Fried Chicken

Preparation Time: 10 minutes | Cooking Time: 15 minutes | Servings: 1

Ingredients:
- 1 ½ pound boneless, skinless chicken thighs
- 2 cups buttermilk
- 1 cup all-purpose flour
- One tablespoon of seasoned salt
- ½ tablespoon ground black pepper
- 1 cup panko bread crumbs
- One serving of cooking spray

Directions:
1. In a shallow casserole dish, place the chicken thighs. Refrigerate the chicken for 4 hours or overnight in buttermilk.
2. Preheat an air fryer to 380°F (190 degrees C).
3. Mix the flour, seasoned salt, and pepper in a large gallon-sized resealable bag. Chicken thighs should be dredged in seasoned flour. Return to the buttermilk and coat with panko bread crumbs.
4. Spray the air fryer basket with nonstick cooking spray. Place half of the chicken thighs in the basket, ensuring none of the contacts. Cooking sprays the tops of each chicken thigh.
5. Cook for 15 minutes in a preheated air fryer. Flip. Spray the tops of the chicken once more. Cook for another 10 minutes until the chicken is no longer pink in the middle and the juices flow clear. In the middle, an instant-read thermometer should read at least 165 degrees F. (74 degrees C). Rep with the remaining chicken.

Air Fryer Blackened Chicken Breast

Preparation Time: 10 minutes | Cooking Time: 15 minutes | Servings: 1

Ingredients:
- Two teaspoons paprika
- One teaspoon of ground thyme
- One teaspoon cumin
- ½ teaspoon cayenne pepper
- ½ teaspoon onion powder
- ½ teaspoon black pepper
- ¼ teaspoon salt
- Two teaspoons of vegetable oil
- 2 (12 ounces) skinless, boneless chicken breast halves

Directions:
1. Mix paprika, thyme, cumin, cayenne pepper, onion powder, black pepper, and salt in a mixing bowl. Place the spice mixture on a flat dish.
2. Rub the oil evenly over each chicken breast. Roll each piece of chicken in the blackening spice mixture, pressing down so the spice adheres to both sides. Allow it to rest for 5 minutes while the air fryer heats up.
3. Preheat an air fryer for 5 minutes at 360 degrees F (175 degrees C).
4. Cook the chicken in the air fryer basket for 10 minutes. Cook for another 10 minutes on the other side. Place the chicken on a platter and let it aside for 5 minutes before serving.

Air Fryer Chicken Satay with Dipping Sauce

Preparation Time: 10 minutes | Cooking Time: 15 minutes | Servings: 1

Ingredients:
- ¼ cup full-fat coconut milk
- Three tablespoons of coconut aminos
- One tablespoon of finely grated fresh ginger
- One tablespoon of fish sauce
- Three cloves of garlic, minced
- Two teaspoons of curry powder
- 1 ½ teaspoon ground turmeric
- ½ teaspoon ground cumin
- ½ teaspoon ground coriander
- salt and ground black pepper to taste
- 2 ½ pounds boneless, skinless chicken thighs, cut into 1-inch pieces
- Dipping Sauce:
- ½ cup teriyaki sauce
- ⅓ cup cashew butter
- Three tablespoons of orange juice
- Two cloves of garlic, minced
- One teaspoon of cayenne pepper
- Two tablespoons chopped raw cashews (Optional)
- 5 cups hot cooked rice
- ½ bunch of cilantro sprigs

Directions:
1. In a gallon-sized resealable bag, combine coconut milk, coconut aminos, ginger, fish sauce, garlic, curry powder, turmeric, cumin, coriander, salt, and pepper. Mix in the chicken pieces. Squeeze off most of the air, seal, and carefully squeeze the chicken pieces until well coated in marinade. Refrigerate for at least 4 hours and up to 24 hours, turning the bag regularly.
2. Prepare the dipping sauce 1 hour before cooking the chicken to allow the flavors to mix. Mix the teriyaki sauce, cashew butter, orange juice, garlic, and cayenne pepper in a small mixing bowl. Refrigerate until ready to serve, well covered.
3. Preheat an air fryer to 400°F (200°C) according to the manufacturer's instructions.
4. Thread chicken chunks onto each skewer and arrange them on a skewer attachment rack.
5. Place the rack in the air fryer basket and cook for 8 minutes. Cook for an additional 8 minutes after carefully turning each skewer. Rep with the remaining chicken. When an instant-read thermometer is put into the center of the chicken and registers 165 degrees F, it is done (74 degrees C).
6. Top the dipping sauce with chopped cashews. Serve the skewers with the dipping sauce on top of hot cooked rice. Garnish with cilantro sprigs if desired.

Mexican-Style Air Fryer Stuffed Chicken Breasts

Preparation Time: 10 minutes | Cooking Time: 15 minutes | Servings: 1

Ingredients:
- Four extra-long toothpicks
- Four teaspoons of chili powder, divided
- Four teaspoons of ground cumin, divided
- One skinless, boneless chicken breast
- Two teaspoons of chipotle flakes
- Two teaspoons of Mexican oregano
- salt and ground black pepper to taste
- ½ red bell pepper, sliced into thin strips
- ½ onion, sliced into thin strips
- One fresh jalapeno pepper, sliced into thin strips
- Two teaspoons of corn oil
- ½ lime, juiced

Directions:
1. Fill a small basin halfway with water and soak toothpicks to protect them from burning during cooking.
2. In a small bowl, combine two teaspoons of chili powder and two tablespoons of cumin.
3. Preheat an air fryer to 400°F (200 degrees C).
4. Place the chicken breast on a flat surface. Cut horizontally through the center. Using a kitchen mallet or rolling pin, pound each half until it is approximately 1/4-inch thick.
5. Sprinkle the remaining chili powder, cumin, chipotle flakes, oregano, salt, and pepper evenly over each breast. In the middle of 1 breast half, place 1/2 of the bell pepper, onion, and jalapeño. Roll the chicken from the tapered end up and fasten with two toothpicks. Repeat with the remaining breast, spices, and veggies, and fasten with toothpicks. Roll each roll-up in the chili-cumin mixture in the shallow dish while drizzling with olive oil until equally coated.
6. Place the roll-ups in the air fryer basket, toothpick side up. Set a 6-minute timer.
7. Flip the roll-ups over. Cook for another 5 minutes in the air fryer, or until the juices flow clear and an instant-read thermometer put into the middle reads at least 165 degrees F (74 degrees C).
8. Before serving, evenly drizzle the roll-ups with lime juice.

Air Fryer Buffalo Chicken Wings

Preparation Time: 10 minutes | Cooking Time: 15 minutes | Servings: 1

Ingredients:
- 2 ½ pounds of chicken wings
- One tablespoon of olive oil
- ⅔ cup cayenne pepper sauce

- ½ cup butter
- Two tablespoons vinegar
- One teaspoon of garlic powder
- ¼ teaspoon cayenne pepper

Directions:
1. Preheat an air fryer to 360°F (182 degrees C).
2. Place the wings in a large mixing basin—drizzle oil over the wings and massage until evenly covered.
3. Cook for 25 minutes with half of the wings in the air fryer basket. Flip the wings with tongs and cook for another 5 minutes. Place the cooked wings in a large mixing dish. Rep with the remaining wings.
4. In a small saucepan over medium heat, mix hot pepper sauce, butter, vinegar, garlic powder, and cayenne pepper while the second batch is cooking. Keep heating until the wings are done.
5. Toss cooked wings with sauce to coat.

Juicy Parmesan-Breaded Air Fryer Chicken Breasts

Preparation Time: 10 minutes | Cooking Time: 15 minutes | Servings: 1

Ingredients:
- One large egg, beaten
- ½ cup all-purpose flour
- ¾ cup dry bread crumbs
- ⅓ cup freshly grated Parmesan cheese
- ¼ cup flax seed meal
- Two teaspoons of lemon zest
- One teaspoon of dried oregano
- ¼ teaspoon ground cayenne pepper
- ¼ teaspoon kosher salt
- freshly ground black pepper to taste
- 3 (6 ounces) boneless skinless chicken breasts, flattened slightly

Directions:
1. Put the beaten egg in a shallow bowl and the flour in another. In a third dish, combine the bread crumbs, Parmesan cheese, flax seed meal, lemon zest, oregano, cayenne pepper, salt, and pepper.
2. Dip each chicken breast into the flour, the egg, and the bread crumb mixture, covering both sides well. Place the coated chicken breasts in the air fryer basket. You may need to cook them in batches depending on the size of your air fryer.
3. Preheat the air fryer to 375°F (190 degrees C). Cook for 10 minutes the chicken breasts. Cook for 5 minutes until the chicken is no longer pink in the center and the juices run clear. An instant-read thermometer in the middle should read at least 165 degrees F if the coating is golden (74 degrees C).

Honey-Sriracha Air Fryer Wings

Preparation Time: 10 minutes | Cooking Time: 15 minutes | Servings: 1

Ingredients:
- 12 fresh chicken wing drumettes
- ½ teaspoon salt
- ½ teaspoon garlic powder
- One tablespoon butter
- ¼ cup honey
- Two teaspoons of rice vinegar
- One tablespoon sriracha sauce

Directions:
1. Preheat an air fryer to 360°F (182 degrees C).

2. Toss the chicken wings in a basin with the salt and garlic powder to coat.
3. Fill the air fryer basket halfway with wings. Cook the wings for 25 minutes, shaking the basket every 7 to 8 minutes. When the timer goes off, switch off the air fryer and leave the wings in the basket for another 5 minutes.
4. Meanwhile, in a small saucepan over medium heat, melt the butter. Bring butter, honey, rice vinegar, and sriracha sauce to a boil. Reduce the heat to medium-low and cook the sauce for 8 to 10 minutes, stirring regularly. Remove from the fire and set aside; the sauce will thicken as it cools.
5. In a mixing dish, combine cooked wings and sauce. Make the extra sauce to serve with the wings.

Air Fryer Frozen Chicken Tenders

Preparation Time: 10 minutes | Cooking Time: 15 minutes | Servings: 1

Ingredients:
- 1 pound frozen chicken tenders
- avocado cooking spray
- salt and freshly ground pepper to taste

Directions:
1. Rinse the chicken tenders under cold running water to remove any ice. Using paper towels, pat dry. Season the chicken tenders with salt and pepper after lightly spraying them with avocado oil.
2. Place the chicken tenders in an air fryer basket, careful not to overlap the pieces.
3. Cook for 15 minutes in an air fryer at 360 degrees F (180 degrees C). Turn the chicken tenders over and cook for another 8 minutes until the chicken is no longer pink in the middle and the juices run clear. In the middle, an instant-read thermometer should read at least 165 degrees F. (74 degrees C).

Quick Air Fryer Chicken Parmesan

Preparation Time: 10 minutes | Cooking Time: 15 minutes | Servings: 1

Ingredients:
- 1 (8 ounces) package of spaghetti
- ½ tablespoon salt
- Two fully cooked breaded chicken fillets (such as Kirkwood®)
- ½ (8 ounces) can of marinara sauce
- 1 (8 ounces) package of fresh mozzarella cheese, sliced
- One tablespoon of fresh basil, cut into very thin strips

Directions:
1. Preheat an air fryer for 5 minutes at 400 degrees F (200 degrees C).
2. Warm up a big saucepan of gently salted water. Cook the spaghetti in boiling water for 12 minutes, tossing periodically until cooked yet firm to the biting.
3. In the meantime, place two chicken fillets in the air fryer basket.
4. Six minutes in the air fryer with chicken fillets. Cook for 6 minutes on the opposite side after flipping the fillets. Distribute marinara sauce over fillets. Top each fillet with a piece of mozzarella. Three minutes longer in the air fryer until the cheese is melted.
5. Drain the spaghetti noodles and divide them between two dishes. Add a chicken fillet to each bowl with care. Garnish with basil if desired.

Air Fryer Lemon-Pepper Wings

Preparation Time: 10 minutes | Cooking Time: 15 minutes | Servings: 1

Ingredients:
- Two tablespoons of olive oil
- One tablespoon lemon-pepper seasoning, divided
- ¼ teaspoon garlic powder
- ¼ teaspoon paprika
- 1 pound party chicken wings

Directions:
1. In a mixing dish, combine olive oil, two tablespoons of lemon-pepper seasoning, paprika, and garlic powder. Toss in the wings to coat.
2. Allow the remaining one teaspoon of the lemon-pepper spice to stay on the wings for 5 minutes while you warm the air fryer to 360 degrees F. (180 degrees C).
3. Place the wings around the edges of the air fryer basket, careful not to crowd them.
4. Cook the wings in the air fryer for 25 minutes, or until the chicken is no longer pink at the bone and the juices flow clear. Allow the wings to rest within the closed basket for 5 minutes after the timer goes off.

Air Fryer Parmesan Chicken Bites

Preparation Time: 10 minutes | Cooking Time: 15 minutes | Servings: 1

Ingredients:
- 1 (6 ounces skinless chicken breasts, cut into bite-size pieces
- One large egg
- Two tablespoons of heavy whipping cream
- ¼ teaspoon salt, divided
- ½ cup panko bread crumbs
- ¼ teaspoon Catanzaro herbs (such as Savory Spice Shop®) or Italian seasoning
- Two tablespoons of shredded Parmesan cheese
- nonstick cooking spray

Directions:
1. Preheat an air fryer for 5 minutes at 400 degrees F (200 degrees C).
2. In a mixing dish, combine the egg, whipping cream, and 1/2 teaspoon salt. Whisk until the mixture is golden and foamy.
3. Mix panko, herbs, and remaining salt in a shallow dish until thoroughly blended.
4. Dip the chicken pieces in the egg mixture first, then in the panko, and place in the air fryer basket.
5. Air-fry the basket for 13 minutes, shaking it after 5 minutes. Coat with frying spray and top with Parmesan cheese. Cook for two until the chicken is no longer pink in the juices, run clear, and the Parmesan has melted. In the middle, an instant-read thermometer should read at least 165 degrees F. (74 degrees C).

Air Fried Maple Chicken Thighs

Preparation Time: 10 minutes | Cooking Time: 15 minutes | Servings: 1

Ingredients:
- 1 cup buttermilk
- ½ cup maple syrup
- One Oneg
- One teaspoon of granulated garlic
- Four skin-on, bone-in chicken thighs
- Dry Mix:
- ½ cup all-purpose flour
- ¼ cup tapioca flour

- One tablespoon salt
- One teaspoon of sweet paprika
- ½ teaspoon smoked paprika
- One teaspoon of granulated onion
- ¼ teaspoon ground black pepper
- ¼ teaspoon cayenne pepper
- ½ teaspoon granulated garlic
- ½ teaspoon honey powder (such as Savory Spice®)

Directions:
1. In a resealable bag, combine buttermilk, maple syrup, egg, and a teaspoon of granulated garlic. Marinate the chicken thighs for at least 1 hour or overnight in the refrigerator.
2. In a shallow bowl, combine flour, tapioca flour, salt, sweet paprika, smoked paprika, granulated onion, pepper, cayenne pepper, 1/2 teaspoon granulated garlic, and honey powder.
3. Preheat an air fryer to 380°F (190 degrees C).
4. Remove the chicken thighs from the marinade and set them aside. Dredge the chicken in the flour mixture and brush off any excess. Cook the chicken for 12 minutes, skin side down, in a preheated air fryer. Fry the thighs for a further 13 minutes.

Air Fryer Stuffed Chicken Breasts

Preparation Time: 10 minutes | Cooking Time: 15 minutes | Servings: 1

Ingredients:
- Two tablespoons of extra-virgin olive oil
- ½ cup diced red onion
- ½ cup diced red bell pepper
- ½ cup diced fresh mushrooms
- One teaspoon of minced garlic
- ½ cup chopped fresh spinach
- ½ teaspoon dried Italian seasoning
- One pinch of salt and ground black pepper to taste
- ½ cup crumbled feta cheese
- Four boneless, skinless chicken breasts
- Four slices prosciutto
- 12 toothpicks
- ¾ cup grated Parmesan cheese
- ¾ cup fine dry bread crumbs
- One teaspoon of dried parsley
- One egg, beaten
- 1 serving avocado oil cooking spray

Directions:
1. In a small pan over medium heat, heat the olive oil until it is hot—Cook and stir for 3 minutes, or until the onion is softened. Cook, stirring periodically, for 3 minutes more after adding the red bell pepper and mushrooms. Remove the skillet from heat and add spinach and garlic. Continue to stir until the spinach has wilted somewhat. Cool for 10 minutes after seasoning with salt, and pepper.
2. Mix in the crumbled feta cheese, breaking up any big bits.
3. Place the chicken pieces on a secure cutting board. Insert a knife into the thickest section of each breast and slice parallel to the cutting board, leaving about 1 inch at each tip. Be cautious not to cut through the breast's thinnest edge.
4. If the manufacturer recommends it, preheat the air fryer to 370 degrees F (190 degrees C).
5. Place the prosciutto slices on a clean prep surface. Place two tablespoons of the vegetable-feta mixture on top and twist it into an oblong bundle. Tuck one prosciutto-wrapped bundle into each cut chicken breast and secure with toothpicks.

6. Combine the Parmesan cheese, breadcrumbs, parsley, salt, and pepper on a dish. Dredge each filled chicken breast in the breadcrumb mixture after dipping it in the beaten egg. Apply avocado oil spray.
7. Cook until browned in the air fryer basket, about 15 minutes on each side. In the middle, an instant-read thermometer should read at least 165 degrees F. (74 degrees C).

Air Fryer Old Bay® Chicken Wings

Preparation Time: 10 minutes | Cooking Time: 15 minutes | Servings: 1

Ingredients:
- Two pounds chicken wings
- Two tablespoons of seafood seasoning (such as Old Bay®)
- ¼ teaspoon freshly cracked black pepper
- ½ cup cornstarch

Sauce:
- Four tablespoons butter

Directions:
1. Preheat the air fryer to 400°F (200 degrees C).
2. Toss the chicken wings with two tablespoons of Old Bay® seasoning and black pepper in a large mixing dish. Toss the wings in cornstarch until well covered. Shake each wing before placing it in the air fryer basket, making sure they don't contact; cook in batches if necessary.
3. Fry for 10 minutes in a hot air fryer, shake the basket and cook for another 8 minutes. Cook until the chicken is cooked and the juices run clear, 5 to 6 minutes longer.
4. Meanwhile, in a small saucepan, add butter and one teaspoon of Old Bay® flavor for the sauce. Bring to a boil, frequently stirring, over medium heat.
5. Each wing should be dipped in the sauce. Serve with any leftover sauce on the side.

Air-Fried Breaded Chicken Thighs

Preparation Time: 10 minutes | Cooking Time: 15 minutes | Servings: 1

Ingredients:
- Four medium bone-in, skin-on chicken thighs
- 1 cup buttermilk
- ¼ cup all-purpose flour
- ¼ cup plain bread crumbs
- Two tablespoons of grated Parmesan cheese
- ½ teaspoon ground paprika
- One teaspoon of garlic powder
- One teaspoon salt
- ½ teaspoon onion powder
- ½ teaspoon black pepper
- nonstick cooking spray

Directions:
1. Combine the chicken thighs and buttermilk in a nonreactive container with a cover or a resealable plastic bag. Marinate for at least 1 hour or overnight in the refrigerator.
2. Take the chicken out of the refrigerator. Pour out the buttermilk and let the chicken aside to rest while preparing the breading mixture.
3. In a wide, shallow dish or pie plate, whisk or mix the flour, bread crumbs, Parmesan cheese, paprika, garlic powder, salt, onion powder, and black pepper until equally blended.
4. Preheat the air fryer from 375°F to 380°F (190 to 195 degrees C). Lightly coat the air fryer basket with nonstick spray.

5. Once the air fryer is heated, dip the chicken thighs, one at a time, into the breading mixture, making sure the breading adheres to both sides as much as possible. Place gently in the air fryer basket. Repeat until all thighs have been breaded and placed in the basket. They should not be stacked on top of one other.
6. Preheat the air fryer for 25 minutes. When the timer goes off, use an instant-read thermometer to check the temperature. The inside temperature should be 180 degrees Fahrenheit (82 degrees C). If they aren't quite done but the breading is turning black, close the basket and let them rest, or put the air fryer back on for a few minutes and check again. Serve right away.

Air Fryer Chicken and Waffle Kabobs

Preparation Time: 10 minutes | Cooking Time: 15 minutes | Servings: 1

Ingredients:
- 16 pieces of frozen popcorn chicken
- 15 ounces frozen mini waffles
- 20 4- to 6-inches wooden skewers
- 1 cup halved fresh strawberries
- ¼ cup fresh blueberries
- ¼ cup fresh raspberries

Directions:
1. Preheat the oven to 200° F. (93 degrees C). Preheat an air fryer to 400°F (200 degrees C).
2. Arrange the popcorn chicken in the air fryer basket in a single layer. Cook for 7 minutes, then turn and cook for another 2 to 3 minutes, or until lightly browned and crispy. Place the chicken pieces on a baking pan and keep warm in a preheated oven.
3. Meanwhile, stack half of the waffles in the air fryer basket in a single layer. Cook for 90 seconds, then turn and cook for another 20 seconds, or until light brown in places and crispy. Place on a baking sheet. Rep with the remaining waffles.
4. Thread 2 waffles and two chicken pieces onto each of 8 skewers. Thread the remaining 12 skewers with berries.

CHAPTER 5:
Beef, Pork & Lamb

Creamy Pork

Preparation Time: 10 minutes | Cooking Time: 22 minutes | Servings: 6

Ingredients:
- 1 tablespoon olive oil
- 1 minced garlic clove
- 3 cups chicken broth
- 1 ½ cups sour cream
- 2 tablespoons white flour
- 2 chopped yellow onions
- 2 tablespoons chopped chives
- 2 tablespoons sweet paprika
- Salt & black pepper as needed
- 2 oz. boneless & cubed pork meat

Directions:
1. Combine pork with oil, salt, and pepper in a pan that fits the air fryer.
2. Add to the air fryer and cook for 7 minutes at 360 degrees Fahrenheit.
3. Toss in the remaining ingredients and cook for an additional 15 minutes at 370 degrees Fahrenheit.
4. Serve once done, and enjoy!

Provencal Pork

Preparation Time: 10 minutes | Cooking Time: 15 minutes | Servings: 2

Ingredients:
- 1 sliced yellow onion
- ½ tablespoon dijon mustard
- 1 tablespoon olive oil
- 7 oz. pork tenderloin
- 1 strip-cut yellow bell pepper
- 1 strip-cut green bell pepper
- 2 teaspoons Provencal herbs
- Salt & black pepper as needed

Directions:
1. Combine all the bell peppers, salt and pepper, onion, Provencal herbs, and half oil in a pan that fits the air fryer.
2. Combine pork with salt and pepper, remaining oil, and mustard separately and add to the baking dish of veggies.
3. Add to the air fryer and cook for 15 minutes at 370 degrees Fahrenheit.
4. Toss in the remaining ingredients and cook for an additional 15 minutes at 370 degrees Fahrenheit.
5. Serve once done, and enjoy!

Easy Air Fried Pork Shoulder

Preparation Time: 30 minutes | Cooking Time: 1 hour 20 minutes | Servings: 6

Ingredients:
- 4 oz. pork shoulder
- 3 tablespoons canola oil
- 3 tablespoons minced garlic
- Salt & black pepper as needed

Directions:
1. Combine all the ingredients except pork in a bowl and brush the pork shoulder with this mixture.
2. Transfer to a preheated air fryer and cook for 10 minutes at 390 degrees Fahrenheit.
3. After, lower the temperature to 300 degrees and roast the pork shoulder for 1 hour and 10 minutes.
4. Slice before serving and enjoy!

Couscous Pork

Preparation Time: 10 minutes | Cooking Time: 35 minutes | Servings: 6

Ingredients:
- ¾ cup chicken broth
- 1 teaspoon dried basil
- 2 tablespoons olive oil
- 2 cups cooked couscous
- 1 teaspoon dried oregano
- 2 ¼ dried teaspoon sage
- ½ tablespoon sweet paprika
- ½ tablespoon minced garlic
- ¼ teaspoon dried rosemary
- ¼ teaspoon dried marjoram
- Salt & black pepper as needed
- 2 ½ oz. boneless & trimmed pork loin

Directions:
1. Combine all the ingredients except couscous in a bowl, add pork loin last, toss and set aside for an hour.
2. Add everything to a pan that fits the air fryer and cook for 35 minutes at 370 degrees Fahrenheit.
3. Serve once done with couscous and enjoy!

Beef & Green Onions Marinade

Preparation Time: 10 minutes | Cooking Time: 20 minutes | Servings: 4

Ingredients:
- ½ cup water
- 1 oz. lean beef
- 1 cup tamari sauce
- ¼ cup brown sugar
- ¼ cup sesame seeds
- 5 minced garlic cloves
- 1 teaspoon black pepper
- 1 cup chopped scallions

Directions:
1. Whisk all the ingredients in a bowl except beef.
2. Add beef to the mixture, toss and set aside for 10 minutes.
3. Drain the beef and add to the preheated air fryer to cook for 20 minutes at 390 degrees Fahrenheit.
4. Slice before serving and enjoy!

Marinated Lamb With Veggies

Preparation Time: 10 minutes | Cooking Time: 30 minutes | Servings: 4

Ingredients:
- 1 sliced onion
- ½ grated apple
- 1 chopped carrot
- 3 oz. bean sprouts
- 1 tablespoon sugar
- 1 minced garlic clove
- 8 oz. sliced lamb loin
- ½ tablespoon olive oil
- 5 tablespoons tamari sauce
- 2 tablespoons lemon juice
- 1 tablespoon grated ginger
- 1 grated small yellow onion
- Salt & black pepper as needed

Directions:
1. Combine grated onion, apple, garlic, ginger, tamari sauce, lemon juice, sugar, and black pepper in a bowl thoroughly.
2. Toss in the lamb and set aside for 10 minutes.
3. Heat oil in a pan that fits the air fryer over medium heat.
4. Stir in sliced onion, carrot, and bean sprouts to cook for 3 minutes.
5. Add the lamb with the mixture to the pan and transfer the pan to the air fryer.
6. Cook for 25 minutes at 360 degrees Fahrenheit.

87

7. Serve once done, and enjoy!

Air Fried Lamb Shanks

Preparation Time: 10 minutes | Cooking Time: 45 minutes | Servings: 4

Ingredients:
- 4 bay leaves
- 4 lamb shanks
- 5 oz. dry sherry
- 2 teaspoons maple syrup
- 1 tablespoon olive oil
- 1 chopped yellow onion
- 2 ½ cups chicken broth
- Salt & pepper as needed
- 2 tablespoons white flour
- 4 teaspoons crushed coriander seeds

Directions:
1. Marinate lamb shanks with half oil, salt, and pepper.
2. Place it in the air fryer to cook for 10 minutes at 360 degrees Fahrenheit.
3. Heat oil in a pan that fits in the air fryer over medium heat.
4. Stir in and cook onion and coriander for 5 minutes.
5. Stir in the remaining ingredients, including the lamb, let it boil, and add everything to the air fryer.
6. Cook again at 360 degrees Fahrenheit for half an hour.
7. Serve once done, and enjoy!

Fennel Flavored Pork Roast

Preparation Time: 10 minutes | Cooking Time: 1 hour | Servings: 10

Ingredients:
- ¼ cup canola oil
- 3 minced garlic cloves
- 1 teaspoon ground fennel
- 1 tablespoon fennel seeds
- Salt & black pepper as needed
- 2 teaspoons crushed red pepper
- 5 ½ oz. trimmed pork loin roast
- 2 tablespoons chopped oregano

Directions:
1. Blend all the ingredients except pork in a food processor until you get a paste.
2. Marinate the pork with the paste and add to the air fryer.
3. Cook it for half an hour at 350 degrees Fahrenheit.
4. Lower heat to 300 degrees Fahrenheit to cook for an additional 15 minutes.
5. Slice pork before serving and enjoy!

Mustard Marinated Beef

Preparation Time: 10 minutes | Cooking Time: 45 minutes | Servings: 6

Ingredients:
- 6 bacon strips
- 3 oz. beef roast
- ¾ cup red wine
- 1 ¾ cup beef broth
- 2 tablespoons butter
- 1 tablespoon dijon mustard
- 3 minced garlic cloves
- 1 tablespoon horseradish
- Salt & black pepper as needed

Directions:
1. Combine butter, mustard, garlic, horseradish, salt, and pepper in a bowl and marinate beef with this mixture.
2. Place bacon strips over a cutting board with beef on top.
3. Fold the bacon over the beef and add to the air fryer basket to cook for 15 minutes at 400 degrees Fahrenheit.

4. Remove it to a pan that fits the air fryer and add broth and wine to it.
5. Add the pan to the air fryer and cook for an additional 30 minutes at 360 degrees Fahrenheit.
6. Slice before serving and enjoy!

Lamb & Creamy Brussels Sprouts

Preparation Time: 10 minutes | Cooking Time: 1 hour 10 minutes | Servings: 4

Ingredients:
- ½ cup Greek yogurt
- 2 oz. scored lamb leg
- 1 minced garlic clove
- 2 tablespoons olive oil
- 1 melted tablespoon of butter
- Salt & black pepper as needed
- 1 tablespoon chopped thyme
- 1 ½ oz. trimmed Brussels sprouts

Directions:
1. Marinate lamb leg with rosemary, thyme, salt, and pepper, and brush with oil.
2. Transfer to the air fryer basket to cook for an hour at 300 degrees Fahrenheit.
3. Remove to a plate and keep it warm.
4. Combine Brussels sprouts, garlic, butter, sour cream, salt, and pepper in a pan that fits the air fryer.
5. Add the pan to the air fryer and cook for 10 minutes at 400 degrees Fahrenheit.
6. Serve the lamb with the Brussels sprouts mixture and enjoy!

Crispy Lamb

Preparation Time: 10 minutes | Cooking Time: 30 minutes | Servings: 4

Ingredients:
- 1 egg
- 28 oz. lamb rack
- 1 tablespoon olive oil
- 1 minced garlic clove
- 1 tablespoon Italian bread crumbs
- Salt & black pepper as needed
- 1 tablespoon chopped oregano
- 2 tablespoons toasted & crushed macadamia nuts

Directions:
1. Combine oil and garlic in a bowl thoroughly, marinate lamb with this mixture, and season with salt and pepper.
2. Combine nuts, oregano, and breadcrumbs in another bowl.
3. Whisk the egg in a separate bowl.
4. Take the lamb and dip it first in the egg, then in the nuts mixture.
5. Add the coated lamb to the air fryer basket to cook for 25 minutes at 360 degrees Fahrenheit.
6. Turn up the temperature to 400 degrees Fahrenheit and cook for an additional 5 minutes.
7. Serve warm and enjoy!

Oregano Pork Roll

Preparation Time: 8 minutes | Cooking Time: 50 minutes | Servings: 8

Ingredients:
- 1 teaspoon sea salt
- 1 oz. pork leg roll
- 1 teaspoon dried oregano
- 1 tablespoon avocado oil

Directions:

1. Use a knife to pierce a pork leg roll five times.
2. Marinate it with salt and oregano.
3. Brush with avocado oil next.
4. Transfer to the air fryer and cook for 50 minutes at 375 degrees Fahrenheit.
5. Flip after 35 minutes and slice into 8 servings.
6. Serve immediately and enjoy!

Beef Strips With Snow Peas

Preparation Time: 10 minutes | Cooking Time: 22 minutes | Servings: 2

Ingredients:

- 7 oz. snow peas
- 1 teaspoon olive oil
- 2 strip-cut beef steaks
- 1 ring-cut red onion
- 2 tablespoons tamari sauce
- Salt & black pepper as needed
- 8 oz. halved white mushrooms

Directions:

1. Combine olive oil and soy sauce in a bowl thoroughly and marinate beef strips with it.
2. Combine snow peas, mushrooms, onion rings, oil, salt, and pepper in a pan that fits the air fryer.
3. Cook it at 350 degrees Fahrenheit for 16 minutes.
4. After, place the beef strips in the pan and cook for an additional 6 minutes at 400 degrees Fahrenheit.
5. Serve once done, and enjoy!

Simple Thyme Lamb

Preparation Time: 10 minutes | Cooking Time: 15 minutes | Servings: 3

Ingredients:

- 1 teaspoon salt
- 12 oz. lamb rack
- 1 tablespoon canola oil
- 1 tablespoon dried thyme

Directions:

1. Marinate the rake of lamb with thyme and salt thoroughly.
2. Finish by sprinkling canola oil and transferring it to the air fryer basket.
3. Cook at 355 degrees Fahrenheit for 15 minutes.
4. Once done, let it cool before cutting.
5. Serve onto plates and enjoy!

Chinese Steak & Broccoli

Preparation Time: 45 minutes | Cooking Time: 12 minutes | Servings: 4

Ingredients:

- ⅓ cup sherry
- 1 teaspoon sugar
- 1 oz. broccoli florets
- ⅓ cup oyster sauce
- 1 teaspoon tamari sauce
- 1 minced garlic clove
- 1 tablespoon canola oil
- 2 teaspoons sesame oil
- ¾ oz. strip-cut round steak

Directions:

1. Marinate beef with sesame oil, oyster sauce, tamari sauce, sherry, and sugar, and set aside for half an hour.
2. Add the beef to a pan that fits the air fryer along with broccoli, garlic, and oil.

3. Combine everything well and transfer to the air fryer to cook for 12 minutes at 380 degrees Fahrenheit.
4. Serve once done, and enjoy!

Tasty Pork Rolls

Preparation Time: 10 minutes | Cooking Time: 15 minutes | Servings: 3

Ingredients:

- 3 egg roll wraps
- ¼ teaspoon kosher salt
- 7 oz. ground pork
- 1 teaspoon olive oil
- 1 chopped scallions
- 1 teaspoon tahini sauce
- ¼ teaspoon minced garlic
- ¾ teaspoon ground ginger

Directions:

1. Heat olive oil in a pan and add all the ingredients except wraps.
2. Cook it for 10 minutes while stirring with a spoon in between.
3. Take an egg roll wrap and fill with a spoon of the cooked pork mixture.
4. Roll into an egg roll and place it in the air fryer basket as you go.
5. Once all are done, cook them in the air fryer at 400 degrees Fahrenheit for 3 minutes.
6. Flip to the other side and cook for a minute more.
7. Serve with any choice of sauce.

Garlic Lamb Chops

Preparation Time: 10 minutes | Cooking Time: 10 minutes | Servings: 4

Ingredients:

- 8 lamb chops
- 3 tablespoons olive oil
- 4 minced garlic cloves
- Salt & black pepper as needed
- 1 tablespoon chopped rosemary
- 1 tablespoon ground coriander

Directions:

1. Combine all the ingredients in a bowl.
2. Add the lamb chops to the air fryer to cook for 10 minutes at 400 degrees Fahrenheit.
3. Serve once done, and enjoy!

Baked Pork Sausages

Preparation Time: 15 minutes | Cooking Time: 5 minutes | Servings: 4

Ingredients:

- 4 slices cheese
- 7 oz. sourdough
- 4 pork sausages
- 2 teaspoon BBQ sauce
- Bamboo skewers as needed

Directions:

1. Roll up sourdough and cut it into 4 triangles using a knife.
2. Put each sausage on each one of the triangles.
3. Top with cheese and roll the triangles into wraps.
4. Use bamboo skewers to skew the rolled sausages and place them in the air fryer basket.
5. Bake at 385 degrees Fahrenheit for 5 minutes or until cooked and lightly golden-brown.
6. Serve with any choice of sauce.

Lamb Stew

Preparation Time: 5 minutes | Cooking Time: 30 minutes |
Servings: 4

Ingredients:
- 1 cup cubed eggplant
- 2 minced garlic cloves
- 3 chopped celery ribs
- ½ cups tomato puree
- 1 tablespoon canola oil
- 1 oz. cubed lamb stew meat
- Salt & black pepper as needed

Directions:
1. Heat canola oil in a pan that fits the air fryer over medium heat.
2. Toss in the lamb with garlic, salt, and pepper and cook for 5 minutes.
3. Add the remaining ingredients, combine and transfer the pan to the air fryer.
4. Cook for 25 minutes at 370 degrees Fahrenheit.
5. Serve once done, and enjoy!

Smoked Beef Strips

Preparation Time: 10 minutes | Cooking Time: 1.5 hours |
Servings: 2

Ingredients:
- 6 oz. round beef strips
- ½ teaspoon brown sugar
- ¼ teaspoon liquid smoke
- ⅓ teaspoon minced onion
- ¼ teaspoon minced garlic
- 2 tablespoons tamari sauce
- ¼ teaspoon cayenne pepper

Directions:
1. Combine all the ingredients, except beef strips.
2. Add the beef strips and marinate.
3. Leave the strips in the marination in the fridge overnight.
4. Preheat the air fryer to 180 degrees Fahrenheit.
5. Transfer the beef strips to the air fryer and cook for 1.5 hours.
6. Once cooked, serve on plates and enjoy!

Garlic & Sprouts Pork Stew

Preparation Time: 5 minutes | Cooking Time: 25 minutes |
Servings: 4

Ingredients:
- 2 cubed tomatoes
- ¼ cup veggie broth
- ¼ cup tomato puree
- 2 minced garlic cloves
- 2 tablespoons olive oil
- 1 oz. cubed pork stew meat
- 1 tablespoon chopped chives
- ½ oz. halved Brussels sprouts
- Salt & black pepper as needed

Directions:
1. Heat olive oil in a pan that fits the air fryer over medium heat.
2. Toss in the meat with garlic, salt, and pepper and cook for 5 minutes.
3. Add the remaining ingredients except for chives, combine and transfer the pan to the air fryer.
4. Cook for 20 minutes at 380 degrees Fahrenheit.
5. Serve once done and enjoy with a sprinkling of chives on top!

Beef Vinegar Chops

Preparation Time: 10 minutes | Cooking Time: 14 minutes |
Servings: 3

Ingredients:
- 3 beef steaks
- ¼ teaspoon salt
- 1 teaspoon olive oil
- 1 tablespoon paprika
- 1 teaspoon white wine vinegar
- ¼ teaspoon ground black pepper

Directions:
1. Mix olive oil and vinegar in a bowl.
2. Combine the rest of the ingredients in a separate bowl except steaks.
3. Marinate the steaks in the dry ingredients bowl.
4. Finish by sprinkling the vinegar mixture onto the steaks.
5. Transfer the steaks to the air fryer.
6. Cook for 7 minutes at 400 degrees Fahrenheit from each side.
7. Cook for 5 minutes more for a golden-brown crust.
8. Serve once done, and enjoy!

Pork & Okra Stew

Preparation time: 5 minutes | Cooking time: 20 minutes |
Servings: 4

Ingredients:
- 1 cup okra
- 1 tablespoon canola oil
- 4 minced garlic cloves
- 2 teaspoons sweet paprika
- Salt & black pepper as needed
- 1 ½ oz. cubed & browned pork stew meat

Directions:
1. Toss in all the ingredients in the pan of the air fryer.
2. Combine well and cook for 20 minutes at 370 degrees Fahrenheit.
3. Serve once done, and enjoy!

Ham & Pineapple Sandwich

Preparation Time: 5 minutes | Cooking Time: 5 minutes |
Servings: 2

Ingredients:
- 2 pineapple rings
- 2 whole-wheat buns
- 2 tablespoons tomato paste
- 2 slices of smoked ham
- 2 teaspoons shredded cheddar cheese

Directions:
1. Preheat the air fryer to 320 degrees Fahrenheit.
2. Halve the buns and transfer them to the air fryer basket.
3. Cook to make the buns crispy and remove once done
4. Add ham, a single pineapple ring, and cheese onto each half of the bun.
5. Transfer to the air fryer basket.
6. Cook for 3 minutes until the cheese is slightly melted.
7. Serve immediately with ketchup and enjoy!

Beef & Tomato Mix

Preparation Time: 5 minutes | Cooking Time: 25 minutes |
Servings: 4

Ingredients:
- 15 oz. tomato puree
- 1 minced garlic clove
- 1 ½ oz. cubed beef stew meat
- ½ cup chopped scallions

- 3 tablespoons melted butter
- ½ cup chopped celery stalks
- ½ teaspoon Italian seasoning
- Salt & black pepper as needed

Directions:
1. Heat butter in a pan that fits the air fryer over medium heat.
2. Toss in the meat and cook for 5 minutes.
3. Add the remaining ingredients, combine and transfer the pan to the air fryer.
4. Cook for 20 minutes at 390 degrees Fahrenheit.
5. Serve once done, and enjoy!

Beef Ravioli

Preparation Time: 10 minutes | Cooking Time: 15 minutes | Servings: 4

Ingredients:
- 2 beaten eggs
- 1 oz. grated pecorino cheese
- 7 oz. frozen beef ravioli
- ½ teaspoon minced garlic
- ½ teaspoon minced onion
- 1 teaspoon chopped parsley
- 2 tablespoons Italian breadcrumbs

Directions:
1. Add breadcrumbs, onion, garlic, pecorino, and parsley to a bowl and combine.
2. Dip the ravioli in the eggs and coat them with the dry mixture.
3. Place the coated ravioli in the air fryer pan and close the lid.
4. Cook it for 15 minutes at 385 degrees Fahrenheit and flip after 7 minutes.
5. Once it's tender, remove it and serve with any sauce you prefer.

Cardamom Lamb Mix

Preparation Time: 30 minutes | Cooking Time: 20 minutes | Servings: 2

Ingredients:
- ¼ teaspoon salt
- 10 oz. lamb sirloin
- 1 oz. sliced fresh ginger
- ½ teaspoon red pepper flakes
- ½ teaspoon fennel seeds
- 1 tablespoon sesame oil
- 2 oz. chopped spring onions
- ¼ teaspoon ground cinnamon
- ½ teaspoon ground cardamom

Directions:
1. Blend all the ingredients except lamb in a blender until you obtain a smooth paste.
2. Make small cuts in the lamb and marinate it with the mixture.
3. Set it aside for 20 minutes and preheat the air fryer to 350 degrees Fahrenheit.
4. Place the lamb in the air fryer and cook for 20 minutes, flipping the meat after 10 minutes.
5. Slice before serving and enjoy!

Mini Pork Burgers

Preparation Time: 5 minutes | Cooking Time: 25 minutes | Servings: 4

Ingredients:
- 1 egg
- Fresh cilantro
- Salt as needed

- All spices powder
- 500g minced pork
- Garlic powder as needed
- Ground pepper as needed
- 1 tablespoon panko breadcrumbs
- Mini bread burgers as needed

Directions:
1. Combine all the ingredients except buns.
2. Shape into small patties out of the mixture.
3. Cook in the air fryer for 20 minutes at 220 degrees Fahrenheit.
4. Put the cooked patties onto the buns and serve immediately.

Bacon Shrimp Snack

Preparation Time: 10 minutes | Cooking Time: 10 minutes Servings: 4

Ingredients:
- 14 oz. sliced bacon
- 16 oz. peeled deveined shrimp

Directions:
1. Preheat the air fryer to 390 degrees Fahrenheit for 4 minutes.
2. Wrap the bacon over the shrimp and put it in the fridge for 20 minutes.
3. After, add it to the air fryer basket and cook for 6 minutes.
4. Remove and serve immediately.

Bacon Avocado Fries

Preparation Time: 5 minutes | Cooking Time: 10 minutes | Servings: 5

Ingredients:
- 10 thin strips of bacon
- ½ teaspoon ranch dressing
- 1 sliced into 10 pieces avocado

Directions:
1. Wrap every 8 slices of avocado with bacon strips.
2. Cut off excess bacon strips.
3. Cook in the air fryer at 400 degrees Fahrenheit for 8 minutes.
4. Serve immediately with ranch dressing.

Ginger Bacon Partridges

Preparation Time: 15 minutes | Cooking time: 20 minutes | Servings: 6

Ingredients:
- 1 teaspoon kosher salt
- 3 oz. sliced bacon
- 1 tablespoon olive oil
- 1 teaspoon minced ginger
- ½ teaspoon garlic powder
- 18 oz. trimmed partridges
- ½ teaspoon smoked paprika

Directions:
1. Marinate the partridges with minced ginger, garlic powder, salt, and smoked paprika.
2. Wrap the partridges over sliced bacon and brush with avocado oil.
3. Add the wrapped partridges to the air fryer basket to cook for 20 minutes at 375 degrees Fahrenheit.
4. Flip on the other side after 10 minutes.
5. Serve once done, and enjoy!

Beef Steak & Chimichurri

Preparation Time: 5 minutes | Cooking Time: 20 minutes | Servings: 5

Ingredients:
- 16 oz. steak
- 20g parsley
- 20g ground coriander
- 1 lemon juice
- 1 small onion
- 20g fresh basil
- 4 anchovy fillets
- 2 peeled garlic cloves
- Salt & pepper as needed
- 1 tablespoon canola oil
- A pinch of crushed red pepper
- 6 tablespoons extra virgin olive oil

Directions:
1. Add all the ingredients to a blender.
2. Mix until you reach the desired consistency and preheat the air fryer at 360 degrees Fahrenheit.
3. Rub vegetable oil on the steak and season with salt and pepper.
4. Add to the air fryer basket and cook the steak for 6 minutes.
5. Allow cooling for 5 minutes when finished.
6. Top with chimichurri sauce and serve immediately.

Delicious Beef Kabobs

Preparation Time: 10 minutes | Cooking Time: 30 minutes | Servings: 4

Ingredients:
- 1 bell pepper
- 8 6-inch skewers
- ½ medium onion
- ¼ teaspoon pepper
- 2 tablespoons tamari sauce
- ⅓ cup Greek yogurt
- 16 oz boneless beef chuck ribs

Directions:
1. Cut the ribs into pieces 1-inch wide
2. Combine the tamari sauce, ribs, and Greek yogurt in a lidded tub, making sure the meat is fully covered.
3. Refrigerate for half an hour at least.
4. Soak the wooden skewers for approximately 10 minutes in water.
5. Preheat the air fryer to 400 degrees Fahrenheit.
6. Slice onion and bell pepper into 1-inch pieces.
7. Remove the meat from the marinade and drain.
8. Layer the onions, beef, and bell peppers on the skewers and dust with pepper.
9. Cook for 10 minutes in the air fryer, ensuring you spin the skewers 5 minutes before the cooking time ends.
10. Serve hot immediately, and enjoy!

Air Fried Roast Beef

Preparation Time: 10 minutes | Cooking Time: 45 minutes | Servings: 8

Ingredients:
- Seasonings of choice
- 1 tablespoon olive oil
- Roast beef as needed

Directions:
1. Preheat the air fryer to 160 degrees Fahrenheit.
2. Combine roast beef with olive oil and seasonings of choice.
3. Add to the air fryer basket and cook for half an hour or until tender.

4. Flip if the air fryer alerts or do it after 15 minutes.
5. Cook for another 15 minutes and slice before serving!

Homemade Pork Buns

Preparation Time: 20 minutes | Cooking Time: 25 minutes | Servings: 8

Ingredients:
- 1 beaten egg
- Diced pulled pork
- 1 teaspoon tamari sauce
- 1 cup barbecue sauce
- Parchment paper as needed
- 3 thinly-sliced scallions
- 16 ⅓ oz. refrigerated buttermilk biscuits dough

Directions:
1. Preheat the air fryer to 325 degrees Fahrenheit.
2. Line the baking tray with parchment paper.
3. Add scallions to the pork and combine.
4. Separate and press the dough to form 8 four-inch rounds.
5. Add two tablespoons of pork mixture to each biscuit round's center.
6. Cover the dough edges by pinching close.
7. Carefully place the buns on the sheet.
8. Brush a mixture of soy sauce and egg on top.
9. Cook for 25 minutes until tender and golden-brown.
10. Serve immediately and enjoy!

Delicious Lamb Meatballs

Preparation Time: 5 minutes | Cooking Time: 30 minutes | Servings: 8

Ingredients:
- 1 lime zest
- 1 lime juice
- 3 beaten eggs
- ½ cup almond meal
- Cooking spray as needed
- 2 chopped spring onions
- 1 tablespoon minced garlic
- 2 ½ oz. ground lamb meat
- A pinch of salt & black pepper
- 2 tablespoons chopped mint
- 2 tablespoons chopped parsley

Directions:
1. Combine all the ingredients except cooking spray in a bowl and shape medium-sized meatballs out of the mixture.
2. Transfer the meatballs to the air fryer and grease them with cooking spray.
3. Cook for 15 minutes at 390 degrees Fahrenheit on each side.
4. Serve once done, and enjoy!

Hot Paprika Beef

Preparation Time: 5 minutes | Cooking Time: 20 minutes | Servings: 4

Ingredients:
- 4 beef steaks
- 1 tablespoon chipotle powder
- 1 tablespoon melted butter
- Salt & black pepper as needed

Directions:
1. Marinate the beef with the remaining ingredients in a bowl and add to the air fryer basket.
2. Cook for 10 minutes on each side at 390 degrees Fahrenheit.

3. Serve once done, and enjoy!

Cumin Pork Steak
Preparation Time: 10 minutes | Cooking Time: 25 minutes | Servings: 4

Ingredients:
- ½ teaspoon sea salt
- 1 tablespoon sesame oil
- ½ teaspoon dried garlic
- ½ teaspoon ground coriander
- ½ teaspoon ground paprika
- 16 oz. (4 oz. each) pork steak

Directions:
1. Combine steak with all the ingredients and brush with sesame oil in the end.
2. Add the marinated steak to a preheated air fryer and cook for 15 minutes at 400 degrees Fahrenheit.
3. Flip to the other side and cook for an additional 10 minutes.
4. Serve once done, and enjoy!

Cheeseburger Pockets
Preparation Time: 10 minutes | Cooking Time: 8 minutes | Servings: 2

Ingredients
- 1 biscuit can be sliced into 8 pieces
- 1 pound ground beef, cooked
- 1 cup of American cheese, shredded

Directions
1. Take the biscuit dough out of the can, lay it flat on the surface, and roll it using a rolling pin till thin, slicing it into 8 equal pieces.
2. Put beef and cheese on four of the dough pieces and lay the remaining four over it, pulling the dough and closing it from the ends using a fork.
3. Grease the air fryer basket with some oil and arrange the burger pockets in a single layer.
4. Drizzle some olive oil over the pockets and cook them for about 8 minutes at around 360 degrees F.
5. Once they get nice and brown, take them out and serve with a dipping sauce of choice.

Air Fryer Hamburgers
Preparation Time: 15 minutes | Cooking Time: 10 minutes | Servings: 4

Ingredients
- 1.5-pound lean ground beef, 80/20
- Salt and black pepper, to taste
- 1 teaspoon minced onion
- ½ teaspoon minced garlic
- ½ cup barbecue sauce, optional
- 4 hamburger buns for serving
- Desired toppings, as needed

Directions
1. First, preheat the air fryer to around 370 degrees F.
2. Mix the lean ground beef, salt, pepper, garlic, and onion in a bowl.
3. Oncc the beef is properly mixed with the seasoning, divide the mixture into four portions and flatten them to make patties, each about ½ inch thick. Use a brush and coat the patties with barbecue sauce if used.
4. Place the patties in a single layer in the air fryer basket and cook them for 5 minutes on each side.

5. If the burgers have cheese, place them on the patties and cook for an additional minute and serve on a bun with toppings of your choice.

Mint Lamb with Toasted Hazelnuts and Peas
Preparation Time: 15 minutes | Cooking Time: 25 -30 minutes | Servings: 4

Ingredients
- 2 ounces hazelnuts
- 2 pounds lamb shoulder, cut into 1-inch strips
- 2 tablespoons avocado oil
- 4 tablespoons mint leaves, chopped
- ½ cup green peas
- Olive oil, for greasing
- 1 tablespoon white wine
- Salt and pepper, according to taste

Directions
1. Add the hazelnuts to a skillet and roast them till fragrant.
2. Once done, take them out and set them aside.
3. Mix oil, salt, and pepper in a bowl and add the lamb strips, tossing to coat all the lamb strips evenly.
4. Grease the inside of the air fryer basket with oil and shift the lamb strips in it.
5. Garnish strips with mint and roasted hazelnuts.
6. Drizzle the white wine over all the ingredients and mix the peas in it, coating everything with a layer of oil and cooking it for about 25 minutes at 400 degrees F.
7. Once done, serve.

Empanadas
Preparation Time: 15 minutes | Cooking Time: 20 minutes | Servings: 2

Ingredients
- 1 pound of ground beef
- 1 bell pepper
- 1 pack of taco seasoning
- ¼ cup beef stock
- 2 packs pie crust, room temperature
- 1 cup cheddar cheese, shredded
- ½ red onion, diced
- 1 egg, whisked

Directions
1. Begin by cooking the beef over medium heat with onions and pepper until the beef is cooked and translucent.
2. Then mix in the taco seasoning and stock.
3. Take the pie crust and lay it flat on a greased surface.
4. Roll it flat using a rolling pin to about 5 inches in diameter and cut 3 equal circles from the dough.
5. Mix the leftover dough with the other pie crust dough and lay it flat on the surface, flattening it like the previous dough.
6. Make three other 3 circles from the dough and do the same with the remaining dough until 8 total dough circles are made.
7. Take 4 to 6 teaspoons of the beef mixture and place it in the center of the dough.
8. Add the cheese as you add the meat filling.
9. Close the empanadas.
10. Brush the edges of the dough with water and close the edges, using a fork and pressing shut the edges.
11. Crack and whisk the egg in a bowl and brush it on all the empanadas.
12. Place the empanadas inside a greased air fryer and cook it for 5 to 7 minutes at around 350 degrees F.

13. Once done, take them out and serve with a side of choice.

Steak Fajita with Onions and Peppers

Preparation Time: 15 minutes | Cooking Time: 8 minutes | Servings: 2

Ingredients
- 1.5-pound tenderloin steak, thin cut
- Salt and pepper, according to taste
- 1/3 cup red onions, sliced
- 1 pack of fajita seasoning, gluten-free
- Olive oil, for greasing
- 4 corn/flour tortillas, gluten-free

Directions
1. Start by covering the air fryer basket with aluminum foil and greasing it with oil.
2. Cut the steak into ¼-inch slices.
3. Season the steak with salt, pepper, fajita seasoning, and onions.
4. Place it inside the baking dish and cook it for about 8 minutes at 390 degrees F, making sure to flip it halfway.
5. Once done, take them out and serve them with the side of the tortilla of your choice.

Air Fryer Nachos

Preparation Time: 15 minutes | Cooking Time: 5 minutes | Servings: 2

Ingredients
- 4 cups corn tortilla chips
- 1 ½ cups ground beef chili, cooked
- 2 cups cheddar cheese, shredded

Directions
1. Add the tortilla chips to the air fryer basket, filling it up to about 1/3.
2. Top the chips with half of the cheese and beef chili.
3. Add the remaining chips and fill the air fryer basket to 2/3.
4. Top the chips with the remaining beef chili and cheese.
5. Place the air fryer basket back in the air fryer and cook it for about 3 to 5 minutes at 350 degrees F.

Air Fryer Taco Pie

Preparation Time: 15 minutes | Cooking Time: 25 minutes | Servings: 2

Ingredients
- 1 tablespoon oil
- 1 cup onions, diced
- 1 pound of ground beef/ vegetarian protein
- 1 tablespoon taco seasoning
- ½ cup corn kernels
- ½ cup Bisquick
- 1 cup almond milk
- 2 eggs
- 1 cup cheddar cheese, shredded
- 1 cup romaine lettuce, chopped
- 1 ½ cup tomatoes, diced

Directions
1. Heat oil over medium heat in a skillet and add the onions, sautéing them for about 3 minutes.
2. Once the onions start turning translucent, mix in the meat and cook it till done.
3. Then stir in the seasoning and corn.
4. Meanwhile, add milk, egg, and Bisquick to a bowl and mix, pouring them inside the skillet once properly mixed.
5. Grease the air fryer basket and lay foil over it.

6. Shift the mix in it, and top with cheese.
7. Cook it for 16 minutes at about 370 degrees F, making sure to stir it occasionally.
8. Once done, top it with tomatoes and lettuce and serve.

Air Fryer Beef and Bean Taquitos

Preparation Time: 15 minutes | Cooking Time: 20 minutes | Servings: 2

Ingredients
- 1.5-pound ground beef
- 1 pack of taco seasoning, gluten-free
- 1 can of refried beans
- 1 cup cheddar cheese, shredded
- 8 flour tortillas
- Oil spray, for greasing

Directions
1. Start by cooking the beef in a skillet.
2. While cooking, add the taco seasoning and stir it.
3. Place the tortillas on a skillet and heat them when the meat is done.
4. Cover the air fryer basket with foil and grease it with oil.
5. Top each tortilla with some cheese, beans, and cooked beef.
6. Wrap it as tight as possible and place it in the greased air fryer basket, making sure to keep the seam side down.
7. Grease the tortilla wrap with some oil and cook it for about 12 minutes at around 390 degrees F.

Keota Kebabs

Preparation Time: 15 minutes | Cooking Time: 12 minutes | Servings: 2

Ingredients
- 1.5 pound beef, grounded
- ½ pound lamb, grounded
- 2 onions, finely diced
- 4 cloves garlic, minced
- 1/3 cup cilantro, chopped
- 2 teaspoons ground coriander
- 1 teaspoon allspice
- ¼ teaspoon nutmeg
- 1/3 teaspoon paprika
- ¼ teaspoon cinnamon
- salt and black pepper, to taste

Directions
1. Add all the ingredients inside a food processor and pulse them till everything is mixed and forms a smooth mixture
2. Scoop some of the meat mix and form patties resembling patties.
3. Mist the patties with oil spray.
4. Arrange them inside the baking dish in a single layer and cook them for 12 minutes at around 380 degrees F, making sure to turn them halfway through the cooking.

Beef Chimichangas

Preparation Time: 15 minutes | Cooking Time: 10 minutes | Servings: 4

Ingredients
- 1 pound beef, grounded
- 1 pack of taco seasoning
- ½ cup refried beans
- ½ cup Mexican cheese, shredded
- 10 flour tortillas
- Taco toppings of choice

Directions

1. Cook the beef in a skillet and stir in the taco seasoning while cooking.
2. When done, add the refried beans and stir them.
3. Divide the mixture in each tortilla and top it with the desired seasoning, making sure not to overflow.
4. Wrap the tortilla as tight as possible.
5. Grease the inside of the air fryer basket with oil and place the tortillas in it, keeping the seam side down.
6. Grease the chimichangas with some oil and cook them for about 10 minutes at around 360 degrees F.

Zucchini Stuffed With Hamburgers

Preparation Time: 15 minutes | Cooking Time: 15 minutes | Servings: 4

Ingredients

- 4 zucchinis
- 1 pound beef, grounded
- 1 cup tomato puree
- Salt and peppers, according to taste
- 1 tablespoon Italian seasoning
- 1 tablespoon garlic, minced
- 1 cup cheddar cheese, grated

Directions

1. Begin by thoroughly washing the zucchinis and cutting them in half.
2. Scoop out the zucchini flesh, leaving a bowl shape of zucchini.
3. Season the zucchini bowl with salt, pepper, and ½ tablespoon of Italian seasoning.
4. Cook the beef in a pan with garlic, remaining Italian seasoning, salt, and pepper, and add the tomato puree once it begins to brown.
5. Stuff the zucchinis with it and top with cheese equally.
6. Cover the inside of the air fryer basket with foil and grease it with oil.
7. Place the stuffed zucchinis basket and cook for 16 minutes a 400 degrees F.
8. Once done, serve.

Pizza Burgers

Preparation Time: 15 minutes | Cooking Time: 25 minutes | Servings: 2

Ingredients

- 1 pound meatloaf beef, veal, and pork
- 2 tablespoons onions, minced
- ½ cup pepperonis, chopped
- 2 tablespoons tomato puree
- 1 teaspoon Italian seasoning
- salt and black pepper, to taste
- 1 cup marinara sauce
- 1 cup of mozzarella, shredded
- 4 crusty focaccia bread

Directions

1. Begin by preheating the air fryer to around 370 degrees F.
2. Add the meatloaf mix, pepperonis, onions, tomato puree, Italian seasoning, salt, and pepper in a bowl and mix till everything is thoroughly combined.
3. Divide the mixture into 4 parts, make patties with them, and make a slight indent in the center of each patty.
4. Cut the rolls in half and coat them with some olive oil.
5. Place the patties inside the air fryer basket and cook them for about 15 minutes, making sure to flip them halfway.

6. When done, add a spoon of marinara sauce and mozzarella cheese on top of the patties and cook them for 3 more minutes.
7. When done, take the patties out and place the rolls in them, cooking them for about 3 minutes.
8. Once the rolls are also done, take them out, place the cooked patties on top, sprinkle a bit of Italian seasoning, and serve.

Roasted Bacon Brussels sprouts

Preparation Time: 15 minutes | Cooking Time: 20 minutes | Servings: 2

Ingredients

- 1 pound Brussels sprouts
- 1/3 cup bacon bits
- 1 tablespoon olive oil
- Salt and pepper, according to taste

Directions

1. Begin by trimming the bottoms of Brussels sprouts, rinsing them, and patting them dry using a paper towel.
2. Place them in a bowl and toss with olive oil, salt, and pepper.
3. Once all the Brussels sprouts are evenly coated, shift them to the air fryer basket and cook them for about 20 minutes at 400 degrees F.
4. When done, top it with bacon bits, sprinkle some salt and pepper, and serve.

Roasted Lamb Rack with Lemon Cumin Crust

Preparation Time: 15 minutes | Cooking Time: 25 minutes | Servings: 4

Ingredients

- 2 pounds Frenched lamb rack
- Salt and pepper, according to taste
- 6 ounces of panko breadcrumbs
- 2 teaspoons garlic, grated
- ¼ teaspoon salt
- ¼ teaspoon coriander
- 1 teaspoon ground coriander
- Lemon rind, grated
- 1 egg, beaten

Directions

1. Start by preheating the air fryer to around 350 degrees F.
2. Season the lamb rack with salt and pepper generously.
3. Add grated garlic, and breadcrumbs in a bowl, ½ teaspoon salt, coriander, ground coriander, oil, and lemon rinds, and mix them until thoroughly mixed.
4. In another bowl, crack and whisk the egg.
5. Then dip the lamb rack in the whisked egg and coat them with the breadcrumbs mix.
6. Shift them to the air fryer basket and cook them for 20 minutes at around 350 Degrees.
7. Once the time is up, crank the heat to around 390 and cook the rack for another 5 minutes.
8. When done, take the lamb rack out and rest for 10 minutes before serving.

Cabbage and Beef Rolls

Preparation Time: 15 minutes | Cooking Time: 10 minutes | Servings: 2

Ingredients:

- 8 egg roll wraps
- 1-pound corned beef, shredded
- 1 cup cabbage, stewed
- ½ cup Dijon mustard

Directions

1. Add corned beef and cabbage together in a bowl and mix till evenly mixed.
2. Lay the egg roll wrap on a flat surface and add a spoonful of the beef and cabbage mix in the center.
3. Brush the edges of the rolls with a bit of water and roll them, making sure to seal the edges properly.
4. Grease all the rolls with oil and palace them inside the air fryer basket, cooking them for about 10 minutes at around 390 degrees F.
5. When done, take them out and serve with a side of mustard.

Steak Kebab

Preparation Time: 15 minutes | Cooking Time: 10 minutes | Servings: 4

Ingredients

- 1 pound sirloin steak
- ¼ cup olive oil
- ¼ cup tamari sauce
- 1 tablespoon garlic, minced
- 1 teaspoon brown sugar
- ½ teaspoon ground coriander
- ¼ teaspoon black pepper
- 10 ounces of mushrooms, stems removed
- 1 onion, diced into 1-inch cubes
- 1 green bell pepper, diced into 1-inch cubes
- Salt and pepper, according to taste

Directions

1. Add the steak pieces to the bowl and toss with tamari sauce, oil, garlic, brown sugar, ground coriander, salt, and pepper, letting the pieces marinate in the mixture for at least 30 minutes.
2. When the steak has marinated for enough time, take them out and skewer them through the skewer with Bella mushrooms, green peppers, and onions.
3. Place the skewers in the air fryer in a single layer and cook them for about 10 minutes or till done.

Mediterranean Rib eye

Preparation Time: 15 minutes | Cooking Time: 70 minutes | Servings: 2

Ingredients:

- 4 cloves minced garlic
- Pinch of salt and pepper
- 2 beef steaks, rib eye
- 3 tablespoons chopped basil
- 1 tablespoon minced thyme
- 1 tablespoon olive oil
- ½ lime's juice
- 2 tablespoon cottage cheese crumbles

Directions

1. Add water to the pot and heat it to 230 degrees F; make sure the water is exactly 230 degrees F as it will be used to cook the steak by the sous-vide method.
2. While the water reaches the temperature, season the steak generously with salt and pepper. Mix minced garlic with basil and thyme and coat the steak with it.
3. Place the seasoned steak inside a zip lock bag, remove as much air as possible and close the bag.
4. Place the bag in the heated water, cover the pot, and let the steak cook for about 1 hour.
5. When done, take out of the zip lock bag and wipe it dry using a paper towel.
6. Put a rack inside the air fryer and place the steak on it, drizzling some oil over it and cooking it for about 10 minutes at around 390 degrees F.

7. Monitor the steak's internal temperature and take it out once the internal temperature reaches 140 degrees F.
8. Sprinkle some crumbled cheese on the steak, drizzle some lemon juice, and serve.

Skirt Steak with Balsamic Shallots

Preparation Time: 25 minutes | Cooking Time: 15 minutes | Servings: 2

Ingredients

- 4 tablespoons balsamic vinegar
- 2 teaspoon brown sugar
- Salt and pepper, according to taste
- 2 cloves garlic, chopped
- ½ avocado oil
- 1 pound steak, skirt
- 10 shallots, peeled

Directions

1. Add all the ingredients, except the steak, to a bowl and give them a mix.
2. Once all the ingredients are mixed, add the steak to the marinade and rest in it for about 30 minutes.
3. Place an airflow rack inside the air fryer and place the steak over it once it has rested in the marinade for enough time.
4. Cook the skirt steak in the air fryer for about 15 minutes at 400 degrees F.
5. Once done, take the steak out of the air fryer, let it rest for at least 10 minutes, and serve with the side of your choice.

Quick Kofta

Preparation Time: 15 minutes | Cooking Time: 15 minutes | Servings: 4

Ingredients

- 2 onions
- 1/3 cup breadcrumbs
- 4 tablespoons mint
- ½ teaspoon salt, or according to taste
- 1 teaspoon garlic clove, crushed
- 2 tablespoons tomato paste
- 1/3 teaspoon ground coriander
- 1/3 teaspoon cinnamon
- 1/3 teaspoon chili flakes
- 1/3 teaspoon allspice powder
- 1 .5 pound beef, grounded
- 1 egg
- 10 tomatoes, sliced
- 4 pita bread
- 8 tablespoons yogurt

Directions

1. Add the first 13 ingredients to a bowl and give them a mix.
2. Divide the ingredients into 8 equal portions and make patties from the portions.
3. Grease the inside of the air fryer with oil and arrange the patties in it, cooking for 8 minutes and flipping them halfway.
4. When done, take them out and serve them with a side of yogurt and bread and tomato slices.

Lamb Chops with Dijon Garlic Marinade

Preparation Time: 15 minutes | Cooking Time: 14 minutes | Servings: 4

Ingredients

- ½ tablespoon Dijon mustard
- 2 teaspoon olive oil

- 2 teaspoons tamari sauce
- 1 teaspoon garlic clove, minced
- 1 teaspoon ground coriander
- 1 teaspoon cayenne pepper
- 1 teaspoon Italian seasoning
- Pinch of salt
- 6-10 lamb chops

Directions
1. Begin by making the marinade for the lamb chops; for that, add Dijon mustard, tamari sauce, ground coriander, salt, cayenne pepper, Italian seasoning, garlic cloves, and olive oil in a bowl and give them a good mix.
2. Place the chops inside a bag and add the marinade inside it, massaging it all over the chops, covering all the edges.
3. Let the lamb chops rest in the Dijon garlic marinade for at least 30 minutes or overnight.
4. Once the chops have rested in the marinade for enough time, take them out and place them in the air fryer basket, cooking for 14 minutes at around 380 degrees F and flipping them halfway.
5. When done, take them out of the air fryer and serve with a garnish of cumin and salt to taste

Pistachio Crusted Lamb Rack

Preparation Time: 15 minutes | Cooking Time: 20 minutes | Servings: 2

Ingredients:
- 1 lamb rack
- 1 teaspoon sea salt
- ¼ teaspoon black pepper, or according to taste
- 1 ounces breadcrumbs
- 1/4 tablespoon oregano, chopped
- 1 tablespoon melted butter
- 4 tablespoons pistachio, crushed finely
- 4 tablespoons of Dijon mustard

Directions
1. Begin by seasoning the lamb rack with salt and pepper.
2. Put the split on the meaty side of the rack and place it on the rotisserie fork, tightening the knobs so that the rack is firmly held.
3. Place a drip pan underneath and cook the lamb rack for about 12 minutes at a temperature of 380 degrees F.
4. Meanwhile, add pistachios, herbs, breadcrumbs, and butter to a bowl and give them a thorough mix.
5. Once the lamb rack is cooked, take it out and give it a coat of Dijon mustard, making sure to cover all the edges. Once the rack is coated, rub the pistachio mix all over it.
6. Put it back in the air fryer and let it cook for 7 more minutes.
7. Once the internal temperature of the meat reaches 140 degrees F, take it out and serve with sides of your choice.

Kofta Lettuce Wraps

Preparation Time: 12 minutes | Cooking Time: 25-35 minutes | Servings: 2

Ingredients
- 1/3 cup Breadcrumbs
- ½ pound beef, grounded
- 1/2 cup onions
- 2 tablespoons cilantro
- 5 ounces grounded lamb
- 1 tablespoon mint
- ½ teaspoon cinnamon, powder
- ½ teaspoon allspice powder

- 1 egg
- Salt and pepper, according to taste
- 1 tablespoon olive oil
- 10 ounces of Greek yogurt
- 1 cucumber
- 1 pack of brown rice, precooked
- 1 teaspoon chili powder
- 2 tablespoon vegetable oil

Directions
1. Start by mixing the breadcrumbs with cilantro, onion, beef, lamb, mint, and the next ingredients till olive oil.
2. Once all the ingredients are properly mixed, divide the batter into 8 portions and flatten them to make patties.
3. Arrange them inside the air fryer in a single layer and cook them for 10 minutes, flipping them halfway.
4. Meanwhile, add yogurt, salt, pepper, onions, and cucumbers to a bowl and give them a good mix.
5. Cook the rice according to the packaging instruction and mix them with chili powder and oil.
6. When the patties are done, take them out and place them on a plate with lettuce on the bottom, top it with rice and yogurt and serve.

Greek-Style Meat Loves with Arugula Salad

Preparation Time: 15 minutes | Cooking Time: 20-25 minutes | Servings: 2

Ingredients
- 1 pound. beef, grounded
- 1 pound lamb meat, grounded
- 4 tablespoons breadcrumbs
- 1 onion
- 1 tablespoon mint leaves
- 1 tablespoon oregano
- 1 teaspoon salt, or according to taste
- ¼ teaspoon mixed spice
- ¼ teaspoon chili flakes
- 3 cloves garlic, crushed
- 1 egg
- 10 ounces Greek yogurt
- 5 ounces. feta cheese
- 1 tablespoon mint and thyme
- ½ lemon's juice
- 1 tablespoon extra-virgin olive oil
- 1 teaspoon black pepper, or according to taste
- toppings or sides
- 4 cups arugula leaves
- 2 cucumbers, diced

Directions
1. Start by heating the air fryer to around 400 degrees F.
2. Add lamb, beef, onions, and breadcrumbs in a bowl and mix them, then add oregano, salt, chili flakes, mixed spice, egg, and garlic in it and mix them thoroughly.
3. Grease the inside of some ramekins with oil and fill them with the meat mix.
4. Arrange those cups inside the air fryer basket and cook them for 20 minutes at around 400 degrees F.
5. While the meat is cooking, add all the remaining ingredients to a bowl and whisk well.
6. Add arugula leaves to a bowl and toss it with salt, pepper, and oil till evenly coated.
7. Once the meatloaf is done, take it out and serve it with the side of arugula salad and a drizzle of dressing sauce.

Lamb Chops with Lime, Farro, and Thyme Vinaigrette

Preparation Time: 15 minutes | Cooking Time: 8 minutes | Servings: 2

Ingredients
- 9 lamb chops
- 4 tablespoons of olive oil
- ½ lime, juice, and zest
- 2 tablespoon extra-virgin olive oil
- ½ shallot
- 1 tablespoon maple syrup
- 1 teaspoon Dijon mustard
- ½ cup farro, precooked
- 4 ounces of arugula
- Salt and pepper, according to taste

Directions
1. Season the lamb with salt and pepper and rub olive oil all over.
2. Grease the inside of the air fryer basket with oil and place the lamb chops in it, cooking them for about 8 minutes and making sure to flip them halfway.
3. Meanwhile, add the next 7 ingredients into a bowl, and season it with salt and pepper accordingly.
4. Once the lamb is done cooking and toss to coat evenly.

Air Fryer Stuffed Pork Chops

Preparation Time: 12 minutes | Cooking Time: 10 minutes | Servings: 1

Ingredients
- ½ teaspoon olive oil
- 1 chopped celery rib
- 4 tablespoon onions, chopped
- 4 white bread slices, diced
- 2 tablespoon cilantro
- Pinch of salt
- ¼ teaspoon sage
- ¼ teaspoon white pepper
- ¼ teaspoon marjoram, dry
- ¼ teaspoon thyme, dry
- 1/3 cup chicken stock, reduced-sodium
- For the pork chops
- 6 pork chops
- ¼ teaspoon salt and pepper, or according to taste

Directions
1. Begin by preheating the air fryer to around 325 degrees F.
2. Heat oil in a skillet over medium heat and sauté the onions and celery in it till tender. When done, remove them from the heat and set them aside.
3. Add bread, slices, seasoning, herbs, and stock to a bowl and give it mix, adding sautéed onion and celery and coating evenly.
4. Make a slit in each pork chop and fill it with bread mix, using a toothpick to close the slit if required.
5. Coat the pork chops with salt and pepper, making sure to coat all the edges, and place them in the air fryer basket, cooking them for 10 minutes or till the internal temperature reaches 145 degrees.
6. When done, take the chops out and let them rest for at least 5 minutes before serving; make sure to remove the toothpicks when serving.

Easy Pork Chops

Preparation Time: 14 minutes | Cooking Time: 10 minutes | Servings: 2

Ingredients
- 1 cup parmesan cheese, grated
- 1 teaspoon chili powder
- 1 teaspoon garlic powder
- 1 teaspoon salt
- 1 teaspoon cilantro, dried
- ½ teaspoon ground black pepper, or according to taste
- 6 pork chops, center cut, 5 ounces each
- 2 tablespoons extra virgin olive oil

Directions
1. Begin by preheating the oven to around 380 degrees F.
2. Add parmesan cheese, garlic powder, chili powder, cilantro, salt, and pepper in a shallow bowl and mix them till thoroughly combined.
3. Drizzle olive oil over the pork chops and massage them around them.
4. Then coat the chops with parmesan mix, making sure to coat all edges with the rub.
5. Arrange 2 chops in the air fryer basket, making sure they are not touching each other, and cook them for about 10 minutes, flipping them over halfway through the cooking.
6. Once the pork chops are done, take them out, let them rest for at least 5 minutes and serve.

Mongolian Beef

Preparation Time: 15 Minutes | Cooking Time: 17 Minutes | Servings: 3

Ingredients
- 1.5 pounds steak, flank cut
- 4 tablespoons cornstarch
- 4 tablespoons olive oil
- 4 garlic cloves, chopped
- 2 tablespoons ginger, chopped
- 1 cup tamari sauce
- ½ cup water
- 4 tablespoons of brown sugar
- 4 tablespoons of scallions, chopped

Directions
1. Slice the steak into thin strips and coat them evenly with cornstarch.
2. Heat the air fryer to about 400 degrees F, grease the inside of the air fryer basket with oil and place the steak in it.
3. Cooking the steaks for about 10 minutes at 400 degrees F.
4. While the steak is cooking, sauté the ginger and garlic in a pan with some oil and add tamari sauce, water, and brown sugar in it, giving them a mix and cooking them for another 7 minutes or till the sauce has thickened to desire.
5. Once the steak is done, shift it to the sauce and toss it to coat evenly.
6. Once it is coated evenly with the sauce, place it on the serving plate a serve it with a garnish of scallions and a drizzle of sauce on top.

Parmesan and Lime with Schnitzels

Preparation Time: 25 minutes | Cooking Time: 20 minutes | Servings: 2

Ingredients
- 4 veal steak, schnitzel
- 2 tablespoon lime juice
- 2 teaspoon lime zest
- 2 tablespoon dill, chopped
- 5 tablespoons parmesan cheese
- 1 cup breadcrumbs

- ½ cup almond flour
- 2 eggs
- 4 tablespoons olive oil
- ½ cup Greek yogurt
- 1 tablespoon baby capers, chopped

Directions

1. Add breadcrumbs, lime zest, parmesan cheese, and dill to a shallow bowl and give it a mix.
2. Add flour to another bowl and whisk the egg into the third bowl.
3. Pat dries the veal steak with a paper towel, first dips it in flour, then dries it with eggs, and finally gives it a coat of breadcrumb mixture.
4. Do this for all the veal and arrange them inside the air fryer oven, cooking them for about 20 minutes at 400 degrees F.
5. When done, take the veal out of the air fryer and cover it with a paper towel.
6. Add yogurt, lime juice, and cappers to a mixing bowl and give everything a good mix.
7. Arrange the cooked veal on a serving plate and serve with yogurt dressing, a garnish of chives, and a side of lemon wedges.

Pork Schnitzel

Preparation Time: 15 minutes | Cooking Time: 6-8 minutes | Servings: 2

Ingredients

- ½ cup all-purpose flour
- Salt and black pepper, to taste
- 2 eggs
- 2 tablespoons milk
- ¾ cup breadcrumbs
- 1 teaspoon chili powder
- 4 pork cutlets

For dill sauce:

- 2 tablespoons all-purpose flour
- 8 ounces of chicken stock
- ½ cup sour cream
- ¼ teaspoon dill weed

Directions

1. Begin by preheating the oven to around 400 degrees F.
2. Mix flour, salt, and pepper in a bowl, crack and whisk the egg with milk in another, and mix breadcrumbs and chili powder in the third bowl.
3. Coat the pork first with flour, then drench them with egg, and coat them with breadcrumbs, making sure to coat all the edges.
4. Place the coated pork in the air fryer basket, grease with cooking spray, and cook for 4 to 5 minutes.
5. When done, take the cooked pork out and let it rest.
6. Add flour and chicken stock to a saucepan and brings it to a boil, boiling it for about 2 minutes.
7. Once the sauce has thickened to desire, add dill and sour cream to the saucepan and take it off the heat.
8. Place the pork on a serving plate and serve with a drizzle of sauce.

Beef Crumble Schnitzel

Preparation Time: 14 minutes | Cooking Time: 10 minutes | Servings: 2

Ingredients

- 2 beef schnitzel crumbed
- 1 cup of mushroom sauce
- ½ cup of pepper sauce

Directions

1. Begin by preheating the oven to around 400 degrees F.

2. Place the beef schnitzel in the air fryer basket and cook them for about 10 minutes.
3. When done, take the beef out and serve with mushroom sauce or pepper sauce.

Teriyaki Beef and Pineapple Kabobs

Preparation Time: 19 minutes | Cooking Time: 20 minutes | Servings: 4

Ingredients

- 2 pounds cubed beef
- ½ pound pineapple chunks

Teriyaki sauce Ingredients:

- 4 tablespoons tamari sauce
- 4 tablespoons brown sugar
- 2 tablespoons pineapple juice
- 1 tablespoon garlic, minced
- 2 tablespoons ginger, minced

Slurry Ingredients:

- ½ tablespoon water, cold
- ½ tablespoon cornstarch

Directions

1. Add all the ingredients for the sauce to a saucepan and bring them to a simmer.
2. Then divide the sauce in ½ and save half of it for later use, and use the rest to marinate the steak for at least 30 minutes or overnight.
3. Add water and cornstarch slurry to the remaining sauce and heat it for about 5 minutes.
4. Take a wooden skewer and thread it with beef and pineapple alternatingly.
5. Coat the skewers with some oil and arrange them inside the air fryer basket in a single layer, cooking them for about 20 minutes at 400 degrees F.
6. When done, take the skewers out and serve with the side of sauce made earlier.

Steak Bites

Preparation time: 12 minutes | Cooking time: 8 minutes | Servings: 2

Ingredients

- 20 ounces of tenderloin steak, diced into bite-size pieces
- 4 teaspoons of steak seasoning
- Salt and pepper, according to taste
- Olive oil, according to need

Directions

1. Begin by preheating the oven to around 400 degrees f.
2. Mix steak seasoning, salt, and pepper in a bowl and toss the steak pieces in it, making sure the steak is properly coated with the rub.
3. Then rub olive oil over the steak bites, arrange them in the air fryer basket in a single layer, and cook them for about 4 minutes, flipping them and cooking for another 4 minutes.
4. Once it's done, take the steak bites out and let them rest for at least 10 minutes before serving.

Vegetables and Sirloin Steak with Sour Cream

Preparation Time: 15 minutes | Cooking Time: 15 minutes | Servings: 4

Ingredients

- 2 pounds beef sirloin, cut into strips
- 6 tablespoons beef stock
- 2 tomatoes, diced
- 8 ounces string beans, halved
- 8 ounces frozen onions, thawed

- 1 tablespoon paprika
- 10 ounces sour cream
- Salt and pepper, according to taste

Directions
1. Begin by preheating the oven to around 400 degrees F.
2. Add beef stock, string beans, tomatoes, onions, paprika, salt, and pepper in a bowl mixing them.
3. Add the sirloin steak and let it rest for some time.
4. Grease the inside of the air fryer basket with oil and add the mixture to it, cooking it for about 15 minutes.
5. Once done, take the steak out and serve with a side of sour cream.

Spicy Beef Fillet

Preparation Time: 15 minutes | Cooking Time: 15-20 minutes | Servings: 2

Ingredients
- 12 ounces beef fillet
- Salt and pepper, according to taste
- 6 teaspoon butter, melted
- 1 teaspoon lime juice
- 1 teaspoon rosemary, chopped
- 1 teaspoon oregano, chopped

Directions
1. Begin by rubbing salt, pepper, rosemary, lime juice, and oregano all over the steak, making sure to coat all the edges of the steak.
2. Once the steak is properly coated, place it in the air fryer oven and cook it for about 15 minutes at 400 degrees F, making sure to flip it halfway and topping it with butter in between cooking.
3. When done, take the steak out and put butter on top.
4. Let it rest for at least 10 minutes before serving.

Easy Beef Ribs

Preparation Time: 15 minutes | Cooking Time: 18 minutes | Servings: 2

Ingredients
- ½ cup BBQ sauce (divided)
- Salt and pepper, according to taste
- 4 ounces brown sugar
- 2 pounds beef ribs, cut to 1/3s
- Oil spray, for greasing

Directions
1. Begin by preheating the oven to around 400 degrees F.
2. Place the ribs in a bowl and coat them with salt, pepper, half of the BBQ sauce, and brown sugar.
3. Then arrange the steak in the air fryer basket and cook it for about 16 to 18 minutes at 400 degrees F.
4. When done, take the steak out and rest for at least 10 minutes before serving.

Sweet Beef Ribs with Baked Potatoes

Preparation Time: 15 minutes | Cooking Time: 16 minutes | Servings: 2

Ingredients
- 6 short ribs
- 2 teaspoon garlic powder
- 4 tablespoons brown sugar
- 2 tablespoon oyster sauce
- Salt, according to taste
- 2 teaspoons avocado oil
- 2 potatoes, baked

Directions
1. Begin by heating the oven to around 400 degrees F 5 minutes before cooking.

2. Add beef ribs to a bowl and toss it with all the listed ingredients, except the potatoes.
3. Arrange the ribs in the air fryer basket and cook them for about 16 minutes at 400 degrees F.
4. When done, take the ribs out and serve with the side of a baked potato.

Veal Shank Fricassee

Preparation Time: 15 minutes | Cooking Time: 60 minutes | Servings: 4

Ingredients
- 1.5 cups of almond flour
- Salt and black pepper, to taste
- ½ teaspoon oregano, dried
- ½ teaspoon cilantro, dried
- ¼ teaspoon of cayenne pepper
- 2 pounds veal shanks
- ½ cup water (divided)
- 2 onions, chopped
- 2 celery ribs, chopped
- 1 bay leaf, chopped
- 2 big carrots, sliced into 1-inch slices
- 2 potatoes, peeled, diced to 1-inch cubes
- 2 tablespoons cornstarch

Directions
1. Add flour and seasoning in a zip lock bag and give them a good mix.
2. Place the veal in the zip lock bag and toss it around to coat the edges evenly.
3. Place the veal in a Dutch oven and brown the veal.
4. Add 1 ¼ cup water, bay leaf, onions, and celery to it, and bring it to a simmer, letting it simmer for about 1 hour.
5. Then add potatoes and carrots to the oven and cook it for another 30 minutes with the lid on it, or till the vegetables are tender and the meat is cooked.
6. When done, take the vegetables and meat out and place them in the air fryer basket.
7. Skim the fat and throw away the bay leaf.
8. Add it to the air fryer and cook for 10 minutes.
9. Strain the loosened browned bits and the drippings in a measuring cup.
10. Mix cornstarch and ¼ cup of water in a saucepan and stir them to make a slurry.
11. Slowly pour the dripping into the slurry and keep stirring, cooking it for about 5 minutes or thickened to desire.
12. Once the sauce reaches desired consistency, pour the sauce over the meat and vegetables and serve.

Veal Parmigiano

Preparation Time: 15 minutes | Cooking Time: 20-25 minutes | Servings: 4

Ingredients
- 14 ounces eggplant
- Salt, to taste
- Olive oil, for spraying
- 8 veal rump steak, 8 oz each
- 2 cups marinara sauce
- 1 cup parmesan cheese, grated
- Green vegetables or salad leaves, for serving

Directions
1. Begin by preheating the grill to medium.
2. Thinly slice the eggplant, sprinkle salt all over them and let them rest for at least 1 hour.

3. After the time is up, rinse and dry the eggplants and coat them with oil.
4. Place them on the grill and cook them for 2 to 4 minutes on each side or until golden.
5. Place the veal rump steak in an air fryer basket and add it to the air fryer, and cook them in batches over high heat for 6 minutes on each side.
6. Arrange them on the baking dish and place the eggplant over it.
7. Top it with 3 cups marinara sauce and 1 cup parmesan cheese.
8. Place it on the grill and cook it for about 5 to 7 minutes or until the cheese is completely melted.
9. Once done, take it out and serve it with a side of green vegetables or salad.

Air Fryer Beef Steak

Preparation Time: 10 minutes | Cooking Time: 15 minutes | Servings: 1

Ingredients:
- 2 lb. Ribeye steak
- Salt and pepper to taste
- 1 tbsp. Olive oil

Directions:
1. Select air fry mode to preheat the Power XL Air Fryer Grill.
2. Set the temperature to 356°F and the timer to 5 minutes.
3. Season the steak with salt, pepper, and olive oil.
4. Place in the Power XL Air Fryer Grill.
5. Cook for 7 minutes in the air, then turn and cook for another 6 minutes.
6. Serve and have fun!
7. Suggestions for Serving: Serve with your favorite sauce.
8. Allow the steak to marinade for a few minutes before cooking.

Air Fryer Meatballs

Preparation Time: 10 minutes | Cooking Time: 15 minutes | Servings: 1

Ingredients:
- 2 lb. Ground beef
- 2cloves garlic, minced
- 2 tbsp. Chopped parsley
- 2 eggs
- Salt and black pepper to taste
- 1-1/2 cup grated parmesan cheese
- 1/4 cup of minced onions
- 1/2 tsp. red pepper flakes
- 1/2 tsp. Italian seasoning

Directions:
1. Select air fry mode to preheat the Power XL Air Fryer Grill.
2. Set the temperature to 350°F and the timer to 5 minutes.
3. In a mixing dish, combine all of the ingredients.
4. Make little balls.
5. Place on an Air fryer baking pan.
6. Place in the Power XL Air Fryer Grill.
7. Air-fried for 8 minutes, then turn and cook for another 5 minutes.
8. Serve and have fun!
9. Suggestions for Serving: Serve with sauce or dips.
10. Directions: & Cooking Hints: Ensure all ingredients are thoroughly blended.

Mushroom Meatloaf

Preparation Time: 10 minutes | Cooking Time: 15 minutes | Servings: 1

Ingredients:
- 14 oz. Lean ground beef
- 1 chorizo sausage, chopped
- 1 egg
- 1 small onion, chopped
- Salt and freshly ground black pepper to taste
- 3 Tbsp. Olive oil
- 2 tbsp. fresh mushrooms, sliced thinly

- 1 garlic clove, minced
- 2 tbsp. fresh cilantro, chopped
- 3 tbsp breadcrumbs

Directions:
1. Select pizza/bake mode to preheat the Power XL Air Fryer Grill.
2. Set the temperature to 390°F and the timer to 10 minutes.
3. In a mixing dish, combine all of the ingredients except the mushroom.
4. Smooth with a spatula into the Air fryer baking tray.
5. Place the mushroom on top of the transfer in the Power XL Air Fryer Grill.
6. 25 minutes in the oven
7. Serve and have fun!
8. Suggestions for serving: garnish with cilantro
9. Directions: & Cooking Tip: Make sure that all of the ingredients are thoroughly blended.

Cheese Stuffed Meatballs

Preparation Time: 10 minutes | Cooking Time: 15 minutes | Servings: 1

Ingredients:
- 1/3 cup bread crumbs
- 1 lb. Lean ground beef
- 1 egg
- 3 tbsps. milk
- 1/2 tsp. Marjoram
- 1 tbsp ketchup
- salt and freshly ground black pepper
- 20 (1/2-inch) cubes of cheese
- Olive oil for misting

Directions:
1. Select air fry mode to preheat the Power XL Air Fryer Grill.
2. Set the temperature to 390°F and the timer to 10 minutes.
3. In a mixing dish, combine all of the ingredients except the cheese.
4. Make 20 meatballs.
5. Each meatball should be shaped around the cheese.
6. Arrange in the baking pan of the Air fryer.
7. Place in the Power XL Air Fryer Grill.
8. 15 minutes in the oven
9. Serve and have fun!
10. Suggestions for serving: sprinkle with cheese
11. Serving Suggestions: Serve with marinara sauce

Carrot and Beef Cocktail Balls

Preparation Time: 10 minutes | Cooking Time: 15 minutes | Servings: 1

Ingredients:
- 1 lb. ground beef

- 2 carrots,
- 1 red onion, peeled and chopped
- 3/4 cup breadcrumbs
- Salt and black pepper to taste
- 1/2 tsp dried rosemary, crushed
- 2 cloves garlic, minced
- flour as needed
- 1/2 tsp dried basil
- 1 Egg
- 1 tsp dried oregano

Directions:
1. In a food processor, combine carrot, onion, and garlic.
2. Add the remaining ingredients, except the flour, to a mixing bowl.
3. Form into a ball and place in the refrigerator for 20 minutes.
4. Roll in flour and place on the baking pan of an Air fryer.
5. Select the air fryer mode on the Power XL Air Fryer Grill.
6. Preheat the oven to 390°F.
7. The Time is set at 20 minutes.
8. Use toothpicks to serve.
9. Suggestions for Serving: Serve with sauce and garnish with parsley.
10. & Cooking Hints: Pulse the carrot till smooth.

Marinated Cajun Beef

Preparation Time: 10 minutes | Cooking Time: 15 minutes | Servings: 1

Ingredients:
- 1lb. Beef tenderloins
- 1/3 cup beef broth
- 1/2 tsp. garlic powder
- 2 tbsp Cajun seasoning, crushed
- 1-1/2 tbsp. Olive oil
- 1/2 tbsp apple cider vinegar
- /3 tsp cayenne pepper
- 1 tsp. Salt
- 1 tsp. Freshly ground black pepper

Directions:
1. In a mixing dish, combine all of the ingredients.
2. Allow the steak to marinade for 40 minutes.
3. Switch to the Power XL Air Fryer Grill.
4. Choose the air fryer/grill mode.
5. Preheat the oven to 390°F.
6. 22 minutes on the grill, turning halfway through
7. Serve and have fun!
8. Suggestions for Serving: Serve with tomato sauce.

Beef and Potatoes

Preparation Time: 10 minutes | Cooking Time: 15 minutes | Servings: 1

Ingredients:
- 1 lb. Ground beef
- 3 cups of mashed potatoes
- 1 cup sour cream
- 2 eggs
- 2 tbsp. Garlic powder

Directions:
1. Select bake/pizza mode to preheat the Power XL Air Fryer Grill.
2. Set the temperature to 350°F and the timer to 5 minutes.
3. In a mixing dish, combine all of the ingredients.
4. Pour onto the baking pan of an air fryer.
5. Place in the Power XL Air Fryer Grill.
6. 6 minutes in the oven
7. Serve and have fun!

8. Suggestions for Serving: Serve with your favorite toppings.

Breaded Beef Schnitzel

Preparation Time: 10 minutes | Cooking Time: 15 minutes | Servings: 1

Ingredients:
- 4 beef schnitzel
- 2 tbsp. Olive oil
- 1 egg
- 5 cups of breadcrumbs

Directions:
1. Select grill mode to preheat the Power XL Air Fryer Grill.
2. Set the temperature to 350°F and the timer to 5 minutes.
3. In a mixing dish, combine the egg and olive oil.
4. Another basin should be filled with breadcrumbs.
5. In the egg mixture, coat the meat schnitzel.
6. after that, coat with the breadcrumb mixture
7. Place in the Power XL Air Fryer Grill.
8. 12 minutes on the grill, rotating halfway through
9. Serve and have fun!
10. Suggestions for Serving: Serve with ketchup.

Quick & Easy Steak Tips

Preparation Time: 10 minutes | Cooking Time: 15 minutes | Servings: 1

Ingredients:
- 1 1/2 lbs. steak, cut into 3/4-inch cubes
- 1/8 tsp cayenne
- 1 tsp Montreal steak seasoning
- 1/2 tsp garlic powder
- 1 tsp olive oil

Directions:
1. Cooking sprays the air fryer basket.
2. Preheat the air fryer to 400 degrees Fahrenheit.
3. Toss the steak cubes in a bowl with the oil, cayenne pepper, steak seasoning, garlic powder, pepper, and salt.
4. Cook the steak cubes in the air fryer basket for 4-6 minutes.

Simple Sirloin Steaks

Preparation Time: 10 minutes | Cooking Time: 15 minutes | Servings: 1

Ingredients:
- 2 sirloin steaks
- 2 tbsp steak seasoning

Directions:
1. Season steaks with steak seasoning after spraying with cooking spray.
2. Place the steaks in the air fryer basket and cook for 12 minutes at 400 F. Halfway through, turn the steaks.

Flavorful Steak

Preparation Time: 10 minutes | Cooking Time: 15 minutes | Servings: 1

Ingredients:
- 2 steaks, rinsed and pat dry with a paper towel
- 1 tsp olive oil
- 1/2 tsp garlic powder
- 1/4 tsp onion powder

Directions:
1. Season steaks with garlic powder, onion powder, pepper, and salt after rubbing them with oil.
2. Place the steaks in the air fryer basket and cook for 18 minutes at 400 F. Halfway through, turn the steaks.

Italian Beef Roast

Preparation Time: 10 minutes | Cooking Time: 15 minutes |
Servings: 1

Ingredients:
- 2 1/2 lbs. beef roast
- 2 tbsp Italian seasoning
- 1 tsp olive oil

Directions:
1. Season the beef roast with Italian seasoning, pepper, and salt after rubbing it with oil.
2. Place the beef roast in the air fryer basket and cook for 45 minutes at 350 F.
3. Cut into slices and serve.

Rosemary Thyme Beef Roast

Preparation Time: 10 minutes | Cooking Time: 15 minutes |
Servings: 1

Ingredients:
- 2 lbs. beef roast
- 1 tsp dried rosemary
- 1 tsp dried thyme
- 1/4 tsp onion powder
- 1 tsp olive oil

Directions:
1. Season the beef roast with rosemary, thyme, onion powder, pepper, and salt after rubbing it with oil.
2. Place the beef roast in the air fryer basket and cook for 15 minutes at 390 F. After 10 minutes, turn the roast.
3. Cut into slices and serve.

Italian Meatballs

Preparation Time: 10 minutes | Cooking Time: 15 minutes |
Servings: 1

Ingredients:
- 1 egg
- 1 lb. ground beef
- 1 tsp Italian seasoning
- 1 tbsp onion, minced
- 1/4 cup marinara sauce, sugar-free
- 1/3 cup parmesan cheese, shredded
- 1 tsp garlic, minced

Directions:
1. Cooking sprays the air fryer basket.
2. Mix all of the ingredients in a mixing bowl until completely blended.
3. Form meatballs from the ingredients and place them in the air fryer basket for 12 minutes at 350 F.

Burgers Patties

Preparation Time: 10 minutes | Cooking Time: 15 minutes |
Servings: 1

Ingredients:
- 1/2 lb. ground beef
- 1/4 tsp onion powder
- 1/4 tsp garlic powder
- 2 drops of liquid smoke
- 1/2 tsp hot sauce
- 1/2 tsp dried parsley
- 1/4 tsp black pepper
- 1/2 tbsp Worcestershire sauce
- 1/4 tsp salt

Directions:
1. Cooking sprays the air fryer basket.

2. Mix all of the ingredients in a large mixing basin.
3. Form patties from the mixture and set them in the air fryer basket for 10 minutes at 350 F. Halfway through, flip the patties.

Tasty Beef Patties

Preparation Time: 10 minutes | Cooking Time: 15 minutes |
Servings: 1

Ingredients:
- 1/2 lb. ground beef
- 1 tsp ginger, minced
- 1/2 tbsp soy sauce
- 1 tbsp gochujang
- 1/4 tsp salt
- 1 tbsp green onion, chopped
- 1/2 tbsp sesame oil

Directions:
1. Combine ground beef and additional ingredients in a large mixing basin. Refrigerate the mixture for one hour.
2. Form patties from the beef mixture and place them in the air fryer basket for 10 minutes at 360 F.

Meatloaf

Preparation Time: 10 minutes | Cooking Time: 15 minutes |
Servings: 1

Ingredients:
- 1 egg
- 1/2 lb. ground beef
- 1/2 tsp turmeric
- 1 tsp garam masala
- 1/2 tbsp garlic, minced
- 1/2 tbsp ginger, minced
- 1 tbsp cilantro, chopped
- 1/8 tsp ground cardamom
- 1/4 tsp ground cinnamon
- 1/2 tsp cayenne
- 1/2 cup onion, chopped
- 1/2 tsp salt

Directions:
1. In a large mixing basin, blend all ingredients until thoroughly incorporated.
2. Place the beef mixture in an air fryer-safe pan, then in the air fryer basket.
3. Cook for 15 minutes at 360°F.
4. Cut into slices and serve.

Spicy Air Fryer Pork Chops with Apricot Glaze

Preparation Time: 10 minutes | Cooking Time: 15 minutes |
Servings: 1

Ingredients:
- 4 cups water
- Two tablespoons of kosher salt
- Two tablespoons of white sugar
- 4 (5 ounces) bone-in center loin pork chops, about 3/4-inch thick
- One teaspoon chili powder, or to taste
- One teaspoon of onion powder
- ½ teaspoon salt
- ¼ teaspoon white pepper
- Glaze:
- ½ cup apricot all-fruit spread
- Three tablespoons of hoisin sauce
- 1 (1 inch) piece ginger root, peeled and grated
- Two cloves of minced garlic
- 1 ½ teaspoon Asian chili-garlic sauce

- ½ medium lime, juiced
- cooking spray
- Two tablespoons of finely minced fresh parsley

Directions:

1. In a mixing bowl, combine the water, salt, and sugar and whisk until the crystals are dissolved. Refrigerate the pork chops for at least 2 hours or up to 4 hours.
2. Shake off any extra brine from the pork chops. Remove any residual brine. Place the chops on a platter or cutting board and pat dry with paper towels.
3. Mix chili powder, onion powder, salt, and white pepper in a small bowl. Distribute half of the rub mixture among the four chops and massage it. Repeat with the remaining chops. Allow 30 minutes for the chops to come to room temperature.
4. Meanwhile, in a medium microwave-safe bowl, mix the apricot all-fruit spread, hoisin sauce, ginger, garlic, chili-garlic sauce, and lime juice for the glaze.
5. Microwave for 3 minutes on high, stirring halfway through. Remove the glazing with care and keep it aside.
6. If the manufacturer recommends it, preheat the air fryer to 400 degrees F (200 degrees C). Cooking spray should be sprayed on both sides of the seasoned and rubbed chops.
7. Place the chops in a single layer in the air fryer and cook for 8 minutes, flipping halfway through.
8. Brush the tops of the chops with the prepared glaze and air-fry for 2 to 3 minutes, or until the pork chops are no longer pink in the middle. In the center, an instant-read thermometer should register 145 degrees F. (63 degrees C).
9. Serve the chops with the remaining glaze and garnish with chopped parsley.

Air Fryer Oven Pork Jerky

Preparation Time: 10 minutes | Cooking Time: 15 minutes | Servings: 1

Ingredients:

- 2 pounds of ground pork
- One tablespoon of sesame oil
- One tablespoon Sriracha
- One tablespoon of soy sauce

- One tablespoon of rice vinegar
- ½ teaspoon salt
- ½ teaspoon black pepper
- ½ teaspoon onion powder
- ½ teaspoon pink curing salt

Directions:

1. Add ground pork, sesame oil, Sriracha, soy sauce, rice vinegar, salt, black pepper, onion powder, and pink curing salt in a large mixing bowl. Refrigerate for 8 hours, covered.
2. Form as many sticks as possible on all three air fryer oven racks with a jerky gun. They will shrink nearly instantly, allowing you to stack them close together and use the whole length of the racks. On the first try, I was able to acquire 21 sticks.
3. Preheat the air fryer to 160 degrees Fahrenheit. Cook for 1 hour using all three racks.
4. Remove the oven racks and dab any excess moisture with paper towels—Cook for another hour after flipping each stick.
5. Step 4 should be repeated for a total cooking duration of 3 hours. Place the jerky sticks on a baking sheet lined with paper towels. Cover with another layer of paper

towels and set aside for 8 hours to dry completely. Rep with the remaining jerky mixture.

6. Refrigerate the jerky for up to 30 days in an airtight container.

Air Fryer Keto Pork Chops

Preparation Time: 10 minutes | Cooking Time: 15 minutes | Servings: 1

Ingredients:

- Four each boneless pork chops, 1/2-inch thick
- One pinch of salt and ground black pepper to taste
- One egg
- ⅓ cup grated Parmesan cheese
- ⅓ cup almond flour
- ½ teaspoon salt
- ¼ teaspoon pepper
- ¼ teaspoon garlic powder
- 1 serving avocado oil cooking spray

Directions:

1. Season the pork chops on both sides with salt & pepper.
2. In a medium mixing basin, beat the egg. In a separate dish, combine the Parmesan cheese, almond flour, 1/2 teaspoon salt, 1/4 teaspoon pepper, and garlic powder.
3. To coat, dip each pork chop in an egg, then in a Parmesan-flour mixture. Spray with avocado oil and place in the air fryer basket.
4. Cook for 8 to 10 minutes in an air fryer at 375°F (190°C) until lightly browned. Then, for 3 to 4 minutes more, flip pork chops over, spritz with avocado oil, and cook until meat is no longer pink in the center.

Air Fryer Chinese Sweet and Sour Pork

Preparation Time: 10 minutes | Cooking Time: 15 minutes | Servings: 1

Ingredients:

- 1 ½ pound pork cutlets, cut into bite-sized pieces
- Three tablespoons cornstarch
- One teaspoon of sesame oil
- 1 serving nonstick cooking spray
- Sauce:
- ¼ cup white sugar
- ¼ cup rice vinegar
- Four tablespoons ketchup
- Two tablespoons of soy sauce

Directions:

1. Toss the pork in a bowl with the cornstarch and sesame oil to coat. Allow for a 5-minute rest.
2. Meanwhile, prepare the air fryer to 350°F (175 degrees C).
3. Coat the air fryer basket with cooking spray. Place the pork in the air fryer basket and coat the top with cooking spray.
4. Ten minutes in the oven. Shake the basket and cook the pork until it reaches the desired crispness, about 10 minutes longer.
5. In a saucepan over medium-high heat, mix the sugar, vinegar, ketchup, and soy sauce while the pork is cooking. Stir frequently until the sugar dissolves and the mixture comes to a boil. Reduce to low heat and keep the sauce warm until ready to use.
6. Place the meat in a bowl. Toss the meat in the sauce to coat it.

Smoked Paprika Pork Loin Chops

Preparation Time: 10 minutes | Cooking Time: 15 minutes | Servings: 1

Ingredients:
- 1 pound pork loin chops
- 1 tablespoon olive oil
- Sea salt and ground black pepper to taste
- 1 tablespoon smoked paprika

Directions:
1. In a lightly oiled Air Fryer cooking basket, combine all ingredients.
2. Cook the pork loin chops for 15 minutes at 400 degrees F, flipping them halfway through.
3. Good appetite!

Classic Center Cut Pork Roast

Preparation Time: 10 minutes | Cooking Time: 15 minutes | Servings: 1

Ingredients:
- 1 ½ pounds center-cut pork roast
- 1 tablespoon olive oil
- Sea salt and freshly ground black pepper to taste
- 1 teaspoon garlic powder
- 1 teaspoon hot paprika
- 1/2 teaspoon dried parsley flakes
- 1/2 teaspoon dried rosemary

Directions:
1. Toss all ingredients in an Air Fryer cooking basket that has been lightly oiled. Cook the pork for 55 minutes at 360 degrees F, turning it over halfway through.
2. Enjoy when still warm!

Classic Pork Spareribs

Preparation Time: 10 minutes | Cooking Time: 15 minutes | Servings: 1

Ingredients:
- 2 pounds pork spareribs
- 1 teaspoon coarse sea salt
- 1/3 teaspoon freshly ground black pepper
- 1 tablespoon brown sugar
- 1 teaspoon cayenne pepper
- 1 teaspoon garlic powder
- 1 teaspoon mustard powder

Directions:
1. Toss all ingredients in an Air Fryer cooking basket that has been lightly oiled.
2. Cook the pork ribs for 35 minutes at 350 degrees F, turning them over halfway through.
3. Good appetite!

Country-Style Pork Belly

Preparation Time: 10 minutes | Cooking Time: 15 minutes | Servings: 1

Ingredients:
- 1 ½ pound pork belly, cut into pieces
- 1/4 cup tomato sauce
- 1 tablespoon tamari sauce
- 2 tablespoons dark brown sugar
- 1 teaspoon garlic, minced
- Sea salt and ground black pepper to season

Directions:
1. Toss all contents into the cooking basket of your Air Fryer.
2. Cook the pork belly for about 17 minutes at 400 degrees F, shaking the basket halfway through.
3. Good appetite!

Italian-Style Burgers

Preparation Time: 10 minutes | Cooking Time: 15 minutes | Servings: 1

Ingredients:
- 1 pound ground pork
- Sea salt and ground black pepper to taste
- 1 tablespoon Italian herb mix
- 1 small onion, chopped
- 1 teaspoon garlic, minced
- 1/4 cup parmesan cheese, grated
- 1/4 cup seasoned breadcrumbs
- 1 egg
- 4 hamburger buns
- 4 teaspoons Dijon mustard
- 4 tablespoons mayonnaise

Directions:
1. Combine the pork, seasonings, onion, garlic, parmesan, breadcrumbs, and egg in a mixing bowl. Make four patties out of the mixture.
2. Cook the burgers for about 15 minutes at 380 degrees F, or until cooked through; flip them over halfway through the cooking time.
3. Burgers should be served with hamburger buns, mustard, and mayonnaise. Enjoy!

Blue Cheese Pork Loin Filets

Preparation Time: 10 minutes | Cooking Time: 15 minutes | Servings: 1

Ingredients:
- 1 ½ pound pork loin filets
- Sea salt and ground black pepper to taste
- 2 tablespoons olive oil
- 1 pound of mushrooms, sliced
- 2 ounces blue cheese

Directions:
1. Combine the pork, salt, black pepper, and olive oil in a lightly oiled Air Fryer cooking basket.
2. Cook the pork loin filets for 10 minutes at 400 degrees F, flipping them halfway through.
3. Serve the mushrooms on top of the pork loin filets. Continue to cook for another 5 minutes. Serve the heated pork with blue cheese on top.
4. Good appetite!

Bacon Salad with Croutons

Preparation Time: 10 minutes | Cooking Time: 15 minutes | Servings: 1

Ingredients:
- 1 pound bacon, cut into thick slices
- 1 head lettuce, torn into leaves
- 1 tablespoon fresh chive, chopped
- 1 tablespoon fresh tarragon, chopped
- 1 tablespoon fresh parsley, chopped
- 2 tablespoons freshly squeezed lemon juice
- 2 garlic cloves, minced
- Coarse sea salt and ground black pepper, to taste
- 1 teaspoon red pepper flakes, crushed
- 2 cups bread cubes

Directions:
1. Place the bacon in the frying basket of the Air Fryer. Then, cook the bacon for about 10 minutes at 400 degrees F, tossing the basket halfway through the cooking time; set aside.
2. Air-fried the bread cubes at 390°F for about 6 minutes, or until the bread is toasted.

3. Toss the remaining ingredients in a salad dish; top with the bacon and croutons. Good appetite!

Pork Sausage with Brussels Sprouts

Preparation Time: 10 minutes | Cooking Time: 15 minutes | Servings: 1

Ingredients:
- 1 pound sausage links, uncooked
- 1 pound Brussels sprouts, halved

Directions:
1. Place the sausage and Brussels sprouts in a lightly oiled Air Fryer cooking basket.
2. Air-fried the sausage and Brussels sprouts for about 15 minutes, flipping the basket midway during the cooking time.
3. Good appetite!

Holiday Picnic Ham

Preparation Time: 10 minutes | Cooking Time: 15 minutes | Servings: 1

Ingredients:
- 1 ½ pounds picnic ham
- 2 tablespoons olive oil
- 2 garlic cloves, minced
- 2 tablespoons rice vinegar
- 1 tablespoon tamari sauce

Directions:
1. Begin by preheating your Air Fryer for around 13 minutes at 400 degrees F.
2. Toss the ham with the remaining ingredients; cover in aluminum foil, and place in the Air Fryer cooking basket.
3. Reduce the heat to 375°F and cook the ham for about 30 minutes.
4. Remove the foil, increase the temperature to 400 degrees F, and cook for another 15 minutes until the chicken is cooked through.
5. Good appetite!

Rosemary and Garlic Pork Butt

Preparation Time: 10 minutes | Cooking Time: 15 minutes | Servings: 1

Ingredients:
- 1 ½ pound pork butt
- 1 teaspoon butter, melted
- 2 garlic cloves, pressed
- 2 tablespoons fresh rosemary, chopped
- Coarse sea salt and freshly ground black pepper, to taste

Directions:
1. Toss all ingredients in a lightly oiled Air Fryer cooking basket.
2. Cook the pork for 55 minutes at 360°F, rotating halfway through.
3. Serve hot, and enjoy!

Fall-Off-The-Bone Ribs with Zucchini

Preparation Time: 10 minutes | Cooking Time: 15 minutes | Servings: 1

Ingredients:
- 1 ½ pound pork loin ribs
- 2 cloves garlic, minced
- 1 tablespoon olive oil
- 4 tablespoons whiskey
- 1 teaspoon onion powder
- Sea salt and ground black pepper to taste
- 1/2 pound zucchini, sliced

Directions:

1. Toss the pork ribs with the garlic, olive oil, whiskey, and spices; place the ingredients in an Air Fryer cooking basket that has been lightly oiled.
2. Cook the pork ribs for 25 minutes at 350 degrees F, turning them over halfway through.
3. Cook for 12 minutes after adding the sliced zucchini to the pork ribs. Serve right away.
4. Good appetite!

Lamb Sliders

Preparation Time: 10 minutes | Cooking Time: 15 minutes | Servings: 1

Ingredients:
- One tablespoon of minced garlic
- ¼ teaspoon ground cumin
- ¼ teaspoon ground coriander
- ¼ teaspoon ground allspice
- ¼ teaspoon salt, or to taste
- ¼ teaspoon ground black pepper, or to taste
- 1 pound ground lamb
- Eight small slider-size rolls, split
- 1 cup baby spinach
- ½ cup tzatziki sauce
- ¼ cup sliced red onion
- ¼ cup crumbled feta cheese

Directions:
1. Preheat an outside grill over medium-high heat and grease the grate liberally.
2. Mix garlic, cumin, coriander, allspice, salt, and pepper; add lamb and stir thoroughly. Make 2-ounce patties out of the mixture.
3. Grill patties on a hot grill until cooked, 2 to 3 minutes on each side. In the middle, an instant-read thermometer should read at least 160 degrees F. (70 degrees C). Place the rolls on the grill and toast for 1 to 2 minutes.
4. Make a slider by layering spinach, tzatziki sauce, a lamb patty, red onion, and feta cheese in each bun.

Simple Grilled Lamb Chops

Preparation Time: 10 minutes | Cooking Time: 15 minutes | Servings: 1

Ingredients:
- One onion, thinly sliced
- ¼ cup distilled white vinegar
- Two tablespoons of olive oil

- One tablespoon of minced garlic
- Two teaspoons salt
- ½ teaspoon black pepper
- 6 (6 ounces) lamb chops

Directions:
1. In a large resealable bag, combine the onion, vinegar, oil, garlic, salt, and pepper. Seal the bag and throw the lamb in it to coat. Marinate for 2 hours in the refrigerator.
2. Heat an outside grill to medium-high.
3. Remove the lamb from the marinade, leaving any onions stuck to the meat; discard the marinade. Wrap exposed bone ends with aluminum foil to prevent them from burning.
4. Cook until done to preference on a hot grill, roughly 3 minutes per side for medium. (Alternatively, the chops can be broiled in the oven for about 5 minutes per side for medium.)

Braised Lamb Shoulder Chops

Preparation Time: 10 minutes | Cooking Time: 15 minutes |
Servings: 1

Ingredients:
- One tablespoon of olive oil
- 2 pounds lamb shoulder chops, or more to taste
- salt and ground black pepper to taste
- One small yellow onion, sliced
- Four cloves of garlic, minced
- Two tablespoons chopped fresh rosemary
- 1 cup beef broth
- 1 cup red wine
- Two tablespoons cornstarch
- ½ cup water

Directions:
1. Preheat the oven to 300°F (150 degrees C).
2. In a pan over medium-high heat, heat the olive oil. Season the lamb chops with salt and pepper to taste. 1 to 2 minutes per side, sear meat in hot oil until browned. Transfer the chops to a platter to drain, leaving the drippings in the pan.
3. Cook until the onion and garlic are soft, approximately 5 minutes, in the saved drippings.
4. Place the drained lamb chops in a baking tray and top with the onion mixture. Season the chops with rosemary. Fill the baking dish halfway with beef broth and red wine. Wrap the dish with aluminum foil.
5. Bake for 3 hours in a preheated oven.
6. Transfer the lamb to a serving plate. Drain the liquid from the baking dish into a saucepan over medium heat. In a mixing bowl, whisk together the cornstarch and water to ensure no lumps remain; add to the liquid in the saucepan. Cook, constantly stirring, until the liquid thickens into a gravy, approximately 5 minutes.

Oven-Roasted Lamb Chops

Preparation Time: 10 minutes | Cooking Time: 15 minutes |
Servings: 1

Ingredients:
- 4 (4 ounces) lamb chops
- One tablespoon olive oil, or as needed
- One clove of garlic, minced
- ½ tablespoon crushed fresh rosemary leaves
- sea salt and freshly ground black pepper to taste
- ¼ cup mint jelly

Directions:
1. Preheat the oven to 425° F. (220 degrees C).
2. Remove any extra fat from the lamb chops (some fat does add flavor). Lightly coat each chop in olive oil. Garlic, rosemary, salt, and pepper should be sprinkled over lamb chops. In a cast-iron pan, brown the lamb chops.
3. Bake uncovered in a preheated oven for 8 to 10 minutes, or until well done. An instant-read thermometer in the middle should read at least 140 degrees F (60 degrees C) for medium-well doneness.
4. Remove from the oven and tent with foil for 8 to 10 minutes to rest. Serve with a side of mint jelly.

Mozzarella-Stuffed Leg of Lamb

Preparation Time: 10 minutes | Cooking Time: 15 minutes |
Servings: 1

Ingredients:
- 2 cups small dried bread cubes or plain croutons
- ½ cup shredded mozzarella cheese
- Two teaspoons of finely chopped mint leaves
- ½ cup Heinz® Chili Sauce
- 1 (3 pounds) boneless, butterflied leg of lamb, trimmed
- ¾ teaspoon salt
- ¾ teaspoon pepper

Directions:
1. Preheat the oven to 325°F (160 degrees C). Toss the bread pieces with the cheese, mint, and chile sauce until thoroughly blended.
2. Sprinkle salt and pepper all over the meat, fat side down. Spread the bread mixture evenly, leaving a 1-inch (2.5-cm) border at one end. Roll up the meat jellyroll manner, beginning at the thin end.
3. Tie the coiled roast with kitchen string. Roast, basting regularly, for 1 1/2 hours or until a meat thermometer inserted in the center of the flesh registers 140 degrees F (60 degrees C) for rare or 160 degrees F (70 degrees C) for medium doneness. Rest the roast for ten minutes. Thickly slice This recipe serves eight people.

Braised Lamb Shanks

Preparation Time: 10 minutes | Cooking Time: 15 minutes |
Servings: 1

Ingredients:
- Two large white onions, chopped
- Four lamb shanks
- 2 cups dry red wine
- 1 cup balsamic vinegar
- ⅓ cup olive oil
- Four cloves of garlic, pressed
- Two lemons, quartered
- 2 (14.5 ounces) cans of diced tomatoes
- One bunch of fresh basil, chopped
- One tablespoon of kosher salt
- One tablespoon of cracked black pepper

Directions:
1. Preheat the oven to 350° F. (175 degrees C).
2. In the bottom of a Dutch oven or medium roasting pan with a cover, stack the onions. On top of the onions, arrange the lamb shanks. Over the meat, drizzle with the wine, balsamic vinegar, and olive oil. Place a crushed garlic clove and a quarter of a lemon on each side of each shank—season with salt, pepper, and basil after pouring the tomatoes over everything.
3. Place in the preheated oven, covered. Three hours in the oven, use the pan juices to make a delicious gravy.

Baked Lamb Meatballs

Preparation Time: 10 minutes | Cooking Time: 15 minutes |
Servings: 1

Ingredients:
- 1 pound ground lamb
- Two slices of bread, torn into small pieces
- ¼ cup yogurt
- ¼ cup raisins
- ¼ cup fresh cilantro
- One clove of garlic, minced
- ¼ teaspoon dried oregano
- ¼ teaspoon dried basil
- ⅛ teaspoon salt
- ⅛ teaspoon ground black pepper

Directions:
1. Preheat the oven to 375° F. (190 degrees C).
2. Combine the lamb, bread, yogurt, raisins, cilantro, garlic, oregano, basil, salt, and pepper in a mixing dish. Form

into 1-inch balls and set on a baking sheet that has been buttered.

3. Bake for 20 minutes, until the meatballs are browned on the outsides and very slightly pink in the centers.

Slow Roast Leg of Lamb

Preparation Time: 10 minutes | Cooking Time: 15 minutes | Servings: 1

Ingredients:

- Three carrots, coarsely chopped
- One head of garlic, split but not peeled
- 1 (5 pounds) leg of lamb
- One ¼ cup of red wine
- One ¼ cups lamb stock
- salt and freshly ground black pepper to taste

Directions:

1. Preheat the oven to 250° F. (120 degrees C).
2. In a roasting pan large enough to hold the leg of lamb, combine the carrots and garlic. Put the lamb on top. Pour in the wine and the lamb stock. Heat the roasting pan over medium-low heat until the liquid is boiling. Place the roasting pan in the oven and cover it securely with aluminum foil, using oven gloves to protect your hands.
3. Roast in a preheated oven for 7 hours, or until an instant-read thermometer inserted into the middle registers 130 degrees F (54 degrees C) for medium. Take it out of the oven.
4. Raise the oven temperature to 400°F (200 degrees C). Place the lamb in a second roasting pan.
5. Roast the lamb uncovered for 15 to 20 minutes or until the skin is crispy. Allow resting before slicing.
6. Pour the cooking liquids from the first roasting pan into a saucepan while the lamb rests. Bring to a boil, then reduce to a gravy, approximately 5 minutes—season with salt and pepper to taste.

Stuffed Greek Leg of Lamb

Preparation Time: 10 minutes | Cooking Time: 15 minutes | Servings: 1

Ingredients:

- 1 (3 1/2) pound leg of lamb, butterflied
- olive oil, or as needed
- Two tablespoons of chopped fresh oregano
- Two tablespoons of chopped fresh basil
- 1 (12 ounces) jar of marinated artichoke hearts, drained and chopped
- 1 (8 ounces) package of crumbled feta cheese
- 1 (6 ounces) jar of sun-dried tomatoes packed in oil, drained and chopped
- Three cloves of garlic, minced
- salt and ground black pepper to taste

Directions:

1. Preheat the oven to 350°F (175 degrees C).
2. Place the leg of lamb on a chopping board, with the interior facing you—drizzle olive oil over the lamb in an equal layer. Season the lamb with oregano and basil. Season the lamb with salt and pepper and top with artichoke hearts, feta cheese, sun-dried tomatoes, and garlic.
3. Wrap the lamb with the filling. To protect the lamb from unraveling, wrap it with kitchen twine. Next, wrap the lamb in foil and lay it in a baking dish.
4. Roast in a preheated oven for 90 minutes, or until done to your liking, or at an internal temperature of 150 degrees F (70 degrees C) for medium. Set aside for 10 minutes in a warm place before slicing. Keep the pan juices aside for dishing.

Irish-Style Lamb Stew

Preparation Time: 10 minutes | Cooking Time: 15 minutes | Servings: 1

Ingredients:

- 1 pound cubed lamb meat
- One large onion, halved and sliced
- 1 pound baking potatoes, peeled and sliced
- One carrot, peeled and sliced
- One large stalk of celery, sliced
- Two tablespoons of chopped fresh parsley
- salt and pepper to taste
- 2 cups beef stock
- One tablespoon of chopped fresh parsley for garnish

Directions:

1. Preheat the oven to 325° F. (165 degrees C).
2. Layer the lamb meat, onion, potatoes, carrot, and celery in an ovenproof saucepan or casserole dish. Season each layer with parsley, salt, and pepper as you continue. Cover and set aside the beef stock.
3. Bake for 1 1/2 to 2 hours, until veggies and meat are extremely soft, in a preheated oven. Divide into bowls and top with more parsley.

Ballymore Irish Lamb Stew

Preparation Time: 10 minutes | Cooking Time: 15 minutes | Servings: 1

Ingredients:

- 2 pounds of boneless lamb chops
- salt and freshly ground black pepper to taste
- Two tablespoons of vegetable oil
- ½ cup Irish stout beer (such as Guinness®)
- 1 pound of new potatoes
- 1 pound of baby carrots
- 1 (8 ounces) package of pearl onions
- 4 cups lamb stock
- Two tablespoons of brown roux
- Two tablespoons of finely chopped parsley

Directions:

1. Season the lamb chops with salt and pepper to taste.
2. In a large Dutch oven, heat oil over medium heat until heated but not smoking; add chops. For 2 to 3 minutes on each side. Set aside after removing from the pan.
3. Pour in the beer and heat for 1 minute, scraping up any browned parts from the pan with a wooden spoon. Return the lamb to the pot.
4. In a mixing bowl, season the potatoes, carrots, and onions with salt and pepper and add to the saucepan. Bring to a boil with the lamb stock. Reduce the heat to medium-low and cover. Simmer for 2 hours, or until the lamb slips off the bone—Cook for 10 minutes after adding the roux. Stir in the parsley before spooning it into the serving dishes.

Lamb Burgers

Preparation Time: 10 minutes | Cooking Time: 15 minutes | Servings: 1

Ingredients:

- 1 pound ground lamb
- One tablespoon of garlic powder
- One 4-inch sprig of rosemary, chopped
- Four sprigs of thyme, chopped
- One pinch salt
- One pinch of ground black pepper
- Three tablespoons mayonnaise

- One tablespoon of Dijon mustard
- Four hamburger buns, split and toasted
- Four thick slices of tomato
- 1 cup baby mixed salad greens

Directions:

1. Preheat an outside grill to medium heat and grease the grate liberally.
2. In a large mixing basin, combine ground lamb, garlic powder, rosemary, thyme, salt, and pepper until fully blended; form into four patties.
3. Cook over a hot grill until the patties are firm and slightly pink in the center, about 5 minutes per side. A thermometer in the middle should read 140 degrees Fahrenheit (60 degrees C). Alternatively, cook the patties to your preferred level of doneness. While arranging the toppings, rest the patties.
4. In a small mixing dish, combine the mayonnaise and mustard. One tablespoon on the bottom of each hamburger bun; top with a lamb patty, tomato slice, and greens. To serve, place the sandwich on the top bread.

Slow Cooker Leg of Lamb

Preparation Time: 10 minutes | Cooking Time: 15 minutes | Servings: 1

Ingredients:

- zest of 1 small lemon
- Two tablespoons chopped fresh rosemary
- Five cloves of garlic, minced
- One tablespoon of chopped fresh thyme
- One tablespoon of chopped fresh parsley
- One tablespoon of olive oil
- One teaspoon of sea salt
- One teaspoon of ground black pepper
- ¼ teaspoon onion powder
- 1 (3 pounds) leg of lamb
- ½ cup vegetable broth

Directions:

1. In a mortar, combine the lemon zest, rosemary, garlic, thyme, parsley, olive oil, sea salt, black pepper, and onion powder. Using a pestle, grind the ingredients into a paste.
2. Pat the lamb dry and rub the herb mixture all over it. Place the lamb in a 3-quart slow cooker and drizzle with lemon juice. Cover with broth.
3. Cook for 6 to 8 hours on low heat.

Easy Herbed Lamb Chops

Preparation Time: 10 minutes | Cooking Time: 15 minutes | Servings: 1

Ingredients:

- Two tablespoons of chopped fresh basil
- One tablespoon chopped fresh rosemary
- One tablespoon of chopped fresh oregano
- One tablespoon of garlic powder
- Two teaspoons of ground black pepper
- 12 raw chop with refuse, 160 g; yields excluding refuses lamb chops
- ½ cup olive oil
- One medium onion, chopped
- leaves from 1 celery stalk, chopped
- Two tablespoons salt
- 1 cup water, or as needed
- Two tablespoons of chopped fresh parsley

Directions:

1. Combine basil, rosemary, oregano, garlic powder, and pepper in a mixing dish. 1/2 of the seasoning mixture should be applied to one side of the lamb chops.

2. Heat the olive oil in a big, deep frying pan over medium-high heat.
3. Place each chop in the hot pan and seasoned side down. Season the lamb chops on the second side with the remaining spice mixture. 3 to 5 minutes to brown both sides. Reduce the heat to medium and add the onions. Cook and stir for 5 minutes, or until the onions sweat and begin to become translucent.
4. Add the celery leaves, salt, and enough water to cover the chops. Allow to simmer and reduce over medium heat for 20 to 30 minutes, or until the water has evaporated. In the middle of a chop, an instant-read thermometer should read at least 140 degrees F. (60 degrees C).
5. Serve the leftover reduction as a sauce on a dish, family-style. Garnish with parsley.

Lamb Meatballs Over Tandoori Naan

Preparation Time: 10 minutes | Cooking Time: 15 minutes | Servings: 1

Ingredients:

- ¼ cup Italian-seasoned bread crumbs
- ¼ teaspoon garlic powder
- ¼ teaspoon ground paprika
- ¼ teaspoon dried mint
- ¼ teaspoon dried basil
- ¼ teaspoon dried parsley
- 1 pound ground lamb
- One egg
- Two tablespoons of finely chopped onion
- Two cloves of garlic, minced
- ½ teaspoon olive oil
- salt and ground black pepper to taste
- 1 (26 ounces) jar of tomato sauce
- One tablespoon capers
- 4 leaves fresh basil leaves, torn
- ¼ teaspoon dried mint
- salt and ground black pepper to taste
- Remaining Ingredients:
- Four pieces of tandoori naan bread
- Eight slices of Muenster cheese, or as needed

Directions:

1. Preheat the oven to 400°F (200 degrees C). A baking sheet should be greased.
2. In a large mixing bowl, combine bread crumbs, garlic powder, paprika, 1/4 teaspoon mint, dried basil, and parsley. Mix in the ground lamb, egg, onion, garlic, olive oil, salt, and pepper until well combined. Form the ground lamb into 1-inch balls and place them on the prepared baking sheet in a single layer.
3. Bake for 15 minutes in a preheated oven. Cook until the meatballs are cooked through, about 10 minutes longer. Remove the meatballs from the oven and decrease the temperature to 350°F (175 degrees C).
4. Over low heat, combine tomato sauce, capers, fresh basil, 1/4 teaspoon mint, salt, and pepper. Cook sauce, stirring periodically, for 5 to 10 minutes, or until heated through and flavors have combined.
5. Arrange the naan bread on a baking pan. Cover with Muenster cheese slices after spooning tomato sauce and meatballs over the naan.
6. Bake for 5 to 10 minutes, or until the cheese is melted.

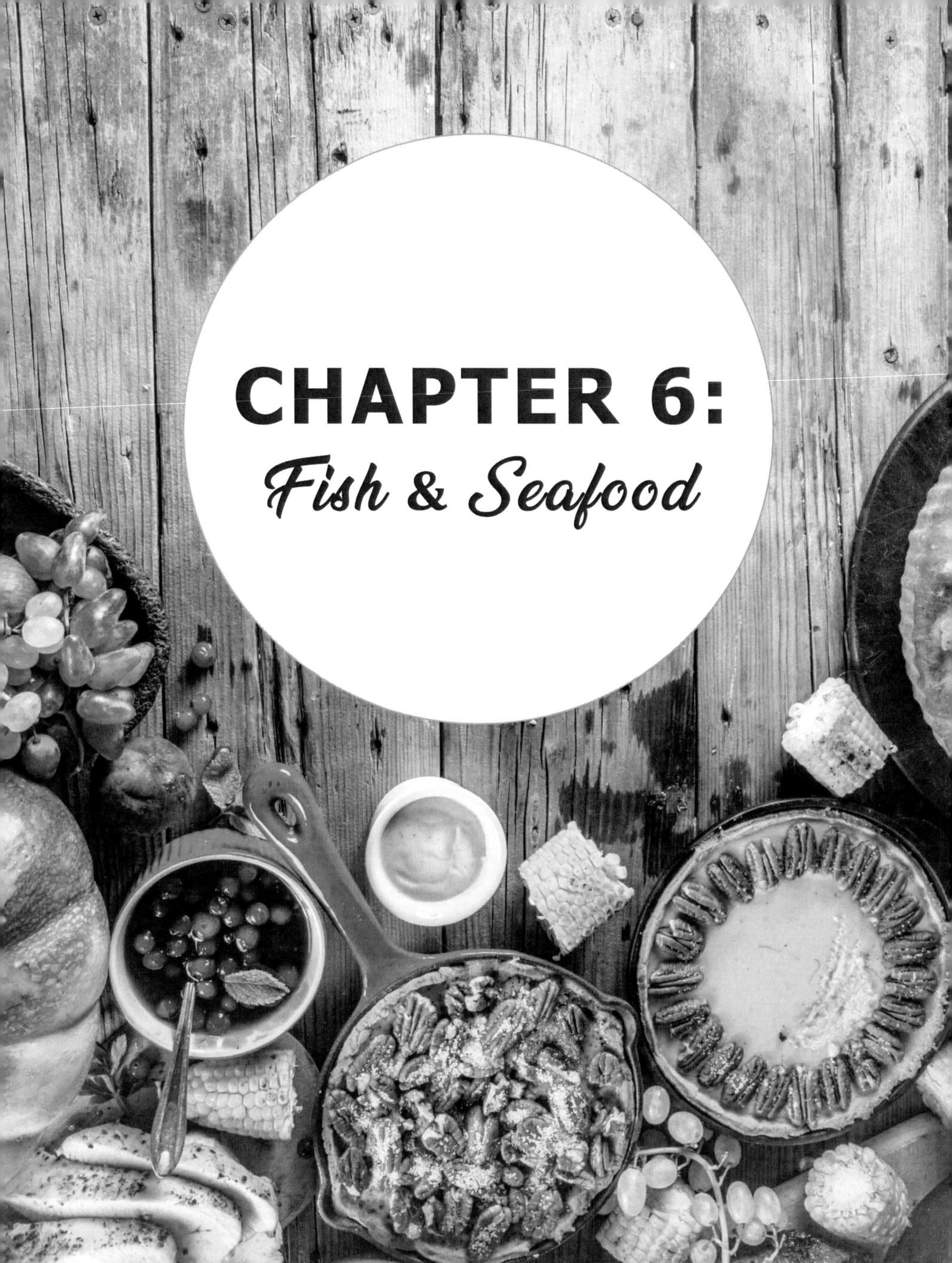

CHAPTER 6:
Fish & Seafood

Savory Lemon Shrimp

Preparation Time: 20 minutes | Cooking Time: 15 minutes | Servings: 2

Ingredients:
- 10 oz. peeled shrimps
- 2 tablespoons lemon juice
- ¼ teaspoon diced garlic
- 1 teaspoon olive oil
- 1 teaspoon grated lemon rind
- 1 tablespoon Cajun seasonings

Directions:
1. Rub the shrimp with Cajun seasoning.
2. Whisk olive oil, lemon juice, garlic, and lemon rind in a bowl.
3. Marinate the shrimp with this liquid and leave it for 15 minutes.
4. Transfer them to the air fryer and bake at 400 degrees Fahrenheit for 4 minutes.
5. Shake the shrimp in between and remove it once cooked.
6. Serve immediately with any choice of dip.

Asian Style Salmon Cubes

Preparation Time: 10 minutes | Cooking Time: 15 minutes | Servings: 4

Ingredients:
- 1 oz. salmon fillet
- 1 teaspoon avocado oil
- 1 tablespoon tandoori seasonings

Directions:
1. Cut salmon into large cubes and season with tandoori powder carefully.
2. Transfer the cubes to the air fryer basket and drizzle avocado oil on top.
3. Close the lid and cook salmon cubes at 365 degrees Fahrenheit for 15 minutes.
4. Serve once done, and enjoy!

Shrimp Celery Salad

Preparation Time: 10 minutes | Cooking Time: 5 minutes | Servings: 4

Ingredients:
- 3 oz. chevre
- ½ teaspoon kosher salt
- 8 oz. peeled shrimps
- 1 teaspoon avocado oil
- ½ teaspoon red pepper flakes
- 1 teaspoon melted butter
- 4 oz. chopped celery stalk
- ½ teaspoon dried thyme

Directions:
1. Top the shrimp with oregano and butter and place them in the air fryer.
2. Cook them for 5 minutes at 400 degrees Fahrenheit.
3. Meanwhile, crumble the chevre and add it to a salad bowl with celery red pepper flakes, salt, and avocado oil.
4. Toss well and serve with air-fried shrimps.

Cod & Kale Leaves

Preparation Time: 10 minutes | Cooking Time: 15 minutes | Servings: 2

Ingredients:
- ½ cup pecans
- 2 black cod fillets
- Olive oil as needed
- 1 cup halved grapes
- 1 thinly sliced fennel bulb
- 3 cups shredded kale leaves
- 2 teaspoons balsamic vinegar
- Salt & ground black pepper as needed

Directions:
1. Transfer the cod to the air fryer basket and season with salt and pepper.
2. Drizzle olive oil on top and cook for 10 minutes at 400 degrees Fahrenheit.
3. Remove the cod from the air fryer and transfer it to a plate.
4. Mix a tablespoon of oil, salt, pepper, grapes, pecans, and fennel in a bowl.
5. Toss to combine and cook this mixture in an air fryer for 5 minutes at 400 degrees F.
6. Meanwhile, mix kale with vinegar, ½ teaspoon of oil, salt, and pepper.
7. Serve fish on a plate and add the cooked mixture to the side with the vinegar and kale leaves.

Simple Cajun Shrimps

Preparation Time: 10 minutes | Cooking Time: 6 minutes | Servings: 4

Ingredients:
- 1 beaten egg
- ½ teaspoon sea salt
- 8 oz. peeled shrimps
- 1 teaspoon olive oil
- 1 teaspoon Cajun spices
- 1 teaspoon cream cheese

Directions:
1. Marinate the shrimp with Cajun and salt.
2. Meanwhile, whisk egg and cream cheese in a bowl.
3. Coat the shrimp with the egg mixture and add to a preheated air fryer with a sprinkle of olive oil.
4. Cook it in the air fryer for 6 minutes at 400 degrees Fahrenheit, shaking after 3 minutes for even cooking.
5. Serve immediately with any choice of sauce.

Seafood Mix

Preparation Time: 15 minutes | Cooking Time: 5 minutes | Servings: 4

Ingredients:
- 1 tofu skin
- Sriracha sauce
- Lettuce leaf
- 1 nori seaweed sheet
- 1 pack of crab sticks
- 1 tablespoon sesame oil

Directions:
1. Place crab sticks onto the nori seaweed sheet.

2. Next, place tofu skin and drizzle oil on top.
3. Transfer to the air fryer and cook at 350 degrees Fahrenheit for 5 minutes.
4. Remove once done and serve on the lettuce leaf alongside sriracha sauce.

Basil & Paprika Cod

Preparation Time: 5 minutes | Cooking Time: 15 minutes | Servings: 4

Ingredients:
- 4 boneless cod fillets
- 2 tablespoon olive oil
- 1 teaspoon dried oregano
- ½ teaspoon hot paprika
- 1 teaspoon chili flakes
- Salt & black pepper as needed

Directions:
1. Combine and toss cod with all the ingredients.
2. Transfer it to the air fryer basket and cook for 15 minutes at 380 degrees Fahrenheit.
3. Serve immediately and enjoy with any sauce!

Calamari Rings

Preparation Time: 15 minutes | Cooking Time: 8 minutes | Servings: 2

Ingredients:
- ⅓ cup heavy cream
- ½ teaspoon salt
- ½ cup corn flour
- 1 tablespoon olive oil
- 7 oz. trimmed calamari
- ¼ teaspoon chili powder
- ¼ teaspoon ground turmeric

Directions:
1. Cut calamari into rings with a knife, add to a heavy cream bowl and mix well.
2. Combine the remaining ingredients in a separate bowl except for calamari rings and oil.
3. Coat the rings with the dry mixture, transfer them to the air fryer basket, and drizzle them with olive oil.
4. Cook at 360 degrees Fahrenheit for 8 minutes, shaking after 4 minutes.
5. Serve with your favorite sauce.

Shrimp Spaghetti

Preparation Time: 10 minutes| Cooking Time: 25 minutes | Servings: 3

Ingredients:
- 5 oz. spaghetti
- 1 tablespoon butter
- 5 minced garlic cloves
- 1 teaspoon red pepper flakes
- 2 tablespoons sesame oil
- ½ teaspoon chicken bullion
- 8 oz. peeled & deveined shrimp
- Salt & ground black pepper as needed

Directions:
1. Cook spaghetti according to package instructions, drain, and set aside

2. Combine shrimp with 1 tablespoon sesame oil butter, and add to the air fryer.
3. Cook at 350 degrees Fahrenheit for 10 minutes in the air fryer.
4. After, add spaghetti, garlic, bullion, and red pepper flakes and season with salt and pepper.
5. Toss to combine and cook in the air fryer for 5 more minutes.
6. Serve hot once done, and enjoy!

Staple Fish & Chips

Preparation Time: 5 minutes | Cooking Time: 15 minutes | Servings: 3

Ingredients:
- 1 egg
- 6 oz. tilapia fillets
- ½ cup panko breadcrumbs
- 2 tablespoons all-purpose flour
- Old bay seasoning as needed
- Frozen crinkle-cut fries as needed

Directions:
1. Add flour to one bowl and whisk the egg in another bowl.
2. Add breadcrumbs and seasoning to another bowl.
3. Coat tilapia with flour, then egg, and then with breadcrumbs in the end.
4. Place the coated tilapia in the air fryer with the fries.
5. Cook at 390 degrees Fahrenheit for 15 minutes.
6. Serve immediately once golden-brown and enjoy!

Wrapped Scallops

Preparation Time: 15 minutes | Cooking Time: 7 minutes | Servings: 4

Ingredients:
- 16 oz. scallops
- ¼ teaspoon salt
- 4 oz. sliced bacon
- 1 teaspoon sesame oil
- ½ teaspoon chili powder
- 1 teaspoon ground cumin

Directions:
1. Marinate scallops with all the ingredients except oil and bacon.
2. After, wrap the scallops in the bacon slices and hold them securely with toothpicks.
3. Drizzle over the oil and preheat the air fryer to 400 degrees Fahrenheit.
4. Place the scallops in the air fryer basket and cook for 7 minutes.
5. Serve once done and enjoy with your favorite sauce.

Thyme Catfish

Preparation Time: 10 minutes | Cooking Time: 12 minutes | Servings: 4

Ingredients:
- 2 beaten eggs
- ½ teaspoon salt
- ⅓ cup coconut flour
- 1 teaspoon avocado oil
- 1 teaspoon dried oregano

- ¼ teaspoon cayenne pepper
- 1 teaspoon white wine vinegar
- 20 oz. (4 oz. each) catfish fillet

Directions:
1. Marinate the catfish with all the ingredients and add avocado oil at the end over the catfish.
2. Preheat the air fryer to 385 degrees Fahrenheit.
3. Place the catfish in the air fryer basket and cook for 8 minutes.
4. Turn over the catfish to the other side and cook for an additional 4 minutes.
5. Serve once done and enjoy with your favorite sauce.

Salmon With Creamy Chives Sauce

Preparation Time: 5 minutes | Cooking Time: 20 minutes | Servings: 4

Ingredients:
- ¼ cup melted ghee
- ½ cup cooking cream
- 2 minced garlic cloves
- 1 teaspoon lemon juice
- 1 teaspoon chopped scallions
- 4 boneless salmon fillets
- A pinch of salt & black pepper
- 1 tablespoon chopped chives

Directions:
1. Whisk all the ingredients except salmon in a bowl.
2. Place the salmon in a pan that fits the air fryer and add the bowl mixture over it.
3. Add the pan to the air fryer and cook for 20 minutes at 360 degrees Fahrenheit.
4. Serve once done, and enjoy!

Tilapia With Tomato Salsa

Preparation Time: 5 minutes | Cooking Time: 15 minutes | Servings: 4

Ingredients:
- 1 tablespoon olive oil
- 4 boneless tilapia fillets
- 12 oz. chopped tomatoes
- A pinch of salt & black pepper
- 1 tablespoon red wine vinegar
- 2 tablespoons chopped scallions
- 2 tablespoons chopped sweet red pepper

Directions:
1. Place tilapia fillets on a baking sheet that fits the air fryer.
2. Season the fillets with salt and pepper, combine all the remaining ingredients in a bowl, and add over the fillets.
3. Toss well and add the baking sheet to the air fryer to cook for 15 minutes at 350 degrees Fahrenheit.
4. Serve once done, and enjoy!

Simple Salmon With Sauce

Preparation Time: 5 minutes | Cooking Time: 10 minutes | Servings: 2

Ingredients:
- 1 cup water
- Salt as needed
- ½ cup cream cheese
- 6 oz. fresh salmon

- 2 teaspoon olive oil
- ½ cup plain Greek yogurt
- 2 tablespoon finely chopped dill

Directions:
1. Add water to the air fryer tray and heat at 285 degrees Fahrenheit.
2. Drizzle oil over fish and add salt.
3. Put it on the tray and cook for 10 minutes.
4. Combine yogurt, cream, dill, and salt to make the sauce.
5. Serve the fish with the sauce once done.

Tangy Grilled Salmon

Preparation Time: 5 minutes | Cooking Time: 10 minutes | Servings: 3

Ingredients:
- ⅓ cup sugar
- 2 salmon fillets
- ⅓ cup tamari sauce
- 1 tablespoon sesame oil
- Salt & pepper as needed
- ½ teaspoon lemon pepper
- ½ teaspoon garlic powder

Directions:
1. Combine fillets with garlic powder, lemon, pepper, and salt.
2. Combine ⅓ of water, sesame oil, tamari sauce, and sugar in a bowl.
3. Add the salmon to the bowl and marinate.
4. Seal with cling film and put in the fridge for an hour.
5. Preheat the air fryer to 350 degrees and add the fish to the air fryer for 10 minutes or until tender.
6. Serve hot with lemon wedges and enjoy!

Garlic Shrimp Mix

Preparation Time: 10 minutes | Cooking Time: 5 minutes | Servings: 3

Ingredients:
- 1 oz. peeled shrimps
- 1 teaspoon ground coriander
- ½ tablespoon avocado oil
- ½ teaspoon dried cilantro
- ½ teaspoon garlic powder
- ¼ teaspoon minced garlic
- ¼ teaspoon grated lemon zest

Directions:
1. Marinate the shrimp with all the ingredients and add avocado oil at the end over the shrimp.
2. Preheat the air fryer to 400 degrees Fahrenheit.
3. Place the shrimp in the air fryer basket and cook for 5 minutes.
4. Serve once done and enjoy with your favorite sauce!

Catfish & Spring Onions With Avocado

Preparation Time: 5 minutes | Cooking Time: 15 minutes | Servings: 4

Ingredients:
- 4 catfish fillets
- 2 teaspoons olive oil
- 1 peeled & cubed avocado
- 2 tablespoons lemon juice

- 2 teaspoons dried oregano
- 2 teaspoons ground coriander
- 2 teaspoons sweet paprika
- A pinch of salt & black pepper
- ½ cup chopped spring onions
- 2 tablespoons chopped parsley

Directions:
1. Combine all the ingredients except fish thoroughly in a bowl.
2. Place the ingredients in a pan that fits the air fryer and put the fish on top.
3. Add the pan to the air fryer to cook for 15 minutes at 360 degrees Fahrenheit, flipping the fish to the other side after 7 minutes.
4. Serve once done, and enjoy!

Smoked Paprika Tilapia

Preparation Time: 5 minutes | Cooking Time: 20 minutes | Servings: 4

Ingredients:
- 2 tablespoons capers
- 4 boneless tilapia fillets
- 2 tablespoons lime juice
- 3 tablespoons melted ghee
- ½ teaspoon garlic powder
- ½ teaspoon dried thyme
- A pinch of salt & black pepper
- ½ teaspoon smoked paprika

Directions:
1. Combine all the ingredients except fish thoroughly in a bowl.
2. Place the fish in a pan that fits the air fryer and add the contents of the bowl over it.
3. Add the pan to the air fryer to cook for 20 minutes at 360 degrees Fahrenheit, shaking it after 10 minutes to ensure even cooking.
4. Serve once done, and enjoy!

Delicious Lemon Cod

Preparation Time: 5 minutes | Cooking Time: 14 minutes | Servings: 4

Ingredients:
- 1 lemon juice
- 4 boneless cod fillets
- 1 tablespoon sesame oil
- 2 teaspoons sweet paprika
- Salt & black pepper as needed

Directions:
1. Combine all the ingredients in a bowl thoroughly.
2. Transfer the fish to the air fryer basket to cook for 7 minutes at 350 degrees Fahrenheit.
3. Serve once done, and enjoy!

Crispy Smoked Fish Fillets

Preparation Time: 5 minutes | Cooking Time: 15 minutes | Servings: 4

Ingredients:
- 1 beaten egg
- 1 teaspoon chili powder
- 2 halved fish fillets

- 1 teaspoon celery seed
- ½ teaspoon seasoned salt
- ½ cup seasoned breadcrumbs
- 1 tablespoon red wine vinegar
- ½ teaspoon ground black pepper

Directions:
1. Add all the ingredients to the food processor except fish and egg and process for 30 seconds.
2. Coat the fish with egg and then the processed breadcrumb mixture.
3. Place the fish on a pan that fits the air fryer and add it to the air fryer.
4. Cook it for 15 minutes at 350 degrees Fahrenheit, flipping to the other side after 7 minutes.
5. Serve hot once done, and enjoy!

Basic Tuna Cobbler

Preparation Time: 15 minutes | Cooking Time: 25 minutes | Servings: 4

Ingredients:
- ⅓ cup cold water
- Chili powder as needed
- 10 oz. can have drained tuna
- 1 tablespoon lime juice
- Cooking spray as needed
- 10 ¾ oz. cream of chicken soup
- 2 oz. sliced & drained pimientos
- 2 tablespoons sweet pickle relish
- 1 ⅓ cup frozen mixed vegetables

Directions:
1. Preheat the air fryer to 375 degrees Fahrenheit.
2. Grease a dish that fits the air fryer with cooking spray.
3. Mix all the ingredients and add to the air fryer to cook for 25 minutes.
4. Remove to a casserole dish and serve hot!

Spinach Tilapia

Preparation Time: 5 minutes | Cooking Time: 20 minutes | Servings: 4

Ingredients:
- 1 crushed bunch of spinach
- 2 minced garlic cloves
- 9 tablespoons olive oil
- 4 boneless tilapia fillets
- 1 teaspoon fennel seeds
- Salt & black pepper as needed
- ½ teaspoon chili flakes

Directions:
1. Combine all the ingredients in a pan that fits the air fryer thoroughly.
2. Add the pan to the air fryer to cook for 20 minutes at 360 degrees Fahrenheit.
3. Serve once done and enjoy hot!

Gingered Salmon

Preparation Time: 5 minutes | Cooking Time: 12 minutes | Servings: 4

Ingredients:
- 4 teaspoons olive oil
- 2 tablespoons lemon juice

- 1 tablespoon grated ginger
- 1 tablespoon soy sauce
- 1 tablespoon chopped chives
- 1 tablespoon toasted sesame seeds
- 1 oz. boneless, skinless & cubed salmon fillets

Directions:
1. Combine all the ingredients in a pan that fits the air fryer thoroughly.
2. Add the pan to the air fryer to cook for 12 minutes at 360 degrees Fahrenheit.
3. Serve once done and enjoy hot!

Coconutty Shrimp

Preparation Time: 5 minutes | Cooking Time: 12 minutes | Servings: 4

Ingredients:
- ¼ cup coconut cream
- 1 tablespoon melted ghee
- A pinch of chili flakes
- A pinch of salt & black pepper
- 1 tablespoon chopped dill
- 1 tablespoon chopped parsley
- 1 oz. peeled & deveined shrimp

Directions:
1. Combine all the ingredients except parsley in a pan that fits the air fryer thoroughly.
2. Add the pan to the air fryer to cook for 12 minutes at 360 degrees Fahrenheit.
3. Serve once done with a sprinkling of parsley on top!

Pecorino Salmon Fillets

Preparation Time: 5 minutes | Cooking Time: 15 minutes | Servings: 4

Ingredients:
- 1 teaspoon dijon mustard
- ½ cup coconut flakes
- 4 skinless salmon fillets
- Cooking spray as needed
- A pinch of salt & black pepper
- 1 tablespoon grated pecorino

Directions:
1. Combine all the ingredients except fish and cooking spray in a bowl thoroughly.
2. Dip the fish in the mix and use cooking spray to grease it before placing it in the air fryer basket.
3. Cook it for 15 minutes at 400 degrees Fahrenheit.
4. Serve once done, and enjoy!

Tuna Skewers

Preparation Time: 5 minutes | Cooking Time: 12 minutes | Servings: 4

Ingredients:
- Olive oil as needed
- 1 minced red pepper
- 4 chopped scallions
- 2 tablespoons lemon juice
- Salt & black pepper as needed
- 1 oz. boneless & cubed tuna steaks

Directions:
1. Combine all the ingredients with a drizzle of olive oil in a bowl thoroughly.
2. Thread the tuna cubes on skewers and add them to the air fryer basket.
3. Cook them for 12 minutes at 370 degrees Fahrenheit.
4. Serve once done, and enjoy!

Cod With Mustard

Preparation Time: 10 minutes | Cooking Time: 14 minutes | Servings: 4

Ingredients:
- 4 boneless cod fillets
- 1 tablespoon dijon mustard
- 1 cup grated pecorino
- Salt & black pepper as needed

Directions:
1. Combine all the ingredients except cod thoroughly in a bowl.
2. Add the contents of the bowl over the cod and place it in the air fryer basket.
3. Cook for 7 minutes from both sides at 370 degrees Fahrenheit
4. Serve once done, and enjoy!

Paprika Cod With Endives

Preparation Time: 5 minutes | Cooking Time: 20 minutes | Servings: 4

Ingredients:
- 2 shredded endives
- 2 tablespoons sesame oil
- 4 boneless salmon fillets
- ½ teaspoon sweet paprika
- Salt & black pepper as needed

Directions:
1. Combine all the ingredients in a pan that fits the air fryer thoroughly.
2. Add the pan to the air fryer to cook for 20 minutes at 350 degrees Fahrenheit, flipping to the other side after 10 minutes.
3. Serve once done, and enjoy!

Buttered Mussels

Preparation Time: 10 minutes | Cooking Time: 2 minutes | Servings: 5

Ingredients:
- 2 oz. mussels
- 1 teaspoon salt
- 1 chopped shallot
- ½ teaspoon red pepper flakes
- 1 teaspoon sunflower oil
- 1 tablespoon minced garlic
- 1 tablespoon melted butter
- 1 tablespoon chopped fresh cilantro

Directions:
1. Clean the mussels by washing them and adding them to a large bowl.
2. Add the remaining ingredients except for cilantro and toss everything together well.

3. Preheat the air fryer to 390 degrees Fahrenheit and place the mussels in the air fryer basket.
4. Cook it for 2 minutes before transferring it to a serving bowl.
5. Sprinkle cilantro on top and enjoy!

Parsley Cod Mix

Preparation Time: 5 minutes | Cooking Time: 15 minutes | Servings: 4

Ingredients:
- 2 tablespoons olive oil
- 1 cup halved grape tomatoes
- Salt & black pepper as needed
- 4 skinless & boneless cod fillets
- 2 tablespoons chopped parsley

Directions:
1. Combine all the ingredients in a pan that fits the air fryer thoroughly.
2. Add the pan to the air fryer to cook for 15 minutes at 370 degrees Fahrenheit.
3. Serve once done, and enjoy!

Lemon & Oregano Tilapia Mix

Preparation Time: 5 minutes | Cooking Time: 20 minutes | Servings: 4

Ingredients:
- ¼ cup tomato puree
- 1 cup cubed tomatoes
- 2 tablespoons olive oil
- 1 tablespoon lime juice
- 1 teaspoon garlic powder
- 1 teaspoon dried oregano
- Salt & black pepper as needed
- 1 cup chopped roasted peppers
- 4 boneless & halved tilapia fillets

Directions:
1. Combine all the ingredients in a pan that fits the air fryer thoroughly.
2. Add the pan to the air fryer to cook for 20 minutes at 380 degrees Fahrenheit.
3. Serve once done, and enjoy!

Fried Oregano Crawfish

Preparation Time: 10 minutes | Cooking Time: 5 minutes | Servings: 4

Ingredients:
- 1 oz. crawfish
- 1 tablespoon avocado oil
- 1 teaspoon minced onion
- 1 tablespoon chopped oregano

Directions:
1. Start by preheating the air fryer at 340 degrees Fahrenheit.
2. Add the crawfish to the air fryer basket and gently combine the remaining ingredients.
3. Cook it for 5 minutes at the preheated temperature.
4. Serve once done, and enjoy!

Buttered Lobster

Preparation Time: 10 minutes | Cooking Time: 6 minutes | Servings: 4

Ingredients:
- ½ teaspoon salt
- 4 peeled lobster tails
- ½ teaspoon dried oregano
- 1 tablespoon olive oil
- 4 teaspoons almond butter

Directions:
1. Make a single cut on the back of each lobster's tail.
2. Sprinkle oregano salt and lastly follow with olive oil over them.
3. Start by preheating the air fryer at 380 degrees Fahrenheit and adding the lobster tails to the basket.
4. Cook them for 5 minutes, and after, brush each of them with almond butter.
5. Cook them for an additional minute before serving right away.

Shrimp With String Beans

Preparation Time: 5 minutes | Cooking Time: 15 minutes | Servings: 4

Ingredients:
- 1 lime juice
- ¼ cup melted ghee
- A pinch of salt & black pepper
- 1 oz. peeled & deveined shrimp
- 2 tablespoons chopped parsley
- ½ oz. trimmed & halved string beans

Directions:
1. Combine all the ingredients in a pan that fits the air fryer thoroughly.
2. Add the pan to the air fryer to cook for 15 minutes at 360 degrees Fahrenheit.
3. Serve once done, and enjoy!

Italian Shrimp

Preparation Time: 3 minutes | Cooking Time: 12 minutes | Servings: 4

Ingredients:
- 1 tablespoon olive oil
- A pinch of salt & black pepper
- 1 teaspoon Italian seasoning
- 1 oz. peeled & deveined shrimp
- 2 tablespoon toasted sesame seeds

Directions:
1. Combine all the ingredients thoroughly in a bowl.
2. Add the shrimp to the air fryer basket.
3. Cook for 12 minutes at 370 degrees Fahrenheit
4. Serve once done, and enjoy!

Sea Bass With Coconut Sauce

Preparation Time: 5 minutes | Cooking Time: 20 minutes | Servings: 4

Ingredients:
- 1 lime juice
- ½ cup okra
- 2 diced tomatoes

- 2 minced red chilies
- 1 minced garlic clove
- 2 cups coconut cream
- 2 chopped scallions
- 4 boneless sea bass fillets
- A pinch of salt & black pepper
- A handful of chopped coriander

Directions:
1. Add coconut cream and the remaining ingredients except sea bass in a pan that fits the air fryer.
2. Bring it to a simmer over medium-low heat and cook for 5 minutes.
3. Toss in sea bass carefully and add the pan with the contents to the air fryer.
4. Cook for 15 minutes at 380 degrees Fahrenheit.
5. Serve once done, and enjoy!

Salmon With Olives
Preparation Time: 5 minutes | Cooking Time: 15 minutes | Servings: 4

Ingredients:
- 1 lemon juice
- ⅓ cup avocado oil
- 4 boneless salmon fillets
- Salt & black pepper as needed
- 1 tablespoon grated lemon zest
- 1 cup pitted & sliced green olives

Directions:
1. Combine all the ingredients thoroughly in a dish that fits the air fryer.
2. Add the dish to the air fryer to cook for 15 minutes at 370 degrees Fahrenheit.
3. Serve once done, and enjoy!

Cajun Salmon
Preparation Time: 14 minutes | Cooking Time: 8 minutes | Servings: 2

Ingredients
- 2 salmon fillets, each about
- 2 teaspoons Cajun seasoning
- 2teaspoons jerk seasoning
- 2 teaspoons of lime juice
- Oil spray, for greasing
- ½ cup blue cheese dressing, optional

Directions
1. Add lime juice, Cajun, and jerk seasoning to a bowl and mix.
2. Drizzle oil over the salmon fillet and coat it with the earlier spice mix.
3. Arrange the fillets in the basket, ensuring they don't touch each other, and cook them for about 8 minutes at around 390 degrees F.
4. When done, take the fillets out and serve with blue cheese dressing if used.

Cajun Scallops
Preparation Time: 15 minutes | Cooking Time: 10 minutes | Servings: 2

Ingredients
- 12 scallops
- 1 teaspoon olive oil
- Salt, according to taste

- ½ tablespoon Cajun seasoning
- 4 teaspoons garlic butter dip

Directions
1. Add the scallops, salt, and Cajun seasoning to a bowl and toss them together.
2. Once the scallops are evenly coated, place them in the oil-coated air fryer basket and cook them for 10 minutes at 400 degrees F.
3. When done, take the scallops out and serve with a side of garlic butter dip.

Mediterranean Style Fish
Preparation Time: 15 minutes | Cooking Time: 10-15 minutes | Servings: 4

Ingredients
- 2 cod fillets
- 12 cherry tomatoes, halved
- 6 olives, sliced
- 2 teaspoon lime zest
- 1 lime, juiced
- 2 tablespoons extra virgin olive oil
- 4 cloves garlic, minced
- Salt and pepper, according to taste

Directions
1. Begin by preheating the oven to around 400 degrees F.
2. Add olives, tomatoes, lime juice, minced garlic, zest, salt, and pepper to a bowl and mix them thoroughly.
3. Pat dry the cod fillet using a paper towel, drizzle olive oil all over it, and season accordingly with salt and pepper.
4. Take 4 pieces of parchment paper every 14 inches, and wrap the cod with it.
5. Place the wrapped cod in the air fryer basket and cook it for about 10-15 minutes.
6. When done, take the fillet out of the parchment paper and serve with the side of rice or as per liking.

Mediterranean Scallops
Preparation Time: 15 minutes | Cooking Time: 20 minutes | Servings: 2

Ingredients
- 2 shallots, diced
- 5 tablespoons of olive oil, as needed
- ½ red bell pepper, sliced into strips
- ½ green bell pepper, sliced into strips
- 4 tablespoon garlic cloves
- 10 cherry tomatoes, halved
- 1 capper, drained
- Black pepper and Kosher salt, according to taste
- 16 ounces of sea scallops
- 2 teaspoons of lime juice
- 2 tablespoons of cilantro, chopped

Directions
1. Add 3 tablespoons of extra virgin olive oil to a cast-iron skillet and heat it over medium heat, adding red bell peppers, green bell peppers, garlic, and shallots in it once it becomes hot.
2. Cook the vegetables for about 3 minutes, then mix in tomatoes, capers, and seasoning of salt and pepper, letting them cook for about 7 minutes.
3. Cook scallops in an air fryer basket by misting them with oil spray for 8 minutes at 400 degrees F.
4. When the scallops are done, shift them to the tomato mixture, drizzle some lime juice over it, garnish it with cilantro and serve.

Salmon Kebob

Preparation Time: 15 minutes | Cooking Time: 8 minutes | Servings: 2

Ingredients:
- 1 ½ pound salmon fillet, diced into 1-inch cubes
- 6 ounces. zucchini, sliced into thin rounds
- 2 large onions, diced

Ingredients For marinade
- 4 tablespoons extra virgin olive oil
- 2 teaspoons lime zest
- 3 cloves garlic
- ½ tablespoon thyme leaves
- ½ tablespoon dry oregano
- 1 teaspoon ground coriander
- 1 teaspoon chili powder

Directions:
1. Mix all the listed ingredients for the marinade, season with salt and pepper accordingly, and mix thoroughly.
2. Place the salmon and zucchini in another bowl and pour the marinade over them, letting them rest in the marinade for at least 15 minutes.
3. Once the time is up, take them out and begin threading them through a skewer, interchanging them with salmon, zucchini, and onions.
4. Place the skewer on a grill and cook them for 6 to 8 minutes, making sure to flip them while cooking.
5. When done, take them off the grill and serve.

Shrimps and Scallops Pizza

Preparation Time: 15 minutes | Cooking Time: 10 minutes | Servings: 4

Ingredients
- 12 ounces of pizza crust
- Oil spray, for greasing

For the toppings
- 8 shrimps, uncooked
- 1/3 cup marinara sauce
- ½ pound mozzarella cheese, shredded
- 6 ounces parmesan cheese, shredded
- 5 ounces scallops
- ½ cup basil leaves, chopped
- Some garlic cloves

Directions
1. Place the pizza crust on a greased pan.
2. Top the crust first with marinara sauce, then with scallops, shrimps, cloves, and cheeses.
3. Place the pizza inside the air fryer and cook it for 10 minutes at a temperature of 400 degrees F.
4. Once done, take it out, top it with chopped basil and garlic cloves, and serve.

Scallops Crab Pizza

Preparation Time: 15 minutes | Cooking Time: 20 minutes | Servings: 2

Ingredients
- 10 ounces of scallops, uncooked, peeled, deveined
- 1 cup water
- 1 lime juice only
- 1 tablespoon butter
- 6 mushrooms, chopped
- 2 small onions, chopped
- 2 sweet red peppers, sliced into strips
- 2 cloves of garlic, minced
- Salt, to taste
- ½ pound crabmeat, chopped
- 10 ounces pizza crust

- 2 cups of Alfredo sauce
- 2 cups parmesan cheese, shredded

Directions
1. Begin by mixing scallops, lime juice, and a few tablespoons of water in a bowl and setting it aside for some time.
2. Then heat butter in a skillet or wok and add onions, mushrooms, and peppers in it once the butter is melted, cooking them for about 4 minutes.
3. Then add garlic, salt, and pepper to the skillet and mix.
4. Drain out the scallops and add them to the skillet with crabmeat, cooking for 1 to 2 minutes.
5. Meanwhile, grease a pizza pan with the oil, and place the pizza crust on top.
6. Add the Alfredo sauce over the crust and top it with the skillet mixture.
7. Then top it with cheese and place it in the air fryer cooking them for 10 minutes at 400 degrees F.
8. When done, take it out and serve with the side of Alfredo sauce.

Korean BBQ Salmon

Preparation Time: 15 minutes | Cooking Time: 8-12 minutes | Servings: 4

Ingredients
- 14 ounces salmon, sliced into equal quarters
- 4 tablespoon Korean BBQ sauce
- Oil spray

Directions
1. In a zip lock bag, place the salmon and mix it with ¾ of the Korean BBQ sauce, letting it sit there for at least 30 to 1 hour.
2. Grease the inside of the air fryer basket and place the salmon fillet in it, cooking it for 8 to 12 minutes at 400 degrees F, making sure to flip the fillet halfway in the cooking.
3. Once done, take the salmon fillet out and serve it with the remaining BBQ sauce.

Korean Crab Cakes with Gochujang Tartar Sauce

Preparation Time: 15 minutes | Cooking Time: 10 minutes | Servings: 2

Ingredients
- 2 cups crab meat
- 1 cup breadcrumbs
- 2 eggs
- 1 teaspoon of maple syrup
- 2 ½ tablespoon mayonnaise
- 2 ½ tablespoon Korean chili pepper
- ½ tablespoon honey mustard
- 1 tablespoon Korean seafood seasoning

Tartar sauce Ingredients
- 2 tablespoon chives, minced
- 1 lime, juiced, zest
- 1 teaspoon kosher salt and pepper.
- ¼ teaspoon Korean chili flakes

Directions
1. Mix all the tartar sauce ingredients in a bowl and set aside.
2. Crack and whisk the egg with honey mustard, mayonnaise, salt, seafood seasoning, and black pepper.
3. Then add the crab meat and breadcrumbs, mix them, cover them, and place them in the fridge for about 1 hour.
4. Once it has rested in the fridge for enough time, take it out and portion it into equal portions of 1-inch thick cakes.

5. Preheat the air fryer to around 375 degrees F and grease the inside of the basket with cooking spray.
6. Place the crab meat cake in the air fryer basket and cook it golden brown.
7. Once done, take them out and serve them with gochujang tartar sauce.

Korean Spicy Yellow Croaker Fish

Preparation Time: 15 minutes | Cooking Time: 10 minutes | Servings: 2

Ingredients
- 6 yellow croaker fish
- 4 teaspoon rice wine
- 1/3 tablespoon Korean hot pepper paste
- 1 ounce of maple syrup
- 1 teaspoon tamari sauce

Directions
1. Begin by rubbing the fish with rice wine and resting for at least 5 minutes.
2. Once it has rested, dry it out using a kitchen towel.
3. Mix gochujang, tamari sauce, and maple syrup in a bowl and set aside.
4. Line the inside of the air fryer basket with foil and place the fish on it, cooking it for 5 minutes at 400 degrees F.
5. When the time is up, take the fish out, brush the rub made earlier, and cook it for another 5 minutes at 400 degrees F.

Bang Shrimp

Preparation Time: 15 minutes | Cooking Time: 5 minutes | Servings: 4

Ingredients
- 10 ounces potato-starch
- Salt and pepper, as needed
- 16 ounces of shrimps, peeled, deveined
- 1 cup buttermilk
- Cooking spray for greasing
- 2 eggs, whisked with 1 tablespoon of water

Ingredients For sauce
- 6 tablespoons sweet and sour sauce
- 5 tablespoons sour cream
- 5 tablespoons mayonnaise
- 1 ounce of buttermilk
- 1 tablespoon hot sauce
- 1 teaspoon of dill weed, dried

Directions
1. Add potato starch to a bowl and season it with salt and pepper; add buttermilk to another bowl.
2. Dip the shrimps first in buttermilk and then coat them with corn starch.
3. Shake off the excess, arrange them in the air fryer bowl, brush them with oil and egg, and cook them for 5 minutes at 400 degrees F.
4. Meanwhile, mix sauce ingredients.
5. Once the shrimp are cooked, place them in the serving dish and serve with a side of sauce.

Cheesy Tuna Flautas

Preparation Time: 25 minutes | Cooking Time: 8 minutes | Servings: 3

Ingredients
- 6 flour tortillas, small
- 6 ounces of tuna
- Pinch of salt
- ¼ teaspoon garlic powder
- ¼ teaspoon paprika

- ½ teaspoon parsley, chopped
- 4 ounces cheddar cheese, shredded
- 4 ounces guacamole, optional
- 4 ounces sour cream, optional

Directions
1. Add tuna to a bowl and mix it with garlic powder, salt, paprika, and parsley.
2. Layer the tortillas with cheddar cheese, a tablespoon of tuna, and some more cheese.
3. Place it in the air fryer in a single layer and cook it for 5 to 8 minutes at about 350 degrees F.
4. Once cooked, take it out and serve with guacamole and sour cream.

Air Fried Salmon with Hoisin Ginger Marinade

Preparation Time: 15 minutes | Cooking Time: 6-8 minutes | Servings: 1

Ingredients
- 8 ounces of salmon fillet
- For the marinade
- 5 tablespoons hoisin sauce
- 1-ounce ginger paste
- 1 garlic clove, minced
- 1 teaspoon hot sauce
- 3 teaspoon sesame oil
- 1 ½ ounces honey
- 2 tablespoons soy sauce
- 1 ½ tablespoon rice wine vinegar

Directions
1. Add all the ingredients listed for the marinade and give them a mix.
2. Place the salmon fillet inside a zip lock bag and pour the marinade over it, closing the bag and letting it rest in the fridge for at least 1 hour or overnight.
3. Preheat the air fryer for 3 minutes before 400 degrees F, and line the inside of the basket with parchment paper. Once the fillet has rested in the marinade for enough time, take it out of the bag and place it in the air fryer basket, cooking it for 6 to 8 minutes.

Maple Teriyaki Salmon

Preparation Time: 25 minutes | Cooking Time: 12-24 minutes | Servings: 1-2

Ingredients
- ½ cup teriyaki, reduced-sodium
- ¼ cup maple syrup
- 2 garlic cloves, minced
- 2 tablespoon avocado oil
- 6 small wild salmon fillets

Directions
1. Add all the ingredients for the marinade to a bowl and whisk them together, place the salmon fillet in it, and let them marinate for some time.
2. Once the filets have marinated for enough time, take them out and place them in the air fryer basket, 3 at a time, and cook them for 12 minutes at around 350 degrees F.
3. Cook in batches according to the capacity of the air fryer.

Korean Grilled Shrimp Skewers

Preparation Time: 25 minutes | Cooking Time: 8 minutes | Servings: 2

Ingredients
- 2 teaspoons olive oil
- 1 ounces tamari sauce

- 3 tablespoons honey
- 3 tablespoons Korean gochujang
- 1 lemon's juice
- ¼ teaspoon of chili flakes, or to taste
- 1 teaspoon garlic, minced
- 2-3 pound shrimps, peeled, cleaned

Directions
1. Begin by soaking some bamboo sticks in water
2. Add tamari sauce, olive oil, Korean gochujang, garlic, lemon juice, and chili flake in a bowl and whisk everything together.
3. Add all the shrimps to the bowl and toss to coat evenly, letting them marinate in it for at least 30 minutes.
4. Preheat the oven to around 350 degrees F, and thread five shrimps through each soaked bamboo stick.
5. Place the skewers in the air fryer basket and cook them for 5 to 8 minutes, making sure to flip them halfway.

Salmon Patties

Preparation Time: 25 minutes | Cooking Time: 12 minutes | Servings: 2

Ingredients
- 12 ounces salmon fillet, without skin
- 6 ounces of all-purpose flour
- 1 egg, large
- 1 onion, medium-sized, chopped
- 1 tablespoon chives, chopped
- 1 lime juice
- 1 teaspoon garlic powder
- 1 teaspoon salt and pepper, or according to taste

Directions
1. Slice the salmon fillet into manageable pieces and add them to the food processor, blending them with all the other listed ingredients until everything is mixed, but the onions, chives, and salmon are still chunky.
2. Divide the batter into four equal parts and flatten them to make 4 patties, each around 3 inches in diameter.
3. Let the patties rest in the fridge for at least 1 ½ hours before cooking.
4. Grease the inside of the air fryer with cooking spray and arrange the patties in it, making sure they are not touching; spray some cooking spray over them and cook them for 10 to 12 minutes at around 400 degrees F.

Blackened Shrimps

Preparation Time: 25 minutes | Cooking Time: 5-8 minutes | Servings: 2

Ingredients
- 16 ounces shrimps, large, peeled, deveined
- 1-ounce canola oil
- 1 tablespoon blackened seasoning
- Dipping sauce of choice
- Lemon wedges
- Cilantro, chopped

Directions
1. Begin by preheating the air fryer to around 400 degrees F five minutes before cooking.
2. Place the shrimps in a bowl and toss it with canola oil, making sure to coat all the shrimps with oil evenly.
3. Drain the extra oil and toss the shrimp with blackened seasoning.
4. Grease the inside of the air fryer with oil and add the shrimps to it, cooking them for 5 to 8 minutes, giving it a shake halfway in the cooking.
5. Once the shrimps are pink and curled, take them out and serve with a dipping sauce of choice, a side of lemon wedges, and a garnish of cilantro.

Bacon-Wrapped Shrimp

Preparation Time: 15 minutes | Cooking Time: 8-10 minutes | Servings: 2

Ingredients
- 24 shrimps, deveined
- 8 bacon slices, sliced to 1/3
- 3 teaspoon olive oil
- 1 teaspoon chili powder
- 2 garlic cloves, minced
- 1 tablespoon cilantro, chopped

Directions
1. Add olive oil, garlic, and cilantro to a bowl and give them a good mix.
2. Add the shrimps with their tails to the bowl and toss to coat evenly.
3. Wrap the middle of the shrimp with bacon and arrange them in a baking dish, refrigerating them for at least 30 minutes.
4. Preheat the air fryer to 400 degrees F. place the shrimps in the air fryer basket, seam side down, and cook them for about 8 to 10 minutes or till the bacon is cooked completely. Make sure the shrimps are not touching each other, so try to cook them in batches.

Coconut Shrimp with Honey Sriracha Sauce

Preparation Time: 25 minutes | Cooking Time: 4-7 minutes | Servings: 2

Ingredients
- 1 pound shrimps
- 2 eggs
- 6 tablespoons almond flour
- ½ teaspoon garlic powder
- ½ teaspoon sea salt, or according to taste
- ¼ teaspoon cayenne pepper
- 1 cup coconut shreds, sweetened

For Honey Sriracha sauce
- ¼ cup honey
- 1 tablespoon Sriracha sauce
- ½ lemon juice

Directions
1. Begin by greasing the inside of the air fryer with oil.
2. Add flour, garlic, cayenne, salt, and pepper in a shallow bowl and give it a mix, crack and whisk the egg in another bowl, and put coconut shavings in the third bowl.
3. Coat the shrimps first in flour, then drench them in egg and finally dip them in coconut and make sure to coat all the edges.
4. Gently push the coconut on the shrimps, so they stick and don't fall off, and arrange them in the air fryer, cooking them for 3 to 6 minutes or until they are crispy and golden brown.
5. Meanwhile, add all the ingredients to the sauce and serve it with the shrimp once they are done.

Tilapia

Preparation Time: 25 minutes | Cooking Time: 10 minutes | Servings: 2

Ingredients
- 2 (6 ounces) tilapia fillets
- 1 tablespoon olive oil
- ½ tablespoon dill, chopped
- 1 tablespoon cilantro, chopped
- ½ tablespoon garlic, minced
- Salt, according to taste

Directions

1. Begin by preheating the oven to around 400 degrees F.
2. Add olive oil, cilantro, garlic, pepper, and dill to a bowl and give them a good mix.
3. Use a kitchen towel and pat dry the fillet, brushing the olive oil mixture once the fillet is dry.
4. Place it in the air fryer basket and cook them for 8 to 10 minutes or till cooked.
5. Once done, take it out and serve.

Blackened Salmon

Preparation Time: 25 minutes | Cooking Time: 7-10 minutes | Servings: 2

Ingredients:

- 1 ½ tablespoon keto blackened salmon seasoning
- 1.5-pound salmon fillet, sliced into 3 to 4 fillets
- 2 tablespoon canola oil

Directions

1. Begin by preheating the oven to around 400 degrees F.
2. Coat the salmon fillets with oil, making sure to evenly coat both sides, and add blackened seasoning onto the fillet, making sure to season both sides evenly.
3. Arrange the fillets in the air fryer basket and cook them for 7 to 10 minutes or till cooked to desire.

Tuna Patties

Preparation Time: 25 minutes | Cooking Time: 10 minutes | Servings: 2

Ingredients

- 1 ½ tablespoon oil
- 1 ½ tablespoon butter
- 2 onions, chopped
- 1 red bell pepper, chopped
- 2 teaspoon garlic, minced
- 2 cans albacore tuna fish, 7 ounces can, water drained
- Juice of one lime
- 1 celery
- ¼ cup cilantro, chopped
- 4 tablespoons parmesan cheese, grated
- 1 teaspoon oregano
- 2 teaspoons of hot sauce
- ½ teaspoon salt, or according to taste
- Black pepper, according to taste
- ½ cup breadcrumbs
- 2 eggs, whisked
- Cooking spray

Directions

1. Add butter and oil to a skillet and heat them over medium-high heat, adding the onions, garlic, and bell peppers in it, and cooking them for 5 to 10 minutes or till the onions start turning translucent.
2. Drain the tuna and shift it to a medium bowl, adding lime juice over it.
3. Shift the sautéed vegetables to the bowl and mix with celery, cheese, eggs, cilantro, and breadcrumbs.
4. Season it with salt, pepper, oregano, and hot sauce.
5. Mix everything well and make patties from the batter, placing them in the fridge and letting them rest in there for at least 30 minutes or overnight.
6. Once they have rested in the fridge for enough time, take them out and give them a coat of breadcrumbs and cheese.
7. Spray cooking spray over each patty, arrange them in the air fryer, cook them for 4 to 5 minutes at around 390 degrees F, turn it around, and cook for another 4 minutes.

8. When done, take it out and serve with a garnish of parsley.

Oysters

Preparation Time: 25 minutes | Cooking Time: 6 minutes | Servings: 2

Ingredients

- 2 pounds oyster, shucked
- 1 cup almond flour
- 2 teaspoon Cajun seasoning
- 1 teaspoon Kosher salt
- ½ teaspoon black pepper
- 2 eggs
- 2 tablespoon cooking cream
- 2 cups breadcrumbs
- Lemon wedges, to serve
- Garlic butter, melted, to serve

Directions

1. Begin by preheating the air fryer to around 350 degrees F.
2. Then shuck the oyster, rinse them in a colander and use a kitchen towel to pat them dry.
3. Add flour, salt, pepper, and Cajun seasoning to a bowl and give it a mix. Crack and whisk the egg with cream in another bowl, and add breadcrumbs to the final bowl.
4. Take the oysters, dip them in a flour mixture, drench them in egg, and finally give them a coat of breadcrumbs.
5. Arrange the breaded oysters in the basket, grease them with oil and cook for 3 minutes on each side.
6. Serve with lemon wedges and garlic butter.

Pecan Crusted Halibut

Preparation Time: 25 minutes | Cooking Time: 8-10 minutes | Servings: 2

Ingredients

- 1 pound Halibut fillet
- ½ cup pecans
- ½ cup breadcrumbs
- 1 cup almond flour
- 1 tablespoon lemon pepper
- 2 eggs
- ½ cup cornstarch
- ½ cup white wine
- Lemon wedges, for serving

Directions

1. Begin by removing the skin of the fish fillet and setting it aside.
2. Crack and whisk the eggs in a bowl with cornstarch.
3. Add flour, white wine, and lemon pepper to another bowl and mix to combine.
4. Add pecans to a food processor and pulse them till they form a fine powder.
5. Add the pecans and breadcrumbs to a bowl and mix them.
6. Drench the fillet first in the flour mixture, then dip it in the egg, and finally give it a coat of breadcrumbs.
7. Heat the air fryer to around 350 degrees F, and place the fillet in it, cooking it for about 8 minutes or till done.
8. Once it is cooked, take it out and serve with the side of lemon wedges.

Fish Fillet with Onion Rings

Preparation Time: 25 minutes | Cooking Time: 12 minutes | Servings: 2

Ingredients

- 1 cup onion rings
- 1 cod fillet, about 8 oz.
- Salt and pepper, according to taste
- 1 teaspoon lime juice
- Cooking spray to grease

Directions

1. Begin by drying the fish fillet with a kitchen towel.
2. Then season it accordingly with lime juice, salt, and pepper.
3. Coat the fillet with oil; also grease the inside of the air fryer with oil, and place the fillet and onion rings in it, cooking it for 12 minutes at around 350 degrees F.
4. Once done, serve.

Whitefish with Garlic and Lemon

Preparation Time: 25 minutes | Cooking Time: 12 minutes | Servings: 1

Ingredients

- 8 ounces tilapia fillet
- 1 tablespoon sesame oil
- ½ teaspoon garlic powder
- ½ teaspoon lemon pepper seasoning
- Salt and pepper, according to taste
- Cilantro, chopped
- Lemon wedges

Directions

1. Begin by preheating the air fryer to around 350 degrees F, five minutes before cooking.
2. Add oil, garlic powder, lemon pepper, salt, and pepper to a bowl and give it a mix.
3. Brush this mixture over the fish fillet.
4. Line the inside of the air fryer with parchment paper or coat it with oil and put the fish fillet in it, cooking it for 12 minutes at 350 degrees F.
5. When done, take the fillet out, season it according to taste and serve with a garnish of cilantro and a side of lemon wedges.

Lime Caper Cod

Preparation Time: 25 minutes | Cooking Time: 8 minutes | Servings: 2

Ingredients:

- 1 cod fillet, about, 8 ounce
- Salt and black pepper, to taste
- Juice from one lime
- 1 tablespoon olive oil
- 2 teaspoon capers
- ¼ teaspoon lime zest

Directions

1. Grease the inside of the air fryer basket with oil, season the fillet with salt and pepper, and place it in the basket.
2. Coat the fillet with a teaspoon of olive oil and cook it for about 4 minutes at around 350 degrees F.
3. While the fillet is cooking, add capers, lime zest, remaining oil, and lime juice to a bowl and mix thoroughly.
4. Once the time is up, brush the mixture on the fillet and let it cook for another 4 minutes.
5. Once done, serve and enjoy.

Fried Calamari

Preparation Time: 25 minutes | Cooking Time: 8-10 minutes | Servings: 2

Ingredients

- 8 ounces calamari rings
- ½ cup buttermilk
- 1 cup almond flour
- ¼ cup cornstarch
- ½ teaspoon thyme, dried
- ½ teaspoon salt and pepper, or according to taste
- ½ teaspoon sweet paprika
- ¼ teaspoon cayenne
- oil spray, as needed
- Lemon wedges, for serving
- ¼ cup marinara sauce

Directions

1. Add buttermilk and calamari rings to a bowl and place them in the refrigerator, letting them refrigerate for at least 1 hour.
2. Preheat the air fryer to around 400 degrees F.
3. Add flour, salt, pepper, cornstarch, paprika, thyme, and cayenne pepper in a shallow bowl and mix.
4. Take the calamari out of the buttermilk and dip them in a flour mixture, making sure to coat all the edges evenly, shake off the excess, and arrange them in the air fryer.
5. Mist some oil over the calamari rings and cook them for about 4 minutes, flipping them and cooking for another 4 minutes.
6. When done, take the calamari rings out and enjoy with the side of lemon wedges and marinara sauce.

Mediterranean Fish

Preparation Time: 25 minutes | Cooking Time: 15 minutes | Servings: 2

Ingredients

- 16 ounces cod fillet
- 16 ounces cherry tomatoes
- 3 ounces olives, sliced
- 1 teaspoon lime zest
- 1 lime, juiced
- 4 cloves garlic, crushed
- 2 tablespoons extra virgin olive oil
- Salt and pepper, according to taste

Directions

1. Begin by preheating the air fryer to around 350 degrees F and lining the inside of the air fryer with parchment paper.
2. Add garlic, tomatoes, olives, lime zest, salt, and pepper to a bowl and mix them.
3. Pat dries the fillet with a kitchen towel and coats it with salt, pepper, and olive oil.
4. Place the fillet, along with the tomatoes and olives mix in the air fryer basket lined with foil, sealing tightly and cooking for about 15 minutes or till the fish is cooked.
5. Once done, serve and enjoy.

Greek Salmon

Preparation Time: 15 minutes | Cooking Time: 10-12 minutes | Servings: 2

Ingredients

- 8 ounces salmon fillet
- ½ tablespoon olive oil
- 1 tablespoon lemon juice
- 1 garlic clove
- ½ teaspoon thyme, dried
- ¼ teaspoon dill, dried

- ¼ teaspoon red pepper flakes
- Salt, to taste

For Greek salad
- 2 tablespoons extra virgin olive oil
- 1 tablespoon red wine vinegar
- ½ teaspoon thyme, dried
- 2 tomatoes
- ½ English cucumber
- ½ onion
- 2 ounces black kalamata olives
- Cilantro
- Salt and pepper, according to taste
- Feta cheese

Directions
1. Mix oil, garlic, dill, lemon juice, salt, oregano, and red pepper flakes in a bowl and toss the fillet with it, letting it rest in the marinade for at least 15 minutes.
2. Grease the inside of the air fryer with some oil and place the marinated fillet in it, cooking it for 10-12 minutes.
3. While the fish is cooking, add all the ingredients for the Greek salad in a bowl and toss to coat everything evenly.
4. When the fish is done, take it out and serve it with the side of the Greek salad.

Crispy Tilapia

Preparation Time: 15 minutes | Cooking Time: 10 minutes | Servings: 2

Ingredients
- 6 tilapia Fish fillet
- 3 cups Italian breadcrumbs
- 1 egg
- 2 teaspoon water, warm

Seasoning:
- 2 ½ tablespoons Lemon Pepper Seasoning
- 2 tablespoon chili powder
- 1 teaspoon garlic powder
- Salt, according to taste
- Oil spray for greasing

Directions
1. Crack and whisk the egg in a bowl with water.
2. Mix breadcrumbs and seasoning in another bowl.
3. Line the bottom of the air fryer basket with foil.
4. Drench the fish fillet first in egg, and then give them a coat of breadcrumbs.
5. Shake off the excess and arrange them on the air fryer basket.
6. Spray some oil over the fillet and cook them for 10 minutes at 350 degrees F, making sure to flip them halfway.
7. When done, take the fillets out and serve with a salad of choice.

Spiced Salmon

Preparation Time: 15 minutes | Cooking Time: 8 minutes | Servings: 2

Ingredients
- 2 pounds of tilapia fillets
- 1 tablespoon avocado oil
- 1 teaspoon garlic powder
- 1 teaspoon of old bay seasoning
- ½ teaspoon of chili powder
- 1 teaspoon of onion powder
- 1 teaspoon lemon pepper seasoning
- Salt and pepper, according to taste

Direction
1. Preheat the air fryer to around 400 degrees F.
2. Pat dry the fillets using a paper towel and brush them with oil, salt, old bay, onion powder, chili powder, pepper, lemon pepper, and garlic powder.
3. Once coated, arrange them inside a greased air fryer basket and cook them for 12 minutes.
4. When done, take them out and serve.

Pistachios Crusted Fish

Preparation Time: 15 minutes | Cooking Time: 8 minutes | Servings: 2

Ingredients
- ½ cup cottage cheese, crumbled
- 2 ½ tablespoon pistachios, chopped
- 2 ½ tablespoon breadcrumbs
- 1 scallion, chopped
- 1 teaspoon lime zest
- 3 halibut fillets
- 2 teaspoon olive oil
- 1/3 teaspoon garlic powder
- Salt, according to taste

Directions
1. Begin by preheating the air fryer to around 400 degrees F, 5 minutes before cooking.
2. Add cottage cheese, scallions, pistachios, breadcrumbs, and lime zest to a bowl and give them a good mix.
3. Dry the fillets using a paper towel and give them a seasoning of oil, salt, and garlic powder.
4. Once seasoned, place it in the air fryer basket and cook it for 8 minutes at 350 degrees F.
5. When done, take the fish out and serve with cheese and breadcrumb mix on top.

Salmon with Lemon Caper Sauce

Preparation Time: 15 minutes | Cooking Time: 10-12 minutes | Servings: 2

Ingredients
- 4 salmon fillet
- Olive oil, as needed
- For seasoning
- 3 teaspoon chili flakes
- 1 teaspoon thyme
- 1 ½ teaspoon onion powder
- 1 teaspoon garlic powder
- Salt and pepper, according to taste
- 1 teaspoon chili powder
- ¼ teaspoon cayenne

For lemon Caper Sauce
- ½ Greek yogurt
- 2 tablespoon lemon juice
- 2 teaspoon lemon zest
- 1 garlic clove, minced
- ½ tablespoon caper
- 1 tablespoon cilantro
- Salt and pepper, according to taste

Directions
1. Add all the ingredients for lemon caper sauce to a bowl and keep aside.
2. Add all the ingredients for the seasoning to a bowl and give them a good mix.
3. Season the fillets of salmon with the rub and grease them with oil.
4. Grease the inside of the air fryer with oil and put the fillet in it.

5. Cook in batches according to the capacity of your air fryer
6. Cook for 8-12 minutes at 400 degrees F
7. Flipping halfway.
8. Once done, serve with sauce.
9. Enjoy.

Eggs Omelet with Tuna and Avocado

Preparation Time: 25 minutes | Cooking Time: 7 minutes | Servings: 2

Ingredients
- 8 ounces tuna fish, without bone
- 2 small tomatoes, diced
- Sea salt, according to taste
- 1-ounce olive oil
- 6 eggs, beaten
- 2 teaspoons of whole milk
- 1 avocado, diced

Directions
1. Crack and whisk the eggs in a big bowl with all the remaining ingredients.
2. Once properly mixed, add the egg to a round pan and place the pan inside the air fryer basket, cooking it for about 7 minutes at 400 degrees F.
3. When done, take it out and let it cool slightly before serving.
4. Serve with diced avocado slices.

Steamed Salmon with Lemon and Herbs

Preparation Time: 25 minutes | Cooking Time: 10 minutes | Servings: 4

Ingredients:
- 2 small white onions, sliced
- 4 spring onions, sliced lengthwise
- 18 ounces salmon fillet, with skin, sliced into 4 portions
- Salt and black pepper, according to taste
- 1/2 teaspoons coriander, grounded
- ½ teaspoon cumin
- 2/3 teaspoon red pepper flakes
- 4 garlic cloves, chopped
- 4 tablespoons of canola oil

Directions
1. Line parchment paper onto the baking pan.
2. Place onion on the bottom of the pan.
3. Tip with salmon skin side down.
4. Season the salmon with salt and pepper.
5. Mix coriander, cumin, salt, and red pepper in a bowl.
6. Top it on to salmon.
7. Then put parsley, garlic, spring onions, lemon slices, and oil drizzle.
8. Fold the pepper all over fish
9. Cook for 8 minutes at 400degres F.
10. Serve once done

Air Fryer Blackened Fish Tacos

Preparation Time: 10 minutes | Cooking Time: 15 minutes | Servings: 1

Ingredients:
- 1 (15 ounces) can of seasoned black beans, rinsed and drained
- Two ears of corn, kernels cut from the cob
- One tablespoon of olive oil
- One tablespoon of lime juice
- ½ teaspoon salt
- 1 pound tilapia fillets
- cooking spray
- ¼ cup blackened seasoning
- 4 (6-inch) corn tortillas
- One lime, cut into wedges
- One teaspoon Louisiana-style hot sauce (Optional)

Directions:
1. Preheat the oven to 400° F. (200 degrees C).
2. Mix black beans, corn, olive oil, lime juice, and salt in a mixing dish. Set aside after gently stirring until the beans and corn are uniformly covered.
3. Pat fish fillets dry with paper towels on a clean work surface. Spray each fillet lightly with cooking spray and sprinkle with 1/2 of the blackened seasoning. Spray the fillets with cooking spray and sprinkle with the remaining spice.
4. Place the fish in the air fryer basket in a single layer, working in batches if required. 2 minutes in the oven. Cook for 2 minutes more on the other side before transferring to a platter.
5. Cook for 10 minutes, stirring halfway through, in the air fryer basket with the bean and corn mixture.
6. Fill corn tortillas with fish and top with bean and corn mixture. Serve with lime wedges and spicy sauce on the side.

Air Fryer Crispy Fish Tacos with Slaw

Preparation Time: 10 minutes | Cooking Time: 15 minutes | Servings: 1

Ingredients:
- nonstick cooking spray
- 4 cups cabbage slaw mix
- One tablespoon chopped fresh jalapeno pepper
- One tablespoon of lime juice
- One tablespoon of olive oil
- One tablespoon of apple cider vinegar
- ½ teaspoon salt
- ¼ teaspoon ground black pepper
- ¼ teaspoon ground cayenne pepper
- ¼ cup all-purpose flour
- ¼ cup yellow cornmeal
- Two tablespoons of taco seasoning mix
- 1 pound cod fillets, cut into bite-sized pieces
- 8 (6-inch) corn tortillas

Directions:
1. Preheat an air fryer to 400°F (200 degrees C). Coat the air fryer basket with cooking spray.
2. In a large mixing bowl, combine cabbage slaw, jalapeño pepper, lime juice, olive oil, vinegar, salt, pepper, and
3. cayenne pepper. Set aside after mixing until evenly blended.
4. Combine the flour, cornmeal, and taco spice in a separate basin. Toss the fish pieces until well covered, removing any excess spice ingredients. Place in the air fryer basket and lightly coat with cooking spray.
5. Cook the fish for 5 minutes in a preheated air fryer. Cook until the salmon is crispy and flakes readily with a fork, about 5 minutes longer. Transfer to a plate lined with paper towels.
6. Fill the air fryer basket halfway with the cabbage slaw mixture.
7. Cook until the cabbage is caramelized, about 8 minutes, stirring halfway through.
8. Fill tortillas with cabbage and top with the fish.

CHAPTER 7:
Vegetarian

Vegan Cheese Green Beans

Preparation Time: 10 minutes | Cooking Time: 6 minutes | Servings: 4

Ingredients:
- ¼ cup vegan broth
- 1 teaspoon vegan butter
- ½ teaspoon red pepper flakes
- 1 cup trimmed green beans
- 2 oz. shredded vegan cheese

Directions:
1. Sprinkle red pepper flakes over green beans and add them to the air fryer pan.
2. Add the remaining ingredients and preheat the air fryer to 400 degrees Fahrenheit.
3. Add the pan of contents to the air fryer and cook the green beans for 6 minutes.
4. Serve once done, and enjoy!

Quick Chickpeas Snack

Preparation Time: 5 minutes | Cooking Time: 15 minutes | Servings: 8

Ingredients:
- ½ teaspoon salt
- ½ teaspoon chili powder
- ½ teaspoon dried chives
- 1 cup rinsed chickpeas
- 2 tablespoons olive oil
- ½ teaspoon cayenne pepper
- ½ teaspoon white pepper

Directions:
1. Combine all the ingredients in a bowl.
2. Toss to mix well and transfer to the air fryer.
3. Cook for 15 minutes at 400 degrees Fahrenheit, giving a stir every two minutes.
4. Serve hot once golden and crispy.

Nutmeg Okra

Preparation Time: 10 minutes | Cooking Time: 10 minutes | Servings: 4

Ingredients:
- ½ teaspoon sea salt
- 1 oz. trimmed okra
- 3 oz. sliced pancetta
- 1 teaspoon olive oil
- ½ teaspoon ground nutmeg

Directions:
1. Start by sprinkling nutmeg and salt over okra.
2. Add the okra to the air fryer and drizzle over oil and top with pancetta after chopping it first.
3. Cook it at 360 degrees Fahrenheit for 10 minutes.
4. Serve once done, and enjoy!

Fried Onion Rings

Preparation Time: 10 minutes | Cooking Time: 14 minutes | Servings: 5

Ingredients:
- 1 beaten egg
- ⅓ cup panko breadcrumbs
- 1 tablespoon sour cream
- 1 trimmed & sliced large white onion

Directions:
1. Separate the onion slices into onion rings.
2. Combine the sour cream and egg well.
3. Dip the onion rings in the wet mixture.
4. Next, coat them with breadcrumbs.
5. Transfer to the air fryer basket.

6. Close the lid and let it air fry for 14 minutes at 395 degrees Fahrenheit.
7. Once crispy and golden, remove and serve hot with any sauce you like.

Spicy Kale

Preparation Time: 5 minutes | Cooking Time: 10 minutes | Servings: 4

Ingredients:
- 1 oz. torn kale
- 1 tablespoon canola oil
- 1 teaspoon chili powder
- A pinch of salt & black pepper
- 2 tablespoons chopped oregano

Directions:
1. Combine all the ingredients in a pan that fits the air fryer.
2. Toss the ingredients and add the pan to the air fryer to cook for 10 minutes at 380 degrees Fahrenheit.
3. Serve once done, and enjoy!

Crunchy Tots Snack

Preparation Time: 5 minutes | Cooking Time: 8 minutes | Servings: 4

Ingredients:
- 6 oz. frozen tater tots
- Cooking spray as needed

Directions:
1. Spread the tater tots in the air fryer in a single layer.
2. Spritz the cooking spray on them and close the lid.
3. Cook it for 4 minutes at 400 degrees Fahrenheit.
4. Flip and cook for an additional 4 minutes.
5. Serve hot once done, and enjoy with any favorite sauce!

Paprika Leeks

Preparation Time: 15 minutes | Cooking Time: 8 minutes | Servings: 3

Ingredients:
- 1 beaten egg
- ½ teaspoon sea salt
- Cooking spray as needed
- 2 roughly-sliced big leeks
- 2 tablespoons almond flour
- ½ teaspoon chili powder
- ½ teaspoon ground turmeric

Directions:
1. Start by sprinkling chili powder, salt, and turmeric over the leek slices.
2. After dipping the leek slices first in egg, then almond flour.
3. Preheat the air fryer to 400 degrees Fahrenheit and place the coated leaks inside.
4. Ensure to grease the leeks with cooking spray before cooking them for 8 minutes.
5. Shake after 4 minutes to ensure even cooking.
6. Serve once done, and enjoy!

Sweet Potato Chips

Preparation Time: 10 minutes | Cooking Time: 10 minutes | Servings: 4

Ingredients:
- ¼ teaspoon sea salt
- ¼ teaspoon chili powder
- 1 teaspoon avocado oil
- 1 peeled & sliced sweet potato

Directions:
1. Combine all the ingredients in a bowl.
2. Toss and transfer to the air fryer in a single layer.

3. Cook for 10 minutes at 400 degrees Fahrenheit.
4. Serve once done and enjoy with your favorite sauce!

Broccoli & Cranberries Mix

Preparation Time: 5 minutes | Cooking Time: 25 minutes | Servings: 4

Ingredients:
- 2 chopped shallots
- ½ cup cranberries
- ½ cup chopped pecans
- A pinch of salt & black pepper
- 3 tablespoons red wine vinegar
- 1 floret separated broccoli head
- 6 cooked & crumbled vegan bacon slices

Directions:
1. Combine broccoli with all the remaining ingredients in a pan that fits the air fryer.
2. Toss the ingredients and add the pan to the air fryer to cook for 25 minutes at 380 degrees Fahrenheit.
3. Serve once done, and enjoy!

Paprika Jicama

Preparation Time: 15 minutes | Cooking Time: 7 minutes | Servings: 5

Ingredients:
- ½ teaspoon salt
- 1 teaspoon sesame oil
- ½ teaspoon red pepper flakes
- ½ teaspoon chili powder
- 15 oz. peeled cut into small sticks jicama

Directions:
1. Start by preheating the air fryer at 400 degrees Fahrenheit.
2. Combine jicama sticks with all the remaining ingredients and sprinkle sesame oil over them at the end.
3. Add the jicama sticks to the air fryer and cook for 4 minutes.
4. Shake them well afterward and cook for an additional 3 minutes.
5. Serve once done, and enjoy!

Squash Noodles

Preparation Time: 20 minutes | Cooking Time: 5 minutes | Servings: 4

Ingredients:
- Spiralizer as needed
- 12 oz. scallop squash
- 1 teaspoon sesame oil
- ¼ teaspoon black pepper
- 1 teaspoon softened vegan butter

Directions:
1. Use a spiralizer to make noodles out of scallop squash.
2. Add the noodles into the air fryer and grease with sesame oil.
3. Cook them at 385 degrees Fahrenheit for 5 minutes.
4. Remove to a plate and sprinkle with vegan butter and black pepper.

Lemon Kale & Bell Peppers Bowls

Preparation Time: 5 minutes | Cooking Time: 10 minutes | Servings: 4

Ingredients:
- ¼ cup olive oil
- 2 cups torn kale
- 1 tablespoon yellow mustard
- 2 tablespoons lemon juice
- 1 tablespoon white vinegar
- A pinch of salt & black pepper
- 1 cup sliced red bell pepper
- 1 ½ cups peeled, pitted & cubed avocado

Directions:
1. Combine kale with avocado, half of the olive oil, salt, and pepper in a pan that fits the air fryer.
2. Toss the ingredients and add the pan to the air fryer to cook for 10 minutes at 360 degrees Fahrenheit.
3. Toss well the remaining ingredients with the kale mix before serving.

Paprika Kale & Olives

Preparation Time: 5 minutes | Cooking Time: 15 minutes | Servings: 4

Ingredients:
- ½ oz. torn kale
- 2 tablespoons olive oil
- 1 tablespoon chipotle powder
- Salt & black pepper as needed
- 2 tablespoons pitted & sliced black olives

Directions:
1. Combine all the ingredients thoroughly in a pan that fits the air fryer.
2. Toss the ingredients and add the pan to the air fryer to cook for 15 minutes at 370 degrees Fahrenheit.
3. Serve once done, and enjoy!

Roasted Cauliflower

Preparation Time: 15 minutes | Cooking Time: 25 minutes | Servings: 4

Ingredients:
- ½ teaspoon salt
- 12 oz. cauliflower head
- 1 teaspoon ground turmeric
- ¼ teaspoon black pepper
- 1 chopped vegan bacon slice
- 2 tablespoons melted vegan butter

Directions:
1. Combine all the ingredients except cauliflower and bacon in a bowl.
2. Fill the cauliflower head with chopped vegan bacon and brush the bowl mixture on it.
3. Add it to the air fryer basket and cook it in a preheated air fryer at 365 degrees Fahrenheit for 25 minutes.
4. Serve once done, and enjoy!

Cilantro Broccoli Mix

Preparation Time: 5 minutes | Cooking Time: 15 minutes | Servings: 4

Ingredients:
- 1 lemon juice
- Olive oil as needed
- A pinch of salt & black pepper
- 1 tablespoon chopped parsley
- 1 floret separated broccoli head
- 2 cups quartered cherry tomatoes

Directions:
1. Combine all the ingredients thoroughly except parsley in a pan that fits the air fryer.
2. Toss the ingredients and add the pan to the air fryer to cook for 15 minutes at 380 degrees Fahrenheit.
3. Serve once done and enjoy with parsley on top!

Lemon, Olives & Zucchini

Preparation Time: 5 minutes | Cooking Time: 12 minutes | Servings: 4

Ingredients:
- 4 sliced zucchinis
- 2 tablespoons olive oil
- 2 tablespoons lemon juice
- 1 cup pitted kalamata olives
- 2 teaspoons red wine vinegar
- Salt & black pepper as needed

Directions:
1. Combine all the ingredients thoroughly in a pan that fits the air fryer.
2. Toss the ingredients and add the pan to the air fryer to cook for 12 minutes at 390 degrees Fahrenheit.
3. Serve once done, and enjoy!

Wholesome Veggie Snack

Preparation Time: 8 minutes | Cooking Time: 10 minutes | Servings: 8

Ingredients:
- 2 sliced beets
- 1 sliced carrot
- 1 teaspoon sea salt
- 1 sliced sweet potato
- Cooking spray as needed

Directions:
1. Combine everything in a bowl except cooking spray, shake and transfer to the air fryer.
2. Grease it with cooking spray and cook the veggies for 10 minutes at 365 degrees Fahrenheit.
3. Shake again and cook for an additional 3 minutes.
4. Flip and check if they're cooked; otherwise, cook for 4 more minutes.
5. Serve once done, and enjoy!

String Bean Small Bites

Preparation Time: 10 minutes | Cooking Time: 10 minutes | Servings: 3

Ingredients:
- ½ teaspoon salt
- 6 oz. trimmed string beans
- ½ teaspoon onion powder
- ½ teaspoon garlic powder
- ½ teaspoon ground coriander
- 2 tablespoons sesame oil

Directions:
1. After shaking well, combine everything in a bowl and transfer to the air fryer.
2. Cook it for 7 minutes at 400 degrees Fahrenheit.
3. Shake again and cook for an additional 3 minutes to ensure even cooking.
4. Serve once done, and enjoy!

Tomato Eggplant Casserole

Preparation Time: 5 minutes | Cooking Time: 20 minutes | Servings: 4

Ingredients:
- 2 teaspoons olive oil
- 4 minced garlic cloves
- ½ cup chopped parsley
- 4 chopped spring onions
- Cubed eggplants as needed
- 1 chopped hot chili pepper
- ½ oz. cubed grape tomatoes
- Salt & black pepper as needed

Directions:
1. Use olive oil to grease a pan that fits the air fryer.
2. Combine all the ingredients in it and add to a preheated air fryer.
3. Cook the ingredients for 20 minutes at 380 degrees Fahrenheit.
4. Serve once done, and enjoy!

Tomato Rice Casserole

Preparation Time: 20 minutes | Cooking Time: 14 minutes | Servings: 8

Ingredients:
- 1 cup cooked rice
- 1 teaspoon olive oil
- ¼ cup tomato puree
- 1 cup chopped tomatoes
- 1 tablespoon sour cream
- 1 tablespoon dried parsley
- 1 teaspoon Italian seasonings

Directions:
1. Combine Italian seasoning and cilantro in a bowl.
2. Grease the baking pan with oil, place half of the rice in the pan and flatten.
3. Top with half a cup of tomatoes.
4. In a separate bowl, mix tomato puree and sour cream.
5. Add the remaining rice over the tomatoes.
6. Then place the remaining tomatoes over it and spread the tomato cream mixture
7. Cover with the foil and seal the edges.
8. Transfer the pan to the air fryer.
9. Cook for 14 minutes at 409 degrees Fahrenheit.
10. Cut the casserole and serve onto plates.

Lentil & Green Beans Stew

Preparation Time: 15 minutes | Cooking Time: 15 minutes | Servings: 4

Ingredients:
- 1½ cup lentils
- 1 teaspoon salt
- 1 cup of string beans
- 1 teaspoon harissa
- 4 medium tomatoes
- 1 teaspoon ground cumin
- ½ cup chopped chives
- 2 cups vegetable broth
- 1 tablespoon chicken broth
- 4 peeled & chopped garlic cloves

Directions:
1. Preheat the air fryer to 400 degrees Fahrenheit.
2. Add lentils and both broth to the air fryer basket.
3. Cook for 10 minutes at the same temperature.
4. Add the remaining ingredients to the lentils.
5. Cook for an additional 5 minutes and serve hot!

Honeyed Carrots

Preparation Time: 10 minutes | Cooking Time: 8 minutes | Servings: 6

Ingredients:
- 4 tablespoon water
- 2 tablespoons maple syrup
- 1 teaspoon cardamom
- 1 teaspoon fresh oregano
- ½ teaspoon chili flakes
- 2 tablespoons brown sugar
- 1 teaspoon ground cinnamon
- 5 medium peeled & striped carrots

Directions:
1. Combine well the carrots strips with all the ingredients except honey.
2. Transfer to the air fryer and cook for 7 minutes at 370 degrees Fahrenheit.
3. Drizzle honey and stir to coat and cook for a minute more.
4. Let cool before serving.

Greek Potatoes

Preparation Time: 10 minutes | Cooking Time: 20 minutes | Servings: 4

Ingredients:
- 3.5 oz. sour cream
- 2 tablespoons olive oil
- 1 tablespoon chili powder
- 1½ oz. peeled & cubed potatoes
- Salt & ground black pepper as needed

Directions:
1. Add potatoes to a bowl with enough water and set aside for 10 minutes.
2. Drain, pat dry, and coat with 1 tablespoon oil, chili powder, salt, and pepper.
3. Add to the air fryer basket and cook for 20 minutes at 360 degrees Fahrenheit.
4. Meanwhile, combine sour cream with the remaining oil and season with salt and pepper.
5. Serve the cooked potatoes with sour cream on top.

Cherries, Farro & Green Onions Mix

Preparation Time: 3 minutes | Cooking Time: 15 minutes | Servings: 3

Ingredients:
- Salt as needed
- 1 tablespoon olive oil
- 2 minced scallions
- 1 cup whole-grain farro
- 1 cup apple cider vinegar
- 1 tablespoon lime juice
- 1 cup minced mint leaves
- 1 cup chopped dried cherries
- 2 cups pitted & halved fresh cherries

Directions:
1. Combine all the ingredients except fresh cherries in a bowl.
2. Transfer to the air fryer and cook at 300 degrees Fahrenheit for 15 minutes.
3. Once done, serve and garnish with fresh cherries.

Chickpea & Cauliflower Bowl

Preparation Time: 15 minutes | Cooking Time: 15 minutes | Servings: 4

Ingredients:
- 1 tablespoon canola oil
- 14 oz. canned chickpeas
- 1 teaspoon seasoning of choice
- 1 cup steamed cauliflower florets

Directions:
1. Preheat the air fryer to 350 degrees Fahrenheit.
2. Drain chickpeas and combine them with seasoning of choice, florets, and canola oil.
3. Transfer to the air fryer and cook for 12 minutes.
4. Serve once done, and enjoy!

Cheesy Stuffed Vegan Peppers

Preparation Time: 10 minutes | Cooking Time: 8 minutes | Servings: 8

Ingredients:
- 8 small bell peppers
- 1 tablespoon olive oil
- Salt & ground black pepper as needed
- 3.5 oz. vegan cheese or any better alternative

Directions:
1. Cut vegan cheese into 8 pieces and set aside.
2. Remove the tops of the bell peppers, deseed and set on the cutting board.
3. Mix oil, cheese, salt, and pepper in a bowl.
4. Add the mixture to each bell pepper.
5. Transfer them to the air fryer basket and cook at 409 degrees Fahrenheit for 8 minutes.
6. Remove to a plate and serve hot.

Vegetable Fritters

Preparation Time: 15 minutes | Cooking Time: 25 minutes | Servings: 4

Ingredients:
- 1 beaten egg
- ¼ cup of water
- ½ teaspoon sea salt
- 3 sliced red onions
- 1 chopped jalapeno
- 1 teaspoon avocado oil
- 1 teaspoon melted butter
- 3 tablespoons chickpea flour
- ½ teaspoon ground cumin

Directions:
1. Combine all the ingredients except avocado oil into a bowl.
2. It will create a thick and smooth batter.
3. Grease the air fryer basket with avocado oil.
4. Use a spoon to spoon out the batter onto the basket.
5. Place the basket in the air fryer.
6. Cook for 8 minutes at 365 degrees Fahrenheit.
7. Flip and cook for an additional 4 minutes.
8. Remove once crispy and do the same with the remainder.
9. Serve hot immediately with your favorite dip!

Easy Lemon Broccoli

Preparation Time: 5 minutes | Cooking Time: 13 minutes | Servings: 3

Ingredients:
- 1 teaspoon salt
- 1 cup broccoli florets
- 1 tablespoon canola oil
- 2 tablespoons lime juice

Directions:
1. Combine all the ingredients in a bowl.
2. Transfer to the air fryer basket and cook for 6 minutes at 395 degrees Fahrenheit.
3. Shake and cook for an additional 7 minutes to ensure even cooking.
4. Once crispy, remove and serve hot with your favorite dip!

Easy Eggplant Stew

Preparation Time: 10 minutes | Cooking Time: 13 minutes | Servings: 9

Ingredients:
- 1 green pepper
- 1 cubed eggplant
- 1 cubed zucchini
- 4 oz. chive stems
- 1 teaspoon chili powder
- 1 cup chicken broth
- ½ cup heavy cream
- 1 teaspoon dried dill

- 1 teaspoon turmeric
- 2 peeled garlic cloves
- 1 teaspoon kosher salt
- 1 teaspoon dried parsley

Directions:
1. Mix all zucchini and eggplant with dill, chili powder, parsley, and turmeric.
2. Chop chives, garlic, and green pepper.
3. Preheat the air fryer to 390 degrees Fahrenheit.
4. Add the chicken broth to the air fryer and place the eggplants.
5. Cook it for 2 minutes in the air fryer.
6. Take out and add chopped garlic, chives, green pepper, and cream.
7. Cook it for an additional 11 minutes until soft.
8. Ladle into bowls and serve hot.

Quick Veggie Paella

Preparation Time: 7 minutes | Cooking Time: 15 minutes | Servings: 4

Ingredients:
- 1 diced tomato
- ½ teaspoon turmeric
- ¼ cup vegetable broth
- ½ teaspoon dried oregano
- ½ cup frozen baby peas
- 1 package of frozen-thawed cooked rice
- 1 jar drained & chopped artichoke hearts

Directions:
1. Combine rice, artichoke, broth, turmeric, and oregano in a 6x6x2 inch pan and stir gently.
2. Place it in the air fryer oven to bake for 8 minutes or until the rice is hot.
3. Take it off the air fryer and gently add peas and tomato.
4. Cook for 5 minutes or until the newly added ingredients are hot.
5. Make sure the paella is bubbling.
6. Serve hot and enjoy!

Easy Apple Chips

Preparation Time: 5 minutes | Cooking Time: 24 minutes | Servings: 4

Ingredients:
- 2 teaspoons stevia
- 1 teaspoon cinnamon
- 4 thinly sliced apples

Directions:
1. Mix all the ingredients in a bowl.
2. Transfer to the air fryer basket.
3. Place the apples in one layer
4. Cook it in batches.
5. Cook at 350 degrees Fahrenheit for 12 minutes.
6. Flip every 4 minutes to ensure even cooking.
7. Serve when golden-brown and crispy.

Healthy Madagascan Stew

Preparation Time: 5 minutes | Cooking Time: 19 minutes | Servings: 4

Ingredients:
- Salt as needed
- 1 tablespoon oil
- 1 tablespoon water
- Cooked rice to serve
- 1 cup vegetable broth
- ½ finely diced onion
- 3 minced garlic cloves
- 1 large handful of arugula

- 7 oz. baby new potatoes
- Black pepper as needed
- ½ tablespoon cornstarch
- 2 large chopped tomatoes
- 1 tablespoon tomato paste
- 1 tablespoon pureed ginger
- 1 ¼ cups drained canned black beans
- 1 ¼ cups drained canned kidney beans

Directions:
1. Cut potatoes into quarters and drizzle with oil.
2. Add the potatoes to the air fryer basket with onions and air fry for 4 minutes.
3. Remove and add to a saucepan over medium flame.
4. Add the remaining ingredients except for rice and cornstarch.
5. First, mix the cornstarch with water in a bowl and add to the stew.
6. Let the mixture simmer for 15 minutes.
7. Once done, serve with rice and enjoy!

Quick Leeks Stew

Preparation Time: 5 minutes | Cooking Time: 20 minutes | Servings: 4

Ingredients:
- 2 sliced leeks
- 1 cup veggie broth
- 2 tablespoons olive oil
- 1 tablespoon hot sauce
- 2 minced garlic cloves
- 1 tablespoon tomato puree
- 1 tablespoon sweet paprika
- ½ bunch of chopped cilantro
- Salt & black pepper as needed
- 2 roughly-cubed big eggplants

Directions:
1. Combine all the ingredients thoroughly in a pan that fits the air fryer.
2. Add the pan to the air fryer and cook for 20 minutes at 380 degrees Fahrenheit.
3. Serve once done, and enjoy!

Cabbage Stew

Preparation Time: 5 minutes | Cooking Time: 20 minutes | Servings: 4

Ingredients:
- 4 oz. vegetable broth
- 14 oz. chopped tomatoes
- 2 tablespoon chopped chives
- 1 tablespoon sweet paprika
- Salt & black pepper as needed
- 1 shredded green cabbage head

Directions:
1. Combine all the ingredients thoroughly except dill in a pan that fits the air fryer.
2. Add the pan to the air fryer and cook for 20 minutes at 380 degrees Fahrenheit.
3. Serve once done and enjoy with dill sprinkled on top!

Spinach Salad

Preparation Time: 5 minutes | Cooking Time: 10 minutes | Servings: 4

Ingredients:
- 1 oz. baby spinach
- 1 tablespoon Dijon mustard
- Cooking spray as needed
- ¼ cup white wine vinegar
- 1 tablespoon chopped dill

- Salt & black pepper as needed

Directions:
1. Grease the air fryer pan with cooking spray and mix all the ingredients.
2. Add the pan to the air fryer and cook the mix for 10 minutes at 350 degrees Fahrenheit.
3. Serve your salad, and enjoy!

Turmeric Cauliflower Rice

Preparation Time: 5 minutes | Cooking Time: 20 minutes | Servings: 4

Ingredients:
- 1 tablespoon avocado oil
- 1 ½ cups vegetable broth
- Salt & black pepper as needed
- ½ teaspoon turmeric powder
- 1 floret separated & riced big cauliflower

Directions:
1. Combine all the ingredients thoroughly in a pan that fits the air fryer.
2. Add the pan to the air fryer and cook for 20 minutes at 360 degrees Fahrenheit.
3. Serve once done and enjoy with dill sprinkled on top!

Turmeric Tofu

Preparation Time: 10 minutes | Cooking Time: 9 minutes | Servings: 2

Ingredients:
- 6 oz. cubed tofu
- 1 diced garlic clove
- 1 teaspoon avocado oil
- ½ teaspoon dried parsley
- ¼ teaspoon ground chili powder
- ¼ teaspoon ground turmeric
- 1 teaspoon apple cider vinegar
- ¼ teaspoon grated lemon zest

Directions:
1. Combine all the ingredients except tofu in a bowl.
2. Marinate tofu with this mixture and add tofu to the air fryer.
3. Cook the tofu for 9 minutes at 400 degrees Fahrenheit.
4. Shake occasionally for even cooking and serve once done!

Blacked Eye Peas and Greens

Preparation Time: 15 minutes | Cooking Time: 10 minutes | Servings: 2-4

Ingredients
- 2 pounds of black-eyed peas
- 1 cup collard greens
- 1 tablespoon paprika
- Black pepper and salt, according to taste
- 1-ounce garlic powder
- 2 tablespoon sesame oil

Directions
1. Begin by rinsing and draining the peas under running water and shifting them to a mixing bowl.
2. Then add paprika, garlic powder, salt, and pepper to the peas bowl and toss to coat evenly.
3. Add the peas to the air fryer and cook them for about 5 minutes at 350 degrees F.
4. While the peas are cooking, add the collard greens and sesame oil to a bowl and toss to coat.
5. Halfway through the cooking, mix in the greens and cook for another 5 minutes.

Pineapple Crisp

Preparation Time: 25 minutes | Cooking Time: 20-22 minutes | Servings: 3

Ingredients
- 8 ounces pineapple rings
- Pinch of salt
- Pinch of chili powder
- 2 ounces brown sugar, granulated
- ¼ teaspoon nutmeg
- Olive oil, for greasing

Directions
1. Add pineapple rings, chili powder, salt, brown sugar, salt, and nutmeg to a bowl and toss to coat the pineapple rings evenly.
2. Coat the inside of the air fryer basket with oil and place the seasoned pineapple rings in it, cooking them at 400 degrees F for 20-22 minutes.

Spicy Yellow Squash

Preparation Time: 25 minutes | Cooking Time: 15 minutes | Servings: 4

Ingredients
- 1 pound yellow squash, halved
- 3 teaspoon olive oil
- 1 tablespoon garlic clove, minced
- ¼ teaspoon basil, dried
- ¼ teaspoon thyme, dried
- 1 tablespoon cilantro, chopped

Directions
1. Take a bowl and add all the listed ingredients, tossing them together till evenly combined.
2. Coat the inside of the air fryer basket with oil and place the squash halves in it, making sure that they are not touching each other and are in a single layer.
3. Cook the squash halves for 15 minutes at around 400 degrees F.
4. Once done, serve

Coated Carrot Fries

Preparation Time: 20 minutes | Cooking Time: 12 minutes | Servings: 2

Ingredients
- 2 cups carrots, sliced to ½ inch
- 8 ounces panko breadcrumbs
- 2 eggs
- 4 tablespoons pecorino cheese
- ½ teaspoon garlic powder
- Salt and pepper, according to taste

Directions
1. Begin by cracking the eggs in a bowl and mixing it with salt, pepper, and garlic powder, and add panko breadcrumbs to another bowl.
2. Drench the carrots in the egg and then give them a coat of breadcrumbs.
3. Coat the inside of the air fryer with oil and place the carrots in it, cooking them for 12 minutes at around 400 degrees F.
4. Top with cheese and let the cheese melt over hot fries.
5. Then serve.

Olive and Balsamic Vinegar String Beans

Preparation Time: 15 minutes | Cooking Time: 15 minutes | Servings: 1

Ingredients
- 1 cup of string beans
- 1 tablespoon olive oil

- ½ teaspoon balsamic vinegar
- Salt, to taste (optional)

Directions
1. Take a bowl and all the ingredients in it, tossing to mix everything evenly.
2. Coat the inside of the air fryer basket with sesame oil and add the beans to it, cooking them for 15 minutes at around 400 degrees F.

Grilled Vegetable and Couscous

Preparation Time: 25 minutes | Cooking Time: 15 minutes | Servings: 2

Ingredients
- 1 zucchini
- 1 teaspoon chili powder
- 4 ounces mushrooms
- 4 ounces shrimps
- Salt and pepper, according to taste
- 2/3 tablespoon Italian herb
- 4 ounces couscous
- ½ cup water
- 2 ounces parmesan cheese

Directions
1. Begin by cutting the mushrooms and zucchini and tossing them with chili powder, salt, pepper, and Italian herb seasoning.
2. Place the seasoned zucchini and mushrooms in the air fryer basket and cook it for 6 minutes at 400 degrees F.
3. While the vegetables are cooking, add water to a pan, mix salt in it and bring it to a boil.
4. Once it begins to boil, add the couscous and remain there.
5. Then add the shrimps to the air fryer basket and cook for 4 more minutes.
6. Once done, take the vegetables out, mix them with cheese, and shrimp and serve with cooked couscous.

Zucchini Chips

Preparation Time: 25 minutes | Cooking Time: 30 minutes | Servings: 2

Ingredients
- ½ teaspoon salt
- 1/3 cup of almond meal
- 4 teaspoon semolina
- ¼ cup parmesan cheese, grated
- 4 teaspoon oregano
- ½ teaspoon minced garlic
- ½ teaspoon lemon rind
- 1 egg, whisked
- 2 medium zucchinis, cut into rounds

Directions
1. Begin by preheating the oven to around 400 degrees F and slicing the zucchini into ½-inch thick slices.
2. Place the sliced zucchini in a bowl and coat them with salt, let them rest for 10 minutes, drain the excess water, and dry them using a paper towel.
3. Mix semolina, almond meal, parmesan cheese, oregano, garlic, and lemon rind. In another bowl, crack and whisk the egg.
4. Drench the zucchini slices first in eggs and coat them with the semolina mix.
5. Arrange them in the air fryer in a single layer, grease them with olive oil and cook them for 25 to 30 minutes, making sure to flip them every 10 minutes.
6. Then, take them out, season with salt accordingly, and serve.

Cinnamon Nut Scrolls

Preparation Time: 25 minutes | Cooking Time: 22 minutes | Servings: 2

Ingredients
- 1 ½ cups self-raising flour
- 2 teaspoon caster sugar
- 2 ounces butter, cold
- ½ cup almond milk
- 1 egg
- ½ cup walnuts, chopped
- ½ cup slivered almonds, toasted
- 2 tablespoon brown sugar
- 1 teaspoon cinnamon, grounded
- 1 tablespoon honey

Directions
1. Begin by preheating the oven to around 390 degrees F and greasing the inside of a 1-inch pan.
2. Add flour and caster sugar to a bowl and mix with butter till it forms a coarse breadcrumb mixture.
3. Crack and whisk the egg with milk, and add it to the flour, mixing it till it resembles dough.
4. Then shift it to a floured flat surface and knead it for 30 seconds.
5. Roll this dough into a rectangle that fits inside the basket.
6. Mix remaining ingredients in a bowl and top it over rolls.
7. Add the rolls to an air fryer basket lined with parchment paper.
8. Bake in the air fryer for 18-22 minutes at 400 degrees
9. Once done, serve.

Feta Filo Fingers

Preparation Time: 25 minutes | Cooking Time: 12 minutes | Servings: 2

Ingredients
- 7 ounces creamy feta cheese
- 12 filo pastry sheets
- 1 lime zest
- 2 tablespoon mint, shredded
- 2/3 tablespoon sesame seeds
- Maple syrup, to drizzle
- Lime wedges to serve

Directions
1. Begin by preheating the oven to 390 degrees F and lining the bottom of the air fryer basket with parchment paper.
2. Slice the feta cheese in a crossway pattern, making 8 pieces, each ½ inch thick. Then slice them further into 1/3rds.
3. Grease a flat surface with oil and place 3 filo pastries on it.
4. Grease them with oil and cover them with oil. Cut the sheets crossway and fold them. Spray some more oil and place a feta cheese slice over from the short end, lengthwise, add mint and lime zest, and fold the sides, making sure to close the edges.
5. Do this with all the dough and cheese and arrange them in the air fryer basket in a single layer, sprinkling some sesame seed on top and cooking them for about 12 minutes.
6. When done, take them out and serve with a drizzle of maple syrup and a side of lime wedges.

Crumbed Asparagus

Preparation Time: 15 minutes | Cooking Time: 12 minutes | Servings: 2

Ingredients
- 1 large asparagus bunch, trimmed, cut in half
  4 eggs
- 6 tablespoons almond flour
- 8 ounces panko breadcrumbs
- Oil spray, for greasing
- Aioli, for serving

Directions
1. Start by cracking and whisking the egg in a bowl.
2. Then add flour to another bowl, and place breadcrumbs in the third.
3. Dip the asparagus first in flour, then drench them with egg, and finally give them a coat of breadcrumbs.
4. Shake off the excess and arrange it on the air fryer basket.
5. Add the basket to the unit.
6. Cook for 8 minutes or till golden brown.
7. When done, drain the excess oil and serve with the side of aioli.

Roasted Honey Parsnip with Pecans

Preparation Time: 25 minutes | Cooking Time: 15 minutes | Servings: 2

Ingredients
- 1 tablespoon oil
- 1 ½ pound parsnip, trimmed, peeled, quartered lengthwise
- 2 ounces honey
- 4 tablespoon pecans

Directions
1. Begin by preheating the oven to around 390 degrees F.
2. Place the parsnip in an air fryer basket and bake them for about 8 minutes or till tender.
3. Then drizzle honey and pecans in the pan and roast them for another 7 minutes.
4. When done, take them out, season with salt and pepper accordingly, and serve.

Crispy Chickpeas

Preparation Time: 25 minutes | Cooking Time: 15 minutes | Servings: 2

Ingredients
- 16 ounces canned chickpeas, drained
- 3 teaspoon sesame oil
- 1 teaspoon salt, or according to taste
- ½ teaspoon garlic powder
- ¼ teaspoon onion powder
- ½ teaspoon chili powder

Directions
1. Begin by preheating the air fryer to around 400 degrees F.
2. Add the chickpeas and oil to a bowl and toss with all the spices.
3. Arrange the chickpeas in the air fryer basket and cook for 15 minutes.
4. When done, take them out, season with salt and pepper accordingly, and serve.

Garlic and Herb Roasted Chickpeas

Preparation Time: 15 minutes | Cooking Time: 15 minutes | Servings: 2

Ingredients
- 8 ounces chickpeas

- ½ tablespoon garlic oil
- 1 tablespoon parmesan cheese
- 1 tablespoon garlic powder
- 3 teaspoon mixed herbs
- Salt and pepper, according to taste

Directions
1. Begin by rinsing and drying the chickpeas and placing them in a mixing bowl.
2. Add a few drops of oil to the bowl, add the seasonings and toss to coat evenly.
3. Once the chickpeas are evenly coated, add them to the air fryer basket and cook them for 15 minutes at around 400 degrees F, making sure to stir them halfway.

Garlicky Couscous

Preparation Time: 25 minutes | Cooking Time: 28 minutes | Servings: 2

Ingredients:
- 1 tablespoon butter
- 1 garlic clove
- 1 cup couscous
- 1 cup chicken stock
- 2 tablespoon cheddar cheese, grated
- Salt and pepper, according to taste

Directions
1. Heat the butter in a small pan over medium heat and sauté the garlic in it till fragrant.
2. Then add couscous to the pan and cook it for about 1 minute.
3. Finally, add the chicken stock to the pan and shift it to the air fryer, cooking it for 25 minutes at around 400 degrees F.
4. Sprinkle cheese on top and adjust salt and pepper, then serve.

Black Beans Fitters

Preparation Time: 20 minutes | Cooking Time: 12 minutes | Servings: 2

Ingredients
- Oil, as needed
- 1 pound of black beans
- 1 onion
- ¼ bunch parsley
- 1 egg
- 1 tablespoon ginger
- 1 clove garlic
- 1 teaspoon cumin
- 1 teaspoon coriander
- 1 teaspoon salt
- ½ teaspoon hot pepper sauce
- 4 ounces panko breadcrumbs

Directions
1. Begin by preheating the air fryer to around 400 degrees F.
2. Add all the ingredients to a bowl and pulse them to form a smooth mixture.
3. Take the batter and make a few patties from them.
4. Arrange the patties in the air fryer basket lined with parchment paper, and cook them for 12 minutes at 400 degrees F.
5. Once done, serve.

133

Vegetable Mirepoix Bites

Preparation Time: 25 minutes | Cooking Time: 24 minutes | Servings: 2

Ingredients
- 4 celery stalks
- 1 carrot, peeled, chopped
- 1 onion
- Oil, as needed
- Pinch of salt and pepper, or according to taste
- 1 sweet potato, cooked and mashed
- ¼ cup cassava flour
- ¼ teaspoon minced garlic
- ½ teaspoon minced onion

Directions
1. Toss celery stalk, carrots, garlic, and onions with oil, salt, and pepper.
2. Add them to the air fryer basket and cook them for 12 minutes at 400 degrees F.
3. When done, shift them into a bowl and mix with all the other listed ingredients.
4. Make small nuggets of the mixture and place them in the air fryer, cooking them for 12 minutes at 300 degrees F.

Veggies Tortilla Pizza

Preparation Time: 25 minutes | Cooking Time: 10 minutes | Servings: 2

Ingredients
- 1 teaspoon olive oil
- 2-4 corn tortillas, 12-inch diameter
- 3 teaspoon marinara sauce
- 1/3 cup of porcini mushrooms, sliced
- 4 ounces mozzarella cheese, shredded
- ½ teaspoon Italian seasoning
- 1 bell pepper, sliced
- ½ cup artichokes

Directions
1. Begin by coating the inside of a pizza pan with oil and putting the tortilla wrap in it.
2. Spread the marinara sauce on the tortilla and top it with mushrooms, cheese, artichokes, bell pepper, and Italian seasoning.
3. In the end, add cheese on top.
4. Place in inside the air fryer basket and cook it for 8 minutes at 400 degrees F.
5. once done, serve

All Olives and Cheese Pizza

Preparation Time: 25 minutes | Cooking Time: 10 minutes | Servings: 2

Ingredients
- 1 pizza crust, 12 inches
- 1 garlic clove, minced
- 1/3 tablespoon onion powder
- 1 teaspoon oregano, chopped
- 2 ounces butter, melted
- 1/3 cup ricotta cheese
- 1/3 cup mozzarella cheese
- ¼ cup black olives, sliced
- 1/3 cup green olives, sliced
- 1 yellow onion, sliced

Directions
1. Begin by coating a pizza pan with oil and placing the crust on top.
2. Add butter, garlic oregano, and onion powder to a bowl and mix them.

---

3. Coat the pizza dough with the mix and top it with cheeses, olives, and yellow onions.
4. Add more of the butter mixture at the end and place the pizza in the air fryer.
5. Bake it for 10 minutes at 400 degrees F.
6. Once done, serve.

Frozen Mini Pizza

Preparation Time: 25 minutes | Cooking Time: 10 minutes | Servings: 2

Directions
- 1 pound frozen mini pizzas

Directions
1. Remove the frozen pizzas from the packaging and arrange them in the air fryer basket.
2. Cook them for about 10 minutes at 400 degrees F.
3. Serve and enjoy.

Butter Glazed Pizza

Preparation Time: 25 minutes | Cooking Time: 10 minutes | Servings: 2

Ingredients:
- 12-inch pizza dough
- 2 ½ tablespoon butter
- 2 teaspoon dried parsley
- 1 teaspoon garlic powder
- 1 teaspoon salt
- 1 cup marinara sauce
- 1 cup mozzarella cheese, shredded

Topping (optional)
- 1 cup pepperoni
- ½ cup olives, sliced
- ½ cup tomatoes, diced
- 1 cup kale, chopped
- Basil leaves

Directions:
1. Grease the inside of a pan with some oil and place the pizza dough on it.
2. Add salt, butter, garlic powder, and parsley and give it a mix, brushing it around the pizza dough once everything is mixed.
3. Add the desired ingredients on top and add cheese over them.
4. Place the pizza in the air fryer and cook it for 10 minutes at around 400 degrees F.
5. Once done, drizzle some more butter on top and serve.

Three Cheese Pizza

Preparation Time: 25 minutes | Cooking Time: 10 minutes | Servings: 2

Ingredients
- 12-inch pizza crust, packed
- 2 garlic cloves
- 1 teaspoon oregano, chopped
- 2 tablespoons extra virgin olive oil
- 2/3 cup gorgonzola cheese
- 1 cup mozzarella cheese, shredded
- 1/3 cup parmesan cheese, grated
- Red pepper, crushed

Directions
1. Coat the inside of a pan with oil and lay the pizza crust on it.
2. Add oil, oregano, red pepper, and garlic to a bowl, mix them and brush it over the dough.

3. Add the three kinds of cheese on top of it and place it inside the air fryer, cooking it for 10 minutes at 400 degrees F.

Tortilla Pizza

Preparation Time: 25 minutes | Cooking Time: 8 | Servings: 2

Ingredients

- 1 teaspoon olive oil
- Corn tortilla, 12 inch
- 3 teaspoon marinara sauce
- Pepperoni slices
- 4 ounces mozzarella slices, shredded
- ½ teaspoon Italian seasoning

Directions

1. Start by coating the inside of a pizza pan with oil and placing the corn tortilla on it.
2. Spread the sauce over the pizza and add the topping over it. add the cheese at the end and place it in the air fryer, cooking it for 8 minutes at 400 degrees F

Lentil Tacos

Preparation Time: 25 minutes | Cooking Time: 6-8 minutes | Servings: 2

Ingredients

- 10 taco shells, hard
- 2/3 tablespoon taco seasoning
- 1 pound lentils, precooked
- ½ tablespoon fajita
- ¼ cup grated cheddar cheese
- Romaine lettuce
- 1 tomato, chopped
- 2 tablespoons sour cream
- 1 tablespoon chives

Directions

1. Begin by preheating the air fryer to around 350 degrees F.
2. Add lentils to a bowl and mix taco seasoning in it.
3. Then arrange the hard tacos in the air fryer basket and add the lentils with equally distributed fajita.
4. Top the lentils tacos with cheese and cook them for 6-8 minutes at 400 degrees F.
5. When done, add lettuce, chives, tomatoes, and sour cream on top of the tacos and serve.

Chickpeas Squash Fitters

Preparation Time: 20 minutes | Cooking Time: 6 12 minutes | Servings: 2

Ingredients

- 1 large butternut squash
- 2 onions
- 1 pound chickpea flour
- ½ tablespoon garlic, crushed
- 1 teaspoon lime juice
- 3 tablespoon cilantro
- Oil, as needed

Ingredients for the Spices

- 1 teaspoon cumin powder
- ½ teaspoon turmeric powder
- 1/6 teaspoon red chili powder
- 1/6 teaspoon salt, or according to taste

Directions

1. Add butternut squash, onions, lime juice, chickpea flour, garlic, cilantro, and all the spice in a bowl and mix.

2. Take a spoonful of the mixture and make balls out of it, placing it in the greased air fryer basket and cooking it for 12 minutes, making sure to flip them halfway.
3. When done, give a garnish of cilantro and serve with a dip of choice.

Fried Rice with Sesame Sriracha Sauce

Preparation Time: 20 minutes | Cooking Time: 15-20 minutes | Servings: 2

Ingredients

- 1 cup rice, cooked
- ½ tablespoon vegetable oil
- 1 teaspoon sesame oil
- Salt and pepper, according to taste
- ½ teaspoon hot sauce
- ½ teaspoon tamari sauce
- ½ teaspoon sesame seeds
- 1 egg
- ½ cup peas, frozen
- ½ cup carrots

Directions

1. Add rice, oil, and a tablespoon of water to a bowl.
2. Season the rice with salt and pepper and fill it into a cake pan lined with foil, placing it in the air fryer, and cooking it for about 8 minutes.
3. While the rice is cooking, add hot sauce, sesame oil, tamari sauce, and sesame seeds to a bowl and give it a mix.
4. Crack and whisk eggs in a bowl and add it over rice, cooking for another 4 minutes.
5. When the egg is cooked, add carrots and peas to the rice and cook for 2 minutes before adding the sauce and serving.

Zucchini Corn Fitters

Preparation Time: 25 minutes | Cooking Time: 10 minutes | Servings: 2

Ingredients

- 2 zucchinis
- ½ cup corn, drained
- 1 cup potato
- 2 tablespoons chickpea flour
- 1 minced onion
- Salt and black pepper, to taste
- Tomato sauce, for serving

Directions

1. Grate the zucchini using a grater, and add it to a mixing bowl, mixing it with oil, salt, and pepper.
2. Let it rest for about 15 minutes and drain the excess water.
3. Mash the potatoes using a masher and add them to the bowl, mixing them with onion, zucchini, salt, corn, chickpea flour, and pepper.
4. Make patties from the mixture, arrange them in the air fryer, cook them for 5 minutes, flip them, and cook for another 5 minutes.
5. When done, take the patties out and serve with the side of tomato sauce or dip sauce of choice.

Lupine Beans Fitters

Preparation Time: 25 minutes | Cooking Time: 22 minutes | Servings: 2

Ingredients

- 1 cup Italian breadcrumbs
- 8 ounces Lupine beans
- ½ cup zucchini

- 1 spring onion, sliced
- 1 tablespoon hemp seeds

For the seasoning
- 1 teaspoon chili powder
- ½ teaspoon garlic powder
- ½ teaspoon chili powder
- ½ teaspoon onion powder
- Salt and pepper, according to taste

Directions
1. Drain the beans and peel their skins.
2. Add them to a food processor and pulse them with onions, hemp seeds, zucchini, and seasoning.
3. Take a spoonful of the mixture and make a small ball out of them,
4. Coat it in Italian breadcrumbs, then arrange them in the air fryer and cook them for 18 to 22 minutes at 350 degrees F, making sure to flip them halfway.

Egg Fried Rice

Preparation Time: 25 minutes | Cooking Time: 13-15 minutes | Servings: 2

Ingredients
- 1 cup leftover rice, cooked
- 3 ½ ounces peas
- ½ cup stir fry mix vegetables
- 2 tablespoons sesame oil
- 4 tablespoon tamari sauce
- 2 tablespoon Worcestershire sauce
- 4 tablespoon five-spice powder
- 4 eggs
- 2 teaspoon butter
- Salt and pepper, according to taste

Directions
1. Whisk the eggs, butter, salt, and pepper in ramekins.
2. Put the ramekins in the air fryer basket and cook them for 8 minutes at around 360 degrees F.
3. When the eggs are cooked, add them to a bowl and mix with all the other ingredients, except the rice.
4. When everything is mixed, add the rice and mix properly.
5. Place it again in the air fryer and cook it for 5 minutes.

Buffalo Quinoa Fritters

Preparation Time: 25 minutes | Cooking Time: 10 minutes | Servings: 2

Ingredients
- 1 cup quinoa
- 2 cups water
- 1 cup chickpeas, drained
- ½ cup sriracha sauce
- 1 cup mozzarella cheese
- 1egg
- 1 cup breadcrumbs
- Salt and pepper, according to taste
- Oil, as needed

Directions
1. Add water and quinoa to a saucepan and cook it for 5 minutes.
2. When done, remove it from the heat and let it cool down.
3. Add chickpeas to a food blender and blend them with egg, sriracha sauce, quinoa, breadcrumbs, salt, mozzarella cheese, and pepper.
4. Once the batter is formed, make patties from it and arrange them in the air fryer basket lined with parchment paper, cooking them for 10 minutes at around 350 degrees F.
5. When they become crispy, take them out and serve.

Spiced Chickpeas and Cashew Mix

Preparation Time: 25 minutes | Cooking Time: 25 minutes | Servings: 2

Ingredients
- ½ pound chickpeas, rinsed, dried
- 2 tablespoon olive oil
- 3 teaspoon curry powder
- 3 teaspoon coriander
- ½ tablespoon turmeric
- 1 teaspoon Garam Masala
- ¾ cup cashews, raw
- Sea salt, for serving

Directions
1. Begin by preheating the oven to around 420 degrees F, lining the bottom of the air fryer basket with parchment paper, and patting dry the chickpeas using a kitchen towel.
2. Add oil, coriander, curry powder, turmeric, and Garam Masala to a large bowl and give them a mix. Set aside 1 tablespoon of the mix and add dried chickpeas to it, tossing them to coat evenly.
3. Season the peas with salt and arrange them in the air fryer basket, cooking them for about 25 minutes or till they turn nice and golden brown.
4. Add the cashews to the reserved spice mix and add them to the air fryer basket 10 minutes before the cooking is complete.
5. When done, take them out and serve with a garnish of sea salt.

Chickpeas Fitter with Sweet Spicy Sauce

Preparation Time: 25 minutes | Cooking Time: 8 minutes | Servings: 2

Ingredients
- 8 ounces yogurt
- 1 ounces sugar
- 1 tablespoon maple syrup
- Salt and pepper, according to taste
- ½ teaspoon red pepper flakes

Fitters Ingredients
- 1 ½ pound chickpeas
- ½ teaspoon cumin powder
- ½ teaspoon garlic powder
- ½ teaspoon ginger
- 1 egg
- ½ teaspoon baking soda
- 2 small onions, chopped
- 4 ounces parsley

Directions
1. Begin by preheating the oven to around 400 degrees F.
2. Add the first 5 listed Ingredients to a bowl and mix them.
3. Then add the chickpeas to a food processor with the seasoning and process till finely blended.
4. Shift the mixture to a bowl and mix with egg, onions, and cilantro.
5. Take a spoonful of the chickpeas mixture and make balls out of them.
6. Arrange the chickpeas bowl in the air fryer basket and cook them for 8 minutes.
7. When done, take the chickpeas out and serve with the side of sauce made earlier.

Air Fryer Falafel

Preparation Time: 25 minutes | Cooking Time: 14 minutes | Servings: 2

Ingredients
- 1 pound chickpeas
- 1 garlic clove
- 1 onion
- ½ bunch cilantro
- 1 teaspoon ground coriander
- 2 tablespoon wheat flour
- ½ teaspoon kosher salt, or according to taste
- ¼ teaspoon baking powder
- ¼ teaspoon black pepper, or according to taste
- 1/8 teaspoon cayenne pepper

Directions
1. Mix the chickpeas with garlic, onion, flour, cayenne pepper, baking powder, cilantro, coriander, salt, coriander, and black pepper.
2. Shift it to a food processor and pulse till coarsely chopped.
3. From medium-sized balls from the batter and place them in the air fryer, cooking them for 14 minutes at 350 degrees F.

Blacked Eyed Pea Dumpling Stew

Preparation Time: 25 minutes | Cooking Time: 30 minutes | Servings: 2

Ingredients
- 1 potato
- 1 onion
- 1 tomato
- ½ eggplant
- 2 small carrots
- 1 small sweet potato
- 1 hot pepper
- 1 bay leaf
- 2 cups water
- Salt and pepper, according to taste

For dumplings
- 1 cup of black-eyed peas
- 2 tablespoon all-purpose flour
- 2 teaspoon cilantro
- 1/6 teaspoon salt, or according to taste

Directions
1. Add the ingredients for the stew and cook them for about 20 minutes or till tender.
2. Then add black eye peas, flour, salt, cilantro, and water as needed in a food processor, pulsing them till they form a dough.
3. Take the dough out and make small balls out of it.
4. Place the dough balls in the air fryer basket lined with butter paper, coat them with some oil, and cook them for about 10 minutes.
5. When done, serve with the stew.

Vegetarian Pumpkin Schnitzel

Preparation Time: 25 minutes | Cooking Time: 22minutes | Servings: 2

Ingredients
- 1 pound of potatoes, peeled, diced into 1-inch pieces
- ½ pound turnip or swede, peeled, diced to 1-inch pieces
- 2 tablespoons extra virgin olive oil
- 4 ounces panko breadcrumbs
- 2 ounces cheddar cheese, grated
- 2 tablespoon pecans, chopped
- 1 tablespoon cilantro, chopped
- 1 pound butternut pumpkin, peeled
- 1 egg
- Lemon wedges, for serving

Directions
1. Add the potatoes and turnip those into a pot of salted boiling water and let them boil for 15 minutes or till the potato and turnips are tender. Then drain them, season them with salt and pepper and mash with 2 tablespoons of oil.
2. Heat the air fryer to 350 degrees F.
3. Mix cheddar cheese, cilantro, pecans, breadcrumbs, and oil in a shallow dish. Crack and whisk the egg into a bowl.
4. Slice the pumpkin into ½-inch thick slices, dip it in the egg, and then give it a coat of breadcrumbs.
5. Arrange the coated pumpkin in the air fryer and cook them for 12 minutes.
6. When done, serve them with the side of lemon wedges and garnish with cilantro and mashed potatoes.

Lentil Fritters with Garlic

Preparation Time: 25 minutes | Cooking Time: 10-25minutes | Servings: 3

Ingredients
- 1 cup lentils, cooked
- ½ tablespoon olive oil
- ½ onion
- 2 garlic cloves
- 4 ounces mushrooms, sliced
- ½ cup quinoa, cooked
- ½ cup walnuts
- ½ teaspoon cumin
- ½ teaspoon paprika, smoked
- ½ teaspoon cilantro
- ½ teaspoon salt
- 1 ½ tablespoon water
- 2 teaspoon flax powder
- 1 teaspoon tamari sauce

For garlic sauce
- ½ cup soy milk
- 1 tablespoon nutritional yeast
- 1 garlic, minced
- 2 teaspoon cornstarch
- Salt, according to taste

Directions
1. Begin by cooking the lentils in a pan and letting them cool down.
2. Add garlic, onions, and mushrooms to another pan, and sauté them for 5 minutes at medium-high heat.
3. Add walnuts to a blender and pulse with salt, water, egg, spices, tamari sauce, flax powder, and mushrooms.
4. Then add lentils to the mix and blend till dough is formed.
5. Add all the ingredients for the garlic sauce to a hot pan and mix till thickened.
6. Take the lentil batter and make patties from it, arranging them in the air fryer basket and cooking them for 10 minutes at around 400 degrees F.
7. When the patties are done, take them out and serve with the side of garlic sauce made earlier.

Lentil Ball with Zesty Rice

Preparation Time: 25 minutes | Cooking Time: 30-35 minutes | Servings: 4

Ingredients
- 1 can lentils

- ½ cup walnuts
- 1 ½ tablespoons mushrooms, dried
- 1 tablespoon tomato puree
- 1 ½ tablespoon cilantro
- Salt and pepper, according to taste
- ¼ cup bread crumbs, or as needed

For zesty rice
- 1 ½ cup water
- 1 cup basmati rice
- 1 tablespoon lemon juice
- 1 tablespoon cilantro
- 1 teaspoon lemon zest
- 1/6 teaspoon salt

For garnish
- 1 cup lettuce
- ½ cup cherry tomatoes
- ½ cup onions
- 2 lemon wedges

Directions
1. Begin by preheating the air fryer to around 365 degrees F.
2. Add walnuts, mushrooms, lentils, cilantro, tomato puree, salt, and pepper to a food processor and blend them till smooth. Then add breadcrumbs to the batter and mix.
3. Make balls out of the batter and arrange them in the greased air fryer basket, cooking them for 10 minutes.
4. While cooking, add water and rice to a pot and heat it over medium heat.
5. Let it cook for 20 minutes, then mix lemon zest, parsley, lemon juice, and salt in it.
6. Mix lettuce, onions, and tomatoes in a bowl portion it into a serving plate, and serve with rice, a lentil ball, and a garnish of lemon wedges.

Moroccan Vegetable Couscous

Preparation Time: 25 minutes | Cooking Time: 50 minutes | Servings: 4

Ingredients
- 2-pound chickpeas
- 2 bell peppers, chopped
- 1 onion
- 1 carrot
- 1 zucchini
- 8 ounces kale
- 1 ounces mint
- 16 ounces couscous
- 1 tablespoon harissa
- 2/3 tablespoon garlic salt
- 1 tablespoon ground coriander
- 1 teaspoon turmeric powder
- 2/3 tablespoon chili powder
- Mint, as needed
- 1 tablespoon sumac

Directions
1. Begin by cutting and rinsing the vegetables.
2. Then add chickpeas to a bowl and toss them with chili powder, salt, and coriander.
3. Add them to the air fryer basket and cook them for 15 minutes at around 400 degrees F.
4. While cooking, add onions and zucchini to a pan and sauté them over medium heat.
5. Then mix in harissa and cook for 5 minutes.
6. In another pan, add oil and cook the bell peppers for about 3 minutes.

7. Toss kale with salt and oil, arrange them in the air fryer basket lined with parchment paper, and cook them for 20 minutes.
8. Meanwhile, add couscous to a bowl and mix with turmeric, garlic salt, and coriander.
9. Then add the couscous to a pot of boiling water and let them boil with a lid on top.
10. Add all the ingredients to the couscous and give it a mix.
11. Give it a garnish of mint and sumac, and serve.

BBQ Lentil Meatballs

Preparation Time: 25 minutes | Cooking Time: 50-60 minutes | Servings: 2-4

Ingredients
- 2 cups lentils
- 1 cup mushrooms
- 4 cups vegetable broth
- 4 tablespoons sesame oil
- 2 cups onions
- 2 tablespoons tomato paste
- 2 garlic cloves
- ¼ cup freshly chopped parsley
- 1 cup wheat flour
- ½ cup BBQ sauce
- 2 tablespoon tamari sauce
- 2 teaspoon onion powder
- BBQ sauce

Directions
1. Add mushrooms, lentils, and vegetable broth to a pot and cook them over medium-high heat for about 20 minutes.
2. Heat oils over medium heat in a saucepan and sautés the onions in it for 5 minutes.
3. Then mix in tomato paste and garlic cloves, cooking them for a minute.
4. Add the mushrooms, onion mix, parsley, tamari sauce, onion powder, wheat flour, BBQ sauce, and water in a food blender and blend them till they form a smooth paste.
5. Make balls from the paste and arrange them in the air fryer basket.
6. Drizzle some oil on them and let them cook for 12 minutes at 350 degrees F. When done, take them out and serve with a side of BBQ sauce.

Charred Runner Bean Salad With Mozzarella And Salsa Verde

Preparation Time: 10 minutes | Cooking Time: 15 minutes | Servings: 1

Ingredients:
- 300g runner beans, halved diagonally (see Easy Swaps)
- 1 tbsp olive oil, plus extra to drizzle
- 100g podded peas (fresh or frozen)
- Handful pea shoots
- 200g ball buffalo mozzarella (check it's vegetarian if you need it to be)
- 50g flaked almonds, lightly toasted in a dry pan
- Grilled bread to serve (optional)
- For the salsa verde
- Large handful of soft herbs, finely chopped (we used a mix of parsley, mint, and basil)
- 1 small garlic clove, crushed
- 1 tbsp capers, washed and drained, roughly chopped
- 1 shallot, finely chopped
- 100g pitted green olives, roughly chopped
- Finely grated zest and juice 1 lemon

- 1 red chili, seeds removed, finely chopped
- 75ml olive oil

Directions:
1. To make the salsa verde, combine all ingredients in a small dish and season with salt. Set aside while preparing the salad.
2. Warm a griddle pan over high heat until it is scorching hot. Toss the runner beans with the oil, then grill in batches for 5 minutes, turning once or twice, until browned in areas and soft. If you prefer, cook on a grill.
3. Meanwhile, cook the peas until soft in boiling water (about 30 seconds for frozen, 1 minute for fresh). Drain, then rinse with cold water. Toss the charred beans with the peas and approximately half of the salsa verde, then serve with the pea shoots, roughly shredded mozzarella, and toasted nuts on a dish. Drizzle with the leftover salsa verde and serve with grilled bread, if desired.

Green Bean Casserole

Preparation Time: 10 minutes | Cooking Time: 15 minutes | Servings: 1

Ingredients:
- 2 cans (10-3/4 ounces each) condensed cream of mushroom soup, undiluted
- 1 cup whole milk
- 2 teaspoons soy sauce
- 1/8 teaspoon pepper
- 2 packages (16 ounces each) of frozen green beans, cooked and drained
- 1 can (6 ounces) french-fried onions, divided

Directions:
1. Combine the soup, milk, soy sauce, and pepper in a mixing bowl. Stir in the beans gently. Half of the mixture should be placed in a 13x9-inch baking dish. Half of the onions should be sprinkled on top. Spoon the remaining bean mixture on top. Finish with the remaining onions.
2. Bake at 350° for 30-35 minutes, or until cooked through, and onions are golden and crispy.

Heirloom Tomato & Zucchini Salad

Preparation Time: 10 minutes | Cooking Time: 15 minutes | Servings: 1

Ingredients:
- 7 large heirloom tomatoes (about 2-1/2 pounds), cut into wedges
- 3 medium zucchini, halved lengthwise and thinly sliced
- 2 medium sweet yellow peppers, thinly sliced
- 1/3 cup cider vinegar
- 3 tablespoons olive oil
- 1 tablespoon sugar
- 1-1/2 teaspoons salt
- 1 tablespoon each minced fresh basil, parsley, and tarragon

Directions:
1. Combine the tomatoes, zucchini, and peppers in a large mixing basin. In a small mixing dish, combine the vinegar, oil, sugar, and salt. Mix in the herbs.
2. Drizzle dressing over salad just before serving; toss lightly to coat.

Cheese Smashed Potatoes

Preparation Time: 10 minutes | Cooking Time: 15 minutes | Servings: 1

Ingredients:
- 1 pound of small red potatoes, quartered

- 2/3 cup shredded reduced-fat cheddar cheese
- 1/4 cup reduced-fat sour cream
- 1/4 teaspoon salt

Directions:
1. Cover potatoes in a large saucepan with water. Bring the water to a boil. Reduce heat to low, cover, and simmer for 10 minutes. Cook until the veggies are soft, about 10 minutes more.
2. Mash with cheese, sour cream, and salt after draining.

Buttery Horseradish Corn on the Cob

Preparation Time: 10 minutes | Cooking Time: 15 minutes | Servings: 1

Ingredients:
- 3/4 cup butter, softened
- 1/4 cup shredded pepper jack cheese
- 1/4 cup prepared horseradish
- 1 tablespoon dried parsley flakes
- 3 teaspoons salt
- 2 teaspoons balsamic vinegar
- 1/2 teaspoon pepper
- 1/4 teaspoon dried thyme
- 12 medium ears of sweet corn, husks removed

Directions:
1. Mix the first 8 ingredients in a small dish until well combined; spread over corn. Wrap each securely with a sheet of heavy-duty foil (approximately 14 in. square).
2. Grill the corn over medium heat until tender, about 15-20 minutes. Allow the steam to escape by carefully opening the foil.

Burnt Aubergine Soup With Rice And Herbs

Preparation Time: 10 minutes | Cooking Time: 15 minutes | Servings: 1

Ingredients:
- 3 medium aubergines
- 90ml olive oil
- 1 large onion, chopped
- 1 tbsp cumin seeds
- 3 garlic cloves, grated
- 1 red chili, sliced
- 3 large tomatoes, diced
- 800ml veg stock, plus a little extra (optional)
- 120g long-grain rice, well rinsed and drained.
- 1½ tbsp lemon juice
- 1 tbsp sugar
- 10g dill, finely chopped
- 10g flatleaf parsley, chopped
- 40g crème fraîche
- ½ tbsp grated lemon zest
- 2 tbsp crispy shallots (optional)
- Glug extra-virgin olive oil

Directions:
1. Set up a grill for direct grilling (coals in the center of the grill) or use the flame of a gas stove. (To avoid a mess, line the cooktop with foil.) Pierce the aubergines with a fork before placing them over the embers or directly over the flame on your burner. Char them all over, flipping them frequently until they are blackened and tender (see Know How). Remove from the oven and set aside until cool enough to handle.
2. Remove the skin off the aubergines and cut the meat into bits. Transfer to a bowl, sprinkle with 60ml olive oil, and season to taste. Set aside while you finish preparing the soup.

3. In a large pan, heat the remaining olive oil over medium heat. Cook for 5-7 minutes, often stirring, or until the onion and cumin seeds are softened. Cook for another 2-3 minutes after adding the garlic and chili. Add the tomatoes, followed by the stock, rice, lemon juice, and sugar. Reduce the heat to low and continue to cook for 20-25 minutes, or until the rice is cooked. Add the aubergines to the soup to warm through around 5 minutes before the end of cooking. Season with salt and pepper to taste (if the soup is too thick, you could thin it with a little extra stock).
4. Ladle the soup into bowls and top with the herbs, crème fraîche, lemon zest, and crispy shallots, if desired. Serve immediately with the extra-virgin olive oil.

Warmed Asparagus And Lettuce

Preparation Time: 10 minutes | Cooking Time: 15 minutes | Servings: 1

Ingredients:
- 3 tbsp olive oil
- 2 small onions, cut into eighths and separated into petals
- 500g asparagus, woody ends snapped off, sliced 1cm thick diagonally
- 1 mushroom stock cube, dissolved in 200ml hot water (or mushroom soaking water from 10g dried mushrooms – or vegetable stock)
- 4 little gem lettuces, quartered lengthways
- 5g mint (about ¼ supermarket bunch), leaves picked, finely chopped

Directions:
1. Heat the oil over medium heat in a big, deep frying pan. Cook for 8-10 minutes, often stirring, until the onions soften. They should retain their integrity in the final meal, so don't overcook them.
2. Toss the cut asparagus into the pan to mix. Stir for 1 minute before adding the stock. Cook for 3 minutes.
3. Remove from the fire after the asparagus is cooked and add the lettuce, tossing to mix with the cooking liquid and wilt the leaves. Season with pepper to taste. Finally, toss in the mint before serving.

Grilled Asparagus And Lemon Rice

Preparation Time: 10 minutes | Cooking Time: 15 minutes | Servings: 1

Ingredients:
- 2 tbsp neutral oil (such as groundnut or sunflower)
- 1 onion, finely chopped
- 1 celery stick, finely chopped
- 1 leek, finely chopped
- 3 garlic cloves, sliced
- 500g asparagus, woody ends snapped off
- 250g cooked short grain brown rice (125g dry weight – see Know-how)
- Grated zest and juice 1 lemon
- 100g hard sheep's cheese, such as pecorino, or vegetarian alternative, grated (optional)

Directions:
1. In a big enough pan to hold everything, heat 1 tbsp of the oil over medium heat. Add the onion, celery, and leek, along with a generous amount of salt. Cook for 12 minutes on low heat to soften the veggies. Cook for another 5 minutes after adding the garlic.
2. In the meantime, mix the asparagus with the remaining tablespoon of oil and a teaspoon of salt. Grill for about 5 minutes, rotating once, over a medium-high heat griddle pan, until tender. Pull out a spear and slice off a portion to consume when you believe they're almost done. If they

require more time, return the spear to the pan and try again in about a minute. Remove each spear from the fire and cut it into four or five parts.
3. Add the rice and 100ml water to the onion pan to get things rolling. Stir thoroughly but gently to reheat the rice without breaking it up. Next, add the asparagus, lemon juice, and a couple of generous pinches of pepper. To blend, stir everything together.
4. When the rice is heated, spoon it into plates or place it on the table for everyone to assist themselves. Finish with the lemon zest and, if using, the cheese.

Prassinopita (Celebration Of Greens Pie)

Preparation Time: 10 minutes | Cooking Time: 15 minutes | Servings: 1

Ingredients:
- 400g strong white bread flour, plus extra to dust
- 2 tsp fine sea salt
- 1 tbsp caster sugar
- ½ x 7g sachet fast-action dried yeast
- 4 tbsp olive oil, plus extra to grease
- 1 medium courgette (around 200g)
- 1 leek
- 4 spring onions
- 200g baby leaf spinach
- ¼ tsp fennel seeds
- Bunch dill
- Bunch flatleaf parsley
- 1 tsp freshly ground white pepper
- 1 lemon
- 2 tbsp sesame seeds
- 3 tbsp honey (or agave syrup, if you need the recipe to be vegan)

Directions:
1. In a large mixing basin (or the bowl of a stand mixer), combine the flour and 1 teaspoon of sea salt. Combine the sugar and yeast in a jug with 225ml warm water. Allow for a few minutes. Rub the olive oil into the flour with your fingertips (or a dough hook), then form a well in the center. Mix in the yeast water, adding a few more tablespoons of water if the dough is too dry to come together. Turn the dough onto a lightly floured surface and knead for 8-10 minutes until it is smooth and elastic. Alternatively, a stand mixer fitted with a dough hook can be used. Place the kneaded dough in a clean, lightly oiled basin and set aside for 1 hour to rise.
2. Prepare the filling while the dough is rising. Trim and thinly slice the courgette, then finely slice each half. Trim and slice the leeks the same way, then place in a sieve and thoroughly rinse to remove any grit. Spring onions, finely sliced. Place all the veggies in a large colander with the baby leaf spinach and scrunch in the remaining 1 teaspoon salt, thoroughly turning the vegetables. Allow the colander to sit in the sink for 30 minutes, scrunching it halfway through.
3. Preheat the oven to 200°C fan/gas 7. Using a pestle and mortar, grind the fennel seeds. Dill and flatleaf parsley, finely chopped. Scrunch the mixture in the colander once to strain the extra liquid; the greens should look wilted. Place in a large mixing basin. Mix in the chopped dill and parsley, white pepper, and lemon juice by hand with the greens.
4. Pat the dough into a ball on a lightly floured work surface. Roll or press it into a circle approximately 35cm in diameter, then pile the salted greens in the center. Bring the edges over the filling and unite them in the center to form a large pie.

5. In a 24cm ovenproof frying pan, drizzle a little oil. Flip the pie into it carefully (seam-side down), patting and easing it in. Drizzle a little extra olive oil over the top of the pie, then sprinkle with sesame seeds and powdered fennel seeds. Heat the skillet over medium heat for 2-3 minutes, or until the pie begins to sizzle, before transferring it to the oven. Bake for 25-30 minutes, or until brown on both sides. After baking, remove the pie from the oven and sprinkle with honey/agave. Allow 5 minutes before serving heated or at room temperature.

Orange, Fennel, And Pea Shoot Salad With Walnuts

Preparation Time: 10 minutes | Cooking Time: 15 minutes | Servings: 1

Ingredients:
- 1 fennel bulb, finely sliced
- 3 small oranges, skin and pith cut away with a sharp knife, sliced into rounds
- 100g walnuts, toasted in a dry frying pan
- 80g bag pea shoots
- Handful mixed salad leaves or soft herbs
- For the dressing
- Juice 1 lemon
- 4 tbsp extra-virgin olive oil, plus a glug
- 1 tsp hibiscus powder (from Waitrose or Amazon – or buy dried hibiscus from a health food shop and grind it)
- 1 tsp balsamic vinegar
- 1 tsp Dijon mustard

Directions:
1. Toss the fennel in a little lemon juice for the dressing and a glug of oil, so it doesn't discolor.
2. Combine all the ingredients for the dressing in a small glass or jar, then whisk with a fork or shake until emulsified.
3. Arrange the salad ingredients on a platter, then drizzle with the dressing to serve.

Lemony Roasted Asparagus, New Potato, And Pea Salad

Preparation Time: 10 minutes | Cooking Time: 15 minutes | Servings: 1

Ingredients:
- 400-500g asparagus spears, any woody root ends trimmed
- 3 tbsp olive oil
- Finely grated zest and juice 1 small lemon
- 200g frozen petit pois
- 600-700g small new potatoes, well washed
- 1 tbsp Dijon mustard
- 70-80g baby spinach, lamb's lettuce, or shredded wild garlic leaves if you can get them
- Some parsley, chervil, tarragon (or a mix), finely chopped – be generous
- 4 'soft' hard-boiled free-range eggs, halved (see tips)

Directions:
1. Preheat the oven to 200°C fan/gas 7 and set aside. Scatter the asparagus in a roasting pan, drizzle with 2 tablespoons olive oil, add the lemon zest and half the juice, and season with salt and pepper to taste. Shake everything around to coat the asparagus completely. Roast for approximately 15 minutes - a little less if the asparagus is extremely thin, a little more if it's thick - until tender and charred. Add the frozen peas about 2-3 minutes before the end of the cooking time, then whisk everything together and simmer until done.

2. While the asparagus is roasting, prepare the potatoes until cooked in gently salted boiling water (about 12-16 minutes, depending on their size). Drain and cut them in half when they're warm enough to handle (unless they're incredibly little). Then, combine them in a large mixing bowl with the remaining lemon juice, mustard, and 1 tablespoon of olive oil.
3. When the asparagus and peas are done, combine them gently with the potatoes. Add any green leaves you're using and any herbs you're using. Season with salt and pepper to taste, divide among plates, and top with the half-cooked eggs.

Charred Cabbage With Harissa Butter And Herb Salad

Preparation Time: 10 minutes | Cooking Time: 15 minutes | Servings: 1

Ingredients:
- 1 medium savoy cabbage, cut into 6 wedges (see Easy Swaps)
- 2 tbsp olive oil
- 4 garlic cloves, bashed
- 1 preserved lemon, skin only, finely chopped
- 120g unsalted butter
- 2 tbsp smoked chili harissa paste (see Easy Swaps)
- 2 tsp cumin seeds
- Greek yogurt to serve
- For the herb salad
- 1 small red onion, chopped
- 100ml white wine vinegar
- 2 tbsp caster sugar
- 1 tsp salt
- Small bunch each dill, parsley, and coriander, leaves picked
- 25g flaked almonds, toasted, plus extra to serve
- 1 preserved lemon, skin only, finely sliced

Directions:
1. Preheat the oven to 180oC fan/gas 6 and set aside. To begin, combine the onion, vinegar, sugar, and 1 teaspoon of salt in a small bowl and put aside to quick pickle.
2. Heat a big oven-safe heavy-bottomed frying pan until blazing hot. Cook the cabbage wedges in batches for 3-4 minutes per sliced side until browned. Place aside.
3. Reduce the heat to medium and stir in the oil, garlic, and preserved lemon. Cook for 1 minute, or until the butter, harissa, cumin, and a sprinkle of salt become aromatic. Add the cabbage wedges and flip to coat on both sides before baking for 25-30 minutes or until tender.
4. Toss the pickled onions with the rest salad ingredients after draining. Serve the cabbage alongside the herb salad, additional flaked almonds, and Greek yogurt.

Beetroot And Goat's Cheese Terrine

Preparation Time: 10 minutes | Cooking Time: 15 minutes | Servings: 1

Ingredients:
- 3 raw beetroot (we used a mix of red, purple, and yellow), trimmed and skin scrubbed
- ½ tsp fennel seeds
- ½ tsp cumin seeds
- ½ tsp coriander seeds
- ½ tsp sea salt flakes
- Grated zest and juice 1 lemon, plus extra wedges to serve
- 4 tbsp extra-virgin olive oil, plus extra to drizzle
- 150g soft goat's cheese
- 200g full-fat Philadelphia cream cheese

- 2 tbsp Greek yogurt
- ½ pack dill, chopped, plus extra fronds to serve
- 2 tbsp finely chopped flatleaf parsley
- 1 tbsp snipped chives, plus extra to serve
- hazelnuts to garnish
- Crusty bread and salad leaves
- to serve (optional)

Directions:
1. Preheat the oven to 160°C fan/gas 4 and set aside. Wrap the beets in foil and bake for 45-50 minutes, or until tender when probed with a fork. Allow cooling before slicing thinly. If using different colored beets, divide them into three bowls; otherwise, combine them in a single bowl.
2. In a small dry frying pan, toast the spices for a few minutes until fragrant. Using a pestle and mortar, crush (or use a jug and the end of a wooden rolling pin). In a small bowl, combine the salt, black pepper, half of the lemon zest, lemon juice, and olive oil.
3. Divide the spice marinade among the beetroot bowls, mix to coat, and put away for at least 30 minutes to marinate.
4. Beat the goat's cheese and cream cheese with a touch of salt and pepper in a mixing basin or stand mixer until smooth, then whisk in the Greek yogurt, the remaining lemon zest, and half of the chopped dill.
5. Arrange overlapping beetroot slices on the bottom of a lined loaf pan, then spoon in a third of the cheese mixture. Place another layer of beets on top, followed by half of the remaining cheese mixture. Next, add another layer of beets and parsley, the leftover cheese mixture, and any remaining beets. Wrap in cling film/plastic and place in the refrigerator for 2 hours, or until ready to serve.
6. Unwrap the terrine and flip it onto a board to serve. Remove and dispose of the cling film/plastic. Drizzle with oil and top with the remaining dill, chives, and nuts. If desired, serve with lemon wedges and crusty bread/salad leaves.

Spiced Squash Kitchari (Indian Slow-Cooked Rice And Lentils)

Preparation Time: 10 minutes | Cooking Time: 15 minutes | Servings: 1

Ingredients:
- 500g butternut squash or pumpkin, cut into wedges
- 3 tbsp olive oil
- 130g basmati rice
- 200g split red lentils
- 1 onion, finely chopped
- 1 thumb-sized piece of ginger, grated
- 2 garlic cloves, crushed
- 2 tsp turmeric
- 2 tsp ground coriander
- 2 tsp cumin seeds
- 1-2 tsp medium chili powder (to taste)
- 1.2 liters of vegetable stock (gluten-free if need be)
- 200g spinach leaves
- Yogurt, chili flakes, and lime wedges to serve (optional)

Directions:
1. Preheat the oven to 180°C fan/gas 6 and set aside. Toss the squash with 1 tablespoon of the oil and some salt on a baking sheet. Roast for 20-25 minutes, or until the vegetables are soft.
2. Meanwhile, strain the rice and lentils through a sieve and rinse under cold water for a few minutes or until the water clears.

3. In a saucepan, heat the remaining oil, add the onion and a bit of salt, and cook for 8-10 minutes over medium heat. Cook for 1 minute after adding the ginger, garlic, and seasonings. Combine the lentils, rice, and stock in a mixing bowl. Bring to a simmer and cook, covered, for 25 minutes over low-medium heat, stirring occasionally. If it becomes too thick, add a dash of more water.
4. Allow the spinach to wilt in the rice for a couple of minutes. Season to taste, then divide into bowls, top with squash/pumpkin, and serve with yogurt, chili flakes, and lime wedges for squeezing, if desired.

Garlic And Chili Purple Sprouting Broccoli

Preparation Time: 10 minutes | Cooking Time: 15 minutes | Servings: 1

Ingredients:
- 150ml vegetable oil for frying
- 2 banana shallots, finely sliced
- 4 large garlic cloves, finely sliced
- 2 tsp sesame oil
- 5cm piece ginger, finely sliced into matchsticks
- 1 small chili, finely chopped (optional)
- 300g purple sprouting broccoli, larger stems halved
- 2 tbsp fermented black bean paste (see Know How)
- 1 tbsp light soy sauce
- 1 tbsp Chinese rice wine (optional)
- Finely grated zest and juice ½ small orange

Directions:
1. In a wok over medium heat, cook the vegetable oil and shallots. Bring to a simmer, occasionally stirring, for 2-3 minutes, or until the shallots are brown. Remove the shallots with a slotted spoon and place them on kitchen paper to drain and cool (they'll crisp up as they cool). Fry the garlic slices in the oil for 2-3 minutes, or until lightly golden (don't allow them to brown too much because they'll continue to brown once they're out of the oil). Remove the garlic and set it aside to drain. Set aside beside the shallots.
2. Pour most of the vegetable oil, leaving roughly 1 teaspoon left (save the flavored oil for future frying). Heat the sesame oil, ginger, and chili (if using) in a wok over high heat. Stir-fry for 1 minute, add the broccoli, and cook for 3-4 minutes, swirling and occasionally tossing, until slightly softened and charred in spots.
3. Combine the black bean paste, soy sauce, rice wine (if using), orange zest, and juice in a mixing bowl. Cook the broccoli for another 2-3 minutes in the pan with the sauce until barely tender and the sauce is slightly reduced. Serve immediately, garnished with crispy shallots and garlic.

Mixed Vegetable Pilau (Subz Mutter Pulao)

Preparation Time: 10 minutes | Cooking Time: 15 minutes | Servings: 1

Ingredients:
- 400g basmati rice
- 75g ghee
- 1 cinnamon stick
- 3 bay leaves
- 4 black cardamom pods (available from souschef.co.uk)
- ½ tsp cloves
- 1 tsp cumin seeds
- 2 red onions, finely sliced
- 100g cauliflower, cut into 1cm florets
- 1 carrot, cut into 1cm cubes
- 1 tsp ground turmeric

- 1 tsp sugar
- 4 green chilies, slit lengthways
- 100g frozen petit pois or garden peas
- 2 tbsp raisins
- 2 tbsp freshly chopped coriander
- 2 tbsp freshly chopped mint leaves
- 50g cashew nuts, deep fried and coarsely chopped (or toasted in a hot pan)

Directions:
1. Wash the rice several times under cold running water, then soak for 10 minutes in a dish of cold water.
2. In a small, oven-safe pan, melt the ghee (one with a tight-fitting lid). Allow the cinnamon stick, bay leaves, cardamom, and cloves to crackle for about a minute before adding the cumin seeds. When the spices begin to crackle, add the sliced onions and cook for 3-5 minutes until they change color.
3. Stir in the cauliflower and carrot, then decrease the heat and cook for another 2-3 minutes. Cook for another minute after adding the turmeric, a generous amount of salt, sugar, and green chilies.
4. Stir in the drained rice until all of the ingredients are combined. Overworking the rice may cause the grains to crack. After about a minute, add the peas and raisins (see Make Ahead).
5. Finally, add 1 liter of boiling water to the rice and vegetable combination and return to a boil in the casserole. Stir constantly over medium-high heat (gently, as too much vigor may break the rice grains).
6. When the water has virtually been absorbed, and small holes can be seen on the top of the rice, sprinkle with the coriander and mint, cover the pan with a tight-fitting lid, and cook for 8-10 minutes on low heat. Serve the rice with the curry and cashew nuts on top.

Jodhpuri Mirchi Vada (Spiced Chili Fritters)

Preparation Time: 10 minutes | Cooking Time: 15 minutes | Servings: 1

Ingredients:
- 400g mild banana chilies (or jalapeños)
- Oil for deep frying
- Tamarind chutney to serve (optional)
- For the stuffing
- 250g floury potatoes (such as Maris piper), unpeeled
- ½ tsp fennel seeds, crushed
- ½ tsp coriander seeds, crushed
- 1 green chili, finely chopped
- 2 tbsp chopped fresh coriander leaves
- 1 tsp dried mango powder (see tip) or juice ½ lemon
- ½ tsp ground cumin
- ½ tsp chili powder
- Pinch ground asafoetida
- For the batter
- 120g chickpea (besan) flour
- ¼ tsp chili powder
- Pinch ground asafoetida
- 1 tsp carom seeds
- ½ tsp nigella seeds
- Pinch bicarbonate of soda (optional)
- 1 tsp salt

Directions:
1. Steam or boil the potatoes until soft for the filling. Peel, mash, and set aside while still warm.
2. Meanwhile, slit each chili down one side with the point of a sharp knife, taking care to keep the stalk intact. Work from the stalk end, leaving around 1cm at the bottom uncut to help the chili keep its shape when packed. Using a teaspoon, remove the seeds. Repeat with the remaining chilies.
3. In a frying pan, heat a tablespoon of oil. Stir in the crushed fennel and coriander seeds for 30 seconds. Add the mashed potatoes, then the rest of the stuffing ingredients. Season, combine well, and set aside to cool to room temperature. Stuff the chilies with the mixture (see Make Ahead).
4. Set a deep, heavy-bottomed pan one-third full of oil over medium heat. In a mixing bowl, combine the chickpea flour, chili powder, asafoetida, carom seeds, nigella seeds, and bicarb (if using). To produce a thick batter, combine the salt and 125-150ml water.
5. Dip the stuffed chilies in the batter to coat, then gently add to the heated oil, working in batches, whenever the oil reaches 160°C-170°C on the digital probe (or a cube of bread browns in 40-50 seconds).
6. Fry each batch for 5-6 minutes, or until golden and crisp, before transferring the chilies to a dish lined with kitchen paper to drain. If desired, serve with tamarind chutney.

Smoky Vegan Chili

Preparation Time: 10 minutes | Cooking Time: 15 minutes | Servings: 1

Ingredients:
- One large aubergine
- 2 tbsp olive oil
- One red onion, sliced
- Two red peppers, thinly sliced
- One large garlic clove, crushed
- 2 tsp ground cumin
- 1 tsp ground coriander
- 1 tsp sweet smoked paprika
- 2-3 tbsp chipotle chili paste
- 400g tin chopped tomatoes
- 2 x 400g tins of black beans, rinsed and drained
- 1 tsp white wine vinegar
- 300ml veg stock
- 50g dark chocolate
- Nachos/rice, avocado, and sliced pink pickled onions (shop-bought is fine) to serve

Directions:
1. Grill the aubergine for 15-20 minutes, turning every 5 minutes, until browned and softened. Allow cooling slightly.
2. Meanwhile, in a large nonstick casserole, heat the oil. Fry the onion and peppers for 10 minutes over medium heat. Cook for 2 minutes more after adding the garlic and seasonings. Season with chili paste, tomatoes, black beans, vinegar, and stock.
3. Scoop the eggplant flesh out of its skin in nuggets with a spoon, then add it to the pan. Cook, uncovered, for 30 minutes over low heat. Stir in the chocolate and season with salt to taste.
4. If desired, serve the chili over nachos or rice, topped with avocado and pickled onions.

New Scrambled Eggs (Air Fryer)

Preparation Time: 10 minutes | Cooking Time: 15 minutes | Servings: 1

Ingredients:
- Rinsed and drained 200 grams of red split lentils
- 200 ml of oat milk (we used Oatly Barista)
- Cashew butter, 100 grams
- 1 tbsp. of fresh lemon juice

- 100-milliliter bottle of extra-virgin olive oil
- Rice flour weighs 60 grams.
- Bicarbonate of soda: 12 teaspoon
- Garlic cloves in the amount of four
- coriander seeds, roasted in a dry pan for 1 tablespoon
- the following: 4 tablespoons extra virgin olive oil
- Large leaf spinach, coarsely cut, around 200g
- Mushrooms, 12 portobellini
- Sourdough bread: 4 to 6 pieces
- To serve: Tomato chutney (we like Tracklements)
- Needed additionally:
- a food processor or a blender is an excellent option.

Directions:
1. The golden 'egg' mixture may be formed by cooking the lentils for 20 minutes or following the package instructions.
2. Run cold water through a sieve after draining. Cooked lentils, cashew butter, lemon juice, extra-virgin olive oil, rice flour, bicarb soda, garlic, and coriander seeds are blended or processed until smooth, then season with salt and pepper.
3. Stir-fry the spinach for a minute in a large pan with one tablespoon of regular olive oil heated to medium heat. Place the portobellini mushrooms in the pan once the chicken has been removed from the pan and left aside. A minute or two on either side should be enough.
4. In a large, heavy-bottomed frying pan, heat the remaining olive oil to medium-high heat and add the onion and garlic. It's time to fry and crisp up the "egg" mixture before turning the pancakes over (it will break up). Cook for a further 3-4 minutes, stirring in the spinach.
5. Put vegan scrambled eggs and tomato chutney on toasted bread before serving.

Vegan Tofu Stir-Fry

Preparation Time: 10 minutes | Cooking Time: 15 minutes | Servings: 1

Ingredients:
- 280g block extra-firm tofu
- 2-3 tbsp corn flour
- 4 tbsp sunflower oil
- For the sauce
- 3 tbsp rice vinegar
- 3 tbsp reduced salt soy sauce
- 1 tbsp hoisin sauce (check it's vegan if necessary)
- 1 tbsp soft brown sugar
- 1 tbsp toasted sesame oil
- 2cm piece of fresh ginger, peeled and grated
- Two garlic cloves, thinly sliced
- One red chili, very thinly sliced, plus extra to garnish

Directions:
1. Tofu should be cut into 2cm cubes and dried well on kitchen paper. Mix half of the corn flour with the tofu chunks in a mixing dish. Toss to coat, then toss with the remaining corn flour. Set aside for 5 minutes to allow the sauce to get somewhat sticky.
2. Set aside the rice vinegar, soy sauce, hoisin sauce, and brown sugar in a bowl.
3. In a wok or frying pan over high heat, heat the sunflower oil and cook the tofu for 1-2 minutes on each side, or until golden brown. Remove from the pan and place on kitchen paper to drain. Remove extra oil from the wok.
4. Allow the pan to cool slightly before adding the sesame oil, ginger, garlic, and chili, and gently frying for around

1 minute before adding the sauce mixture and 150ml water. Cook until the sauce is thick and shiny.
5. Toss the tofu in the pan to coat well. Serve with additional chili, steaming rice, and broccoli on the side.

Vegan Chocolate Cake

Preparation Time: 10 minutes | Cooking Time: 15 minutes | Servings: 1

Ingredients:
- 300ml unsweetened soy milk
- 1 tbsp finely ground/milled chia seeds
- 1 tbsp lemon juice
- 1 tsp instant coffee powder
- 2 tsp vanilla extract
- 150g vegan spread, such as Vitalite or Flora 100% Natural, melted
- 3 tbsp agave nectar
- 175g caster sugar
- 35g cocoa powder
- 300g self-rising flour
- For the vegan ganache
- 200g dairy-free dark chocolate (about 45% cocoa solids)
- 250ml plant-based double cream alternative – we used Elmlea Plant
- 1 tbsp agave nectar
- For the vegan buttercream, amaretto, and jam filling
- 90g vegan spread
- 1 tsp vanilla extract
- 1 tbsp unsweetened soy milk
- 2 ½ tbsp cocoa, sifted
- 180g icing sugar, sifted
- 4-8 tbsp vegan amaretto
- 6 tbsp good quality black cherry jam (see Tips)

Directions:
1. Preheat the oven to 160°C fan/gas four and set aside. Line the cake tin's base and sides with parchment paper. Mix the soy milk, chia, lemon juice, coffee powder, vanilla, melted spread, and agave nectar in a large jug. Set aside 5 minutes (don't worry if the mixture seems curdled).
2. To make the buttercream, whip the spread with an electric mixer until it is pale. To blend, whisk in the vanilla and soy milk. Beat in the cocoa and icing sugar until pale and frothy.
3. Cut the cooled cake into three layers using a sharp knife to assemble it. Drizzle 1-2 tbsp amaretto on the cut side of each layer. (If you have time, freeze the drizzled layers for an hour to firm them up and make assembling/decorating simpler.)
4. Spread half the buttercream on top of the bottom and middle layers, then add half the jam, spreading thinly until approximately 1cm from the edge. Stack the cake layers with the undecorated ones and place them on a serving platter.
5. Spread the ganache evenly on the sides using a palette knife, then pile and swirl the remaining on top. Area the cake in a cold place for several hours or until it is stiff enough to cut.

Vegan Hot Dogs

Preparation Time: 10 minutes | Cooking Time: 15 minutes | Servings: 1

Ingredients:
- 3 tbsp olive oil
- One bushy rosemary sprig leaves picked and chopped
- 3-4 medium carrots, halved (or 6-8 baby carrots, whole)

- Four spring onions or one red onion, cut into four thick rings
- Four vegan hot dogs or eight vegan chipolatas (we used Moving Mountains plant-based hot dogs from Sainsbury's and Waitrose)
- Two corn cobs
- 4 tbsp tomato chutney
- Handful basil leaves, mostly torn, plus a few extra wholes to serve
- Four sub rolls
- Mayonnaise (optional – vegan if it needs to be), gherkins, and mixed salad leaves to serve
- You will also need
- Barbecue with a lid (or ridged griddle pan)

Directions:
1. Light the BBQ and spread the embers out evenly. In a bowl, combine the oil, rosemary, salt, and pepper, and then brush over the carrots, spring onions, vegan hot dogs, and corn. Place the carrots on the grill and cook for 10 minutes, flipping halfway through. Cook for 15 minutes, regularly rotating, until the corn cobs, onions, and sausages are cooked.
2. Slice the corn from the cobs using a sharp knife, then combine it with the tomato chutney and shredded basil in a mixing dish. Season with pepper to taste. Warm the sub rolls on the grill, cut them in half, and top them with sweetcorn relish and mayo (if using).
3. Fill each roll halfway with hotdogs and grilled vegetables, then top with additional sweetcorn relish and basil leaves. Serve with gherkins, mayonnaise, and salad leaves.

Vegan Pumpkin Pie

Preparation Time: 10 minutes | Cooking Time: 15 minutes | Servings: 1

Ingredients:
- 450g pumpkin, peeled, seeded, and cubed
- 100g light muscovado sugar
- 1 tbsp vegetable oil
- 150g creamed (block) coconut (we used Bart Creamed Coconut Sachets, four individual 50g sachets, from Waitrose and bartspices.com)
- One vanilla pod split lengthways
- For the pastry
- 300g plain flour, plus extra for dusting
- 150g vegan margarine (such as dairy-free Pure Sunflower, available from major supermarkets), chilled
- 35g icing sugar, sifted
- A little soya milk to bind
- For the topping
- 55g vegan margarine, chilled
- 125g plain flour
- 90g demerara sugar

Directions:
1. Preheat the oven to 180°C/fan160°C/gas mark 3. 4.
2. To make the filling, combine the pumpkin, sugar, and oil in a large roasting pan. 35 minutes, rotating halfway through, until soft and golden.
3. Raise the oven temperature to 190°C/fan 170°C/gas mark 3. 5. In a food processor, combine the syrupy roasted pumpkin and creamed coconut. Scrape the vanilla seeds into the machine and blend until smooth. Spoon into the tart case and evenly distribute.
4. Bake for 25 minutes until the topping is crisp and brown on top of the pumpkin. Allow cooling somewhat before

removing from tin. Slice and serve hot or warm with a sprinkle of coconut milk.

Vegan Pesto Spaghetti With Lemon And Courgettes

Preparation Time: 10 minutes | Cooking Time: 15 minutes | Servings: 1

Ingredients:
- 2 tbsp extra-virgin olive oil, plus extra to serve
- One small onion, finely chopped
- Two garlic cloves, finely chopped
- One medium courgette, thinly sliced
- 400ml vegetable stock
- 150g spaghetti
- 50g broad beans, podded
- 50g runner beans, cut into 2-3cm pieces
- One lemon, zest, and juice of ½, the rest cut into wedges
- 50g green olives
- 130g vegan basil pesto – we used Saclà
- Parmesan-style vegan cheese and basil leaves to serve (optional)
- You'll also need
- Medium saucepan or deep-sided sauté pan with a lid

Directions:
1. Heat one tablespoon of the oil in a large saucepan over medium heat. Cook for 5 minutes or until the onion is softened. Cook for another minute after adding the garlic.
2. Stir in the remaining 1 tbsp oil, then the courgette, and cook for 5 minutes until the edges are roasted, and the zucchini slices are gently browned.
3. Stir in the stock, then bring to a boil with the spaghetti, wide beans, runner beans, and lemon wedges. Simmer for 10 minutes over medium-high heat or until the pasta is soft (al denté).
4. When the pasta is done, and the liquid has been reduced, add the green olives and pesto and gently mix everything to blend. Serve with lemon zest and juice, an extra drizzle of olive oil, vegan parmesan, and basil leaves, if desired.

Vegan Wild Garlic Lasagne

Preparation Time: 10 minutes | Cooking Time: 15 minutes | Servings: 1

Ingredients:
- 200g wild garlic (see Easy Swaps)
- Pinch grated nutmeg
- 10-12 lasagne sheets (egg-free)
- 100g vegan mozzarella (optional)
- For the ragù
- 2 tbsp olive oil
- One onion, finely chopped
- One celery stick, finely chopped
- One small carrot, finely chopped
- One garlic clove, finely chopped
- A few thyme, sage, or rosemary sprigs
- One bay leaf
- 500g frozen vegan mince
- 400g tin crushed tomatoes
- 1 tbsp tomato purée
- 1 tsp soy sauce
- 2 tsp Marmite or 1 tsp of yeast
- 2 tbsp plant-based milk
- For the 'cheese' sauce
- 250g cashews, soaked in boiling water for 1 hour
- 1 tbsp white wine vinegar or cider vinegar

- 2 tbsp nutritional yeast (such as Engevita)
- ¼ tsp celery salt (optional)
- ¼ tsp paprika
- Splash hot chili sauce
- Pinch mustard powder (optional)

Directions:
1. In a heavy-bottomed skillet, heat the olive oil, then add the onion, celery, carrot, and a sprinkle of salt. Cook for 15 minutes to soften, then add the garlic and continue to cook for 10 minutes, or until the vegetables begin to caramelize. Combine the herbs, bay leaf, and black pepper to taste.
2. Stir in the vegan mince to thaw and brown it slightly. Combine the tomatoes, tomato purée, soy sauce, and Marmite in a mixing bowl.
3. Preheat the oven to 1800C fan/gas six and prepare the lasagne sheets as directed on the package. Spread one-third of the ragù on the bottom of a baking dish (about 25cm x 35cm). Cover with a layer of spaghetti and a third of the 'cheese' sauce. Spread half of the wild garlic combination and a third of the mozzarella (if using) equally over the top, then continue the layers and finish with layers of the remaining ragù, pasta, 'cheese' sauce, and mozzarella (if using).
4. 30-40 minutes, or until bubbling and golden. Allow for a 10-minute rest before serving.

Vegan Miso Mushroom, Squash, And Chestnut Wellington

Preparation Time: 10 minutes | Cooking Time: 15 minutes | Servings: 1

Ingredients:
- One butternut squash (about 800g), peeled and deseeded
- Olive oil for drizzling and brushing
- 600g portobellini or chestnut mushrooms, roughly chopped
- 50g walnut halves, chopped
- 180g bag vacuum-packed whole chestnuts, roughly chopped
- A large handful of fresh flatleaf parsley stalks and leaves chopped separately
- Three fresh thyme sprig leaves picked
- 2 tbsp miso paste (see Know-how)
- Four fat garlic cloves, crushed
- Three soft pitted prunes, finely chopped
- 3 tbsp Madeira (check the label to make sure it's vegan)
- 2 tbsp chopped chives
- ¼ tsp soy sauce, plus a splash
- 6 tbsp panko breadcrumbs
- 500g block puff pastry (check the label to make sure it's vegan – we used Jus-Rol)
- Plain flour for dusting
- Sea salt flakes
- Large pinch poppy seeds

Directions:
1. Preheat the oven to 200°C/180°C fan/gas mix and set aside. Toss the squash in a large roasting pan with a drizzle of olive oil and a sprinkling of sea salt and freshly ground black pepper. Roast for 25-30 minutes, or until the vegetables are soft and gently browned. Place aside to cool.
2. Meanwhile, in a separate roasting pan, sprinkle the mushrooms with a splash of olive oil and roast for 15 minutes alongside the squash. Remove from the oven and toss in the walnuts, chestnuts, parsley stalks, thyme

leaves, miso paste (see Know-How), and garlic. Cook for another 5 minutes. Place aside to cool.
3. Then smooth it down carefully with your fingertips to ensure no air bubbles. Finally, brush with oil and set aside for 30 minutes.
4. Brush the pastry with a mixture of a splash of oil and a dash of soy sauce. Bake for 30-40 minutes, or until golden and puffed and the filling is hot and sprinkled with sea salt flakes, freshly crushed black pepper, and poppy seeds. The wellington will stay warm for around 30 minutes.

Vegan Katsu Curry

Preparation Time: 10 minutes | Cooking Time: 15 minutes | Servings: 1

Ingredients:
- 280g block extra-firm tofu (we used The Tofoo Co Naked Tofu, from larger supermarkets)
- 1 tbsp soy sauce
- 50g panko breadcrumbs (check the label to ensure they're vegan)
- 2 tbsp corn flour
- Vegetable or sunflower oil to fry
- Steamed rice, salad leaves, and sushi ginger (from supermarkets) to serve
- For the katsu sauce
- Drizzle vegetable oil
- ½ onion, chopped
- One garlic clove, crushed
- ½ carrot, grated
- ½ small granny smith apple, peeled and grated
- ½ tbsp medium curry powder
- 1 tsp soy sauce
- ½ tbsp miso paste

Directions:
1. Place the tofu on its end and cut it into four even slices vertically. Wrap each slice with kitchen paper and stack it on a baking sheet or pan. Place another sheet or tin on top, then weigh it with full cans. To press extra moisture from the tofu, leave for 5 minutes, replacing the paper halfway through. Unwrap, place in a small dish, and coat with one tablespoon of soy sauce. Leave for 5 minutes.
2. In a frying pan, heat 1cm oil over medium heat. Cook for 3-4 minutes on each side, or until brown and crisp, with two coated tofu pieces. Transfer to a cutting board and repeat. Slice and serve rice, salad, and sushi ginger, then spoon over the sauce.

Creamy Vegan Sausage And Spinach Pasta

Preparation Time: 10 minutes | Cooking Time: 15 minutes | Servings: 1

Ingredients:
- 1 tbsp sunflower oil or olive oil
- Two red onions, thinly sliced
- Eight vegan sausages, thawed if frozen (we like Tesco Plant Chef or Birds Eye Green Cuisine)
- Two garlic cloves, crushed
- 2 tsp fennel seeds, crushed in a pestle and mortar
- 300g dried pasta shapes such as rigatoni or fusilli
- 200g baby leaf spinach (see tip)
- 300ml single soya cream (we used Alpro)
- Handful freshly chopped flatleaf parsley (optional)

Directions:
1. In a large nonstick frying pan, heat the oil. Fry the onions for 3-4 minutes over medium heat. Cut the sausages into tiny slices and combine with the onions, garlic, and

crushed fennel seeds. Cook for 6-8 minutes, occasionally stirring, until golden. If the sausages begin to cling to the pan, add a drop of water.
2. Meanwhile, cook the pasta according to the package directions. Reserve roughly a cup of the cooking water after draining the pasta.
3. To the frying pan, add the spinach and soya cream. Season with salt and black pepper, then simmer, occasionally turning, for 2-3 minutes, or until the spinach has wilted. Add the cooked pasta and enough conserved cooking water to produce a creamy sauce. Serve immediately, garnished with parsley if desired.

Vegan Sausage Plait

Preparation Time: 10 minutes | Cooking Time: 15 minutes | Servings: 1

Ingredients:
- 50g sunflower seeds, soaked in water overnight
- 85g vegan stuffing mix – we used Paxo Sage & Onion
- 100g dried soya mince (we used Clearspring Organic – see tip)
- 2 tsp vegan stock powder (such as Marigold Bouillon Powder)
- Splash olive oil
- One onion, finely chopped
- Two garlic cloves, crushed
- 2 tsp Marmite
- 1 tbsp each chopped fresh rosemary, parsley, and thyme
- 1 tbsp English mustard
- Plain flour to dust
- 500g block puff pastry (check the label to make sure it's vegan – we used Jus-Rol)
- 1 tbsp soy sauce to glaze
- Cranberry sauce to serve
- You'll also need...
- Baking sheet lined with compostable baking paper

Directions:
1. Preheat the oven to 200°C/180°C fan/gas mix and set aside. In a large heatproof dish, combine the soaked sunflower seeds and stuffing mix and cover with 175ml freshly heated water. Set aside after stirring.
2. Roll out the pastry to a rough 30cm × 35cm rectangle on a lightly floured board. The filling should be spooned lengthwise along the center of the pastry. Cut the pastry into strips on either side of the filling, at right angles to the filling, along the length. Plait the strips over the filling alternately from side to side to produce a lattice look.
3. Brush the wellington with soy sauce and bake for 30-35 minutes on a baking pan coated with nonstick baking paper. Serve warm, at room temperature, or cold with cranberry sauce.

Chocolate Hobnob-Style Biscuits (Vegan)

Preparation Time: 10 minutes | Cooking Time: 15 minutes | Servings: 1

Ingredients:
- 100g rolled oats
- 125g whole meal flour, plus extra to dust
- 50g plain flour
- 100g unrefined golden caster sugar (we used Billington's)
- 50g unrefined dark muscovado sugar (we used Billington's)
- 100ml vegetable oil
- 2 tbsp golden syrup
- 1 tsp bicarbonate of soda
- 2 tbsp boiling water
- 150g melted dark vegan chocolate
- You'll also need...
- 2-3 baking sheets, lightly floured

Directions:
1. Preheat oven to 160°C/140°C fan/gas 3. In a mixing dish, combine the rolled oats, flours, and sugars with a pinch of salt.
2. Melt the oil and golden syrup in a large saucepan over medium heat. Take the pan off the heat.
3. Bake for 10-12 minutes until the top is deep golden brown. Remove from the oven and let aside 5-6 minutes to firm up a little. Loosen with a palette knife, then move to a wire rack to cool (see Make Ahead).
4. Once cooled, pour a little melted dark chocolate over each biscuit and spread with the back of a spoon, or form a ridged design with a knife or fork (see tip).

Vegan Coconut Curry

Preparation Time: 10 minutes | Cooking Time: 15 minutes | Servings: 1

Ingredients:
- 2 tbsp light olive oil or coconut oil
- 2 x 280g packs firm tofu, cut into chunks and dried on kitchen paper
- Four large spring onions, white and green parts, sliced separately
- Four garlic cloves, crushed
- 1-2 red chilies, sliced, to taste
- 1 tbsp cumin seeds, bashed
- Ten fresh or 15 dried curry leaves
- 400ml half-fat coconut milk
- 175g frozen peas
- 200g tender stem broccoli
- 1 tbsp tamarind paste, plus extra to drizzle

Directions:
1. Heat the oil in a large, heavy-bottomed skillet over medium heat, then add the tofu and brown for about 2-3 minutes on each side, or until golden. Set aside after removing from the pan.
2. Add the coconut milk and 200ml cold water (or vegetable stock if you have it), then gently simmer for 10 minutes over low-medium heat, taking care not to allow the curry to boil, or it will split. Cook for 5 minutes until the tofu, peas, and broccoli are just cooked. Cook for another 1-2 minutes after adding 1 tbsp tamarind paste.
3. Serve with the green pieces of the spring onion and a dab of tamarind paste on top.

Vegan Spaghetti Bolognese

Preparation Time: 10 minutes | Cooking Time: 15 minutes | Servings: 1

Ingredients:
- One celery stick, roughly chopped
- One small carrot, roughly chopped
- Four plant-based sausages, defrosted if necessary (we like Birds Eye Green Cuisine Succulent Meat-free Sausages)
- Handful fresh thyme and sage
- 1 tbsp tomato purée
- ½ garlic clove, crushed
- 1 tsp fennel seeds
- 2 tbsp olive oil
- 2 tbsp balsamic vinegar
- 1 tsp soy sauce
- 1 tsp nutritional yeast (see Know How)

- 400g tin chopped tomatoes
- 1 tbsp ketchup
- One bay leaf
- One cinnamon stick
- ½ orange
- For the spaghetti...
- 2 tbsp fine sea salt
- 400g spaghetti
- Plant-based parmesan-style cheese to serve
- Extra-virgin olive oil to serve 10cm and 8cm round biscuit cutters
- You'll also need...
- Food processor

Directions:

1. Pulse the celery and carrot with the sausages in a food processor until finely minced. After adding the thyme and sage leaves, tomato purée, garlic, and fennel seeds pulse a couple more times.
2. Heat the olive oil in a large frying pan, then add the mince mixture and stir-fry for a few minutes. In a mixing bowl, combine the balsamic vinegar, soy sauce, nutritional yeast, tomatoes, ketchup, bay leaf, and cinnamon. Squeeze in the orange juice, mix, and allow it to boil while you prepare the pasta.
3. Cook the pasta in salted water until al dente (but still firm), as directed on the package.
4. Remove and discard the cinnamon and bay leaf from the sauce. Slosh the cooked pasta into the sauce in the pan with tongs, bringing some of the pasta water. Mix with tongs, adding additional pasta water as necessary. Serve with a sprinkle of olive oil and plant-based parmesan-style cheese.

Pizzette With Vegan Mozzarella And Onion Relish

Preparation Time: 10 minutes | Cooking Time: 15 minutes | Servings: 1

Ingredients:

- 190g plain flour, plus extra for dusting
- ½ tsp fine sea salt
- 3.5g fast-action dried yeast
- 1 tsp caster sugar
- 4 tbsp olive oil, plus extra for greasing and drizzling
- 110ml warm water
- For the onion relish
- 1.5kg onions, sliced
- Four garlic cloves, sliced
- 1 tbsp soft light brown sugar
- 3 tbsp balsamic vinegar
- 200g non-dairy mozzarella, grated (from good health food shops or goodnessdirect.co.uk – if you're not cooking for vegans, you could use regular mozzarella)

Directions:

1. Mix the flour, salt, yeast, and caster sugar in a dish. Make a well in the center and add one tablespoon of olive oil and warm water. Combine everything with your hands, then tip onto a lightly oiled work surface. Knead the dough for 10 minutes until it is smooth and elastic.
2. Preheat the oven to 2200C/2000C fan/gas and set aside. Roll each dough ball into a 15cm disc on a lightly floured surface, then place on one large or two small baking sheets. Spread the onion mixture evenly on the discs, spreading it to the edges of each. Drizzle with olive oil and top with shredded mozzarella before baking for 10-12 minutes, or until the base is crisp and golden and the topping is bubbling.

CHAPTER 8:
Desserts

Coconut Lime Pie

Preparation Time: 10 minutes | Cooking Time: 35 minutes | Servings: 8

Ingredients:
- 2 beaten eggs
- ¾ cup swerve
- ¼ cup coconut flour
- 1 oz. shredded coconut
- Cooking spray as needed
- 1 teaspoon vanilla extract
- ½ teaspoon lime extract
- 1 teaspoon baking powder
- 2 tablespoons melted butter
- 1 teaspoon grated lime zest

Directions:
1. Combine all the ingredients thoroughly except cooking spray in a bowl.
2. Use the cooking spray to grease a pie pan that fits the air fryer.
3. Pour the bowl mixture into the pan and add the pan to cook for 35 minutes at 360 degrees Fahrenheit.
4. Slice before serving warm!

Pecan Cookies

Preparation Time: 5 minutes | Cooking Time: 15 minutes | Servings: 8

Ingredients:
- 2 beaten eggs
- 2 tablespoons stevia
- 1 ½ cups crushed pecans
- ½ teaspoon baking powder
- ¼ teaspoon almond extract
- Parchment paper as needed

Directions:
1. Whisk all the ingredients in a bowl and scoop out 8 portions of the mixture onto a baking tray that fits the air fryer.
2. Line the baking tray first with parchment paper before adding the mixture scoops.
3. Add the baking sheet to your air fryer and cook for 15 minutes at 350 degrees Fahrenheit.
4. Let it cool before serving and enjoy it with tea!

Coconut Butter Donuts

Preparation Time: 5 minutes | Cooking Time: 15 minutes | Servings: 4

Ingredients:
- 1 beaten egg
- 8 oz. coconut flour
- 2 tablespoons stevia
- 4 oz. coconut milk
- 1 teaspoon baking soda
- ½ tablespoon melted butter

Directions:
1. Whisk all the ingredients in a bowl and shape donuts out of this mixture.
2. Arrange the donuts in the air fryer basket to cook for 15 minutes at 370 degrees Fahrenheit.
3. Serve warm and enjoy it with tea!

Simple Banana Rolls

Preparation Time: 10 minutes | Cooking Time: 5 minutes | Servings: 2

Ingredients:
- 2 wonton wraps
- 1 teaspoon butter
- 1 teaspoon avocado oil

- 1 tablespoon honey
- 1 peeled & chopped banana
- ½ teaspoon ground cinnamon

Directions:
1. Melt butter in a saucepan over medium flame.
2. Throw in chopped banana and add honey and cinnamon.
3. Sauté in the rest of the fruits for 3 minutes.
4. Add the mixture to the wonton wraps and roll them.
5. Brush each roll with oil and transfer to the air fryer.
6. Cook at 400 degrees Fahrenheit for a minute from both sides.
7. Serve once done, and enjoy!

Perfect Coconut Cookies

Preparation Time: 10 minutes | Cooking Time: 11 minutes | Servings: 4

Ingredients:
- 4 tablespoon coconut flour
- 1 tablespoon brown sugar
- 2 tablespoons coconut oil
- ½ teaspoon ground clove
- 2 tablespoons almond meal

Directions:
1. Combine all the ingredients in a bowl except butter.
2. Add butter to create dough while kneading.
3. Roll up the dough and use a knife to cut it into cookie sticks.
4. Transfer the cookies to the air fryer to cook at 365 degrees Fahrenheit for 11 minutes.
5. Remove once lightly golden-brown.
6. Serve with hot tea and enjoy your cookies!

Vanilla Creamy Cake

Preparation Time: 3 minutes | Cooking Time: 20 minutes | Servings: 3

Ingredients:
- 3 eggs
- 2 cups flour
- 1 cup sugar
- 2 cups milk
- Salt as needed
- 2 cups cooking cream
- 14 oz. condensed milk
- 1 cup evaporated milk
- 2 tablespoons vanilla extract
- 2 tablespoons baking soda

Directions:
1. Combine all the ingredients in a bowl except the condensed milk, cream, and evaporated milk
2. Pour the batter into a round baking tray.
3. Place it in the air fryer and cook for 20 minutes at 300 degrees Fahrenheit.
4. Meanwhile, mix the cream and the evaporated and condensed milk.
5. Once the cake is ready, remove and cover with the milk mixture.
6. Slice and serve with tea!

Lovely Vanilla Cookies

Preparation Time: 10 minutes | Cooking Time: 20 minutes | Servings: 12

Ingredients:
- 2 beaten eggs
- ¼ cup swerve
- ¾ cup coconut flour
- ½ cup melted butter
- Cooking spray as needed

- 1 tablespoon cooking cream
- 2 teaspoons vanilla extract

Directions:
1. Combine all the ingredients thoroughly in a bowl.
2. Grease the baking sheet that fits the air fryer with cooking spray.
3. Shape 12 cookie-sized balls out of the bowl mixture.
4. Arrange and flatten them on the baking sheet.
5. Add the baking sheet to the air fryer to cook for 20 minutes at 350 degrees Fahrenheit.
6. Let them cool before serving with hot tea!

Delicious Chocolate Pastry

Preparation Time: 2 minutes | Cooking Time: 15 minutes | Servings: 3

Ingredients:
- 1 cup sugar
- A pinch of salt
- 2 cups cooking cream
- 2 tablespoons butter
- 2 cups melted chocolate
- 2 cups creamy almond butter
- 2 cups graham cracker crumbs

Directions:
1. Combine all the ingredients in a bowl thoroughly.
2. Pour into a round cake pan that fits the air fryer.
3. Bake for 15 minutes at 300 degrees Fahrenheit for 15 minutes in the air fryer.
4. Remove from the pan once cool.
5. Slice and serve with tea.

Cream Cheese Bites

Preparation Time: 25 minutes | Cooking Time: 2 minutes | Servings: 4

Ingredients:
- ½ cup flour
- 1 teaspoon olive oil
- 1 cup mascarpone cheese
- 1 tablespoon heavy cream
- 4 tablespoons Splenda
- Parchment paper as needed

Directions:
1. Add Splenda, heavy cream, and mascarpone cheese to a mixing bowl and beat for 4 minutes.
2. Use a scoop to create balls from the mixture.
3. Transfer to a pan that fits the air fryer lined with parchment paper.
4. Put them in the freezer for 20 minutes until they are solid.
5. Take them out and coat them with flour.
6. Sprinkle olive oil on top and cook in the air fryer for 2 minutes at 400 degrees Fahrenheit.
7. Serve once done with your favorite hot beverage!

Easiest Chocolate Mug Cake

Preparation Time: 5 minutes | Cooking Time: 15 minutes | Servings: 3

Ingredients:
- 1 tablespoon butter
- 1 cup coconut cream
- ½ cup cocoa powder
- ½ cup stevia powder
- 1 tablespoon vanilla extract
- 1 package room temperature mascarpone cheese

Directions:
1. Start by preheating the air fryer at 350 degrees Fahrenheit.
2. Combine all the ingredients in a bowl and mix everything with an egg beater.
3. Grease the heat-proof mugs and pour the batter into them.
4. Add the mugs to the air fryer basket to bake for 15 minutes.
5. Place the mugs in the fridge to chill before serving cool with hot tea!

Healthy Zucchinis Bars

Preparation Time: 10 minutes | Cooking Time: 15 minutes | Servings: 12

Ingredients:
- 6 eggs
- 4 oz. mascarpone cheese
- 3 oz. shredded zucchini
- 2 tablespoons erythritol
- 2 teaspoons vanilla extract
- ½ teaspoon baking soda
- Parchment paper as needed
- 3 tablespoons melted coconut oil

Directions:
1. Combine all the ingredients thoroughly in a bowl and add them into a baking dish that fits the air fryer.
2. Make sure the dish is first lined with parchment paper.
3. Add the dish to the air fryer to bake the mixture for 15 minutes at 320 degrees Fahrenheit.
4. Let it cool before slicing and serving!

Plum Apple Crumble

Preparation Time: 15 minutes | Cooking Time: 20 minutes | Servings: 7

Ingredients:
- ⅓ cup oats
- ⅔ cup almond flour
- 1 cup cranberries
- 1 tablespoon maple syrup
- 2 ½ oz. caster sugar
- ½ stick chilled butter
- 1 tablespoon cold water
- Cooking spray as needed
- 1 tablespoon lemon juice
- ½ teaspoon vanilla paste
- ½ teaspoon ground mace
- ¼ oz. Pitted & chopped plums
- ¼ oz. cored & chopped apples

Directions:
1. Preheat the air fryer to 390 degrees Fahrenheit for 4 minutes.
2. Grease the cake pan that fits the air fryer with the cooking spray.
3. Thoroughly combine sugar, lemon juice, honey, mace, apples, and plum in a bowl.
4. Transfer to the prepared cake pan.
5. In a separate bowl, combine the rest of the ingredients well.
6. Top the fruit mix with this mixture.
7. Add the cake pan to the air fryer basket and cook for 20 minutes.
8. Remove to a serving plate and serve warm.

Nutty Pecan Bars

Preparation Time: 5 minutes | Cooking Time: 16 minutes | Servings: 4

Ingredients:
- 1 egg
- ¼ cup almond flour

- ⅓ cup cocoa powder
- 3 tablespoons swerve
- ¼ cup chopped pecans
- ½ teaspoon baking powder
- 1 teaspoon vanilla extract
- 7 tablespoons melted ghee

Directions:
1. Combine all the ingredients thoroughly in a bowl.
2. Line a baking sheet that fits the air fryer with parchment paper and spread the bowl mixture on it.
3. Add the baking sheet to the air fryer to bake for 16 minutes at 330 degrees Fahrenheit.
4. Let them cool before slicing and serving!

Easy Yogurt Treat

Preparation Time: 10 minutes | Cooking Time: 6 minutes | Servings: 4

Ingredients:
- 2 large eggs
- Butter as needed
- 2 teaspoon maple syrup
- Mixed berries
- Greek yogurt as needed
- 2 slices of sourdough bread
- 1 teaspoon vanilla extract

Directions:
1. Preheat your air fryer to 355 degrees Fahrenheit for 5 minutes.
2. Grease the air fryer basket with cooking oil spray.
3. Thoroughly whisk vanilla and eggs in a bowl.
4. Spread butter on both sides of the bread slices and soak them in the egg batter.
5. Place the slices in the basket and cook for 3 minutes at the same temperature.
6. Remove and serve warm with Greek yogurt and berries you like.

Chocolate Berry Cake

Preparation Time: 10 minutes | Cooking Time: 3 minutes | Servings: 6

Ingredients:
- 2 eggs
- Salt as needed
- ⅓ cup raspberries
- 5 tablespoons sugar
- ⅔ cup unsalted butter
- ⅔ cup almond flour
- Cooking spray as needed
- 1 cup melted chocolate chips

Directions:
1. Preheat the air fryer to 355 degrees Fahrenheit for 5 minutes.
2. Grease 6 ramekins with cooking spray and dust with some sugar.
3. Thoroughly mix sugar and butter in a bowl.
4. Add eggs and whisk till fluffy.
5. Stir in flour and salt.
6. Add in chocolate chips while mixing.
7. Pour the batter into the ramekins about ¾ full.
8. Place the ramekins in the air fryer basket and cook for 3 minutes at the same temperature.
9. Remove from the basket and serve warm with raspberries on top.

Sweet Cinnamon Toast

Preparation Time: 10 minutes | Cooking Time: 5 minutes | Servings: 6

Ingredients:
- 1 cup sunflower oil
- 2 teaspoon pepper
- 1 ½ teaspoon cinnamon
- ½ cup brown sugar
- 12 slices of whole-wheat bread
- 1 ½ teaspoon vanilla extract

Directions:
1. Heat coconut oil until melted and mix with any sweetener until dissolved.
2. Thoroughly mix the rest of the ingredients except the bread.
3. Spread the mixture onto bread slices.
4. Now, place the bread slices into the air fryer rack.
5. Cook at 400 degrees Fahrenheit for 5 minutes until the bread is nicely toasted.
6. Remove and cut into triangles and serve hot with tea!

Almond Aromatic Cup

Preparation Time: 10 minutes | Cooking Time: 15 minutes | Servings: 1

Ingredients:
- 1 whisked egg
- 1 teaspoon Erythritol
- 1 teaspoon lemon juice
- 1 tablespoon almond butter
- ½ teaspoon baking soda
- ½ teaspoon vanilla extract
- 2 tablespoons almond flour

Directions:
1. Combine all the ingredients in a cup until smooth.
2. Preheat the air fryer to 350 degrees Fahrenheit and add the cup to the air fryer to cook for 15 minutes.
3. Eat straight from the cup once a bit cooled!

Fantastic Chocolate Ramekins

Preparation Time: 5 minutes | Cooking Time: 15 minutes | Servings: 6

Ingredients:
- 2 eggs
- 1 cup blackberries
- ½ cup cooking cream
- ½ cup melted ghee
- 1 tablespoons stevia
- ¼ cup melted dark chocolate
- 2 teaspoons baking soda

Directions:
1. Whisk all the ingredients thoroughly in a bowl and divide the batter into ramekins.
2. Add them to the air fryer and bake for 15 minutes at 340 degrees Fahrenheit
3. Serve once cold and enjoy!

Ginger Vanilla Cookies

Preparation Time: 10 minutes | Cooking Time: 15 minutes | Servings: 12

Ingredients:
- 1 egg
- 1 cup swerve
- 2 cups all-purpose flour
- ¼ cup melted butter
- 2 teaspoons grated ginger
- 1 teaspoon vanilla extract
- ¼ teaspoon ground nutmeg
- ¼ teaspoon cinnamon powder

Directions:
1. Combine all the ingredients thoroughly in a bowl.

2. Line the baking sheet with parchment paper that fits the air fryer.
3. Spoon cookie-sized balls out of the bowl mixture onto the baking sheet.
4. Arrange and flatten them on the baking sheet.
5. Add the baking sheet to the air fryer to cook for 15 minutes at 360 degrees Fahrenheit.
6. Let them cool before serving with hot tea!

Cinnamon Raspberry Cupcakes

Preparation Time: 10 minutes | Cooking Time: 20 minutes | Servings: 8

Ingredients:
- 1 egg
- ½ cup swerve
- ¾ cup raspberries
- ¼ cup melted ghee
- ¼ cup coconut flour
- ½ teaspoon baking powder
- Cooking spray as needed
- 3 tablespoons mascarpone cheese
- ½ teaspoon baking powder
- 2 tablespoons almond meal
- 1 teaspoon cinnamon powder

Directions:
1. Thoroughly combine all the ingredients except cooking spray in a bowl.
2. Use the cooking spray to grease a cupcake mold that fits the air fryer.
3. Pour the bowl batter into the cupcake pan and add the pan to the air fryer.
4. Cook for 20 minutes at 350 degrees Fahrenheit.
5. Let it cool before serving!

Lemon Berry Jam

Preparation Time: 10 minutes | Cooking Time: 20 minutes | Servings: 12

Ingredients:
- ¼ cup water
- ¼ cup swerve
- 8 oz. sliced strawberries
- 1 tablespoon lemon juice

Directions:
1. Thoroughly combine all the ingredients in a pan that fits the air fryer.
2. Add the pan to the air fryer to cook for 20 minutes at 380 degrees Fahrenheit.
3. Let it cool before serving on a slice of bread, croissants, or scones!

Blackberry Cream

Preparation time: 4 minutes | Cooking time: 20 minutes | Servings: 6

Ingredients:
- ½ lime juice
- 2 cups blackberries
- 2 tablespoons water
- 2 tablespoons swerve
- 1 teaspoon vanilla extract

Directions:
1. Thoroughly combine all the ingredients in a bowl.
2. Divide the batter into 6 ramekins and place them into the air fryer.
3. Cook for 20 minutes at 340 degrees Fahrenheit.
4. Let it cool before serving!

Coconut Cake

Preparation Time: 5 minutes | Cooking Time: 20 minutes | Servings: 8

Ingredients:
- 1 egg
- 2 tablespoons swerve
- ¼ cup coconut milk
- 10 tablespoons coconut flour
- 1 tablespoon cocoa powder
- ½ teaspoon baking soda
- 2 tablespoons melted coconut oil

Directions:
1. Thoroughly combine all the ingredients in a bowl.
2. Pour the batter into a cake pan that fits the air fryer.
3. Add the pan to the air fryer to cook for 20 minutes at 340 degrees Fahrenheit.
4. Slice and serve with tea!

Coconut Berries Cream

Preparation Time: 5 minutes | Cooking Time: 30 minutes | Servings: 6

Ingredients:
- ¾ cup swerve
- 6 oz. raspberries
- 12 oz. blueberries
- 12 oz. blackberries
- 2 oz. coconut cream

Directions:
1. Thoroughly combine all the ingredients in a bowl.
2. Divide the batter into 6 ramekins and place them into the air fryer.
3. Cook for 20 minutes at 320 degrees Fahrenheit.
4. Let it cool before serving!

Almond Cookies

Preparation Time: 15 minutes | Cooking Time: 5 minutes | Servings: 4

Ingredients:
- 1 whisked egg
- 4 teaspoons stevia
- ¼ teaspoon vanilla extract
- 4 tablespoons almond butter

Directions:
1. Combine all the ingredients in a mixing bowl.
2. Use a fork to stir the mixture, and after, create four cookies.
3. Preheat the air fryer to 355 degrees Fahrenheit and add the cookies to the air fryer.
4. Cook it for 5 minutes and serve once done!

Simple Air Fryer Brownies

Preparation Time: 10 minutes | Cooking Time: 25 minutes | Servings: 6

Ingredients:
- 3 beaten eggs
- ¼ cup almond flour
- ¼ cup coconut flour
- ½ cup almond milk
- 3 tablespoons swerve
- ¼ teaspoon baking powder
- 1 teaspoon vanilla extract
- Cooking spray as needed
- 2 tablespoons cocoa powder
- 6 tablespoons soft cream cheese
- 2 tablespoons melted coconut oil

Directions:
1. Thoroughly combine all the ingredients except cooking spray in a bowl.
2. Use the cooking spray to grease a pan that fits the air fryer.
3. Pour the bowl batter into the pan and add the pan to the air fryer.
4. Cook for 25 minutes at 370 degrees Fahrenheit.
5. Let it cool before slicing and serving!

Cream Cups

Preparation Time: 5 minutes | Cooking Time: 10 minutes | Servings: 6

Ingredients:
- 3 eggs
- 2 tablespoons swerve
- 8 oz. soft mascarpone cheese
- 2 tablespoons melted butter
- 2 tablespoons shredded & unsweetened coconut

Directions:
1. Thoroughly combine all the ingredients in a bowl.
2. Divide the batter into small ramekins and place them into the air fryer.
3. Cook for 10 minutes at 320 degrees Fahrenheit.
4. Let it cool before serving!

Avocado Cream Pudding

Preparation Time: 5 minutes | Cooking time: 25 minutes | Servings: 6

Ingredients:
- 2 beaten eggs
- ¾ cup swerve
- 1 cup coconut milk
- ½ teaspoon ginger powder
- 1 teaspoon cinnamon powder
- 4 peeled, pitted & mashed small avocados

Directions:
1. Thoroughly combine all the ingredients in a bowl.
2. Pour the bowl batter into the pudding mold and add it to the air fryer.
3. Cook for 25 minutes at 350 degrees Fahrenheit.
4. Serve warm with tea!

Almond Bars

Preparation Time: 5 minutes | Cooking Time: 12 minutes | Servings: 12

Ingredients:
- 1 egg
- 2 tablespoons stevia
- 1 cup soft almond butter
- 1 teaspoon vanilla extract
- Parchment paper as needed

Directions:
1. Combine all the ingredients thoroughly in a bowl.
2. Line a baking sheet that fits the air fryer with parchment paper and spread the bowl mixture on it.
3. Add the baking sheet to the air fryer to bake for 12 minutes at 350 degrees Fahrenheit.
4. Let them cool before slicing and serving!

Healthy Chia Jam

Preparation Time: 10 minutes | Cooking Time: 30 minutes | Servings: 12

Ingredients:
- ¼ cup swerve
- 2 cups blackberries
- 4 tablespoons chia seeds

- 2 tablespoons lime juice

Directions:
1. Thoroughly combine all the ingredients in a pan that fits the air fryer.
2. Add the pan to the air fryer to cook for half an hour at 300 degrees Fahrenheit.
3. Let it cool before serving on a slice of bread, croissants, or scones!

Yummy Berry Pudding

Preparation Time: 5 minutes | Cooking Time: 15 minutes | Servings: 6

Ingredients:
- 1 grated lemon zest
- ⅓ cup blackberries
- ⅓ cup blueberries
- 2 tablespoons swerve
- 2 cups coconut cream

Directions:
1. Blend all the ingredients in a blender and divide the batter into 6 small ramekins.
2. Place the ramekins in the air fryer to cook for 15 minutes at 340 degrees Fahrenheit.
3. Let them cool before serving cold!

Plum Almond Cake

Preparation Time: 10 minutes | Cooking Time: 30 minutes | Servings: 8

Ingredients:
- 3 eggs
- ½ cup swerve
- ½ cup soft butter
- ¾ cup almond milk
- ½ cup coconut flour
- 1 ½ cups almond flour
- 4 pitted & chopped plums
- Parchment paper as needed
- 2 teaspoons baking soda
- ¼ teaspoon almond extract
- 1 tablespoon vanilla extract

Directions:
1. Thoroughly combine all the ingredients in a bowl.
2. Pour the batter into a cake pan that fits the air fryer, but first line it with parchment paper.
3. Add the pan to the air fryer to cook for half an hour at 370 degrees Fahrenheit.
4. Let it cool before slicing and serving with tea!

Cinnamon Fried Plums

Preparation Time: 5 minutes | Cooking Time: 20 minutes | Servings: 6

Ingredients:
- 10 drops of brown sugar
- 6 wedgie-cut plums
- 1 grated lime zest
- 2 tablespoons water
- 1 teaspoon ground ginger
- ½ teaspoon cinnamon powder

Directions:
1. Thoroughly combine all the ingredients in a pan that fits the air fryer.
2. Add the pan to the air fryer to cook for 20 minutes at 360 degrees Fahrenheit.
3. Let it cool before serving cold!

Lemon Berries Stew

Preparation Time: 10 minutes | Cooking Time: 20 minutes |
Servings: 4

Ingredients:
- 1 ½ cups water
- 4 tablespoons stevia
- 1 oz. halved strawberries
- 1 tablespoon lime juice

Directions:
1. Thoroughly combine all the ingredients in a pan that fits the air fryer.
2. Add the pan to the air fryer to cook for 20 minutes at 340 degrees Fahrenheit.
3. Let it cool before serving cold!

Toasted Marshmallow Fluff Waffles

Preparation Time: 25 minutes | Cooking Time: 10-15 minutes |
Servings: 2

Ingredients
- 16 marshmallows
- 4 Belgian waffles
- 1 cup maple syrup

Directions
1. Begin by coating the inside of the air fryer basket with non-stick spray so that the food does not stick to it.
2. Arrange the marshmallows in the basket in an upright position and cook them for 8 minutes at 350 degrees F.
3. Meanwhile, cook the Belgian waffles according to instructions.
4. Once the marshmallows are done, scoop some out using a blunt blade and place them on each waffle.
5. Drizzle some maple syrup, top with chocolate chips if desired, and serve.

Air Fryer Cake Box Mix Cupcakes

Preparation Time: 25 minutes | Cooking Time: 10-12 minutes |
Servings: 2

Ingredients
- 1 cake mix box
- other ingredients listed on the cake box

Directions
1. First, pick the cake mix you want to cook.
2. Then arrange all the ingredients and add them to a mixing bowl in appropriate portions.
3. Fill some silicon muffin liner with the batter filling only ¾ of it.
4. Arrange each of them in the air fryer and cook them for 12 minutes at 350 degrees F.
5. Use a toothpick and check whether the muffins are done by inserting them in the center and checking if it is clean or not.
6. When the toothpick comes out clean, the cupcakes are ready to be served.
7. Take them out and let them cool down before serving them with frosting, sprinkles, or toppings of choice.

Carrot Coffee cake

Preparation Time: 25 minutes | Cooking Time: 25 minutes |
Servings: 2

Ingredients
- 2 eggs, beaten
- 1 cups buttermilk
- 2/3 cup sugar
- ½ cup canola oil
- ¼ cup dark brown sugar

- 2 teaspoon lime zest
- 2 teaspoon vanilla extract
- 1 ¼ cup almond flour
- 2/3 cup whole wheat flour
- 2 teaspoons baking powder
- 2 teaspoon pumpkin pie spice, divided
- ½ teaspoon baking soda
- 1/2 teaspoon salt
- 2 cups carrots, shredded
- ½ cup cranberries, dried
- 2/3 cups walnuts, chopped

Directions
1. Preheating the air fryer to around 350 degrees F and coating a 6-inch baking pan with oil and flour.
2. Add baking powder, whisk flour, egg, and a teaspoon of pumpkin pie spice, salt, and baking soda to a mixing bowl and give it a good mix.
3. Then mix in carrots and cranberries to the mix and shift it into the greased baking dish.
4. Mix walnuts, a teaspoon of pumpkin spice, and 2 tablespoons of sugar in a bowl and mix thoroughly.
5. Place the baking pan in the air fryer basket and add the walnut mixture over it.
6. Cook the cake for about 20-25 minutes, or till it becomes dark from the top.
7. Once done, take it out and rest on a cooling rack 10 minutes before cooking.

Raspberry Shortcake

Preparation Time: 25 minutes | Cooking Time: 15 minutes |
Servings: 2

Ingredients
- 3 cup raspberries, sliced
- ¼ cup sugar, granulated
- 1 ½ cup almond flour
- 4 teaspoon baking powder
- Pinch of baking soda
- ½ tablespoon kosher salt
- 4 tablespoons unsalted butter
- 2/3 cup low-fat buttermilk
- Whipped cream for serving

Directions
1. Mix adding the raspberries to a bowl, mixing them, and setting them aside.
2. Heat the air fryer to around 350 degrees F and grease a baking pan with oil.
3. Add flour, sugar, baking powder, baking soda, and salt to a mixing bowl, mixing it till fully combined.
4. Then add butter and buttermilk to the mixture, slowly adding the buttermilk and mixing it till a sticky dough is formed.
5. Shift this dough to the greased pan and place it inside the air fryer cooking it for 15 minutes.
6. Once it becomes brown on top, take it out and let it rest for 10 minutes before serving it, and serve it with some whipped cream and raspberries on top.

Air Fryer Almond Cupcake

Preparation Time: 25 minutes | Cooking Time: 12 minutes |
Servings: 2

Ingredients
- 1 cup granulated sugar
- 1 cup butter
- 2 eggs
- ¼ cup almond milk
- 1 cup almond flour
- ¼ cup rainbow sprinkles

- ¼ tablespoon vanilla extract

Directions
1. Add butter and sugar to a mixing bowl and mix them till fluffy.
2. Then crack an egg in the bowl one at a time and mix.
3. Finally, add the vanilla extracts, milk, and flour, mixing everything till properly incorporated.
4. Mix some sprinkles in the batter and add them to silicon cupcake liners.
5. Place the liners in the air fryer basket and cook them for 12 minutes at 350 degrees F.

2 Ingredients Strawberry Cobbler

Preparation Time: 25 minutes | Cooking Time: 15 minutes | Servings: 2

Ingredients
- 1 cake mix box
- ¼ cup butter softened
- 1 strawberry can pie filling

Directions
1. Begin by preheating the air fryer to around 400 degrees F.
2. Add the cake mix to a mixing bowl and mix it with butter.
3. Then add the strawberry filling to a baking pan and top it with the cake batter, completely covering the top.
4. Place the baking pan in the air fryer and cook it at 400 degrees F for 15 minutes.
5. When done, take the cake out and serve with the toppings of your choice.

Chocolate Molten Lava Cake

Preparation Time: 25 minutes | Cooking Time: 10 minutes | Servings: 2

Ingredients
- 4 tablespoon butter, unsalted
- ½ cup dark chocolate bar
- 1 egg
- ¼ cup brown sugar
- ½ tablespoon vanilla extract
- 3 tablespoon all-purpose flour
- Pinch of salt

Directions
1. Be by greasing the ramekin's inside with oil and setting it aside.
2. Add butter and chocolate to a microwavable bowl and heat it in the microwave for a minute or until melted.
3. Beat the egg in another bowl with a hand blender and add the brown sugar, mixing till fluffy.
4. Then add the chocolate mix, flour, salt, and vanilla extract to the bowl and mix.
5. Arrange the ramekin in the air fryer oven and cook it for 8 to 10 minutes at 350 degrees F.
6. Insert a toothpick in it; the cake is cooked if it comes out clean.
7. When the toothpick comes clean, take the cake out. Let it rest for a few minutes before serving it with the topping of whipped creams or berries.

Chocolate Cake

Preparation Time: 25 minutes | Cooking Time: 10-12 minutes | Servings: 2

Ingredients
- ¾ cup brown sugar
- ½ cup almond flour
- ¼ tablespoon unsweetened cocoa powder

- ¾ tablespoon baking powder
- ¾ tablespoon baking soda
- ½ tablespoon salt
- 1 egg
- ½ cup almond milk
- ¼ cup canola oil
- 1 tablespoon vanilla extract
- ½ cup hot water with instant coffee

Directions
1. Begin by heating the air fryer to around 400 degrees F for at least 5 minutes.
2. Add sugar, cocoa powder, flour, baking powder, salt, and baking soda to a bowl and mix them thoroughly.
3. Crack and whisk the egg with oil, milk, hot water, and vanilla extract.
4. Add the wet ingredients to the dry ingredients bowl and whisk them together.
5. Pour the batter into a baking pan, covering the batter with foil and making a few holes on the top.
6. Add the baking pan to the air fryer basket and cook it for 10 minutes at 350 degrees F, or till the skewer inserted comes out clean.
7. Once the cake is cooked, take it out and cool for at least 10 minutes before serving.

Angel Food Cake

Preparation Time: 25 minutes | Cooking Time: 15 minutes | Servings: 2

Ingredients
- 4 eggs
- ¾ cup sugar
- ½ teaspoon vanilla
- ½ cup almond flour
- ½ tablespoon baking powder
- 1 tablespoon cream of tartar
- 16 oz. whipped cream
- 2 cup strawberries, shredded

Directions
1. To make the first layer, whisk the eggs with sugar for about 5 minutes.
2. Then add vanilla extract, almond flour, baking powder, and cream of tartar to the bowl and mix them for another minute.
3. Shift the batter in the pan and place the pan in the air fryer, cooking it for 15 minutes at around 350 degrees F.
4. When done, shift the layer to a plate and let it cool down.
5. Repeat the steps to make more layers.
6. Top the first layer with whipped cream and place the second layer on it.
7. Do this with all the layers, give it a garnish of strawberries and serve.

Homemade Coffee Cake

Preparation Time: 25 minutes | Cooking Time: 25 minutes | Servings: 3

Ingredients
- 3 cups almond flour
- 1 cup brown sugar
- 1 tablespoon baking soda
- 2/3 teaspoon salt
- ½ cup butter, melted
- 1 cup milk with 3 tablespoons of coffee
- 1 ½ teaspoon vanilla

For the topping
- ½ cup almond flour
- 1 cup sugar

- 1 tablespoon cinnamon, grounded
- ½ cup butter, melted

Directions
1. Begin by mixing the dry and wet ingredients in separate bowls.
2. Then add the wet ingredients to the dry ingredient bowl and whisk everything together.
3. Coat the inside of the baking pan with oil and pour the batter into it.
4. To the batter with sprinkles and place it in the air fryer, cooking it for 25 to 30 minutes at 350 degrees F.
5. Check if the cake is cooked by inserting a toothpick into it.
6. If the toothpick comes out clean, the cake is cooked.
7. Take it out and let it rest for some time before serving.

Air Fryer Apricot Cake

Preparation Time: 25 minutes | Cooking Time: 12 minutes | Servings: 2

Ingredients
- ½ cup apricots, dried
- ¼ cup lemon juice
- ½ cup self-rising flour
- 1 egg
- ¼ cup granulated sugar
- 2 tablespoons raisins

Directions
1. Begin by preheating the air fryer to 400 degrees F.
2. Add lemon juice and apricots to a food blender and blend them till smooth.
3. Mix flour and sugar in another bowl.
4. Crack the egg in it and whisk it thoroughly.
5. Finally, add the raisins and apricot puree made before.
6. Give everything a mix and shift it into a baking pan.
7. Place the pan in the air fryer oven and cook it for 12 minutes. Once the toothpick comes out clean, the cake is cooked.

Pineapple Cake

Preparation Time: 25 minutes | Cooking Time: 25-30 minutes | Servings: 2

Ingredients
- 1 cup self-rising flour
- ½ cup butter
- ½ cup granulated sugar
- ¼ cup pineapple juice
- 2 cups pineapple pieces
- ¼ cup dark chocolate, grated
- 1 egg
- 2 tablespoon almond milk

Directions
1. Begin by preheating the oven to around 390 degrees F and greasing the inside of the tin with oil.
2. Add flour, butter, and breadcrumbs to a bowl and mix.
3. Then add the dark chocolate, pineapple chunks, juice, and sugar to the bowl and set it aside.
4. Crack and whisk the egg with milk and pour it into the batter until a soft cake batter is formed.
5. Pour this batter into the greased tin and place it in the air fryer basket, cooking it for 30 minutes at 350 degrees F.
6. Once cooked, take it out and set it aside before serving.

3 Ingredients Christmas cake

Preparation Time: 25 minutes | Cooking Time: 2 minutes | Servings: 2

Ingredients
- 3 cups dried mixed fruits
- 1 ½ cup iced coffee
- 1 cup self-rising flour

Directions
1. Begin by adding the dried fruits to a bowl and mixing it with iced coffee.
2. Then cover it using a siren wrap and let it rest in the fridge for at least overnight.
3. Preheat the air fryer to about 350 degrees F and prepare a cake tin by lining some parchment paper with it.
4. Add the self-rising flour and fruit mix to a cake tin and mix it, placing it in the air fryer basket and cooking it for 25 minutes or till a skewer inserted in the center comes out clean.

Fruit Pudding

Preparation Time: 25 minutes | Cooking Time: 25 minutes | Servings: 2

Ingredients
- ½ cup almond flour
- ¼ cup granulated sugar
- 1 egg
- 2 tablespoons milk
- 2 ounces butter
- ½ tablespoon baking soda
- 1 cup sliced fruits or canned

Directions
1. Begin by preheating the air fryer to around 350 degrees F.
2. Add flour, sugar, egg, butter, milk, and baking soda to a bowl and mix them till fully combined and the batter is formed.
3. Add the fruits to a baking pan and pour the flour mixture over it, flattening it using and spatula.
4. Place the baking pan in the air fryer and cook it for 25 to 30 minutes at 350 degrees F.

Peach Cobbler

Preparation Time: 25 minutes | Cooking Time: 15 minutes | Servings: 2

Ingredients
- 2 cups peach pie filling
- 4 tablespoons almond flour
- 1 cup sugar
- 1 cup peaches, drained

For Cobbler Topping
- 1 cup flour
- ¼ cup sugar
- 1 teaspoon baking soda
- 1 teaspoon cinnamon, grounded
- 1 egg
- ¼ cup almond milk

Directions
1. Begin by mixing the peach pie filling, flour, and sugar in a bowl and setting it aside.
2. Then coat the bottom of an air fryer-safe baking pan with olive oil and add the peaches to it.
3. Mix flour, sugar, baking soda, ground cinnamon, egg, and milk in a bowl and pour it over the peaches, flattening them using a spatula.
4. Place the baking pan in the air fryer basket and cook the cobbler for 15-20 minutes at 350 degrees F.
5. When done, take the cobbler out and let it rest for some time before serving.

Pecan Strawberry Rhubarb Cobbler

Preparation Time: 25 minutes | Cooking Time: 10-15 minutes | Servings: 2

Ingredients
- 2 cup rhubarb, frozen or fresh, sliced
- 2 cups strawberries, fresh, sliced
- ½ cup sugar
- 2 tablespoons quick-cooking tapioca
- 2 teaspoon lime juice

For Toppings
- ¾ cup all-purpose flour
- ½ cup pecans, chopped
- ½ cup sugar
- ¼ teaspoon baking soda
- Pinch of salt
- 2 teaspoons of butter
- 2 eggs
- 1 cup vanilla ice cream

Directions
1. Preheat the air fryer to around 350 degrees F.
2. Add the first 6 ingredients listed in two separate ramekins or custard cups. Give them a good mix and let them rest for about 15 minutes.
3. Add flour, pecans, sugar, baking soda, and salt to another bowl and mix it with butter until it forms a mixture resembling breadcrumbs. Then crack an egg in it, add it over the fruit mix, and spread it all over.
4. Put the ramekins inside the air fryer basket and cook the cobbler for 20 minutes.
5. When the inserted toothpick comes out clean, the cobbler is done.
6. While the cobbler is cooking, microwave the ice cream and wine at 50 percent power for 1 to 2 minutes, and give it a mix.
7. When the cobbler is done, take it out and let it rest for some time, and serve it with the side of ice cream.

Lemon Biscuit

Preparation Time: 25 minutes | Cooking Time: 8 minutes | Servings: 2

Ingredients
- ½ cup butter, melted
- 1 cup granulated sugar
- 3 cups self-rising flour
- 2 lemon juice and zest
- 4 eggs
- Avocado oil, as needed

Directions
1. Begin by preheating the oven to around 400 degrees F.
2. Add all the dry ingredients to a bowl and mix them thoroughly.
3. In a different bowl, add the wet ingredients and mix them.
4. Pour the wet ingredients into the dry ingredients bowl and mix them thoroughly, kneading till it forms a dough.
5. Take a spoonful of the dough and roll it flat to make biscuits.
6. Grease the inside of the air fryer basket with oil and arrange the biscuits in it, cooking them for 8 minutes at 400 degrees F, without flipping.

Red Velvet Cookies

Preparation Time: 25 minutes | Cooking Time: 22 minutes | Servings: 2

Ingredients
- 2 cups almond flour
- ¼ cup cocoa powder, unsweetened
- 2 teaspoon baking soda
- Pinch of salt
- ¾ cup butter softened
- ½ cup brown sugar
- ½ cup sugar, granulated
- 3 eggs, whisked
- 1 tablespoon cream cheese
- 2 tablespoon milk
- 1 teaspoon vanilla extract
- 2 tablespoon red food coloring
- ½ pound white chocolate chips

Directions
1. Add salt, cocoa powder, flour, and baking soda to a bowl and mix them, setting aside once mixed.
2. Crack and whisk the eggs with butter, and brown sugar, using a hand blender.
3. Add vanilla, cream cheese, milk, and food coloring to a dish and fold them together.
4. Pour the egg mixture into the dry ingredients bowl and knead till the dough is formed.
5. Then fold in the chocolate chips
6. Make cookies out of the batter and arrange them in the air fryer basket, cooking them for about 22 minutes at 350 degrees F.

Walnut Chocolate Cookies

Preparation Time: 25 minutes | Cooking Time: 15-20minutes | Servings: 2

Ingredients
- 1 cup almond flour
- ¼ cup cocoa powder, unsweetened
- 2 teaspoon baking powder
- 2 eggs,
- 1/3 cup butter, softened
- ½ cup brown sugar
- 3 tablespoons almond milk
- 1 teaspoon vanilla extract
- 2 ounces walnuts, chopped

Directions
1. Begin by mixing cocoa powder with flour and baking powder.
2. Crack and whisk the egg with butter, sugar, milk, and vanilla extract.
3. Pour the egg mixture into the dry ingredients bowl and mix it till the dough is formed.
4. Then fold the walnuts into the dough and shape them into cookies.
5. Arrange the cooking in the air fryer basket and cook it for 15 to 20 minutes at 350 degrees F.

Grill Peaches

Preparation Time: 25 minutes | Cooking Time: 5 minutes | Servings: 2

Ingredients
- 3 peaches
- 4 tablespoon graham cracker crumbs
- 4 tablespoon brown sugar
- 4 tablespoon butter
- Whipped cream for topping

Directions
1. Slice the peaches into wedges.
2. Place a parchment paper at the bottom of the air fryer and place the peach wedges on it, cooking them for 5 minutes at around 350 degrees F.

3. Meanwhile, mix graham crackers, brown sugar, and butter in a bowl, mixing them thoroughly.
4. Arrange the peaches, skin side down, and serve on the graham cracker mix.

Air Fryer Cookies

Preparation Time: 25 minutes | Cooking Time: 10-12minutes | Servings: 2

Ingredients
- ¼ cup butter, melted
- 8 oz. granulated sugar
- 3 cups flour, self-rising
- 1 teaspoon vanilla extract
- ½ cup whole milk
- 1 cup cocoa powder

Directions
1. Preheat the air fryer to around 350 degrees F.
2. Add cocoa powder and flour to a bowl and mix them.
3. Next, mix the vanilla extract and butter in it.
4. Finally, add the coconut milk and mix it till the dough is formed.
5. Make cookie shapes from the batter and arrange them in the air fryer, cooking them for 10 minutes at 350 degrees F.

Oat Sandwich Biscuits

Preparation Time: 25 minutes | Cooking Time: 15 minutes | Servings: 2

Ingredients
- 3 cup oat flour
- ¼ cup butter
- ¼ cup brown sugar
- 2 eggs
- 1 cup desiccated coconut
- 2 cups oats
- 2 cups white chocolate
- 2 teaspoon vanilla extract

Directions
1. Start by mixing sugar and butter using a hand mixer.
2. Then add the egg, chocolate, vanilla extracts, oats, and coconut to the bowl.
3. Finally, mix in the flour until it forms a dough.
4. Make biscuits shaped from the dough and place those biscuits in the air fryer, cooking them for 15 minutes at 350 degrees F.

Low Sugar Brownie

Preparation Time: 25 minutes | Cooking Time: 10 minutes | Servings: 2

Ingredients
- 1 cup almond flour
- ½ cup sweetener
- ½ teaspoon baking soda
- ½ cup unsweetened cocoa powder
- 6 eggs
- ¾ cup butter, melted
- ½ cup chocolate chip
- ½ cup hazelnuts

Directions
1. Preheat the air fryer to around 350 degrees F.
2. Add almond flour, baking soda, cocoa powder, and powdered sweetener to a bowl and mix them.
3. Next, crack the eggs in the dry ingredients bowl and mix till it becomes smooth inconsistently.
4. Finally, fold the pecans and chocolate chips and shift the batter into a greased ramekin.

5. Place the ramekin in the air fryer basket and cook it for 10 minutes.
6. Once done, take the brownie out and let it rest for some time before serving.

Peanut Butter Cupcake

Preparation Time: 25 minutes | Cooking Time: 15 minutes | Servings: 2

Ingredients
- 1 cup almond flour
- ¼ cup cocoa powder
- 1/2 teaspoon baking powder
- ¼ teaspoon baking soda
- Pinch of salt
- 2 eggs
- 1/3 cup granulated sugar
- 1/3 cup almond oil
- 1 teaspoon vanilla extract
- 1/3 cup almond milk

Directions
1. Being cracking and whisking the egg with sugar in a big bowl.
2. Then mix in the milk and vanilla extracts.
3. Add all the dry ingredients to a separate bowl and whisk them together.
4. Pour the wet ingredients into the dry ingredients and mix them.
5. Once it reaches the desired consistency, pour it into muffin cups and arrange the cups in the air fryer basket, cooking them for 15 minutes at 350 degrees F.

Orange Cornmeal Cake

Preparation Time: 25 minutes | Cooking Time: 25 minutes | Servings: 2

Ingredients
- 1 cup almond flour
- ½ cup yellow cornmeal
- ½ cup white sugar
- ½ teaspoon baking powder
- ¼ cup olive oil
- ½ cup orange juice
- 1 teaspoon vanilla extracts
- ¼ cup powdered sugar
- Oil, as needed

Directions
1. Grease the inside of a baking pan with oil and set it aside.
2. Add all the listed ingredients into a bowl and whisk them until a batter is formed.
3. Pour the batter into the greased baking pan and place the pan in the air fryer basket, cooking it for 25 minutes at 350 degrees F.

Vanilla Bean Meringues

Preparation Time: 25 minutes | Cooking Time: 10-15 minutes | Servings: 2

Ingredients
- ¼ cup powdered sugar
- Salt
- 6 egg whites
- 2 vanilla beans

Directions
1. Begin by whisking the egg whites using a hand blender.
2. Once it becomes smooth, mix in vanilla beans, salt, and sugar.
3. Mix it till it forms peaks and pours it into a piping bag.

4. Grease the inside of the air fryer with oil and pour the batter into the pepping bag in it.
5. Cook the meringues for about 20 minutes, 160 degrees F.

Coconut Meringues

Preparation Time: 25 minutes | Cooking Time: 5 minutes | Servings: 2

Ingredients
- ½ teaspoon cream of tartar
- Salt, according to taste
- 6 egg whites
- 1 teaspoon coconut flakes
- 2 tablespoons of powdered sugar

Directions
1. Whisk the egg whites using a hand blender till it becomes smooth.
2. Then add salt, coconut flakes, sugar, and cream of tartar to the egg and whisk them in.
3. Pour the batter into a piping bag and pour it into the air fryer basket, lined with parchment paper. Cook the meringues for 20 minutes at around 170 degrees F in dehydrating mode.

Sweet Cookie

Preparation Time: 25 minutes | Cooking Time: 18 minutes | Servings: 2

Ingredients
- 1 cup almond butter
- 4 tablespoons granulated sugar
- 4 egg whites only
- 1 cup confectioners' sugar
- ½ cup almond

Directions
1. Begin by adding butter, sugar, and egg whites to a bowl and whisking it using a hand blender.
2. Then fold in the confectioner's sugar and almond.
3. Take a spoonful of dough and cookies from it.
4. Arrange the cookies in the air fryer and cook them for 18 minutes at 350 degrees F.

Oreo Chocolate Pudding

Preparation Time: 25 minutes | Cooking Time: 12 minutes | Servings: 2

Ingredients
- 2 ounces chocolate pudding
- 2 cups cooking cream
- 8 Oreos cookies
- 1 tablespoon Nutella
- 2 teaspoon butter

Directions
1. Grease the inside of ramekins with oil.
2. Add butter, chocolate, Nutella, and cream to a bowl and mix them while crushing the Oreos.
3. Shift the crushed oreo batter in the greased ramekin and add pudding and other desired toppings on top like cream
4. Place the ramekin in the air fryer oven and cook it for 12 minutes at around 350 degrees F.

Blueberry Pie

Preparation Time: 25 minutes | Cooking Time: 12 minutes | Servings: 2

Ingredients
- 1 pie dough box
- ½ cup blueberries, cubed

- ¼ cup pistachio
- 1 egg white, wash

Directions
1. Place the dough on a flat surface and cut it into equal-sized circles.
2. Brush the egg whites on the edges of the circles and place the cream, blueberries, and pistachio on top.
3. Fold the dough inwards and close the edges using a fork.
4. Place the pies in the air fryer basket and cook them for 10 to 12 minutes at around 400 degrees F.

Honey Goat Cheese balls

Preparation Time: 25 minutes | Cooking Time: 8 minutes | Servings: 2

Ingredients
- 1 cup goat cheese
- ¼ cup almond flour
- 1/3 cup Italian breadcrumbs
- 1/3 cup maple syrup

Directions
1. Shape the goat cheese into balls and let it refrigerate in the fridge for at least 20 minutes.
2. After resting in the fridge for enough time, take the balls out and coat them with flour, egg, and breadcrumbs.
3. Place the goat cheese balls back in the fridge and let them rest for at least 12 hours.
4. Then take the cheese balls out and arrange them in the air fryer oven.
5. Give them a coat of oil and let them cook for 6 to 8 minutes at 400 degrees F.
6. Once the balls are done, take them out and serve with a drizzle of maple syrup.

Easy Donuts

Preparation Time: 25 minutes | Cooking Time: 25 minutes | Servings: 2

Ingredients
- 2 cup milk
- 3 teaspoon active dry yeast
- ½ cup sugar, granulated
- 1 teaspoon kosher salt
- 2 eggs
- ½ cup butter, melted, unsalted
- 6 cups almond flour
- Oil, as needed

For glaze
- ¾ cup butter, unsalted
- 3 cups powdered sugar
- 4 teaspoon vanilla extract
- ¼ cup hot water

Directions
1. Mix the milk with sugar and yeast.
2. Mix sugar, egg, salt, 4 cups flour, and butter in a bowl. Then once the milk begins to foam, add it to the flour mix and knead it till dough is formed.
3. Cover it with a towel and let it rest till it puffs to double its size.
4. Once it has risen properly, use pizza dough and cut it into portions.
5. Cover the portions with parchment paper and let them rise again.
6. Coat the inside of the air fryer with oil, shape the donuts into shape and arrange them in the air fryer, cooking them for 4 minutes at 350 degrees F.
7. While the donuts are cooking, heat butter in a pan and add sugar and vanilla extract once it is melted.

8. When the donuts are done, take them out and cover them with the glaze and serve after letting them.

Donut Sticks

Preparation Time: 25 minutes | Cooking Time: 5-10 minutes | Servings: 3

Ingredients
- 2 pack crescent roll dough
- ½ cup butter, melted
- 1 cup white sugar
- 1 tablespoon cinnamon, grounded
- 1 cup strawberry jam

Directions
1. Begin by taking out the crescent rolls and cutting them into rectangles.
2. Then, cut them ½ inch thick and arrange them in the air fryer basket.
3. Coat the sticks with butter.
4. Cook the crescent rolls for 4 to 5 minutes at around 400 degrees F.
5. Meanwhile, add sugar and cinnamon to a bowl and mix them.
6. Once the donuts are done, add them to the sugar and cinnamon bowl and toss them to coat.
7. Shake off the excess and serve with the strawberry jam.

Anzac Biscuits

Preparation Time: 25 minutes | Cooking Time: 15 minutes | Servings: 1-2

Ingredients
- 1 cup steel-cut oats
- 1 cup almond flour
- ½ cup brown sugar
- ½ cup desiccated sweet coconuts
- 6 oz. butter
- 4 tablespoon golden syrup
- 1 teaspoon bicarb soda
- Water

Directions
1. Begin by mixing oats, flour, brown sugar, and coconut in a bowl.
2. Melt butter in a pan and add hot water and soda to it.
3. Mix wet ingredients in a bowl and pour the butter over it.
4. Add remaining ingredients as well.
5. Next, pour the wet ingredients over the dry ingredients and knead them until the dough forms.
6. Make small balls out of the dough and shape them into biscuits.
7. Arrange the biscuits in the air fryer oven and cook them for 12 to 15 minutes at 350 degrees F.
8. When done, take the biscuits out and let them rest for 10 minutes before serving.

Lime Macaroons

Preparation Time: 25 minutes | Cooking Time: 10 minutes | Servings: 2

Ingredients
- 4 eggs, whites only
- 5 oz. powdered sugar
- ¼ cup gin
- 1 teaspoon lime zest
- ¼ teaspoon salt
- ¼ teaspoon almond extract
- 1 pack of sweetened shredded coconut
- ½ cup almond flour

- ½ cup dark baking chocolate

Directions
1. Begin by preheating the oven to around 350 degrees F.
2. Crack the egg and whisk it with sugar, gin, lime zest, and almond extracts.
3. In another bowl, add coconut and flour.
4. Pour the egg, mix the flour and mix it.
5. Grease the inside of the air fryer with oil and place the mix in the air fryer rack, dipping the bottom of the macaroons in the melted chocolate and cooking till the macaroons are set.

Coconut Macaroons

Preparation Time: 25 minutes | Cooking Time: 10-12 minutes | Servings: 2

Ingredients
- 1 pack of flaked coconut, sweetened
- 1 cup condensed milk
- ¾ teaspoon sea salt
- ½ teaspoon vanilla extract
- 2 eggs
- ½ cup dark chocolate

Directions
1. Preheating the air fryer to around 320 degrees F for 10 minutes.
2. Mix coconut, condensed milk, salt, and vanilla extracts in a bowl.
3. In another bowl, crack and whisk the egg using an electric beater.
4. Then pour the egg into the coconut mixture and mix.
5. Take a spoonful of the mixture and make balls out of it.
6. Line the bottom of the air fryer basket with parchment paper and place the cookie balls in it, cooking them for 10 minutes or until golden brown.
7. Let them stay in the air fryer for another 20 to 30 minutes when they are done.

Canned Biscuits

Preparation Time: 25 minutes | Cooking Time: 10 minutes | Servings: 2

Ingredients
- 2 biscuit box

Directions
1. Line the bottom of the air fryer with parchment paper and arrange the biscuits on it.
2. Cook them for 2 minutes at around 350 degrees F.
3. After 2 minutes, lower the heat to 330 degrees F and cook them for 8 to 9 minutes.

Cream Puffs

Preparation Time: 25 minutes | Cooking Time: 35 minutes | Servings: 2

Ingredients
- 1 cup almond milk
- ¼ cup sugar
- Salt according to taste
- ¼ cup butter
- 1 cup almond flour
- 6 eggs
- 1 cup vanilla pudding

Directions
1. Start by mixing milk with butter, salt, and sugar.
2. Then shift it into a pan and bring it to a boil.
3. Once it begins to boil, remove it from the heat, add flour, and whisk together.

4. Then crack the eggs and whisk them till it forms a dough.
5. Make balls with the dough and arrange them on the air fryer basket lined with parchment paper, cooking them for 35 minutes at 350 degrees F.
6. When done, take it out and make holes in it, filling the holes with vanilla pudding and serving.

The Ultimate Chocolate Cake

Preparation Time: 10 minutes | Cooking Time: 15 minutes | Servings: 1

Ingredients:
- 2 cups all-purpose flour
- 1 teaspoon salt
- 1 teaspoon baking powder
- Two teaspoons of baking soda
- 3⁄4 cup unsweetened cocoa powder
- 2 cups sugar
- 1 cup vegetable oil
- 1 cup of hot coffee
- 1 cup milk
- Two large eggs
- 1 teaspoon vanilla
- 1 cup milk
- Five tablespoons of all-purpose flour
- 1⁄2 cup butter, softened
- 1⁄2 cup shortening
- 1 cup sugar
- 1 teaspoon vanilla

Directions:
1. Heat the oven to 325°F.
2. Sift together the dry ingredients in a large mixing basin. Mix in the oil, coffee, and milk for 2 minutes on medium speed. Beat in the eggs and vanilla extract for another 2 minutes. The batter will be thin.
3. Cream the butter, shortening, sugar, and vanilla extract in a medium mixing bowl. Beat for 10 minutes with cold milk and flour mixture. Frost the cooled cake and serve! The icing may be overwhelming, but it is well worth it! By the way, we like this cake cooled straight from the refrigerator. This is how the rich chocolate and cold icing seem to taste the finest.

Bananas Foster

Preparation Time: 10 minutes | Cooking Time: 15 minutes | Servings: 1

Ingredients:
- 1⁄4 cup butter (1/2 stick)
- 1 cup brown sugar
- 1⁄2 teaspoon cinnamon
- 1⁄4 cup banana liqueur
- Four bananas, cut in half lengthwise, then halved
- 1⁄4 cup dark rum
- Four scoops of vanilla ice cream

Directions:
1. In a flambé pan or skillet, combine the butter, sugar, and cinnamon.
2. Cook until the sugar melts in the pan over low heat, either on an alcohol burner or on top of the stove.
3. Stir in the banana liqueur before adding the bananas to the pan. When the banana parts start to soften and brown, slowly pour in the rum.
4. Simmer the sauce until the rum is hot, then ignite with a long match or tip the pan slightly.

5. When the flames have died down, remove the bananas from the pan and lay four slices on top of each serving of ice cream.
6. Serve immediately with a generous spoonful of heated sauce on top of the ice cream.

Snickerdoodles

Preparation Time: 10 minutes | Cooking Time: 15 minutes | Servings: 1

Ingredients:
- 1⁄2 cup butter, softened
- 1⁄2 cup granulated sugar
- 1⁄3 cup brown sugar (I used light brown)
- 1 egg
- 1⁄2 teaspoon vanilla
- 1 1⁄2 cups flour
- 1⁄4 teaspoon salt
- 1⁄2 teaspoon baking soda
- 1⁄4 teaspoon cream of tartar
- TOPPING
- Two tablespoons of granulated sugar
- 1 teaspoon cinnamon

Directions:
1. In a large mixing bowl, cream together the butter and sugars at high speed.
2. Beat in the egg and vanilla extract until creamy.
3. In a separate dish, whisk together the flour, salt, baking soda, and cream of tartar.
4. Mix the dry components into the wet ingredients.
5. Preheat the oven to 300°F while the dough rests in the refrigerator for 30-60 minutes.
6. The topping should be combined in a small bowl.
7. Roll roughly 2 1/2 teaspoons of dough into a ball.
8. Roll the dough in the cinnamon/sugar mixture and place it on a cookie sheet that has been buttered.
9. *Cookies may appear uncooked but will develop after 10-12 minutes of baking.
10. Don't roll the dough into too large a ball; if you do, it may take longer to bake.

Cream Cheese Brownies

Preparation Time: 10 minutes | Cooking Time: 15 minutes | Servings: 1

Ingredients:
- 2⁄3 cup flour
- 1⁄2 teaspoon baking powder
- 1⁄4 teaspoon salt
- 1⁄2 cup butter
- 1⁄2 cup cocoa
- 1 cup sugar
- Two eggs
- 3⁄4 teaspoon vanilla

CREAM CHEESE FILLING
- 1 cup cream cheese, softened
- 1⁄3 cup sugar
- 1 egg
- 1⁄2 teaspoon vanilla

Directions:
1. Preheat the oven to 350°F.
2. Combine the flour, salt, and baking powder in a mixing bowl.
3. Remove the butter from the heat.
4. Incorporate the cocoa.
5. Incorporate the eggs, sugar, and vanilla extract.
6. Incorporate the dry ingredients.

7. Pour half the batter into a 9" oiled square casserole dish or baking pan.
8. CAREFULLY spread the Cream Cheese Filling on top!
9. Finish with the remaining chocolate batter.
10. Pull a knife through the layers to get a marbled look.
11. Bake for 40-45 minutes, covered with tin foil or a glass lid, or until a toothpick inserted into the brownies comes clean.
12. Filling: Cream cheese should be whipped.
13. Add the 1/3 cup sugar, one egg, and 1/2 teaspoon vanilla extract until the mixture is extremely smooth.

Strawberry Pie

Preparation Time: 10 minutes | Cooking Time: 15 minutes | Servings: 1

Ingredients:
- 1 cup sugar
- 1 cup water
- Six teaspoons cornstarch
- 3 ounces strawberry Jell-O gelatin dessert
- 1 -2 pint washed and hulled strawberry
- 1 9in. Baked pastry shell, cooled

Directions:
1. Over medium-high heat, boil the sugar, water, and cornstarch.
2. Stir in the Jell-O until it is completely dissolved.
3. Allow cooling before adding the strawberries.
4. Refrigerate for 45 minutes or until the mixture begins to solidify.
5. Cool fully in the pie shell.
6. To serve, top with whipped cream or ice cream.

Chocolate Bundt Cake With Chocolate Glaze

Preparation Time: 10 minutes | Cooking Time: 15 minutes | Servings: 1

Ingredients:
- 1(18 1/4 ounce) package devil's food cake mix
- 1(4 ounces) package of instant chocolate pudding mix
- 2 cups semi-sweet chocolate chips
- 1 3/4 cups water
- Two eggs, beaten
- One teaspoon of vanilla extract
- Three tablespoons cocoa
- Two tablespoons of butter, melted
- 1 cup powdered sugar (10X)
- 2 -3 tablespoons hot water

Directions:
1. Preheat the oven to 350°F.
2. Set aside the bundt pan that has been greased and floured.
3. Combine cake, pudding, and chocolate chips in a large mixing basin.
4. Whisk together the water, eggs, and vanilla extract in a separate dish.
5. Mix the egg mixture into the dry ingredients with a spoon until barely combined.
6. Pour into the prepared baking dish.
7. Bake for 50 to 55 minutes, or until a wooden pick inserted into the center of the cake comes out clean.
8. Allow the cake to cool for 15 to 20 minutes before removing it from the pan.
9. When the cake has completely cooled, sprinkle it with Chocolate Glaze.
10. In a mixing dish, combine all the chocolate glaze ingredients.
11. Blend with a spoon until smooth.

Mexican Weeding Cake

Preparation Time: 10 minutes | Cooking Time: 15 minutes | Servings: 1

Ingredients:
- 1 cup butter, softened
- 1 cup powdered sugar
- 2 cups flour, sifted
- 1 cup nuts, ground
- 1 teaspoon vanilla

Directions:
1. Combine all of the ingredients.
2. Make 1 1/2" balls out of the dough.
3. Bake for 10-15 minutes on a cookie sheet at 350°F, or until firm.
4. While still warm, roll in more powdered sugar.

Homemade Yellow Cake

Preparation Time: 10 minutes | Cooking Time: 15 minutes | Servings: 1

Ingredients:
- 3 1/2 cups cake flour
- One tablespoon of baking powder
- 1 teaspoon salt
- 2 cups sugar
- 1 (3 1/2 ounce) package of instant vanilla pudding
- Six tablespoons of butter softened
- Six tablespoons of butter flavor shortening
- 1 1/2 cups milk
- One tablespoon of vanilla extract
- 1/2 cup sour cream
- Four eggs

Directions:
1. Combine the butter, shortening, sugar, and pudding in a mixing bowl.
2. Add the eggs one at a time.
3. Mix in the sour cream and vanilla extract. Combine thoroughly.
4. Sift the flour, baking powder, and salt together.
5. Alternately add the flour mixture and milk into the butter, beginning and ending with the flour mixture.
6. Pour into a 13x9 pan that has been properly oiled and floured.
7. Bake for 40-50 minutes at 350°F.
8. White Cake Variation: Use four egg whites instead of 3 whole eggs.
9. Spice Cake Variation: To the flour mixture, add 1-1/2 teaspoons cinnamon, 1/4+1/8 teaspoon ground allspice, and 1/4+1/8 teaspoon ground cloves.
10. Chocolate Cake Variation: Use chocolate pudding mix and 1/3 cup cocoa. (I then increase the milk slightly.)

Barefoot Contessa's Carrot Cake

Preparation Time: 10 minutes | Cooking Time: 15 minutes | Servings: 1

Ingredients:
- 2 cups sugar
- 1 1/3 cups vegetable oil
- One teaspoon of pure vanilla extract
- Three extra-large eggs
- 2 cups all-purpose flour
- Two teaspoons of ground cinnamon
- Two teaspoons of baking soda
- 1 1/2 teaspoons kosher salt
- 3 cups grated carrots (less than 1 pound)
- 1 cup raisins

- 1 cup chopped walnuts
- ¾ lb. cream cheese, at room temperature
- ½ lb. unsalted butter, at room temperature
- One teaspoon of pure vanilla extract
- 1 lb. confectioners' sugar

Directions:
1. Preheat the oven to 350 degrees Fahrenheit.
2. In the bowl of an electric mixer fitted with a paddle attachment, combine the sugar, oil, and vanilla.
3. One at a time, add the eggs.
4. Sift together the flour, cinnamon, baking soda, and salt in a separate basin.
5. Add 1/2 of the dry ingredients to the wet components while mixing on low speed.
6. Mix the remaining flour with the grated carrots, raisins, and walnuts before adding it to the batter.
7. Just blend everything.
8. Paper muffin cups should be lined.
9. Scoop the batter into 22 muffin cups, filling them 3/4 full.
10. Bake at 400°F for 10 minutes, then reduce to 350°F for another 35 minutes (**see note at bottom), or until a toothpick comes out clean.
11. Allow cooling on a rack.
12. In the bowl of an electric mixer fitted with a paddle attachment, cream together the cream cheese, butter, and vanilla extract.
13. Beat in the sugar until smooth.
14. Liberally frost them and serve when the cupcakes are cool enough to handle.

Fried Oreos

Preparation Time: 10 minutes | Cooking Time: 15 minutes | Servings: 1

Ingredients:
- 1 bag of Oreo cookies
- 2 cups pancake mix
- 1 ½ cups milk
- Two eggs
- Four teaspoons oil
- plus oil (for frying)

Directions:
1. Preheat the deep fryer to 375°F.
2. Combine the pancake mix, milk, eggs, and oil in a mixing bowl.
3. Mix until no lumps remain.
4. Dip the Oreos into the batter, ensuring both sides are coated, and then place them in the deep fryer.
5. You'll need to keep an eye on them because the cookies tend to float, so flip them frequently.
6. You also don't want them to burn; you simply want them to be golden brown.
7. Remove the cookies and thoroughly drain.
8. The cookies are excellent, fresh from deep frying.

Banana Bread Brownies

Preparation Time: 10 minutes | Cooking Time: 15 minutes | Servings: 1

Ingredients:
- 1 ½ cups sugar
- 1 cup sour cream
- ½ cup butter, softened
- Two eggs
- 3 -4 bananas, mashed
- Two teaspoons of vanilla extract
- 2 cups all-purpose flour

- 1 teaspoon baking soda
- ¾ teaspoon salt
- ½ cup walnuts, chopped (optional)
- ½ cup butter
- 4 cups powdered sugar
- 1 ½ teaspoons vanilla extract
- Three tablespoons milk

Directions:
1. Preheat the oven to 375°F. 15x10-inch jelly roll pan, greased and floured. Mix the sugar, sour cream, butter, and eggs in a large mixing basin until creamy. Mix in the bananas and vanilla essence. Blend in the flour, baking soda, and salt for 1 minute. Mix in the walnuts.
2. Pour batter into the pan in an equal layer. Cook for 20–25 minutes, or until golden brown.
3. Meanwhile, melt the butter in a large saucepan over medium heat until it begins to boil. Allow the butter to develop a delicate brown before removing it from the heat.
4. Mix in the powdered sugar, vanilla essence, and milk. Whisk everything together until smooth (it should be thicker than a glaze but thinner than frosting). Spread the brown butter icing over the heated bars using a spatula (the frosting will be easier to spread while the bars are still warm).

Boston Cream Pie

Preparation Time: 10 minutes | Cooking Time: 15 minutes | Servings: 1

Ingredients:
- Two large eggs
- 2 cups unsifted cake flour
- 1 cup sugar, separated
- 2 ½ teaspoons baking powder
- ½ teaspoon salt
- ⅓ cup vegetable oil
- 1 cup milk
- Two teaspoons of vanilla extract
- 1 ½ cups milk
- Two tablespoons cornstarch
- ¼ cup sugar
- 1 pinch salt
- 1 large egg
- One tablespoon of vanilla extract
- ¼ cup water
- Two tablespoons sugar
- ½ cup semisweet chocolate or 1/2 cup milk chocolate chips

Directions:
1. Preheat the oven to 350°F. Grease and flour two 9" round cake pans, or make things easier on yourself by tracing the bottom of the pans on waxed paper, cutting to fit, and placing them on the bottom of the pans. No need to oil the pan; the cakes will just fall out.
2. To make the cake layers: Separate the eggs; put aside the whites in a small, clean bowl devoid of grease or oil. Combine cake flour, 3/4 cup sugar, baking powder, and salt in a large mixing basin. Place aside.
3. To assemble, place one upside-down cake layer on a serving platter. Spread the cream filling on top. Place the remaining cake layer on top, right side up. Spread glaze around the borders of the cake. Refrigerate.

Peach Cobbler Dump Cake

Preparation Time: 10 minutes | Cooking Time: 15 minutes | Servings: 1

Ingredients:
- 1 (18 1/4 ounce) box of yellow cake mix
- 1 (32 ounces) can of peach in heavy syrup
- ½ cup butter ground cinnamon

Directions:
1. Preheat your oven to 375°F.
2. Fill a 13 x 9-inch baking pan halfway with peaches.
3. Cover with the dry cake mix and firmly press down.
4. Place tiny slices of butter or margarine on top of the cake mix.
5. Sprinkle with cinnamon on top.
6. 45 minutes in the oven

Silky Chocolate Peanut Butter Pie

Preparation Time: 10 minutes | Cooking Time: 15 minutes | Servings: 1

Ingredients:
- 1 cup chocolate chips
- 16 ounces soft silken tofu, drained
- ⅔ cup creamy peanut butter
- ½ cup sugar
- ½ teaspoon vanilla
- One prepared graham cracker crust

Directions:
1. Melt chocolate chips in a small dish in the microwave for 90 seconds on high power.
2. Stir until completely smooth.
3. Allow cooling slightly.
4. Blend or process the tofu, peanut butter, sugar, and vanilla extract until smooth.
5. Blend in the chocolate until smooth.
6. Pour into the pie crust.
7. Refrigerate for several hours, or until the filling is firm, covered with plastic wrap.
8. Garnish with peanuts, melted chocolate, or whipped cream if desired.

Peanut Butter Cookies

Preparation Time: 10 minutes | Cooking Time: 15 minutes | Servings: 1

Ingredients:
- 1 cup peanut butter
- ½ cup sugar
- 1 large egg

Directions:
1. Combine the ingredients.
2. Drop by teaspoon onto a baking sheet.
3. Bake at 325°F for 10 minutes or at 350°F for 8-10 minutes.

Fresh Peach Turnovers

Preparation Time: 10 minutes | Cooking Time: 15 minutes | Servings: 1

Ingredients:
- ½ cup sugar
- Two tablespoons cornstarch
- 2 lbs. fresh peaches, peeled and sliced
- 1 tablespoon butter
- ½ teaspoon cinnamon
- ¼ teaspoon nutmeg
- Two sheets of frozen puff pastry, thawed
- One egg (beaten with one teaspoon of water)
- ½ cup powdered sugar

Directions:
1. Preheat the oven to 400°F.
2. Save the liquid when you slice the peaches.
3. In a saucepan, combine peach juice, sugar, and cornstarch. Cook until the sauce is thick and bubbling.
4. Mix in the peaches, butter, cinnamon, and nutmeg.
5. Allow cooling slightly.
6. Roll out each pastry sheet lightly on a floured board.
7. Each sheet should be cut into four squares.
8. Fill half of each square with peach filling. Brush the edges with the beaten egg. Fold into a triangle (or rectangle) and press the edges to seal (or crimp with a fork).
9. Place on cookie sheets.
10. Bake for 10-15 minutes until gently browned and puffy, at 400°.
11. Allow cooling on racks.
12. Dust with powdered sugar. Alternatively, frost with powdered sugar icing.

Thanks for checking out the air fryer cookbook with its 1500 delicious recipes and helpful information so that you can make an informed decision. With our air fryer guide, you can identify the air fryer that fits both your budget and your needs. In addition, our recipes will show you how to use an air fryer to its fullest! So take care of your air fryer so you can benefit from it for a long time!

Manufactured by Amazon.ca
Acheson, AB

10342446R00098